Democracy and Elitism

DEMOCRACY
and
ELITISM

Two Essays with Selected Readings

❧

HARRY K. GIRVETZ

UNIVERSITY OF CALIFORNIA
SANTA BARBARA

CHARLES SCRIBNER'S SONS   NEW YORK

CONTENTS

PREFACE

As though nagging poverty were not enough, the island of Sicily is the seat of an infamous society known as the Mafia. Since the families generally referred to by this name often wage relentless war on each other until the ranks of their male members are nearly decimated, the sense in which they may be called a "society" is not altogether unassailable. Nevertheless, the Mafia has its hierarchs and henchmen. Its rulers gather occasionally in formal conference, and it appears to conduct itself by a kind of code, albeit one that is as brutal as it is bizarre.

If we are to believe one of its chroniclers,[1] there was a time when the leaders of the Mafia thought of themselves as social benefactors, although, given the nature of their activities, the claim strains credulity. But whatever the past may have contained, the recent crimes of the Mafia have been so heinous as completely to preclude the possibility that the perpetrators could really believe they were promoting the public good. This change, if it was one, resulted at least in part from the repatriation of gangsters like the late Lucky Luciano who imparted a certain American efficiency to the antique methods of his more provincial colleagues. Extortion and graft took on new and ingenious forms; traffic in drugs and assorted rackets became a major industry, and violent death a daily occurrence. We are told that the homicide rate of Palermo is the highest in the world, and since not even the grief-stricken relatives of the victims will brave the vengeance of the Mafia by testifying against the murderers, the crimes go unpunished.

The Mafiosi correspond to those anomic men described by Professor R. M. MacIver who have substituted disconnected urges for moral standards. They are a law unto themselves. They rule by terror. Their sole weapon is the threat

[1] Norman Lewis, *The Honored Society* (New York: G. P. Putnam's Sons, 1964).

of violence. Suffering no pangs of conscience, oblivious of the rules by which most men are governed, impervious to considerations of social justice, they have no need for those rationalizations—transparent or opaque—by which the normal man tries to conceal his baser motives. They would be the first to scorn ideologues and system-makers; their interests and energies are generally exhausted in the act of pillage itself and the immediate conditions that make it possible. Except as objects of plunder their victims are of only marginal interest to them. It seems appropriate, therefore, to coin the term "mafianism" for all exercises of power that seek no extenuation and have no objective other than plunder, no means other than violence or the threat of violence, and no limit other than the satiation of the oppressor and the impoverishment of his victim.

Happily mafianism is a rare phenomenon, partly because it is a highly inefficient method of exploitation, partly because even the most brutal men generally need some formula for legitimizing their activities. The absence of such a felt need may indeed be taken as pathological and as a hallmark of the truly criminal mind. Thus, mafianism is simply organized criminality—almost institutionalized and in complete control of a society, as under a Duvalier or Trujillo in such blighted Caribbean countries as Haiti and the Dominican Republic, hardly structured and lurking in the interstices of a society as in the case of our own Cosa Nostra.[2]

Among those given to rhetorical exaggeration, mafianism as thus described is often confused with totalitarianism. While the difference may be imperceptible to the victims, the distinction is important. The term "totalitarianism" is better reserved for those uses of unrestricted power which are more efficiently organized and are initially justified by appeal to some accepted set of values. The rulers, except for a few cynics among them, successfully persuade themselves that their ascendancy is essential to the public good and that the perquisites of power are merely a happy coincidence or (for the theistically oriented) a divine dispensation. An ideology is evolved to bolster this conviction and convert skeptics. Much attention is given to myth-making and indoctrination. Mild disagreement may be tolerated at the outset, and family and church may be left to their own devices. However, strains and crises attendant on war and revolution or economic collapse soon generate a fear of dissent. In any

---

[2] Social scientists have taken over Durkheim's term "anomie" or "anomy" to designate the state of normlessness described above. According to R. M. MacIver "Anomy signifies the state of mind of one who has been pulled up by his moral roots, who has no longer any standards but only disconnected urges, who has no longer any sense of continuity, of folk, of obligation. The anomic man has become spiritually sterile, responsive only to himself, responsible to no one." *The Ramparts We Guard* (New York: The Macmillan Co., 1950), p. 84. Cf. also David Riesman's *The Lonely Crowd* (New Haven: Yale University Press, 1950), pp. 287 ff. and Robert K. Merton's *Social Theory and Social Structure* (Glencoe, Illinois: The Free Press, 1957), pp. 161–170. Merton makes the point that the psychological concept described by MacIver "is . . . a counterpart of the sociological concept of anomie, and not a substitute for it," p. 162.

case, either because the rulers at the very outset doubt the persuasiveness of their own rationalizations, or because events in the course of time deprive such rationalizations of their initial plausibility, extra-political institutional influences are increasingly regarded as a threat to power. Likewise individual discretion seems increasingly to pose serious hazards. Consequently, the rulers demand a complete monopoly of power, refusing autonomy even to the family, and ignoring all distinctions between public and private in the life of the individual. It may be emphasized that regimes are totalitarian not merely because those in charge of the state acknowledge no rival source of authority, but because they seek in a positive way to regulate all the activities of the individual —the way in which he makes his living and spends his income, his schooling, his recreation, his enjoyment of the arts.

As rationalizations become more and more transparent, the use of force and terror increases and with it recourse to that ultimate rationalization which has invariably been the prelude to man's greatest inhumanities to man, namely, that the end justifies the means. But, "things bad begun make worse themselves by ill." Soon ideology drops more and more into the background. Terror and naked force take over, and full-fledged totalitarianism, familiar to us recently in the forms of Hitlerism and Stalinism, emerges.

Totalitarianism is the condition of a society that is in trouble; it is not generally sought for its own sake, but is the desperate recourse of frustrated and frightened men. While some, a Hermann Göring, for example, may use it for purposes of private plunder, totalitarians, unlike the Mafiosi, may be austere and even ascetic men.

Totalitarianism as thus described is now in eclipse and, while its causes deserve careful study, there is danger that excessive preoccupation with its sins may divert us from the less discernible and less clamorous rivals to which democratic societies may succumb. Totalitarians are all too easy to flog especially when, after a disastrous war, only a handful of psychopaths among them could continue to regard themselves as riding the wave of the future.

The real challenge to democracy comes not from such manifestly disreputable sources, but from philosophies and social systems which, while eschewing the complete regimentation imposed by totalitarian dictatorship, are nonetheless hostile to popular rule. Such systems may be called "elitist" because they share a common belief that enlightened government and a healthy and stable society are unattainable unless a group or class endowed with special gifts preponderates over the majority. Elitism approaches totalitarianism, of course, in proportion as the proposed grant or actual use of authority is unlimited, and often, as classifiers always learn to their dismay, it is difficult to draw a line. However, apart from such borderline cases, elitist regimes are more formidable rivals of democracy than the totalitarian systems into which they sometimes have degenerated, if only because their appeal is so subtle and persuasive that many of us who fancy ourselves democratic are really elitist at heart.

The leadership of any group, academic, commercial, literary, may be called its elite. Strictly speaking, the elite may not necessarily lead; they may simply excel. Nobel prize winners are the elite of the scientific and literary worlds; members of the French Academy are (or were) the elite of the French intellectual world; no doubt in their day the Yankees were the elite of baseball. However, elit*ism* is generally a view concerning how society should be ruled or governed, and the term is therefore primarily political in its import. This, at any rate, will be its meaning as used here where it will refer to the view that only a relative few are qualified to rule and that rule ought to be by those most qualified.

Such a claim is likely to go without serious challenge in a society where the role of an elite is in fact functional and where members of the elite in pursuing their purposes are releasing the productive energies of the society of which they are a part, as was the case, for example, with the mine and mill owners of nineteenth century Britain. It is only when an elite is functionless, as was the eighteenth century French aristocracy whose members were absentee landlords fluttering about the bright lights at Versailles, and where its characteristic activities frustrate the creative energies of a society, that it almost inevitably invites dictatorship or succumbs to the forces of democracy. In any event, a functional and creative elite has no need of totalitarian techniques, even though it rules in its own interest. To the extent that its claims are not fully made good in terms of actual results for society as a whole, myths, ideologies or simple promises of future well-being will suffice to keep grumbling and discontent under control. Accordingly, unlike totalitarianism, elitism generally acknowledges the autonomy of such social institutions as the family and the church, as it acknowledges also an area of autonomy for the individual.

Elitism is very much with us. The reaction of many influential Americans to the Supreme Court decisions on reapportionment suggests that their commitment to democracy is largely a verbal one. The "new" conservatives who very nearly gained control of one of our two major parties, are fond of insisting that the United States is a republic and not a democracy. From the other direction the "thaw" in the Soviet Union that followed the denigration of Stalin suggests that the Kremlin may be groping for a formula somewhere between totalitarianism and democracy. A discussion which concentrates on elitism rather than totalitarianism is therefore surely opportune.

But we are also prodded to rethink the democratic philosophy. Critics constantly impute attributes to democracy which are neither essential to it nor claimed for it by its informed advocates. They readily demonstrate then that a philosophy of government resting on such assumptions cannot work. Much of their case depends on ambiguities that lurk in the terms "rule" and "competence," not to mention such terms as "equality," "power" and even "people." Often they seem only to be protesting against conformity, vulgarity, materialism and what Ortega y Gassett called "the sovereignty of the mediocre." Invariably such critics treat remediable flaws in democracies as though they were inherent and fatal defects. Considerable sophistication is required not only to parry their arguments, but to guard against the oversimplifications perpetrated by many friends of democracy. In any case, the concept of democracy is not a fixed entity (except among incorrigible Platonizers); it is constantly in need of redefinition in the light of new circumstances and new problems. An analysis which deals with democracy as well as elitism would therefore appear to be very much in order.

Accordingly this book is divided into three main sections, one on Democracy, one on Elitism, and a group of selections from distinguished authorities which elaborate upon or document points made by the author in his essays. At appropriate points in the essays reference is made to the selections, so the reader can pursue the issue in greater depth and examine it in one of its classical formulations. The selections are taken from recent (e.g. Pareto, Schumpeter) and living (e.g. Lippmann) authorities, as well as from noted political philosophers of the past (e.g. Plato, Jefferson). These selections retain the punctuation and capitalization of the sources from which they were taken.

The first of the author's essays attempts a fresh definition of democracy, purged of the oversimplifications of its more unsophisticated advocates, and defends democracy against some of the more plausible charges of its elitist critics. Two of these charges—that democracy is sometimes a potential and often an actual tyranny of the majority, and that it involves a rejection of qualified leadership in favor of rule by the average or "mass" man, are examined in some detail. So, too, is the Marxist argument that democracy is unattainable within the framework of a capitalist economy. However, to be meaningful, the author argues, democracy must rest on a basic consensus. The fundamentals of this consensus occupy much of this essay.

On the assumption that we have already been abundantly informed about the nature of totalitarianism, and that elitism poses a greater and subtler challenge to democracy (since the eclipse of Hitler and Stalin), the second essay distinguishes and evaluates several important varieties of elitism from Plato's defense of a rule by philosopher-kings and Nietzsche's apotheosis of the artist-tyrant, to Pareto's and Mosca's so-called neo-Machiavellianism, to a new development which is termed "cybernated bureaucracy."

The volume closes with an epilogue containing two selections and a postscript which focus the argument on the American scene. Do elitist or democratic tendencies now dominate in this country? Which prevails in our society: mass or class? Or, if the dynamics of their interaction in the context of American life is properly understood, may it not be that there is nothing contradictory in answering—both?

H. K. G.

Democracy and Elitism

The prime duty that devolves today upon those who direct society is to enlighten democracy; to revive, if possible, its faith; to purify its morals; to guide its movements; to replace inexperience with expertness and blind instinct with a knowledge of its true interests; to adapt its government to time and place, and to modify it in accordance with circumstance and the actors of the age.

ALEXIS DE TOCQUEVILLE
Democracy in America

PART ONE

✣

Two Essays

DEMOCRACY

*. . . many things are revealed to the humble that are hidden from
the great.*

ADLAI STEVENSON

An account of democracy might proceed by describing what is common to
the forms of government called democratic by those who live under them. But the
procedure is fraught with difficulty. Those who live under a given form of government characterize it variously. And, quite awkwardly, the Soviet Union,
which most Americans view as a dictatorship, is regarded by many if not most of
its citizens as operating under a principle of "democratic centralism," and hence
as a democracy. The People's Republic of Red China presents similar embarrass-
ments which are hardly dispelled by sub-classifications such as "bourgeois democracy" and "socialist democracy." Finally, and perhaps most awkward of all,
many practices in the United States have been only remotely suggestive of democratic procedures if they have not been actually a subversion of them. Such practices have ranged from the disfranchisement of urban populations against which
the Supreme Court's reapportionment decisions were directed, to the exclusion of
Negroes from the voter rolls of Alabama and Mississippi, to a Congressional
committee system which, at least until recently, could effectively keep proposed
legislation from coming to a vote in Congress.

On the other hand, to define the democratic idea without reference to its
putative embodiment in actual governments is to set up an abstraction with little
relevance to the real world and to court charges of being arbitrary. We may, of
course, use words, including the word "democratic," as we please. Wisdom, however, decrees that we use them in such a way as to be understood by others, and
that they not be used in such a way as to obscure important differences.

The Will of the People

The democratic principle will be considered only as applied by a society to
the conduct of its political affairs. Political affairs are those involving policies
regarded by the decision-making group as so crucial to its well-being that they

will not be trusted to informal understandings and private arrangements, or even to established custom, but will be embodied in formal law and enforced. Political affairs, then, are those in the disposition of which the coercive power of the state may be invoked, even though in most instances it may not be needed. In such affairs, as every fledgling student is taught, power in a democracy resides in the people; they make the determination; they are sovereign.

But who are the people? How is their will formed and how ascertained? How is their power exercised? What can be said of their competence to rule? What may their rule embrace?

After a long period of wavering and uncertainty, our answer to the first query is by now fixed and firm—except perhaps in the Deep South—and no one is thought of as excluded from a voice in ruling except the very young, the insane and feebleminded, felons, and transients or aliens. But this is recent. Athenian democracy, the source and font of Western democratic tradition, embraced only its citizens and tolerated slavery. In 1832, almost a century and a half after the publication of Locke's *Second Treatise*, the British, heeding Thomas Macaulay's warning that universal suffrage is "incompatible, not with this or that form of government, but with all forms of government," had only reached the point where they conferred suffrage on the middle class. Even the Reform Bill of 1867, for which Disraeli persuaded Lord Derby and the Conservatives to "shoot Niagra," did not completely abolish property qualifications. In the United States the regulation of suffrage was left to the states which at first limited voting almost exclusively to male property owners. But there has been much change. Indeed, there is change even now as a President, reflecting the aroused conscience of the American people over racial brutalities in Alabama, recently requested and received legislation that strikes down virtually the last state barrier against the participation of Negro citizens in elections at all levels—federal, state and local.[1] The people are no longer "a select society of free individuals." Now we have mass democracy.

Ascertaining the popular will poses more vexing problems quite apart from the metaphysical snares for which notions of a "collective" or "general" will are notorious (pp. 85–87). Since people vary in their interests and preferences, they rarely if ever achieve unanimity. Also, the vigor with which each individual affirms a preference varies in intensity from near indifference to strong conviction. Finally, it is often said that many individuals are in ignorance of their true preference—that their will is, in fact, better understood by others. Communists have claimed that the proletariat—especially its "vanguard"—is better equipped to interpret the will of the masses than peasants, intellectuals or men of property. In an earlier age, hereditary aristocracies claimed to be endowed by birth and training with deeper insight into the will of the people than the people themselves. Historically, property owners have claimed the possession of wealth confers such insight. And, in modern Germany, a führer was able to persuade his

---

[1] Still retained in state elections by Virginia, Mississippi, Alabama and Texas, the poll tax was outlawed by the Supreme Court in 1966.

people that by virtue of superior powers of intuition he was uniquely able to discern their will. When such interpretations have manifestly failed to coincide with the people's wishes it has always been possible to dismiss the popular will as mere caprice or passing whim inimical to their well-being and differing from the "deeper" abiding will of which they are not yet aware; or to distinguish, in the Hegelian language appropriated by Marxists, between what is merely "implicit" in the popular consciousness and what is "explicit." Burke called this the principle of "virtual representation."

The democratic idea as we have come to understand it in the West rejects such claims in behalf of a führer, an hereditary aristocracy, a propertied class, or the proletariat as either spurious or too susceptible of error to be reliable or for ultimately causing civil strife. It was Dean Inge (among others) who said, "although counting heads is not an ideal way to govern, it is better than breaking them." Democracies have appropriated this wisdom. There must be an actual count conducted with an understanding that the majority will prevail. Since the count not only should be accurate, but reflect the true conviction of each individual voting (if only at the moment of voting), a secret ballot must be available at the request of any voter. It should be emphasized finally that, if the poll is to be meaningful, voters must be presented with a choice of real alternatives. This includes a choice of political parties which define issues and candidates who reflect the alternatives, and not, as in Nazi Germany, between the candidates or program of one party and a simple abstinence or "nein."

Competence and the Popular Rule

It is just as well to dispose at the outset of a caricature of democracy at least as ancient as Plato's *Republic*. Under the "form of government in which the magistrates are commonly elected by lot," Plato observes, "a man may say and do what he likes." There is "no necessity for you to govern in this State, even if you have the capacity, or to be governed, unless you like, or to go to war when the rest go to war, or to be at peace when others are at peace, unless you are so disposed. . . ." The spirit of democracy, "never giving a thought to the pursuits which make a statesman, and promoting to honour anyone who professes to be the people's friend," results in "a charming form of government, full of variety and disorder, and dispensing a sort of equality to equals and unequals alike." [2] In his famous parable of the ship, he had already described the people as "a little deaf" with "a similar infirmity in sight" and noted that, in the absence of a philosopher king, "everyone is of the opinion that he has a right to steer, though he has never learned the art of navigation" [3] (pp. 189, 202–03).

These famous words may or may not have been a just description of Athenian democracy—Popper argues that the myths about democratic Athens make

[2] Plato, *The Republic*, Book VIII, 557–58 (Jowett translation).
[3] *Ibid.*, Book VI, 488.

"nonsense of the known facts" [4]—but they have been the inspiration for criticisms which range all the way from identifying democracy with a state of anarchy to confusing it with a rule of the ignorant herd. The argument that democracy leads inevitably to anarchy no longer holds terrors, but it has been and still is fashionable in certain quarters to dwell on the inability of the average citizen to cope with the complexities of the issues on which, in a democracy, he is asked to pass judgment. This inadequacy has occasioned countless jeremiads.

Concededly, the average voter is no authority on public affairs and certainly the issues are surpassingly complex. But let those who scoff from a height of presumed competence consider the predicament of Justice Learned Hand as he confessed his "incapacity to understand and deal with the multitude of questions that increasingly call for answer in a desperately complicated world." The distinguished jurist told the Federal Bar Association,

> I do not know how it is with you, but for myself I generally give up at the outset. The simplest problems which come up from day to day seem to me quite unanswerable as soon as I try to get below the surface. Each side, when I hear it, seems to me right till I hear the other. I have neither the time nor the ability to learn the facts, or to estimate their importance if I knew them; I am disposed to accept the decision of those charged with the responsibility of dealing with them.[5]

Let us grant that Justice Hand was carried away by an excess of modesty. Even so, if we deride the inadequacy of a polity which counts the noses of average men must we not also scoff at the polity which counts the nose of Justice Hand? And all like him, including ourselves? Clearly, something is wrong with an evaluation of democracy based on this kind of supercilious approach.

Another point is worth mentioning. It has been suggested many times as an answer to the elitism to which disillusionment with democracy often leads. John Kenneth Galbraith states it with his usual felicity as applying to a wealthy elite, although his remarks are applicable to all privileged groups:

> Wealth is not without its advantages and the case to the contrary, although it has often been made, has never proved widely persuasive. But, beyond doubt, wealth is the relentless enemy of understanding. The poor man has always a precise view of his problem and its remedy: he hasn't enough and he needs more. The rich man can assume or imagine a much greater variety of ills and he will be correspondingly less certain of their remedy.[6]

Here, indeed, lies the grain of truth in the popular myth concerning the omniscience of the masses (their "nobility" is not here in question). The problem of

[4] Popper, Karl R., *The Open Society* (Princeton: Princeton University Press, 1950), p. 176.

[5] *The Spirit of Liberty* (New York: Alfred A. Knopf, 1952), pp. 92–93.

[6] *The Affluent Society* (Boston: Houghton Mifflin Co., 1958), p. 1.

the masses—at any rate where they are seriously deprived and disadvantaged—is really quite simple: to eat or starve, to live in a hovel or an adequate dwelling, to work 58 hours a week (as they did when Britain was contemplating passage of the Ten Hours Act) or 40 or 35 hours a week. By contrast, members of the middle class have far more complex and baffling problems: finding efficient domestic help, planning a European trip,[7] paying alimony, coping with obesity, maintaining their automobiles, washing machines, vacuum cleaners, television sets, radios, air conditioning units, dishwashers, and hi-fi sets at a reasonable cost despite rapacious repairmen who prey on their helplessness, etc. Wisdom, is, after all, a function of the complexity of the problems we face. If all this fails to persuade, one may ponder the words of Aristotle, who was hardly insensitive to the failings of democracy:

> Now any member of the assembly, taken separately, is certainly inferior to the wise man. But the state is made up of many individuals. And as a feast to which all the guests contribute is better than a banquet furnished by a single man, so a multitude is a better judge of many things than any individual.

> Again, the many are more incorruptible than the few; they are like the greater quantity of water which is less easily corrupted than a little. The individual is liable to be overcome by anger or by some other passion, and then his judgement is necessarily perverted; but it is hardly to be supposed that a great number of persons would all get into a passion and go wrong at the same moment.[8]

There are other ways of stressing the difference between social intelligence and intelligence in its other manifestations. It is not necessary to confront the many difficulties inherent in the word "intelligence" to see that social intelligence involves attributes not necessarily displayed by a brilliant mathematician, a gifted chess player, or a genius of the financial world. It involves, among other traits, a patience with the shortcomings of others, a talent for "taking the role of the other" beyond those routine feats of projection we perform in ordinary intercourse, and above all, that sensitiveness to the needs of others that we call compassion. The most acute minds may or may not display these traits and, lacking them, might well sow chaos and confusion if they were called upon to govern.

However, all this may be ignored as a mere precaution against counting on social intelligence in the wrong places. If democracy means that all or even most

---

[7] In a recent issue of *Harper's* devoted to advice to the traveler, the prospect of insolvency is treated in these terms: "The rich are just as rich and the poor, oddly enough, no poorer when they get home. Neither faces the bedevilling decisions of the middle-income man. Is the four-star restaurant really worth the price once? Is a hired car with a chauffeur the only way to see Turkey? When is an economy flight too uncomfortable to justify the lower fare?" (January, 1965). *Harper's* correspondent volunteered answers to these questions, but in this writer's judgment they are insolubly complex.

[8] "Politica," *The Works of Aristotle*, X, ed. Benjamin Jowett (Oxford: Clarendon Press, 1921), Book III, 15, 1286a.

members of society must partake equally in the determination of public policy, then such a thing never did or will exist. On this score we may agree with the elitists. We may even grant Carlyle that "the few Wise will have, by one method or another, to take command of the innumerable Foolish," and that without this "there is no Society possible in the world." [9] The all-important questions are by *what* "method or another" and *how* the "command" is exercised. There is nothing in the concept of democracy which excludes recourse to the best and most informed leadership. The rejection of authoritarianism need not imply the repudiation of authority. To reduce democracy to a counting of heads, as did Plato, is to confuse the end of a process with the process itself.

It is only at the end that the Benthamite ideal—each to count as one and no one as more than one—is relevant. If there were only a counting of heads we would doubtless find them empty enough. But a great deal happens before the counting begins. Society is not a loose collection of discrete and isolated atoms, although many political philosophers of the eighteenth and nineteenth centuries mistakenly regarded it as such. Individuals are guided by political parties, labor unions, co-operatives, churches, civic organizations, business associations, professional groups, etc. And, if this seems like a Babel of tongues, the tongues are certainly more informed and educated than that "mass man" who is held up in certain anti-democratic parodies as the prototype of every voter. In any case, the energetic, civic-minded, informed citizen surely has far more to do with decision-making than his slothful, apathetic, politically illiterate neighbor, even though each counts as only one when a poll is taken. To be sure, fanatics, opportunists and special interest groups are also not without great energy, and the danger that their counsel may prevail over the counsel of men of wisdom and good will is always present. But this is only to say that democracy is not without its hazards. Let us be the pessimist: It is a good wind that blows no ill. Meanwhile, those who cherish freedom will be guided by the famous dictum of Pericles that "although only a few may originate policy all are able to judge it." The comments in his funeral oration, delivered at least a half century before the *Republic* was written, may surely be applied to democracies other than the democracy of Athens for which he intended them. "Our administration favors the many instead of the few," he said, "and this is why it is called a democracy. But we do not ignore the claims of excellence. When a citizen distinguishes himself, then he will be called to serve the state, in preference to others, not as a matter of privilege, but as a reward of merit."

Finally, there is nothing in the logic of a democratic system that precludes the people from relying on representatives better informed than they for decisions on the complex issues of government, provided such representatives can be replaced. The reference here, it should be understood, is not to mere *delegates* polling their constituents on each issue as it arises. Nor are representatives themselves prevented from relying on experts for technical advice and even granting

[9] Thomas Carlyle, "Latter-Day Pamphlets," *The Works of Thomas Carlyle*, XX (New York: Charles Scribner's Sons, 1901), p. 34.

them quasi-legislative and judicial powers, as is done when experts are recruited to serve on tax review boards, utilities commissions, a civil aeronautics authority, etc. (p. 145). All this is routine in a complex society and, while no one would deny abuses exist the arrangement works reasonably well and in a manner completely consistent with the requirements of democracy. Democracy is not, then, a daily plebiscite, as Rousseau seemed to insist (p. 104), and the people need not and ought not to be called upon for decisions which even the wisest among them could not intelligently make. Democracy does not necessarily imply rule by the people if "rule" implies, as it did to the Greeks, direct participation by the people in government. Democracy, as we understand it, reposes *power*, of a sort, in the people; it is not necessarily government *by* the people, Lincoln's magnificent rhetoric notwithstanding.[10]

Tyranny of the Majority

It is appropriate at this point to dispose of another common criticism of democracy. Taken merely as a procedural principle majoritarianism might seem to mean that, after a poll in which each is reckoned as one, half the group, plus at least one, has a right to commit the other half, less at least one, to any course or policy under consideration. That the case is more complicated becomes evident as soon as one reckons with situations in which there are several alternatives. In such an event the gravity of the issue may well determine whether a plurality or majority shall prevail. Obviously, this introduces a new factor, namely the *importance of the issue to be decided*, which often results, even when there are only two alternatives, in requiring more than a simple majority. Generally hailed as the great majoritarian, Rousseau reckoned with this factor. In his view bare majorities suffice only in an emergency.

> There are two general rules. First, the more grave and important the questions discussed, the nearer should the opinion that is to prevail approach to unanimity. Second, the more the matter in hand calls for speed, the smaller the prescribed difference in the number of votes may be allowed to become: when an immediate decision has to be reached, a majority of one should suffice.[11]

How is importance to be assessed? In the end, if one eschews value judgments and adheres strictly to political terms, such assessment can be made only by reference to whether the minority is likely to abide by the outcome or resist it. (In increasingly rare instances a minority might have the alternative, as with the Mormons, of withdrawal from the community.) To urge that such a determination is difficult is to say only that the survival of a democracy depends on the astuteness of its majorities and, even more importantly, on an inclusive commu-

---

[10] We are helped philologically since *demo-cratia* refers to the *power* of the people. *Archē* is the Greek word for rule. Hence mon*archy*, or the *rule* of one.

[11] *Social Contract*, Book IV, Chapter ii.

nity of interest sufficient to assure the loyalty of minorities made dissident by defeat on a particular issue. On many issues the actual determination of what is important will have been made by constitutional provision, although the fact remains that issues as important as those dividing John F. Kennedy and Richard Nixon were decided in the 1960 presidential election by a majority of hardly more than one!

But what if the majority be so large that it need have no expedient concern about effective resistance to its verdict? May it, consistent with the democratic principle, do with the minorities that remain or with individuals or indeed with itself as it pleases? It is at this point that the task of defining the democratic idea grows more complex, a task rendered unnecessarily difficult if one deals with it as an abstract concept without reference to its origins in specific needs and its linkage with specific and enduring aspirations and convictions.

Much has been made of the potentialities for tyranny in a majoritarian system (p. 122). If the will of the majority is supreme, if there is no higher principle, it would appear that there are no rights, whether of individuals or of groups of individuals, that the majority may not invade or abridge. And, as Benjamin Constant pointed out, from the point of view of the individual it makes no difference whether he is tyrannized by an individual despot or by all the rest of the individuals composing the society of which he is a member; he is oppressed just the same. Indeed, his predicament is more acute in the latter case. Oppressed by an individual despot, he may look to others for understanding or help, and tyrannicide is always a possible way out. Oppressed by a large and tyrannical majority, he has no comparable relief or escape; nothing except his sense of loneliness and perhaps a haunting fear that with so many against him it might even be that he is not without blame.

Beyond such manifestations of tyranny lies the always present possibility that the majoritarian principle may be invoked to destroy itself. The rationale for employing a popular plebiscite to establish a dictatorship was provided long ago in the *Leviathan* where Hobbes, understandably prizing order as the highest good during a period of protracted civil strife, argued that civil society with all its amenities is made possible only when men enter into a covenant to give up to a sovereign the freedom they have by natural right. The decision is made by a majority and the sovereign is given absolute power. Since the contract is entered into only by those who select the sovereign and is not between them and him, there is nothing he can do to violate it. The delegation of power is irrevocable. Such were the delegations of power sought by Napoleon I and Louis Napoleon, and such were the plebiscites by which in our own time the *Führerprinzip* was sustained in Nazi Germany.

Some would provide for such abuses of power under the democratic rubric by distinguishing between totalitarian and constitutional democracy. They would defend the distinction as useful if only because it reminds us of the excesses and follies to which majorities can fall prey. Conservatives not only prefer this line (if the radical right which rejects democracy altogether is excluded), but tend to stress the frequency with which excess and folly prevail. When John Adams, leader of the Federalist party, declared that "the majority has eternally and without one exception usurped over the rights of the minority," he was reflecting the fear of conservatives from his time until now.

Others would urge that totalitarian democracy is a contradiction in terms made plausible because of an impermissible concentration on only one aspect of a democracy, namely, the majoritarian principle, and an oversimplification of that principle besides. This becomes clear when we are reminded that, although physical events are best understood (and, in fact, only understood) by ignoring purposes, we may not deal with social phenomena in the same way. One cannot understand the *idea* of democracy apart from its functioning as an *ideal*, i.e., apart from reference to the purposes which the idea of democracy was intended to serve. And these purposes involved no apotheosis of the state, no mystique about the people as a collectivity. They had to do with certain strong convictions about the individual, his dignity and his freedom. They were inspired by the efforts of individuals to be as free as possible of coercion. And, even though it was with their own freedom that most of them were concerned, the important point is that those who fathered the democratic tradition found it necessary to express their concern in terms of universals applicable to all men. Commenting on this tradition, Harold Laski has written:

> What . . . it is important to realize is the fact that in its making the state was never itself an end, but always a means to an end; that the individual, finite, separate, identifiable, was always regarded as existing in his own right, and not merely as a unit serving the state to which he belonged. His happiness, and not its well-being, was the criterion by which its behaviour was to be judged. His interests, and not its power, set the limits to the authority it was entitled to exercise.[12]

In brief, unless one oversimplifies the idea of democracy and tears it out of its historical context, democracy can hardly be other than constitutional, i.e., inseparably associated with the limitation of power. The majority should rule not because there is some mysterious virtue in majorities, not because they are endowed with intrinsic worth, but because this best serves individuals. If, to be thus served, individuals must give something up, this does not mean they give up everything. What the individual retains has been the subject of much debate, but it is at least as much as he may retain without threatening the welfare of others. In sum, the democratic idea is incompatible with the omnicompetent state. It declares that there are affairs which do not concern the state, including those actions of the state which reflect the will of an overwhelming majority. Such affairs may range all the way from the activities of sports car buffs (provided they obey the traffic regulations) to the beliefs and practices of religious sects. Democracy is the laboriously evolved outcome of a desire to limit sovereignty and control the state, not to make it omnicompetent—although when this has been said we must

[12] *The State in Theory and Practice* (New York: The Viking Press, 1935), p. 36.

be on guard against those who, often for self-serving reasons, would relegate government, through which the state acts, to virtual impotence.

Beyond this, there are other basic considerations which impose limitations on majority rule. Majorities do not form in a vacuum. Certain conditions involving individual rights must prevail. Unless a majority verdict is some miraculous coincidence or spontaneous merger of individual opinions—which it is not—it can come about only if individuals are free to formulate their views, to clarify them and to exchange them. A majority is not a mere mathematical concept and hence a fixed, timeless entity. Majorities emerge, grow and are the outcome of a process *in time*—a circumstance curiously neglected by those who fail to see that implicit in the very concept of majoritarianism are those conditions whereby minorities are free to *become* majorities. Beyond the traditional rights to speak and write freely, this implies in a complex society freedom to associate and organize, and easy access to mass communication. Above all, it assumes freedom from fear of reprisal.

It is of the essence of the democratic idea, then, that the power of the majority be restricted by certain individual rights. Whether such rights are justified by an appeal to nature (Locke, p. 60), history (Burke, p. 233) or utility (Bentham) is not here germane. The point is that sovereignty in a democracy is limited. Often the doctrine of individual rights is set up as something opposed to the democratic principle. If the foregoing is valid, such a polarity is specious. Individual rights are implied by the very nature of the democratic ideal.

If the rule of any given majority is limited by certain acknowledged individual rights, it is also limited by the decisions of earlier majorities, basically by the decisions of what we have come to call a constituent majority, and such specific limitations on the action of subsequent majorities as the constituent majority may have decreed. Thus, the power of a majority of the American people in the last elections was limited by the majority (in this case, not a truly popular majority) which adopted the basic law promulgated by the Founding Fathers. So on that Tuesday in November when Americans last voted in a national election, they could not have ordered the adoption of a nationwide speed limit or a federal divorce law or, directly—since there is no provision for a national referendum—a federal law of any kind. Neither could they have abolished the United States Senate. Even such power as they were allowed to exercise—at the national level, the election (say in 1962) of all the representatives to the lower house of Congress and of one-third of the Senate—was limited by the decision of the majority of two years before which had elected one-third of the Senate and the President of the United States, and a majority two years before that, which had elected the remaining one-third of the Senate.

Such *specific* limitations on the power of an instant majority as federalism and bicameralism are surely not essential to the idea of democracy, as the example of Great Britain demonstrates, even though Madison saw them as guarding against "the propensity of all single and numerous assemblies to yield to the impulse of sudden and violent passions, and to be seduced by factious leaders into intemperate and pernicious resolutions." [13] As far as the idea of democracy is concerned, the only essential limitation, apart from provisions for those individual rights referred to earlier, is implicit in the constitutional principle per se, namely, *that which requires the concurrence of several majorities distributed over a period of time before the basic law, once adopted, can be modified.* In this fashion, no single majority, such as that described by Thomas Hobbes, can surrender its sovereignty and thereby preclude succeeding majorities from enjoying it.

Similarly (lest the issue appear limited to musty treatises in political theory and bygone plebiscites), no single majority voting in Colorado or California can today surrender its sovereignty, as majorities in these states in fact voted to do in 1962 and 1964 respectively when they rejected proposals that would have reapportioned their legislatures on a straight population basis. In *Lucas* v. *The Forty-Fourth General Assembly of the State of Colorado,* Chief Justice Earl Warren declared for the United States Supreme Court that "a citizen's constitutional right can hardly be infringed because a majority of the people choose to do so." [14] This verdict can be undone only by constitutional amendment, that is, the action of a series of majorities, and often, as in this country, more than simple majorities at that.

The people speak through more than any extant majority and, in any case, through more than any instant majority: for the people embrace, if not the generations of yesterday, as Burke never tired of insisting, then of tomorrow and next year and a hundred years hence. Since *ex hypothesi* the generations of the future cannot be consulted, we do the next best and guard against fallibility by giving the majorities of the recent or remoter past a voice. And, if we wisely protect ourselves by reserving the power to override men whose prescience could hardly encompass our predicaments, we limit this power, where the basic law is at issue, by requiring more than a simple or single majority for its exercise. It is surely arbitrary to insist that democracy is dominated only by what Burke called "the vulgar practice of the hour" [15] (p. 134) and speaks only through the voice of a living majority or, worse, a majority of the moment or "momentary aggregation," as he called it. To insist that plebiscitary democracy is the only "pure" democracy is to be guilty of Platonizing with a vengeance.

Restraints on the majority were not, it is clear, contemplated by Rousseau, who believed that spontaneous assemblies of the people, convening in complete independence of the government, are the sole corrective of a tendency on the part of government to subordinate the interests of the people to its own. These are, as he viewed them, constituent, that is, revolutionary assemblies, as evidenced by the two questions they consider: "First, is it the pleasure of the sovereign [people] to preserve the existing form of government; second, is it the pleasure of the

[13] *Federalist Papers,* No. 62.

[14] 377 U.S. 713, 736–737 (1964).

[15] "Reflections on the Revolution in France," *The Writings and Speeches of Edmund Burke,* III, Beaconsfield ed. (London: Bickers and Sons, Ltd., 1901), p. 278.

people to leave the administration to those who at present have it in charge" (p. 108) ? The very functions of government are suspended during their deliberations. But Rousseau was an exception (as was Jefferson on this issue) and ideas of this kind were discredited by the excesses of the revolution that made him its patron saint.

Now it may be argued that constitutions are mere scraps of parchment (and in Britain, hardly that). Hence, if any given majority, or, indeed, any minority has the power and the fancy seizes it, it may well overturn the constitution and thereby ignore the limitation that, especially as regards the basic law, it act only with the concurrence of majorities removed from it in time. Our Founding Fathers did just that when they repudiated the Articles of Confederation. And it is, of course, true that constitutional restraints will prove useless unless the important groups in a society believe in their general fairness and rightness. If the majority is inhibited by constitutional restraints from suppressing a minority, or a minority from revolting against the majority, it is because, as suggested earlier, underlying their differences there is a *basic community of interest* which not only assures a "loyal opposition," but a tolerant majority prepared to contemplate the possibility of its defeat. In the absence of such an agreement among major factions or parties concerning the fundamentals of the social order of which they are a part, either they will war against each other, or one will tyrannize over the other. Neither alternative is compatible with democratic government.

Democracy and the Basic Consensus

The foundations of such a consensus deserve careful attention. It must be built on the understanding that all men shall enjoy the protection of what Thucydides long ago called the "common laws of humanity." Clearly involved is a system of relationships which does not *arbitrarily* exclude members of society from sharing in the amenities of civil life, as the Jews were excluded under Hitler or Negroes have been excluded in the Deep South. It is the arbitrariness of such exclusion that is crucial. Often the worst disabilities will be tolerated if only a rationale is provided. There must be some point or meaning to the exclusion—if only that "natural harmony of interests" which rationalized the brutal exploitation of workers during the murky dawn of the industrial revolution. But no community of interest is possible when normal human aspirations and established expectations are purposelessly and systematically frustrated.

No doubt that is why Negroes are not convinced that "the laws of theft are as important to Negroes as they are to anyone else," although it was a Negro judge, James B. Parsons, the first of his race to be appointed to a federal bench in the continental United States, who said that.[16] The result is a contempt for

---

[16] The occasion was not the wild spree of looting and senseless violence that occurred in the Los Angeles ghetto of Watts, but Martin Luther King's "supralegal" takeover of the rentals from a Chicago slum tenement to renovate the property for the benefit of the tenants (*Time*, March 25, 1966, pp. 18–19).

law among many of them which will be mitigated only when it becomes evident that they are not gratuitously excluded from the benefits which the law is intended to protect. Meanwhile, the fact that many Negroes find no community of interest with the majority group results in a use of force to restrain them which, even where necessary, must acutely trouble the conscience of a democratically oriented society.

Similarly unreasonable denials of opportunity explain why large numbers of talented European youth may be found in the ranks of Western Europe's Communist parties. On a larger scale comparable consequences were invited when, in Europe and the United States, an impoverished and unemployed multitude confronted the paradox of enforced idleness and want in the midst of potential plenty during the depression of the thirties. Men endure what they cannot escape. The combination of idle machines and unmet needs was bound to suggest a way out which they would one day seek even if it meant challenging the accepted order with force. In such circumstances, the dominant group, whether an ascendant class or numerical majority, confronted by subordinate classes or numerical minorities with which it no longer shares any basic purposes—not even the preservation of order—takes fright. And the result is suppression, regimentation, a denial of the democratic process.

At one time religious conformity would have been regarded as an essential part of any basic consensus. But as Jefferson said, "it does me no injury for my neighbor to say that there are twenty gods, or no god." [17] Mankind has learned from bitter experience—at any rate much of it has—that the price of religious conformity runs too high. Even so, there are secular creeds today, equally intolerant of dissent, which is denounced not as heresy, but as disloyalty. In our country the most clamorous of these creeds, once its veneer of patriotism is penetrated, turns out to be concerned with a return to the unregulated capitalism of the early decades of this century. There also clings to most of these creeds a patina of religiosity, but it turns out the spiritual renewal to which we are summoned hinges on undertakings no more uplifting than repeal of the income tax. While, in ordinary circumstances, such a sorry credo would hardly merit serious attention, the charge of disloyalty in a world menaced by Russia or Red China frightens many people as easily today as the people of Salem were frightened by rumors of witchcraft.

What one is dealing with here is, of course, a perversion of the concept of consensus and in the end a suspension of it, for the charge of disloyalty when directed by one party at another ends discussion, argument, negotiation. It replaces the competition of ideas with physical conflict. It is an invitation to civil war. One does not parley with traitors or even with "dupes" of traitors—one destroys them. Those who, in the tradition of the late Senator Joseph McCarthy, impugn the loyalty of all who disagree with them sin against democracy and, indeed, against representative government of all kinds. In the name of an im-

---

[17] *Notes on Virginia*, ed. William Peden (Chapel Hill: University of North Carolina Press, 1955), p. 159. However, Jefferson's critics plagued him endlessly with this statement.

posed and often spurious consensus parading as "loyalty," they destroy that deeper concord without which the political process degenerates into a test of brute force. What could happen is suggested by the famous words of Thucydides describing the "commotion" in the Hellenic world during the years preceding the outbreak of the Peloponnesian war:

> The meaning of words had no longer the same relation to things, but was changed . . . as [was] thought proper. . . . The leaders on either side used specious names. . . . Striving in every way to overcome each other, they committed the most monstrous crimes . . . ; even these were surpassed by the magnitude of their revenges . . . neither side observing any definite limits either of justice or public expediency. . . . An attitude of perfidious antagonism everywhere prevailed; for there was no word binding enough, no oath terrible enough, to reconcile enemies. Each man was strong only in the conviction that nothing was secure; he must look to his own safety, and could not afford to trust others.[18]

Egalitarianism and the Consensus

To what extent must a genuine consensus embrace the egalitarian ideal? Although much of what has been said provides an answer, the question must be considered in its own terms. The democrats have been called levelers, as indeed they are. But they need not and do not assume that all men are equal in strength, intelligence, or any other of the traits (e.g., determination and self-discipline) by virtue of which some men greatly excel others. Nor do they assume each individual, because he has a single vote, has an equal voice in governing, and they do not believe the democratic principle implies equality or even approximate equality of reward. The egalitarian ideal to which they are committed is a limited one compounded, as we all say, of equality of opportunity and equality before the law. This much at least is part of the consensus on which democracy rests.

All too often the account is left here. But in truth, even when understood in this limited sense, egalitarianism has certain implications for the prevailing distribution of rewards which may not be ignored. Quite obviously equality of opportunity involves not only the removal of legal disabilities and of such class barriers and racial or religious restrictions as may prevent individuals from realizing their capacities and enjoying the fruits of their effort. It also involves the availability of means without which individuals are decisively handicapped. These are not only educational resources, but all those other resources generally called living conditions. Even if their schools were much more adequate than they are, it would be sheer self-deception to suggest that children who live in the blighted areas of our large cities enjoy equality of opportunity.

[18] *The Peloponnesian War*, III, pp. 82–84 (Jowett translation).

Equality before the law, to be meaningful, likewise implies access to minimal resources. Still disconcertingly relevant is the 1919 Carnegie Foundation study which found that:

> The administration of American justice is not impartial, the rich and the poor do not stand on an equality before the law, the traditional method of providing justice has operated to close the doors of the courts to the poor, and has caused a gross denial of justice . . . to millions of persons.[19]

After all, it was not until 1963 that the Supreme Court, responding favorably to the handwritten personal appeal of an indigent Florida prisoner named Gideon, reversed the verdict it reached in *Betts* v. *Brady* (1942) and declared that, "in our adversary system of criminal justice, any person hailed into court who is too poor to hire a lawyer cannot be assured a fair trial unless counsel is provided for him." [20]

Beyond all this, however, the democratic ideal, even though it can be reconciled with large disparities in income, may well require the extension of the egalitarian ideal to exclude certain kinds of income, namely, those that are not functionally justifiable. Large incomes are justified in this country mostly on the grounds that they are a reward of skill, that such skill would not be exercised in the absence of large reward, and that all ultimately benefit from its exercise.[21] The merit of the justification is not here under scrutiny. The point is that many forms of income are not functionally justifiable, and that a democratically governed community will not in the long run readily permit individuals to preempt goods and command services—which is what they do when they have large incomes—simply because such favored individuals like or enjoy their privileged status. It will want to be convinced such privileges are at least approximately earned by the discharge of socially useful functions.

This conclusion does not follow as a necessary logical consequence. An overwhelming majority might decide for entirely sentimental reasons to maintain certain favored individuals in the most lavish manner without exacting or expecting comparable services. Conceivably, the British royal family is the beneficiary of some such sentiment. One could not charge that this is inconsistent with democratic practice. Rather, the issue is one involving social psychology: a free people are unlikely to tolerate functionless incomes—for example, the vast incomes derived by a small group of Americans from the ownership of sub-surface resources which they have neither discovered, extracted or distributed and on which, as though to gild the lily, they enjoy special tax privileges. If such incomes are relatively untouched, the suspicion is a proper one that the community

---

[19] R. H. Smith, *Justice and the Poor*, Carnegie Foundation Bulletin 13, 1919. The study by a member of the Boston bar was approved by such eminent lawyers as Elihu Root and Charles Evans Hughes.

[20] *Gideon* v. *Wainwright*, 372 U.S. 335, 344 (1963).

[21] For another justification, see p. 49.

has not been free to act. If the restraint on freedom in such instances is not in America a source of friction affecting the basic consensus, it may well be because a society as opulent as ours can afford free riders.

Democracy and Economic Power

The foregoing discussion of the democratic constitutional ideal and of the consensus on which it depends was prompted by the contention that in essence the democratic idea embraces an inner duality. It is not only a scheme for conferring but also for *limiting* power. In America, apart from certain enumerated rights which shield the individual, this limitation has been accomplished by the several arrangements of the machinery of government that are called federalism, bicameralism, and the separation of powers. Of interest primarily to the student of government, these are mentioned here because they are reminders of the supreme confidence our predecessors reposed in political contrivances as safeguards against tyranny. Victims of despotic Stuarts and Bourbons and later witnesses to the excesses of the French Assembly were understandably preoccupied with abuses of political power and justly intent on devising political mechanisms to thwart such abuses. But this need not deter us from understanding that for the most part our forebears were really political determinists who believed the sum of all felicities could be achieved by evolving the proper forms of government. As such, they were limited in their understanding of the uses and abuses of power.

Any effort to discuss democracy meaningfully without reference to economic power and the arrangements and practices through which such power is exercised and limited must be sterile. There is this much truth in the teaching of Marx. It is a large truth and an important teaching which the political determinism of the eighteenth and nineteenth centuries obscured.

By this time Marx's conception of the bearing of economic institutions on democratic practices is well known. Parliamentary forms, he argued, are a mere pretense so long as there is private ownership of the means of production. Behind the facade provided by suffrage and the party system, owners of the means of production rule, and government is, in Marx's famous phrase, "nothing but the executive committee of the bourgeoisie." One may charge that Marx completely underestimated the possibility of making government responsive to the will of the people within the framework of a capitalist system, as indeed he did. But his economic determinism, though an oversimplification, was not too irrelevant to his time and, in any case, it made those who came after him reckon seriously with economic forces.

Economic determinism, it may be noted, is no monopoly of Marxists. Ironically, many who are most vigorous in execrating Marx, especially for his "materialist" stress on economic forces, insist with equal vehemence that democracy is inseparably linked with private ownership of the means of production and the "free" market as that market operated in the first decades of this century. They add that totalitarianism is not a possible or likely, but an *inevitable* outcome of deviation from such traditional capitalist arrangements. The remarks of Henry Hazlitt are typical: "Capitalism is merely the name for a system of economic liberty. Under it civil and political liberties flourish and are secure. Under a complete or nearly complete socialism neither economic nor political liberty can exist. Freedom is indivisible." [22] The comment takes on great import when we remind ourselves that, for those of Hazlitt's persuasion, virtually every form of government intervention is designated as socialism. Among them is Ludwig Von Mises who says "if history could teach us anything, it is that private property is inextricably linked with civilization." Since, as he goes on to say, "governments have always looked askance at private property," [23] we must conclude that governments represent a principle in opposition to civilization. Whether true or false, this is surely economic determinism with a vengeance and, if this is not to refute the position, at least something is gained by calling it by its right name. Meanwhile, it is safe to say that both the exaggeration and neglect of economic forces have been corrected by most careful thinkers, at any rate in the English-speaking world, and the consequence has been a new understanding of the phenomenon of power as it bears on democracy.

It is now commonplace that the emergence of a highly industrialized society based on the free market and private ownership of the means of production, has resulted in giving individuals enormous power over the lives of others even though such individuals hold no political position, make no laws, command no armies. This was already evident in the day of the "Titans," as Max Lerner has called them, when men like Carnegie, Morgan and the elder Rockefeller wielded power beyond the dreams of any Renaissance prince. It is equally a commonplace since Berle and Means wrote in *The Modern Corporation and Private Property* that the advent of the modern corporation and the separation of ownership and management associated with it have enormously concentrated such power in a few hands. This power no longer derives, primarily, from ownership of the means of production, as was the case in the early and middle periods of the industrial revolution, but for the most part from control by strategically placed managers of the property of absentee owners.

Several circumstances may be considered in connection with this concentration of economic power. First, it was accomplished at the same time that political power was being diffused and limited so that the significant regulation of economic power was for a long period practically precluded. Government was easily brought under economic influence and even when partly free of such influence, it was too restricted in authority to act effectively. This was especially true in America during the decades beginning with the mid-1880's when the Supreme Court, invoking the due process clause—intended for the protection of the Negro—virtually excluded the American people from exercising control over the economic life of the community. These were the days when, as we are always reminded, Justice Holmes felt obliged to inform his colleagues on the bench that

[22] *Newsweek,* August 20, 1962, p. 77.
[23] *Omnipotent Government* (New Haven: Yale University Press, 1944), p. 58.

"the Fourteenth Amendment does not enact Mr. Herbert Spencer's Social Statics."

Second, the concentration of economic power has been associated with a significant weakening of the traditional economic checks by means of which it was supposed to be held in restraint. The decisive check supplied by competition has become more and more attenuated as fixed and "administered" prices have replaced competitive prices in large areas of the economy. Also, large corporations have less and less recourse to the security market to finance replacement and expansion of plant and equipment, relying increasingly on retained earnings, so that this check on corporation policy no longer plays the role assigned it in orthodox economic theory. Most important of all, perhaps, management, as all students of the corporation concede, has become less and less accountable to the shareholders. The point was driven home perfectly by a former vice-president of General Motors who, upon being asked to open the books of the corporation to a government fact-finding commission, responded: "We don't even open our books to our own stockholders."

Nothing has changed since the editors of *Fortune*, surely not biased against corporate management, wrote: "The control of the typical big corporation is now in the hands of 'managers' who do not own it, and its ownership is in the hands of stockholders who do not influence its behavior. The corporation has become a disembodied, almost self-sufficient, socially 'illegitimate' force." [24] If illegitimacy in this context does not mean birth out of wedlock, it does refer to power acquired and wielded without reference to explicitly formulated and acknowledged principles and to an absence of accountability in the exercise of power.

Third, the size of the largest of our corporations has in many instances exceeded the requirements of efficiency and economy in production. Obviously, the size of the modern enterprise is *up to a point* decreed by the conditions of operating in a technologically advanced economy based on mass production. No one denies that the corporation is a functionally indispensable device for the conduct of most enterprises in a modern economy. But, in the judgment of many, the size of our largest corporations has gone beyond the point where it can be said to be functionally justifiable. There is abundant evidence to indicate that small units can produce with equal and often greater efficiency.[25] The late Professor Henry Simons, himself a neo-classicist in economic theory, wrote: "The corporation is a socially useful device for organizing the ownership and control in operating companies of size sufficient to obtain the real economies of large-scale production under unified management." But, he added, "few of our gigantic corporations can be defended on the ground that their present size is necessary to reasonably full exploitation of productive economies: their existence is to be explained in terms of opportunities for promoter profits, personal ambitions of industrial and financial 'Napoleons,' and advantages of monopoly power." [26] *If this is so, and*

---

[24] "The Domestic Economy," insert in *Fortune*, December, 1942, p. 3.

[25] For example, see Professor T. N. Beckman's "The Structure of Postwar American Business," *American Economic Review*, XXXIV (March, 1944), No. 1, Part II, supplement.

[26] *Economic Policy for a Free Society* (Chicago: University of Chicago Press, 1948), pp. 58–60.

*the growth of the large corporation must be viewed, at least in part, as a response
to the desire of its managers for power, then it is a political phenomenon and
must be treated in such terms.*

Fourth, there is evidence that the already great power resident in the large
corporation when it operates within the economic sphere is expanding into other
institutional areas. This has happened as management, no doubt acting from the
most laudable motives, has taken up the ideal of corporate "citizenship,"[27] coming to the rescue, for example, of financially beleaguered institutions of higher
learning, providing for the recreational interests of the corporation's employees,
and even ministering to their spiritual needs.[28] There is, indeed, ample room for
the exercise of civic responsibility in areas not likely to enhance the power of
corporations—control of air and stream pollution, vigorous programs against
mendacity in advertising and cheating in packaging, support of adequate drug
legislation ordinarily blocked in Congressional committees by business lobbies,
and fair employment practices. It is here that those troubled by the issue of
power would wish to see corporate citizenship manifest and they urge that the
other areas be declared out of bounds.

Last, and in the light of recent events perhaps most significant, is the fact
that the power of management is such that the decisions of a small group of men
in a key industry may decisively affect the functioning of the entire economy.
During the Kennedy administration and again during the Johnson administration, decisions of management in the steel industry to raise prices despite vigorous government resistance afforded a spectacular example. Here is power over
the national economy that has not been solicited, and is, in fact, unwanted. But it
is nonetheless real and formidable. Thus men holding no public office, their decisions subject—at any rate, in their judgment—to no review, weighing the effect
of their decision only on their enterprise without reference to the economy as a
whole, are able to set in motion powerful forces of vital concern to the entire
nation. The boldness imputed to President Kennedy when he challenged the management of the steel industry and the traumatic effect of his challenge on the
business community are measures of the extent to which many have thus far
failed to reckon with—the fact that those who wield great power in a democracy
must reconcile themselves to being held accountable. If President Johnson's resistance to unilateral price increases has provoked fewer cries of outrage, this
may be credited to his substantial mandate, the Vietnam war, and unprecedented
prosperity. In any case, his protests now go largely ignored.

It is not for laymen to decide whether the action of management in the steel
industry would have had the consequences cited by the late President and his
successor. Neither is it for them to pass on the hazards of inflation; although
long warned by the business community of the catastrophic (or insidious) conse-

---

[27] For a full exploration of this topic see Richard Eells, *The Meaning of Modern
Business* (New York: Columbia University Press, 1960), pp. 38–67, and A. A. Berle, Jr.'s
20th Century Capitalist Revolution (New York: Harcourt, Brace and World, 1960).

[28] A number of corporations have recently provided churches and chaplains for this
purpose.

quences of inflation, laymen may be pardoned if they fear it disproportionately. The central point is that the business community as a whole regarded President Kennedy's and President Johnson's intervention as unwarranted interference, insisting that the books of the enterprises involved were a private affair, and rejecting proposals for a public fact-finding committee.

Affairs cease to be private once the community concludes that its welfare is in some decisive sense bound up with them, as it surely is in the case of the pricing policies of the steel or aluminum or copper industry. The community did not, in the case of steel, arrive at such a conclusion in response to the manipulations or decrees of planners, meddlers, or foes of free private enterprise. The very size of the steel companies—that same size which the steel companies themselves sought and secured—made it inevitable that a democratically organized community would arrive at this conclusion, especially when these corporations act in concert. Although they are privately owned and privately operated, the great steel companies *have made themselves* quasi-public enterprises. What has been said here of steel may, of course, be said of all comparably large undertakings.

None of this is intended as a criticism of bigness. Neither does it pretend to be a final evaluation of the way in which management has used its power. No doubt in many instances that power has been used responsibly, although there is also a long and continuing record of irresponsibility. The basic point is that *the democratic idea cannot be intelligently discussed without reference to checks on such power* and that, in fact, managerial power will *not* be used responsibly unless a democratic society generates forces that will contain and balance it.

Commenting, in 1834, on America's emerging business elite, Alexis de Tocqueville wrote:

> I am of the opinion . . . that the manufacturing aristocracy which is growing up under our eyes, is one of the harshest which ever existed in the world; but at the same time it is one of the most confined and least dangerous. Nevertheless the friends of democracy should keep their eyes anxiously fixed in this direction; for if ever a permanent inequality of conditions and aristocracy again penetrate into the world, it may be predicted that this is the channel by which they will enter.[29]

The harshness to which de Tocqueville referred has been much softened, and the economic elite of this country surely contrast favorably (if one excludes an all too influential number of parvenu tycoons) with their European counterparts.[30] Even so, the perceptive Frenchman's advice was sound and if, thanks to certain other tendencies at work in our society, the eye need not be anxious, it should be alert.

[29] *Democracy in America*, II (New York: Schocken Books, 1961), p. 194.
[30] Cf. pp. 51–52.

The Limitation of Economic Power

Once the managers or owners who control the means of production have secured their creature comforts, their main objective is bound to be a government hospitable to the continued exercise of their power. And, so long as the economy over which they preside satisfies established expectations, provides reasonable opportunity for the able and talented, and in general appears to be realizing its productive potentialities, they can count on friendly majorities to provide them with just such a government. To be sure, such majorities do not spring into being spontaneously. A job of selling must be done. Moreover, the chance of a challenge to privilege is by no means excluded even in the favorable circumstances described. There will always be some contention, if only because man is refractory and perverse, and so long as the goods of the world are unevenly distributed. But given the circumstances cited, there are a thousand ways to deal with discontent without compromising the foundations of privilege and power or tampering with the forms of democracy.

It was precisely because during the thirties our economic system failed on a vast scale to meet established expectations, to provide opportunity, and to realize its productive potentialities that the power of those in charge was vigorously and successfully challenged. With this challenge came a new and more realistic understanding of the means by which to use and limit the use of power in a democratic society.

It should be noted that the challenge was not mounted easily. Those very checks intended to keep majorities from abusing power had in effect become charters for the use of power by private individuals. At the same time, the majority had been reduced to near impotence so that, while token measures in behalf of the general welfare might be permitted, substantive social legislation was a utopian dream. The dry prose of a 1923 Supreme Court decision striking down state minimum wage laws for women is an eloquent illustration. The provision was found unconstitutional because the basis for determining the wage rates, the Court said (with Justice Holmes dissenting), "is not the value of the services rendered, but the extraneous circumstance that the employee needs to get a prescribed sum of money to insure her subsistence, health and morals."

The larger pattern of which this decision was only a part is well described by Max Lerner:

> If a program is marked for destruction, one path open is a direct assault in the area of public attitude, where the dominant minority has a massive influence in the opinion industries. If they lose there, they can turn their energies to the prevention of a majority for the measure in either house of Congress, using to their advantage the committee system, the rules of parliamentary delay and filibuster, the high-pressure operation of lobbies, and the fact that Congressional representation is badly skewed to favor the rural conservative constituen-

cies as against the urban liberal ones. If they lose there, they can fall back—as they did for a half century from the 1880's to the Roosevelt era—on the protection of the judicial power as interpreted by a property-minded Supreme Court. If they lose there, they can concentrate on weakening the administrative enforcement of the measure or even capturing the administrative machinery and its personnel. And always they have the chance, by their immense wealth and power, of capturing the party machinery and dictating the choice of candidates in both the major parties. In short, the battle for an affirmative democratic program is like an action in which one army, in order to win, has to take every one of a succession of fortified places, while the other army has only to win and hold one such fortified place, even though it loses all the rest.[31]

The danger, it had turned out, was not, as John Adams feared, that the majority would usurp the rights of the minority. The danger was that on essential issues it would not be able to act at all, and that, while preserving the traditional democratic forms, a select minority would usurp the rights of the majority. Only a monumental failure, in the course of which large segments of the business community lost confidence in their own shibboleths, could have liberated the majority from this impotence. The depression of the thirties was such a failure. It prepared the way for a new pattern of power relationships based not on a reorganization of the machinery of government, but on a mobilization of forces outside the operations of government.

To understand what transpired one must seek out the sources of actual or potential power in modern society. These will be found at the point where large groups have vital interests at stake and, because these interests diverge, compete with each other for ascendancy. The power of such groups may derive from mere numbers, from the group's strategic position in the configuration of forces, or from a combination of both. Thus, consumers of goods have a vital interest in buying the best commodity at the lowest possible price. This is in conflict with the interest of sellers, who seek the reverse. Workers have a vital interest in obtaining as large a share of increase in productivity as they can without discouraging the capital investments which are a prerequisite to increased productivity; employers have a contrary interest. Rural agrarian areas have an interest in high prices for agricultural commodities which is resisted by the urban manufacturing areas. In America, ethnic and religious minorities have sought equality of opportunity and status from an unresponsive and often hostile majority.

Similar foci of power and corresponding conflicts have in the past arisen, or arise now elsewhere, in the relation of the military to the civilian interest (as in France during the Algerian crisis); of the clerical to the secular interest; of a state church to disestablishmentarians; or of a government bureaucracy to the average citizen. Recently, Mortimer Adler and Louis Kelso, no doubt recalling an

[31] *America as a Civilization* (New York: Simon and Schuster, Inc., 1957), pp. 368-69.

earlier "manifesto," have issued *The Capitalist Manifesto* in which they call upon shareholders to unite against management. One can imagine societies of the future in which other major conflicts of power and interest would arise.

So long as there are divergences over vital interests, the competing groups, to the extent that they are able, will try to influence government to intervene in their behalf, and, if they are operating within the framework of a democracy, to convert the majority to their persuasion. However, until the thirties, the preponderant power of the managerial-upper income group was reflected in the feebleness of organized labor, the weakness of farmers, the helplessness of the average consumer, and the resignation of racial minorities and such traditionally neglected groups as the aged. It was also mirrored in the party system. Both major political parties were dominated by the business interest, and while, within their notoriously ample confines, reform movements might win minor skirmishes, hardly anyone who counted contemplated radical change in the prevailing pattern of property relationships.[32] Even the intellectuals of the decades preceding the thirties could hardly be described as hostile to the aspirations and ideals of the business community and the few exceptions had little impact on the course of events. The first wave of intellectual protest in the twenties was against propriety rather than property—a noble crusade, but not one calculated to upset the *status quo*.

The first manifestation of the new configuration of forces produced by the great depression was a party system in which the major parties more accurately reflected opposing views and interests. While it is clear that the influence of the business community is still by no means limited to one party, it is also clear that ethnic minorities, workers, the needy aged, and large segments of the population forming the core of our great metropolitan areas—led often by reform-minded patricians and intellectuals—have found a political vehicle only rarely and imperfectly available to them prior to the thirties. By means of it, they have been able to introduce drastic reforms heretofore contemplated only in textbooks. The long delays preceding the adoption of Medicare and federal aid to education testify to the strength of those who oppose reform as do roadblocks in the way of other proposals such as comprehensive tax reform. It may well be that, in the absence of emergency, reforms opposed by the business community are still doomed to defeat, but the contest is far less uneven than it would have been at the turn of the century.

Our Founding Fathers feared a party system as promoting factionalism.[33]

---

[32] The notable exception was the Sixteenth Amendment authorizing income tax legislation which had been outlawed by the Supreme Court—a major reform that warned of untapped strength in the democratic process.

[33] Madison wrote of the "factious spirit [that] has tainted our public administrations," where the faction is understood as "a number of citizens, whether amounting to a majority or a minority of the whole, who are united and actuated by some common impulse of passion, or of interest, adverse to the rights of other citizens or to the permanent and aggregate interests of the community" (*Federalist Papers*, No. 10). On the other hand, he wrote (*Federalist Papers*, No. 50) that an extinction of parties necessarily implies either a universal alarm for the public safety, or an absolute extinction of liberty."

But we have come to understand that a multi-party system functioning, as indicated earlier, within a framework of common ideals and aspirations, is essential to a democratic society. Such a party system, operating independently of the government, is an indispensable way of checking power *in all of its forms and varieties.* Single party systems are, of course, the device by means of which dictatorships perpetuate themselves without reliance on an often fickle military. But a multi-party system makes possible the organization of an effective opposition which can oust governments unresponsive to the wishes of the people. Also, and less obviously, by attracting otherwise diffused and dispersed power to the support of specific policies, programs and personalities, and thereby concentrating it, a party system generates countervailing power to balance those otherwise unchallenged concentrations of power produced by the operations of the economy.

The party system in America achieves these results most imperfectly: Our conglomerate parties, if only to avoid fragmentation, often tend to blur rather than define issues; deals often win out over ideals, and the prize is often more sought than the principle; party discipline often fails to triumph over the resistances built into our system of checks and balances, but the creaking mechanism works and grinds the grain from which we brew democracy.

Another major countervailing force generated during the thirties came about as a result of pooling the power, not in this instance of voters, but of workers. The labor union movement, too, is full of flaws and generally falls short of the expectations of its early prophets. But it represents an essential contribution to a balance of power without which government would still be under the domination of employers—a domination decisively attested to by the early use of troops against strikers (as in the Pullman strike) and the later use of a variety of legislative and judicial devices which severely curtailed union activities. The Magna Carta of the labor union movement was the National Labor Relations Act of 1935, but given the power of employers, it surely would never have been adopted had the economy not been in a state of shock.

As the power of voters and workers has been pooled, so might the diffused power of multitudinous consumers have been concentrated and organized to improve their position *vis à vis* sellers. The great cooperative movements of Europe and the British Commonwealth do in fact provide a counterpoise to the power of producers and sellers, but in America the ultimate buyer, lulled in part by the myth of consumer sovereignty, has not exploited his potential power. The price he pays for this neglect is perhaps best calculated after a reading of the record of the hearings of the Kefauver Committee. The measure of the imbalance is suggested by the fact that even urgently needed legislation to control the drug industry was held up indefinitely in committee until the birth of scores of malformed babies jolted Congress into action.

The last several decades have witnessed the effective organization of farmers, of Negroes, all of whom, once organized, contribute to the new balance of power. Many would urge that the business community still enjoys hegemony as evidenced by the success with which it opposes significant social reform and discourages serious consideration of forthright intervention by the community in the affairs of a still imperfect economy. But, if this is so, the hegemony is precarious and limited, at the mercy these days of minor tremors in the economy, and much more restricted in compass.

It turns out that it has not been exclusively or even primarily by arrangements in the "interior structure of the government" that power is checked and democratically controlled in a modern society, but by "exterior provisions" of the kind which deal with power wherever it appears. In his famous defense of the system of checks and balances Madison wrote "the great security against gradual concentration of the several powers in the same department consists in giving to those who administer each department the necessary constitutional means and personal motives to resist encroachment of others. . . . Ambition," he said, "must be made to counterset ambition," and he added, "it may be a reflection on human nature that such devices should be necessary . . . [but] this policy of supplying, by opposite and rival interests, the defect of better motives, might be traced through the whole system of human affairs, private as well as public." [34] And so it may. Madison's language takes on peculiar relevance once one applies it beyond the departments of government to all those affairs in which men believe they have a vital stake.

Interventionism in a Free Society

At the outset of this discussion, political affairs were defined as those involving issues which the community regards as so crucial to its well-being that it will prescribe the course to be followed by its members and assure itself of conformity, if necessary to the point of using coercion. In such circumstances the community enlists the agency of the state which, in modern society, is accorded an exclusive monopoly in the use of force.

For many years the prevailing view in this country was that such affairs should be limited (with minor exceptions) to defense, the preservation of order, the enforcement of contracts, provisions for facilitating exchange (e.g., a monetary system), and teaching citizens to "read, write and account." For the community to concern itself with more was regarded as involving it in a dictatorial infringement on property rights, and hence on individual freedom with which the unrestricted enjoyment of property rights had come to be identified. As will be noted in detail in the next essay, such a view had the effect of excluding the community from significant intervention in its economic affairs, which is to say, from any direct concern with such basic issues as the allocation of resources and the distribution of income. The view was bulwarked by a description of property rights as absolute and "natural."

However, such a rationalization has never had great appeal to those who are without property,[35] so that it has always been necessary to justify property

[34] *Federalist Papers*, No. 51.

[35] On the other hand, in some contexts the doctrine of natural rights had great appeal—enough to prompt propertyless individuals to contend that they had been deprived of what was theirs by "nature."

rights functionally by reference to their social utility—as Locke, the great exponent of property as a natural right, and Adam Smith, in fact, did (p. 64).
Once one accepts such a criterion, however, the argument that the community
may not intervene in economic affairs without violating basic moral principles is
bound to seem arbitrary. As a matter of fact, if the test of consequences appears
to call for intervention and the community still fails to act, the conclusion is ines-
capable that it is not operating within a framework of democratic principles. A
wise and free society will intervene in economic affairs sufficiently to realize its
productive potentialities and to secure as broad a diffusion of income as may be
compatible with optimum productivity. It will respect (and even expand) occu-
pational freedom of choice. It will also seek the closest possible coincidence between what its citizens produce and what they want. To the extent that these
goals are realized we may be sure that the democratic community is functioning
meaningfully and vigorously, enjoying the substance of democracy as well as its
form.

ELITISM

*The mass crushes beneath it everything that is different, everything
that is excellent, individual, qualified and select.*

JOSÉ ORTEGA Y GASSET

As understood here, elitism is the view that only a few are qualified to rule
—that is, to guide policy and make the basic decisions which must be made in
any society—and that rule, or a preponderant role in ruling, ought to be by those
most qualified. These few must not be understood, however, as restricted to those
actually in charge of the machinery of government; in practice the power to influence basic decisions in a critical sense may be wielded by others not formally
vested with it or involved in the actual execution of it. The elite as a class consists
of those who possess, or are thought to possess, the qualifications for such rule.
In the broader sense, it includes the group from which they come, supplemented
by those individuals—soldiers, artists, physicians, administrators—who possess
relatively rare skills which for one reason or another rulers highly prize.

If an elitist system is to be meaningfully differentiated from a well-governed
democracy, a distinction between governing and ruling must be assumed. An
elite does not merely govern, it rules. In a democracy, able people or people favored or preferred for reasons other than ability may govern. They do not rule,
nor would we refer to them, except in some Pickwickian sense, as our rulers.
They would indeed rule if they served without the consent of those whom they
govern or, as in an elitist system, with only partial or largely token reliance on such
consent.

However, accountability, even though tenuous, is assumed in elitist systems
—at least as elitism is understood here. All responsible men have a sense of their
weakness in the presence of great temptation and of the need to protect themselves and others from the possibility that they might succumb. If some, like
Plato, have been silent about safeguards, it is generally recognized among elitists
that even the best rulers are corruptible and that those over whom they preside
must be provided with some kind of protection. This might be accomplished
through a system of plural voting (which would give at least one vote to the individual as such while weighting it in favor of the ruling class), or through a

system of "mixed government" which may give representatives of the people at least some voice in action taken by the state (p. 246). As envisaged by Montesquieu, for example, such a system would incorporate a separation of powers in government in which its several functions were discharged by individuals representative of different major interest groups in the social order.

In short, elitists, if they are not to be indistinguishable from totalitarians, must be committed in principle to constitutionalism, that is to say, to the limitation of power, which is in essence what constitutionalism means. However, we must remind ourselves that no limitation of power even though embossed on parchment and embodied in institutions and practices is meaningful or durable unless there are (a) groups in the community capable of challenging an abuse of power by those who rule, and (b) a consensus among the groups which count that power ought to be distributed in that particular way. In an elitist society, the achievement of consensus is easy or difficult in proportion as the group in charge is able to exploit the productive possibilities of the society over which it presides, and is disposed to absorb the most creative members of society into its own ranks. Thus, in England, where aristocrats became businessmen and businessmen became aristocrats (while the nobility in general actively managed their estates), an aristocratic regime enjoyed a tenure not vouchsafed the functionless French nobility congregated at Versailles.

Etymologically, the elite are the *elect* (Fr. *élire*, to choose; L. *eligere*, to elect), *select* or *chosen*. Hence the term refers to any group set apart because of some superior quality or condition. The "election" or "selection" may have been made by God, by nature "red in tooth and claw," [1] or by popular recognition based on commonly accepted standards of merit. The developments culminating in such a selection may lie in the recent past or remotely enough in the past to become myth and legend. Although, etymologically, *aristoi* implies no process or act of selection or choice, it too refers to those who excel or are superior, so that the two designations are interchangeable. Historically, however, aristocracy came to stand for the rule of those whose status derived from birth or inherited title. This is obviously a very special kind of basis for excellence and claim to privilege, hence the need for a term like elite or "governing elite" (p. 271) to include groups free of such historical associations.

Common to elitists is some concept of the good which the ascendancy of one or other group is thought to promote and hence a *rationale*: The elite ought not to wield power because they happen to have it or want it, but because society as a whole is thereby better served. On the other hand, the good sought need not necessarily be an improvement of the general level of living. It may be identified with certain "spiritual" or aesthetic values—categories of which some elitists are especially fond—rather than with the "material" welfare of society as a whole (p. 258). Or, the welfare of society as a whole may indeed receive recognition, but only as identified with "stability" or the power to fend off external enemies. The latter appears to be the position of Pareto who placed great store by what he

---

[1] The phrase is Tennyson's and misrepresents Darwin.

called the utility "*of* a community" (for example, its power to repel external rivals), but likened the humanitarian "religion," that is, the utility "*for* a community," to the "intent of the child who kills a bird by too much fondling. . . ." For him social stability is, indeed, so precious that to maintain it even justifies enlisting the "theology of universal suffrage" (p. 273).

It may be noted that elitism as thus far defined involves a judgment about a matter of fact (that only a few are qualified to rule) and a value judgment (that they ought to rule). Several ambiguities and omissions will be considered in their proper place. First a variant of elitism as thus described must be examined which purports to renounce judgments of value and takes its stand upon things as they are rather than as they ought to be.

The Neo-Machiavellians

We commonly distinguish between positive and normative statements. The former are descriptive, the latter prescriptive. Since the sciences are expected to limit themselves to descriptions of matter-of-fact they are often called the *positive* sciences in contrast to ethics, aesthetics, etc., which are disciplines designated as *normative*. Positivism in the narrow sense is the view that the sciences, including the social or behavior sciences, must scrupulously avoid judgments of value. In the broader sense, positivism is the view that only such *wertfrei* generalizations are meaningful because they are the only generalizations that can be confirmed or disconfirmed.

At any rate, whether in the broad or narrow sense, a whole school of thought described as elitist adheres, or seems to adhere, to this positivist position. It claims to be concerned not with what ought to be, only with what is. And it finds that in all societies rule is inevitably exercised by a minority, a ruling class. This is as true under a so-called democracy as under any other form of government. Such a ruling class is properly called an *elite*—the term popularized by Vilfredo Pareto, most celebrated and influential exponent of this point of view (p. 268). Its status as an elite is determined (when exponents of this point of view express themselves consistently) not by a necessarily subjective evaluation of its qualifications, but by the fact that it rules. There is no other test. To be sure, different historical situations call upon differing talents and qualifications so that the character of elites varies. In one age we may have a military elite with the characteristic talents of soldiers; in another, a commercial elite with the interests and skills of merchants and manufacturers, and so on. It is not for the scientist to praise or deplore the circumstances that catapult one or other group into ascendancy. He must be concerned merely to describe what he finds, and always what he finds are two classes, in Pareto's words, "the ruling and subject classes stand[ing] towards each other very much as two nations respectively alien." [2]

[2] Vilfredo Pareto, *The Mind and Society*, IV, trans. Arthur Livingston (New York: Harcourt, Brace, and Co., 1935), p. 1556.

The position thus set forth received one of its classical formulations in Gaetano Mosca's *The Ruling Class,* albeit with some later reservations and misgivings. The distinguished Italian scholar wrote:

> In all societies . . . two classes appear—a class that rules and a class that is ruled. The first class, always the less numerous, performs all political functions, monopolizes power, and enjoys the advantages that power brings, whereas the second, the more numerous class, is directed and controlled by the first, in a manner that is more or less legal, now more or less arbitrary and violent . . . (p. 280).

Presumably if a group of gangsters or Klansmen, or Fascists, or a military junta were able to capture and hold power this would establish it as qualified and it would thereby comprise an elite, although Mosca would have contemplated any of these with dismay. Such a condition has been designated in the Preface to this volume as *mafianism* or *totalitarianism* and should not be confused with elitism. But it is difficult to see how consistent positivists (in the broad sense) could make such a distinction without invoking moral criteria.

The author of *The Ruling Class* does waver and is often an incorrigible moralizer who, contrary to his premises, can be found distinguishing between good and bad elites. Mosca, an acute American commentator notes, "is forever making value judgments which the scientist in him could not accept and must be made to overlook." Fortunately for his reputation as a wise (if not a consistent) statesman and scholar, Mosca, in 1925, in the Italian Senate, defended the parliamentary democracy he had spent a lifetime denigrating. This was when Mussolini and his black-shirted condottieri were dismantling it. Still, in the final version of his view, when he was preoccupied with theoretical issues and not with tragically exigent events, Mosca was quite unequivocal: Those best qualified to govern are "by no means . . . the 'best' individuals intellectually, much less the 'best' individuals morally." Not a heightened sense of justice nor "extent of knowledge" nor "broadness of view," but "perspicacity, a ready intuition of individual and mass psychology, strength of will and, especially, confidence in oneself" determine fitness to rule.[3] Certainly such traits were not wanting in Hitler and the men with whom he surrounded himself, nor can Hitler's downfall be cited as evidence to the contrary; if it were not for one fatal misjudgment—the invasion of Russia—he might now rule the world.

Vilfredo Pareto's words lead to a similar conclusion:

> To say that some members of society possess certain qualities to a more eminent degree than others is not the same as saying that there is a class of people who are absolutely *better* than the rest of the population. And to go on from there to say that those 'better' people

---

[3] J. H. Meisel, *The Myth of the Ruling Class* (Ann Arbor: University of Michigan Press, 1962), p. 9. Cf. also, pp. 208, 223.

'ought' to govern all the rest is to commit that most egregious fallacy:
to make an illogical deduction from a dubious premise [4] (p. 267n).

The ruling class may indeed retort to their restive subalterns as did the lions in
the fable of Demosthenes to the hares who clamored for equality: "Where are
your claws and teeth?" [5]

Mosca and Pareto, along with Robert Michels, who formulated the view
cited above in his "iron law of oligarchy," have been called the "New Machiavellians" by James Burnham, not only because they all purport to be "realists" who
believe in calling a spade a spade, but because Machiavelli appeared to anticipate
the elitist concept when he wrote that "in any city whatsoever, in whatsoever
manner organized, never do more than forty or fifty persons attain positions of
command." [6] Whether expressed in the language of Olympian detachment
affected by "neutral" scientific observers or the hortatory phrases of moralists
and reformers, the fact is that the neo-Machiavellians, so-called,[7] share with all
elitists a hostility to democracy, not only in its socialist manifestations, which
evoke their special ire (p. 289), but in its bourgeois form as well. But their central objection is, as indicated, a peculiar one, apart from whatever other strong
criticisms they may have. It is quite simply that democratic rule is in the nature
of the case impossible to attain and that those who claim democracy has been or
can be attained are engaged in sheer mythologizing.

The new Machiavellians do not deprecate myths or "vital fictions" as they
have also been called. Indeed, George Sorel, who popularized the role of myth in
social action is one of their favorite authors, and Pareto makes much of it in his
notion of "derivations" (p. 273) as does Mosca in his concept of the "political
formula" (p. 285). After all, as Michels points out, "A conservative candidate
who should present himself to his electors by declaring to them that he did not
regard them as capable of playing an active part in influencing the destinies of
the country, and should tell them that for this reason they ought to be deprived
of the suffrage would be a man of incomparable sincerity but politically insane." [8] So, too, Mosca:

[4] Cited by Meisel, *op. cit.*, p. 179. To be sure, ardent admirers of Pareto like James
Burnham are not altogether consistent concerning Pareto's ethical interests. On p. 195 of
The Machiavellians, Burnham says: "Pareto, as well as other Machiavellians, is often
charged by sentimentalists with 'neglecting human goals.' No charge could be more inap-
propriate." It is difficult to reconcile this statement with Burnham's comment on p. 171
that Pareto "is not offering any program for social improvement nor expressing any ideal of
what society and government ought to be. He is merely trying to describe what society is
like. . . . What could or should be done with this knowledge . . . is a question he does
not try to answer."

[5] Cited by Aristotle, *Politica*, Book III, 13, 1284a.

[6] Cited by Gaetano Mosca, *The Ruling Class*, trans. Arthur Livingston (New York:
McGraw-Hill, 1939), p. 329.

[7] Not all authorities are agreed that the designation is apt. Professor Meisel, for example, questions the propriety of the label—regarded by Burnham as an honorific one—for
Mosca. It may be noted here that neo-Machiavellians like Mosca are also critical of the
aristocratic principle in its traditional form.

[8] Robert Michels, *Political Parties* (Glencoe, Ill.: The Free Press, 1949), p. 6.

All those who, by wealth, education, intelligence, or guile, have an aptitude for leading a community of men, and a chance of doing so—in other words, all the cliques in the ruling class—have to bow to universal suffrage . . . and also, if occasion requires, cajole and fool it (p. 291).

Thus, ironically, the democratic myth is one that an elitist society, which despises democracy, *must* perpetrate and preserve. The irony is compounded in that Marx, whom the new Machiavellians revile, had anticipated Mosca, Pareto, *et al.*, in referring to democracy as we have known it as a pretense and a sham, and to democratic institutions as a facade behind which the real rule is exercised by others. No one had stressed the role of classes more than he. However, not even Marx, notorious as he was for acerbity, exceeded Mosca's comment that "a system which affects to be based on the free expression of the will of the majority is perpetrating an unmitigated lie. . . ." Karl Marx differs from the Machiavellians, of course, in that his strictures were limited to social systems in which the means of production are privately owned; he believed in the possibility of a classless society where true democracy would prevail.

There are, as has been seen, numerous weighty objections to democracy other than that it partakes of the character of myth and can never be realized in actual practice. Although these are based on obvious value judgments, positivists—sometimes implicitly, sometimes explicitly—subscribe to them. They are more appropriately reviewed, however, in connection with a discussion of the specific variants of elitism that have been espoused in the course of time. Four such varieties will be distinguished here. Two, timocracy (in Plato's sense as the dominance of the military) and theocracy, will be omitted as having only historical interest.

Racism

One variant of elitism may be disposed of summarily. It is not necessary to dilate on the familiar doctrine of racial superiority and hardly necessary to note that it is without reputable scientific support.[9] The concept of race is used by racists with an elasticity which reached its extreme in the Nordic myth. Thus a self-styled *Herrenvolk,* invoking the doctrines of pseudo-ethnologists like Friedrich von Hellwald, and inspired, among others, by Houston Stewart Chamberlain, Count de Gobineau, and their own Richard Wagner, deluded themselves into distinguishing Slavs, Jews, and others as racially different. Spurious racial distinctions were based on the presence or absence of physical traits hardly acceptable to anthropologists. The possession or lack of such traits marked one as also having or lacking certain vaguely defined moral and personality traits such

[9] Cf. Ruth Benedict, *Race: Science and Politics* (New York: The Viking Press, 1943) ; W. C. Boyd, *Genetics and the Races of Man* (Boston: Little, Brown and Co., 1950) ; L. C. Dunn and Theodosius Dobzhansky, *Heredity, Race and Society* (New York: Mentor Books, 1946) ; Ashley Montagu, *Race, Science and Humanity* (Princeton: Van Nostrand, 1962).

as a high sense of honor, military prowess, courage, daring, gallantry, forth-rightness, and, with all these, fitness to rule.

However, we have been dealing thus far with a pathological manifestation of elitism. Less aberrational, because hallowed by time and anthropologically more plausible, is Caucasian racial elitism with its derogation of Negroes and other dark-skinned peoples. These—with the embarrassing exception of mulattoes and octaroons—*are* identifiable racial groups. And the aboriginal peoples of the world *are* mostly Negroid and not Caucasian. Once it is assumed that their "backward" state is no historical accident, but a proof of racial inferiority, it is easy to conclude that they never become more than superficially "civilized" and that their native handicaps remain with them.

The well-publicized record of brutal exploitation in the Congo and elsewhere has exposed the "White Man's Burden" as a hoax, and it no longer has any responsible advocates, although it retains a certain historical interest. On the other hand, intelligent men in the South, who in any other context would gener-ally be regarded by their critics as men of good will, honestly believe the South-ern Negro would prosper more under their patronage than when, as they say, he achieves the rights enjoyed by an emancipated Negro in a Harlem slum. The new Negro's recent intransigence has generated an atmosphere of hostility which makes it increasingly difficult for Southerners to speak fondly of their Negro de-pendents and to proclaim their solicitude for the Negro's welfare, but many of them still dream of what might have been if Northern meddlers had not inter-fered. In the idyllic version, what might have been was a situation in which the Negro was, in Toynbee's felicitous phrase, *in* but not *of* society, bovinely per-forming all the menial tasks while a white patron provided at a low level for his creature needs, including, so long as he remained submissive and segregated, se-curity from violence. As John C. Calhoun said, "A Mysterious Providence has brought the black and the white people together from different parts of the globe, and no human power could now separate them. The whites are an European race, being masters; and the Africans are the inferior race, and slaves . . . they could exist among us peaceably enough, if undisturbed, for all time." [10] That dream —a part of the plantation mystique—is gone now, even if the wind has blown tardily, and what will replace it no one can say.

It may be noted that in the South, if not in the world as a whole, the white racial elite, unlike other elites, are the majority and not the minority.[11] That this involves the inclusion of back county red-necks among the elect is an interesting and, one might think, a disturbing complication. On the other hand, it helps ex-plain why the fiercest resistance to integration often comes from the lowest stratum of the white population in the South; their color is their only claim to status. The real rulers in the white hierarchy, themselves too fastidious to perpe-trate ugly acts of brutality, thereby have a corps of hoodlums to cow the poten-

[10] *Congressional Debates*, Vol. XIII, Part I, 1836–1837, p. 566.
[11] On the other hand, in Rhodesia a white minority of 217,000 dominates an African majority of 3,750,000.

tially insurgent Negro with occasional acts of violence. By a happy coincidence the white riff-raff can be kept in *their* place by the availability of a cheap and abundant supply of black laborers. One need not postulate a conspiratorial design or explicit intent at work here; things comfortably work out this way and the pattern with its train of welcome consequences becomes part of established usage and rooted custom, although today, even in the Deep South, there are signs of drastic change.

Hereditary Aristocracy

A feature peculiar to racial elitism and to the variety of elitism called hereditary aristocracy is that in both cases the elite groups are almost invariably closed. The principle on which they are based generally (though not always) precludes that "free circulation" of elites, as Pareto called it (p. 270), by which members of the lower strata are absorbed into the higher. Otherwise racial elitism and hereditary aristocracy have little in common. While assumptions about race are no doubt implicit in the ideology of hereditary aristocracies, the rationale is fundamentally different.

We need not linger over the origins of hereditary aristocracies except to note that in most cases the founders of aristocratic lines, themselves not the heirs to power and privilege, no doubt exhibited some kind of talent, in most cases as warriors or in others, as charismatic leaders in Weber's sense.[12] Functioning usually as protectors in the absence of strong governments capable of maintaining order, or as military aides to an overlord, they were rewarded with large areas of land which became the basis of their descendants' wealth and power. The career of aristocracy varies, of course, with each country. In general, the decline of aristocracy begins with the spread of commerce and the rise of industry and, with this, the appearance of a middle-class rivaling and exceeding the nobility in wealth and power.

The rationale behind the claim that birth is a sufficient qualification for fitness to rule or to exercise a numerically disproportionate voice in ruling consists of several propositions: First, a monarch is kept from monopolizing power; second, the refinements of a civilized society, unattainable in the absence of a leisure class, are thereby preserved; and finally, those who rule will understand the art of governing and have a sense of the responsibilities that go with it, since these are inborn traits or are acquired only by those who have been indoctrinated from earliest infancy.

Since an hereditary aristocracy is not likely to be conspicuous among other groups for competence in the arts, sciences or humanities, not to mention technological skills, distinctiveness must be sought in other ways. This is achieved by a great emphasis on honor, duty, display, fashion, manners, "taste," skill at such

[12] See *From Max Weber: Essays in Sociology,* trans. and edit. H. H. Gerth and C. Wright Mills (New York: Oxford University Press, 1946), pp. 245 ff. and p. 45, n. 50 in this volume.

sports as only a leisure class would have the time and money to cultivate, a martial spirit, etc. With this goes an ethic demeaning "trade" and work as marks, not merely of inferior status but of lack of competence. As Thorstein Veblen pointed out, a life of leisure is evidence of superior force "provided always that the gentleman of leisure can live in manifest ease and comfort." Leisure is not indolence; it is simply abstention from productive or useful labor.

> Conspicuous abstention from labour therefore becomes the conventional mark of superior pecuniary achievement and the conventional index of reputability; and conversely, since application to productive labour is a mark of poverty and subjection, it becomes inconsistent with a reputable standing in the community.[13]

Our very language reflects what Reinhold Niebuhr calls the "confusion of manners and morals" prevalent under the regime of an hereditary aristocracy. " 'Gentlemen' and 'noblemen' in English and *'adel'* and *'edel'* in German are significant examples of words to be found in all languages which have the connotation of well-born and well-mannered, on the one hand, and virtuous and considerate on the other." [14] Similarly, the double meanings of "villain," once a feudal tenant; "blackguard," one who looked after the kettles; and "knave," a servant.[15] So, too, the German word *"schlecht,"* for bad or poor, as *"schlicht"* simply designated a plebian as distinguished from an aristocrat.

No one more eloquently rationalized the role of the aristocrat than Edmund Burke in his *Reflections on the Revolution in France* (p. 236) and his *Appeal from the New to the Old Whigs*. The following passage from the latter is worth quoting in full:

> A true natural aristocracy is not a separate interest in the state, or separable from it. It is an essential integrant part of any large body rightly constituted. It is formed out of a class of legitimate presumptions, which, taken as generalities, must be admitted for actual truths. To be bred in a place of estimation; to see nothing low and sordid from one's infancy; to be taught to respect one's self; to be habituated to the censorial inspection of the public eye; to look early to public opinion; to stand upon such elevated ground as to be enabled to take a large view of the wide-spread and infinitely diversified combinations of men and affairs in a large society; to have leisure to read, to reflect, to converse; to be enabled to draw the court and attention of the wise and learned, wherever they are to be found; to be habituated in armies to command and to obey; to be taught to despise

---

[13] Thorstein Veblen, *The Theory of the Leisure Class* (New York: The Modern Library, 1934), p. 38.

[14] *Moral Man and Immoral Society* (New York: Charles Scribner's Sons, 1932), p. 126.

[15] Cf. J. Dewey and J. H. Tufts, *Ethics,* rev. ed. (New York: Henry Holt, 1932), pp. 161–62. Cf., also Friedrich Nietzsche, *The Genealogy of Morals,* trans. H. B. Samuel (New York: Russell and Russell, 1964), pp. 22 ff.

danger in the pursuit of honor and duty; to be formed to the greatest degree of vigilance, foresight, and circumspection, in a state of things in which no fault is committed with impunity and the slightest mistakes draw on the most ruinous consequences; to be led to a guarded and regulated conduct, from a sense that you are considered as an instructor of your fellow-citizens in their highest concerns, and that you act as a reconciler between God and man; to be employed as an administrator of law and justice, and to be thereby amongst the first benefactors to mankind; to be a professor of high science, or of liberal and ingenuous art; to be amongst rich traders, who from their success are presumed to have sharp and vigorous understandings, and to possess the virtues of diligence, order, constancy, and regularity, and to have cultivated an habitual regard to commutative justice: these are the circumstances of men that form what I should call a *natural* aristocracy, without which there is no nation.[16]

Burke was referring, he says, to a "natural" aristocracy, including, it will be noted, the "professor of high science" and the "rich trader," but it was, using Jefferson's distinction (p. 114), an "artificial" aristocracy that he was defending—the aristocrats comprising the British House of Lords and the French aristocracy, the overwhelming majority of whom were not professors of "high" science or, at that time, any other kind of science. Burke conceded that in France "those of the commons who approached to or exceeded many of the nobility in wealth were not fully admitted to the rank and estimation which wealth, in reason and good policy, ought to bestow in every country"—although "not equally with that of other nobility." He granted that "the two kinds of aristocracy were too punctiliously kept asunder." [17] Elsewhere, Burke observed that virtue and wisdom should be recognized wherever they are found and that he did not "wish to confuse power, authority, and distinction to blood and names and titles." But, "the road to eminence and power, from obscure condition, ought not to be made too easy, nor a thing too much of course." [18] Here spoke the voice of a true advocate of hereditary aristocracy; whatever the intrinsic merit of the warning, to caution, as in the last comment cited, against easy vertical mobility in eighteenth-century England was like lecturing the untouchables of Bombay on the vices of over-eating. On balance, Burke's final verdict was that "some decent, regulated preëminence, some preference . . . given to birth, is neither unnatural, nor unjust, nor impolitic." [19] This is the minimal claim of the hereditary aristocrat. And, when compared with the self-made men of commerce and industry who were about to oust him, a member of the nobility may indeed have presented certain advantages. Born to his station, he would not have been brutalized by the struggle for survival which makes men calculating, grasping, greedy, and

[16] "Appeal from the New to the Old Whigs," *The Writings and Speeches of Edmund Burke*, IV, Beaconsfield ed. (London: Bickers and Sons, Ltd., 1901), pp. 174–75.
[17] "Reflections on the Revolution in France," *Ibid.*, III, p. 415.
[18] *Ibid.*, p. 297.
[19] *Ibid.*, p. 299.

oblivious of the public interest; he had a sense of *noblesse oblige*. A parallel is suggested in the United States by the difference in public-mindedness between many of our *arriviste* tycoons and third generation multimillionaires who have achieved a sense of what may be called *richesse oblige*.

Quite apart from the decisive challenge of the emergent middle class, soon to be supplemented by the swelling protest of nameless workers, the aristocrat's rationale was bound to yield to the argument that it is as absurd to have an hereditary legislator as an hereditary physician, if not to the impertinent couplet:

> When Adam delved and Eve span
> Who was then the gentleman?

In his *Notes on the State of Virginia* (1782), Jefferson recalled that in Great Britain, the constitution "relies on the house of commons for honesty, and the lords for wisdom." This, he said, "would be a rational reliance, if honesty were to be bought with money, and if wisdom were hereditary." [20] The logic of Jefferson has prevailed. Today, even the House of Lords, more receptive to commoners than most hereditary bodies, is virtually shorn of its power.

"Natural" Aristocracy

It will be observed that advocates of the hereditary principle sought justification for it in the functions which an aristocracy selected on this basis can perform, both by governing well and by providing those graces and refinements indispensable to a civilized society. But their reasoning never proved persuasive with a long line of critics who, while ardently committed to the principle of aristocracy, preferred an aristocracy of talent to an aristocracy of blood. We have no good term with which to identify this position. "Functional" aristocracy will not do, since advocates of the inheritance principle claim that an hereditary nobility does in fact perform a function. "Meritocracy" is really quite barbarous. Jefferson's distinction between natural and artificial aristocracies is perhaps the most useful. He called aristocracies "founded on wealth and birth" artificial as distinguished from natural aristocracies based on "virtue and talents."

It may be agreed at the outset that an hereditary system has two advantages. First, it respects the principle of historical continuity. True, respect becomes reverence and this induces ossification, but in all fairness the kernel of virtue in this vice must be recognized; there is at least no agonizing break with the past and no naive belief that a new society can be initiated *de novo* without influence from what has preceded. Aristocracies of talent, on the other hand, are generally in the utopian *genre* and, as such, postulate impossible departures from history, fresh starts with no legacy from the past. Plato's rulers "will rub out the picture, and leave a clean surface." [21]

---

[20] *Notes on Virginia*, ed. William Peden (Chapel Hill: University of North Carolina Press, 1955), p. 119.

[21] *The Republic*, 501. Wise though he was, Jefferson believed that "Our Revolution . . . presented to us an album on which we were free to write as we pleased." (Letter to John Cartwright, June 5, 1824).

Also, barring such confusions as occur in *Tom Jones*, descent and order of descent by blood are easily determinable. Thus the nagging problem of selection and succession is easily solved. But who are those with the talent to rule? What is such talent? As John Adams said in responding to Jefferson, "Fashion has introduced an indeterminate use of the word talents." [22]

Political theory is largely the work of philosophers and they have a strong bias in favor of their kind. Thus, Plato tells us that "neither cities nor States nor individuals will ever attain perfection until the small class of philosophers . . . are providentially compelled, whether they will or not, to take care of the State, and until a like necessity be laid on the State to obey them. . . ." [23] Such men are no ordinary mortals. They are not specialists who love a part of wisdom, but men who love the whole of it; men who scorn opinion and seek only knowledge; who alone "are able to grasp the eternal and unchangeable" in contrast to those "who wander in the region of the many and the variable." [24] In Plato's famous phrase they are "spectators of all time and all existence" [25] (pp. 185–88).

Such excellence is not the result of accident. Those who are to become guardians—unlike hereditary aristocrats, their biological fathers and mothers are unknown to them—are carefully educated from the age of twenty to thirty-five, first in arithmetic, then geometry and astronomy, and, finally, in dialectic, the "coping stone" of the sciences. Thereafter, they are sent into the world to acquire practical experience ("sent down into the den") [26] for fifteen years until, at fifty, if they have survived temptation and distinguished themselves they must

> raise the eye of the soul to the universal light which lightens all
> things, and behold the absolute good; for that is the pattern accord-
> ing to which they are to order the State and the lives of individuals,
> and the remainder of their own lives also; making philosophy their
> chief pursuit, but when their turn comes, toiling also at politics and
> ruling for the public good. . . . [27]

This vision of enlightened rulers who, having no family and precluded from owning property, are thereby free of the temptations of nepotism and wealth, obviously inspired the Middle Ages. The baronage and commoners corresponded to Plato's warriors and artisans, and the medieval clergy to his guardians, except that the clergy found the truth by which they governed in divine revelation, while Plato's guardians find theirs in understanding the Idea of the Good.

The rise of modern science prompted its great seventeenth century prophet, Francis Bacon, to prefer a college of scientific investigators for his *New Atlantis*

[22] Letter to Jefferson, Nov. 15, 1813.
[23] *The Republic*, Book VI, 499, Jowett translation.
[24] *Ibid.*, VI, 484.
[25] *Ibid.*, VI, 486.
[26] *Ibid.*, VII, 539.
[27] *Ibid.*, VII, 540.

to Plato's philosophers and Campanella's priest-magistrates.[28] With scientists, St. Simon many years later, included artists and industrialists in the group that should be charged with responsibility for managing the national interest.[29] His ideas were propagated by numerous disciples, most notably by Auguste Comte, father of positivism, who, writing in the mid-nineteenth century, urged that control over society be assumed by what he called a scientific priesthood.

It should be emphasized that many of the post-eighteenth century advocates of rule by the able have been as uneasy about the new captains of industry, commerce and finance as about vesting power in the people. Competent though the new capitalists might be in the management of their enterprises and the accumulation of wealth, they are not qualified to govern and are even a threat to good government, according to these elitist critics. It was no Marxist, but John Quincy Adams who, castigating the idleness of the rich, referred to them as "mere burdens of human society, mere cumberers of the ground." [30] His patrician descendants, Henry and Brooks Adams, were as critical as socialists of the titans of industry and commerce of their day. Henry's disenchantment led him to escape into the past (see his *Mont-Saint-Michel and Chartres*). In a letter to his brother, he referred contemptuously to "the capitalists [who] have abandoned their old teachers and principles, and have adopted socialist practices," adding "there seems to be no reason why the capitalist should not become a socialist functionary. Solidarity is now the law . . . I belong to the nineteenth century." [31] And his brother, Brooks, wrote "the modern capitalist . . . is not responsible, for he is not a trustee for the public. If he be restrained by legislation, that legislation is in his eye an oppression and an outrage, to be annulled or eluded by any means which will not lead to the penitentiary." [32]

Later, the conservative Irving Babbitt, in his *Democracy and Leadership* (1924) complained bitterly of "standardized mediocrity," and a conservative philosopher, George Santayana, echoing Emerson's dolorous verdict that "things are in the saddle and ride mankind," noted that industrialization was "complicating life prodigiously without ennobling the mind." He added, "it has put into rich men's hands facilities and luxuries which they trifle with without achieving any magnificence in living, while the poor, if physically more comfortable than formerly, are not meantime notably wiser or merrier." [33]

In Britain the authoritarian Thomas Carlyle sourly commented that "this Mamon-Gospel of Supply-and-Demand, Competition, *Laissez-faire*, and Devil

---

[28] These comprised the governing assembly of Tommaso Campanella's *City of the Sun* (1623).

[29] See St. Simon's *Social Organization, the Science of Man and Other Writings*, trans. and ed. Felix Markham (New York: Harper Torchbooks, 1964).

[30] Cited by G. A. Lipsky, *John Quincy Adams* (New York: Thomas Y. Crowell, 1950), p. 112.

[31] Cited by Charles Beard in his introduction to Brooks Adams, *The Law of Civilization and Decay* (New York: Alfred A. Knopf, 1951), p. 39.

[32] *Theory of Social Revolutions* (New York: The Macmillan Co., 1914), p. 209.

[33] "Reason and Society," *Works*, Triton Edition, III (New York: Charles Scribner's Sons, 1936), p. 273.

take the hindmost, begins to be one of the shabbiest gospels ever preached.
. . ." [34] He was echoed by Ruskin, who denounced capitalism as substituting
exploitation and the cash-nexus for pride in workmanship and sought a society
paternalistically organized along Platonic principles.[35] And re-echoed in our
own time by T. S. Eliot who deplored "the tendency of unlimited industrialism
. . . to create bodies of men and women—of all classes—detached from tradition, alienated from religion and susceptible to mass suggestion; in other words,
a mob." [36]

Clearly, all of these writers were as hostile to industrial capitalism, with its
mechanistic regimentation of life, its stress on acquisition and competition and
its preoccupation with material goods, as they were to democracy. As for democracy, by flouting the principle of inequality, it neglects excellence, degrades taste,
and glorifies the average. From the same womb as capitalism, it is similarly immersed in satisfying creature needs—presumably such material concerns as the
feeding, housing and medical care of the masses—and is steeped in a vulgar
hedonism no less gross for being called "utilitarianism." Such were the strictures
of men who thought of themselves as members of an aristocracy of taste and talent more concerned with the state of the arts than with the size of the gross national product (pp. 196–98).

Writers like Carlyle and Ruskin were if anything vehement, but they were
mild and mellow by comparison with Nietzsche who, while scorning trade ("Not
to understand trade is noble. . . .") [37] and urging that "those who own too
much are fraught with danger to the community," [38] stormed that "the will to
lowliness, abasement, and equalization" [39] had captured Europe. The supermen
whom Nietzsche would place in charge were not, to be sure, like the Nazi elite-
guardists who later saw themselves reflected in his murky mirror. Neither were
they hereditary noblemen. They were artist-tyrants, spiritual aristocrats, "dare-
devils of the spirit" who have climbed the highest and most dangerous peaks.[40]

"Spirituality" is, of course, an imponderable. For Nietzsche, these higher
men are ascetics who find their joy in self-conquest and their happiness in "hardness against themselves and others" (p. 261).[41] Their spirituality is not other-
worldliness. It manifests itself in an affirmation of life and the will to power. As
such, it is the opposite of Christian and Jewish spirituality which cravenly denies
the life impulse. The incarnation of spirituality as conceived by Nietzsche is to be

[34] *Past and Present* (London, 1843), p. 8.
[35] See John Ruskin's *Unto This Last* (1876), *Time and Tide* (1886), and *The Crown of Wild Olive* (1888).
[36] "The Idea of a Christian Society," *Christianity and Culture* (New York: Harvest, 1940), p. 17.
[37] "The Dawn of Day," *Complete Works*, ed. Oscar Levy, trans. Helen Zimmerman (New York: Russell and Russell, 1964), 308.
[38] "Human, All Too Human," *Ibid.*, p. 285.
[39] "The Genealogy of Morals," *Ibid.*, p. 16.
[40] "Nietzsche Contra Wagner," *Ibid.*, Epilogue.
[41] "The Antichrist," *Ibid.*, p. 57.

found in those "virile, noble natures" [42] who were masters of Rome until they were undermined through the Jew, Paul, and by the Judaic-Christian conspiracy —that same cabal which also "trampled down" the "noble" and the "male" instincts of Islam. There were moments of renewal, in the Renaissance man of *virtu,* in France during the reign of Louis XIV, and for an instant with the appearance of Napoleon, "that synthesis of Monster and Superman." [43] But, alas, Judaea conquered Rome, priests have worsted proconsuls, and the slave morality of those who believe in the "prerogative of the most" has won out over a master morality. European man has been dwarfed and levelled. In some age other than this "rotting and introspective present" we may once again have spirits of "sublime malice, spirits rendered potent through wars and victories, to whom conquest, adventure, danger, even pain, have become a need," who are habituated "to sharp, rare air, to winter wanderings, to literal and metaphorical ice and mountains." [44] Meanwhile, all that one can say is "O nausea! Nausea! Nausea," thereby siring twentieth-century existentialism as well as a strange and—for some—morbidly attractive variety of elitism.

It was perhaps the crowning paradox of this paradoxical life that one day in Turin, in January 1899, this man whose diatribes against the weak, sick and lowly were perhaps the harshest ever written saw a coachman flog a horse, rushed toward the animal, threw protective arms around it, and collapsed of a madness from which he never recovered. Conceivably, this was a prophetically symbolic enactment of the career of a Third Reich which, for two terrible decades during what Nietzsche might have called the "deep midnight of its soul," sought vindication in his reckless hyperboles and dark parables.

To turn from Nietzsche's apocalyptic visions to the humdrum devices of bureaucrats is like leaving the angry screams of a flamboyant bird for the busy silence of burrowing moles. And yet of all the aristocracies of merit, it is not Plato's philosopher-kings, nor Campanella's priest-magistrates, nor Bacon's college of scientific investigators, nor Nietzsche's supermen, but plodding bureaucrats who are likeliest to take over, if a so-called natural aristocracy ever prevails at all.

It is commonplace to note that the routine functioning of modern society is of such enormous complexity that it can be accomplished only by virtue of the services of a body of experts highly trained for a broad range of specialized tasks. Such experts, appropriately equipped and organized, constitute a bureaucracy, although they are more commonly designated "management" when the private sector of the economy is under discussion.

Bureaucracy is hardly new. But, as Max Weber observed in an essay that is a *locus classicus,* the full development of bureaucracy is a phenomenon of the modern state and, in the private sector, of the most advanced stage of capital-

---

[42] *Ibid.,* p. 56.
[43] "The Genealogy of Morals," *Ibid.,* p. 16.
[44] *Ibid.,* p. 24.

ism.[45] The corps of public or private officials who comprise a bureaucracy are hierarchically organized with precisely defined jurisdictions and responsibilities. Such officials or managers are selected because of special competence acquired through apprenticeship or formal training. As bureaucracy grows more mature it tends increasingly to enlist those with sufficient formal schooling in public or business administration to qualify for processional status. Indeed, modern administration has taken on the character of a discipline or applied science and, as such, makes possible the efficient management of complex affairs on a scale completely ignored by ideological critics of large scale bureaucracy (pp. 145–46).

Generally, vertical mobility prevails within a bureaucratic system, no one is dismissed without cause, and benefits are available upon retirement. In consequence, service and ascent in the hierarchical order is thought of as a *career*. The bureaucratization of government, business, the military, schools, churches, trade unions, and political parties, has produced what William H. Whyte, Jr. has called the "Organization Man." As Whyte describes him, the organization man does not merely work for the "organization"; he *belongs* to it. "They are the ones of our middle class who have left home, spiritually as well as physically, to take the vows of organization life, and it is they who are the mind and soul of our great self-perpetuating institutions." [46] With the organization man there goes, of course, an apparatus, varying in scope and complexity with the size of the undertaking, of offices, clerks, files, salary schedules, rules and regulations, qualifying examinations, etc.

A bureaucracy is essentially *impersonal* so that the consequences of the rules by which it operates are *calculable*. Whim, caprice, or what Bentham called *ipse-dixitism*, are reduced to a minimum. As Weber points out, "the more the bureaucracy is 'dehumanized,' the more completely it succeeds in eliminating from official business love, hatred, and all purely personal, irrational, and emotional elements which escape calculation. This is the specific nature of bureaucracy and it is appraised as its special virtue." [47] The bureaucratic ideal, in short, is to reduce favoritism, personal sympathy, and the like to a minimum. Committed as it is to maximum rationality in the execution of its given task, the bureaucratic apparatus tends to shun tradition and the legacy of extraneous privileges, loyalties, usages, and the like which come in the train of tradition. Thus, in breaking sharply with the past and destroying the *ancien régime*, the French revolution and Bonapartism quite naturally created a powerful bureaucracy. In Britain, where traditional institutions were adapted to new needs, the pace of bureaucratization was correspondingly slow.

As thus far described, bureaucracy does not make policy much as it may alter policy in the course of executing it. The supreme example of bureaucratization is to be found, of course, in the Soviet Union where two factors contributed

[45] Reprinted in *From Max Weber: Essays in Sociology*, Chapter III.

[46] *The Organization Man* (New York: Simon and Schuster, 1956), p. 3.

[47] *From Max Weber: Essays in Sociology*, p. 216. For a discussion stressing departures in actual practice from this ideal, see Peter M. Blau, *Bureaucracy in Modern Society* (New York: Random House, 1956), Chapter III.

to a vast proliferation of bureaucratic personnel: a sharp revolutionary break with the past, and the assumption by government of both economic and political functions. There, however, the bureaucracy is no longer an instrument or mechanism in the classical mechanical sense, passively implementing decisions that have been made for it. With the disappearance of the old Bolsheviks (through natural death or execution), there has emerged a new kind of bureaucracy analogous to the kind of machine that can "program" itself, a *self-maintaining* system. We might call it a *"cybernated" bureaucracy*.[48]

The point deserves elaboration. Weber points out, "the decisive reason for the advance of bureaucratic organization has always been its purely technical superiority over any other form of organization. The fully developed bureaucratic mechanism compares with other organizations exactly as does the machine with the non-mechanical modes of production." [49] As such the bureaucratic mechanism is not, as is so often alleged, inconsistent with democracy. On the contrary, in a complex society it is indispensable to democracy, for not to use it (if this were possible) would be to deprive democracy of the means for efficiently executing its decisions. But, what one encounters now in the Soviet Union is a mechanism which never had articulate majorities to give it direction and which no longer has masters in the person of charismatic leaders such as Lenin or Stalin.[50] The striking development may be that the bureaucracy in Russia not only carries on and operates itself for those calculable and recurrent needs which all bureaucracies are instituted to meet, but adjusts itself to new needs and even defines them. It is analogous, in other words, to those higher-order machines described by Norbert Wiener and others which can do things not foreseen by their makers.

It is common among those who emphasize the difference between the brain and the machine, Wiener observed, to say "that the machine cannot do anything original but is merely an executory enlargement of the scope of the human beings who have made it. It has even been supposed that those who have made a machine must have automatically a full comprehension of all the possibilities of performance of the machine and that the dangers mentioned by Samuel Butler that

---

[48] The term "cybernetics" was coined by Norbert Wiener to designate the processes of communication and control in man and the computer machines involved in automation. "Cybernated systems," says Donald N. Michael, "perform with a precision and a rapidity unmatched in humans. . . . They can be built to detect and correct errors in their own performance and to indicate to men which of their components are producing the error. They can make judgments of instructions programmed into them. They can remember and search their memories for appropriate data, which either has been programmed into them along with their instructions or has been acquired in the course of manipulating new data. Thus, they can learn on the basis of past experience with their environment." From "Cybernation: The Silent Conquest," *A Report to the Center for the Study of Democratic Institutions* (Santa Barbara, Calif., 1962).

[49] *From Max Weber: Essays in Sociology*, p. 214.

[50] The charismatic authority in Weber's sense is the opposite of the specialized, bureaucratic officeholder trained to perform a particular function. He is the "natural" leader, endowed with the gift to charm, inspire, move his followers. Viewed in these terms, Khrushchev was a transitional figure.

the machines may to some extent control humanity are absurd and empty." To this Wiener responded, "now that the machines are stepping up one or more stages in their functions, this idea of the machine is already insufficient and the difficulties and dangers conceived by Samuel Butler assume a new actuality."

Wiener, and many others have followed him in this, goes on to speak of machines; for example, a game-playing machine, in which, "while the general policy will be put into the machine by a person, the detailed applications of this policy in particular instances may not and in general will not be known to those who have programmed it." Indeed, "they may go beyond the complete comprehension of those who have constructed them." [51] If one substitutes "bureaucracy" for "machine" in the foregoing passages one may well have an accurate description of the development bureaucracy has undergone in the Soviet Union, a development which could well overshadow the ideological innovations which have usually monopolized our attention. Even if the "general policy" fed or "programmed" into the bureaucratic machine might be some such democratic formula as "maximum diffusion of goods consistent with optimum productivity," such cybernated bureaucracy, as we may now call it, would not, of course, be in the democratic tradition. It would be a new and strange manifestation of elitism. Hannah Arendt has called such bureaucracy the "rule of nobody" and wisely cautioned that it "is not necessarily no-rule [and] . . . may indeed, under certain circumstances, even turn out to be one of its cruelest and most tyrannical versions." [52]

To a lesser degree, and, because its activities are largely limited to the economic sphere, on a smaller scale, the operation of large private corporations has undergone a similar development. The charismatic founders and leaders have passed on. A self-perpetuating regime called "management" has taken over the decision-making powers often including decisions on issues unrelated to the regular operational routine. Such a regime might well be called cybernated management or cybernated bureaucracy, American-style. If its decision-making powers included those areas commonly demarcated as political it would, of course, be a plutocracy.

Plutocracy

In a plutocracy those who command economic power wield political power as well. The tern preferred by Plato and Aristotle was "oligarchy" (pp. 195, 220), although, strictly speaking, oligarchy simply means rule by a few. If, as distinguished from aristocracy, oligarchical rule is for corrupt and selfish purposes, this connotation, as in the case of plutocracy, is acquired and not original.

Economic power derives from the ownership and, increasingly in our time,

[51] *Dimensions of Mind,* ed. Sidney Hook (New York: Collier Books, 1961), pp. 109–12.
[52] *The Human Condition* (Garden City: Doubleday and Co., Inc., 1959), p. 37. See also, p. 41.

from the *control* of property. Property may, of course, be of many kinds: property in slaves, property in land, property as represented by wages, salaries or royalties, property in the physical means of production other than land, or property in rents and interest. As R. H. Tawney pointed out long ago, there are many kinds of property, and much confusion concerning the property *right* can be caused by treating them as one.[53] Nevertheless, the several kinds of property all have this in common: they involve a pre-emptive *right* to the use of goods; and they involve the *power* to command services. Since the industrial revolution, ownership of the means of production has superseded ownership of land as the most prominent form of property. With the advent of large-scale production and absentee ownership, a derivative property right, stemming from the *control* of property that others own, has become the most prominent of all.[54] This is not, however, the place to comment on such developments and their implications,[55] except to note that the manner in which the property right is justified, i.e., whether as *functional* and therefore on a utilitarian basis, as *natural*, or as *traditional*, is bound to vary with the kind of property involved and the relationship of the owner to it.

Of concern here is not the justification of the property right as such, nor the merits of such justification, nor even the way in which its several forms have influenced other institutional arrangements and practices. The topic is a political thesis, the contention, namely, that a stable and progressive social order is possible only if society is governed by the owners of property—in brief, the merits of a plutocracy. John Jay stated the thesis bluntly: "Those who own the country ought to govern it." Our Founding Fathers had in mind primarily the owners of land; others made no discrimination. The difference, while historically interesting, need not cause delay at this point. More important—and confusing—is the *amount* of property regarded as rendering one eligible for participation in the ruling class, and what is meant by "stability" and "progress."

The question of eligibility is generally left vague. When the rule of property owners has not been seriously challenged and has therefore been openly avowed, it has usually expressed itself in limitations on suffrage which restrict the voting right to taxpayers (or some similar device). However, one is dealing here with a mere formality, important as forms may be in reflecting the underlying realities of a social system. Once one accepts the basic thesis that property owners should rule, the corollary follows easily in the case of a qualification lending itself so readily to quantification as property: the more property the greater the power to rule. And, as advocates of this point of view tacitly recognize (even though they may shun explicitness on this issue), such increase in power need not be formal-

[53] *The Acquisitive Society* (New York: Harcourt, Brace and Co., 1920), Chapter V. For example, the right to property in royalties from a play can be justified functionally in a sense in which one can hardly justify the ownership of sub-surface resources.

[54] Cf. A. A. Berle and Gardner Means, *The Modern Corporation and Private Property* (New York: The Macmillan Co., 1933).

[55] The author has done so in some detail in his *Evolution of Liberalism* (New York: Collier Books, 1963).

ized as in a system of plural voting; it is built into the institution of property itself. To be specific, the majority of Americans are taxpayers and own *some* property, even if those who pay only sales or excise taxes and own only personal property are excluded. But of that majority, surely the power of the one-tenth of one per cent of the families (with annual incomes in excess of $75,000) receiving, in 1929, an aggregate income approximately equal to the aggregate income of the 42 per cent of the families at the bottom of the scale, was far greater than that of any other segment on the scale. The year 1929 is chosen because, as will be seen shortly, it antedates the introduction in our country of certain decisive limitations on a regime of property, even though (contrary to popular assumption) no significant change has since taken place in the pattern of income distribution.[56]

What do advocates of this point of view have in mind when they speak of a more "stable" and "progressive" society? An answer to this question is crucial in explaining why it is thought that political power should be made a function of the ownership of property.

To begin with, unlike an aristocracy, an economic elite is open-ended. Circumstances of birth do not in principle exclude entry and lack of title is no barrier, any more than is racial or religious origin. To reach the top requires only competence. Hence such a system allays discontent and the instability that frustration breeds. Also it is selective. Admittedly, luck sometimes plays a role in the acquisition of wealth, but luck, a wise man has said, is infatuated with ability and, in any case, luck is the exception rather than the rule. Hence, a society that gives a preponderant voice in *all* areas of social concern to the wealthy forthwith assures itself of competence in its decision-makers. Indeed, the system screens for other virtues as well as competence, such as assiduity, thrift, prudence, all of which are much needed in government. To be sure, many have inherited wealth and therefore possess it without having demonstrated ability (or other virtues), but in many if not most of the cases they have inherited the competence of their fathers along with the property.[57]

Apart from all this, whether as the heirs or founders of fortunes, the wealthy have a large stake in a settled social order and are therefore a stabilizing influence in a world all too often given to impetuous and intemperate action, and hence verging often on the edge of chaos. The poor, having nothing to lose, act on impulse; consequently, in a democracy, decisions are likely to be capricious and irrational (pp. 123, 235).

Also, extravagance is bound to prevail in a democracy. The disadvantaged will try to obtain by political action the subsistence they have been unable to earn, or that society as a whole has been unable to produce. In the former case, they will succeed only by taxing the owners of property, but this will penalize initiative and destroy incentive, thereby reducing the total amount of wealth pro-

[56] Cf. *Evolution of Liberalism*, pp. 225–31.
[57] Recently a mass circulation weekly devoted extensive coverage to the sons who, taking over the management of their fathers' enterprises, at least equal if they do not excel their elders. *Time*, Atlantic Edition, May 28, 1965.

duced. In the latter case, they will precipitate a ruinous inflation from which all will suffer. The latter hazard is especially acute in under- or semi-developed countries and can be witnessed today on a disastrous scale in countries like Brazil. Aristocrats who never had to learn the lesson of thrift can do no better.

Finally, after affirming that a regime of property is bound to preserve prevailing inequalities in the distribution of income and even to exacerbate them, its advocates will note that (a) it thereby preserves the incentive that encourages the production of wealth, and (b) it supplies a source of capital formation. The latter claim requires brief elaboration.

In every society some allocation of resources must be made between the production of consumer and the production of capital goods. The production of capital goods will consist of the repair and replacement of existing tools and the making of new tools. Traditionally, in a capitalist society, the production of capital goods has been funded from the profits earned by entrepreneurs. In nineteenth-century England and the United States, the profit system provided businessmen and proprietors with lavish incomes. These, after generous expenditures on "conspicuous consumption," were invested in the means of production. Lacking such symbols, trappings, and realities of power as titles, fiefs and sinecures, merchants and manufacturers could satisfy their desires for power and status only in that way. In any case, there is a limit on what one can spend for strictly creature gratification. Beyond this, kings and aristocrats sought gratification in ways—many of them an enduring legacy to culture—now familiar to us in Paris and Versailles, in Rome and the Vatican, in Florence, etc. Merchants and manufacturers had another way—expanding the avenues of commerce and the means of production. The result was the most rapid growth of productive capacity in the history of the world.

However, this could happen only if the working and consuming masses were unable through economic or political organization to get a larger share of the available income for themselves. If they had a larger share they would spend it because of their always exigent need for consumer goods. Such income, that is to say, would not be saved and invested in producer goods. Thus, progress became synonymous with the large disparities in income made possible in a society dominated by merchants and manufacturers.

The culmination of this line of thought was Adam Smith's "natural harmony of interests," the alchemy which transmutes individual greed into public welfare, or, in Mandeville's famous phrase, "private vices into public virtues." For, as Adam Smith showed, in a society where there is a division of labor and exchange, the very avarice of producers prompts them—since they are also rational—to serve others in order to serve themselves. Others will be served, to be sure, only if free *competition* prevails. The fear of preemption by rivals who are more efficient spurs men to do their best, and the threat that another may sell for less, whether the commodity be goods, capital or labor, bridles their greed. Here, in the sovereignty of the free market governed solely by the law of supply and demand is to be found the ultimate curb on what might otherwise be the unlimited avarice of incompetent men. Thus it is that we find in the dynamics of a market economy the key to automatic progress.

An economy in which the market is sovereign requires absence of interference not only by private individuals acting collectively, but by society as a whole acting through government. Thus, the negative state (though it may be invoked surreptitiously) is an essential premise of the natural harmony of interests. The market is not only thereby left free, but—no doubt quite incidentally—the wealthy are freed of the threat of a rival source of power.

Initially and for most of the history of such a regime, the rule of a propertied elite, as noted earlier, has manifested itself politically in limitations on suffrage. Most of our Founding Fathers defended such limitations believing with Benjamin Franklin that "as to those who have not landed property the allowing them to vote is an impropriety." It was not until the first quarter of the nineteenth century that most states provided for universal white male suffrage, despite Daniel Webster's warning that equal suffrage is incompatible with inequality in property.

In England, the Reform Act of 1832 extended the franchise to the middle class only. The possibility of including the working class was too remote to inspire serious debate. As noted earlier, even the Reform Act of 1867, by which Disraeli sought to seize the initiative from the Whigs ("I caught the liberals in bathing and ran off with their clothes."), retained some property qualifications, although by this time England was clearly moving in the direction of popular suffrage.

In France, the ideal of universal suffrage proclaimed by the Revolution of 1789 was not to be realized for more than brief intervals until 1875. The French *bourgeoisie*, rejecting the democratic aspirations of 1789 and 1830, opposed lowering property qualifications for voting so that, during the reign of the "Citizen King," Louis Phillipe, the electorate numbered only some 200,000 in a population of about 30 million.

Many contend that the United States—to limit the discussion to this country—is still ruled by an economic elite. While the late C. Wright Mills, for example, emphasizes the concentration of power in a combination of three groups— "the political directorate, the corporate rich and the high military" (p. 307), it is the corporate rich who emerge in his stimulating book as the real power. Despite the "moral uneasiness of our time," there is "still one old American value that has not markedly declined: the value of money and of the things money can buy. . . . Money is the one unambiguous criterion of success, and such success is still the sovereign American value." [58]

Nevertheless, it may well be that Mills and others underestimate the extent to which power has come to be shared in our country. The issue will be explored later.[59] Certainly the mere removal of property qualifications for voting, as suggested earlier, would not have been very significant so long as devices other than

[58] *The Power Elite* (New York: Oxford University Press, 1956), pp. 344–46.
[59] See pp. 341 ff.

the denial of suffrage were available for preventing the state from intervening effectively in economic affairs. For a long time, thanks to our system of checks and balances, to federalism and to the domination of our major political parties by the economically privileged, the people acting collectively could not make decisions in the areas that concerned them most, namely, the distribution of income and the allocation of resources. The Supreme Court could strike down a state minimum wage law for women as a "naked and arbitrary exercise of power." Congressional committees could be cemeteries in which legislative proposals wanted by the majority might be buried without prospect of disinterment. One legislative chamber could refuse approval of the action of the other, and a President, acting on Calvin Coolidge's philosophy that the best government is no government, could veto the action of both. The market—as managed by property owners—was sovereign. Consequently, universal suffrage hardly posed the challenge to upper income groups anticipated by Daniel Webster. Whatever the trend may be now, the United States surely bore close resemblance to a plutocracy.

How, then, may one evaluate the accomplishments of a plutocratic regime both in this country and elsewhere? The price of generalization on so complex an issue is likely to be oversimplification. Nevertheless, evaluation is much needed of a kind of regime which, whether it does or does not continue to enjoy hegemony in this country, is still very much with the western world, and a number of generalizations may be ventured.

Certainly when the rich were in almost unchallenged ascendancy, American production and productivity (the latter refers to labor efficiency) expanded at a rate without precedent in the history of the world. No doubt this was accomplished in part as a result of the incentives built into the system, even though pecuniary incentives are far from playing the role attributed to them by capitalist ideologues. American entrepreneurs, after appropriate deductions for lavish living, *did* pour their profits back into improving and expanding the means of production, with the results we now know. Although the prevalence of vertical mobility in our system has been greatly exaggerated and is the subject of much mythologizing, the able and talented were able to rise with impressive frequency from the humblest beginnings. Competition, although systematically subverted, was prevalent in significant areas of the economy and attempts were made (e.g., the Clayton Act) to outlaw the more flagrant monopolistic practices. Although our tax laws have been and still are notoriously biased in favor of the rich, there has been no wholesale evasion of the taxes levied. Finally, as already noted, many wealthy entrepreneurs and their descendants developed what we earlier called a sense of *richesse oblige* and, while their benefactions have inspired much hyperbole, they have in fact endowed universities, museums, libraries, institutes and the like on a grand scale.

But while the American entrepreneurial class has been exceptional in virtually every one of these respects, their European counterparts have exhibited no comparable generosity in aiding public projects. The well-to-do of Italy, for example, are notorious tax-evaders, and the same holds true for many if not most other countries. There is very little room at the top for the able and talented in Europe. Monopolistic practices have been taken for granted and, in the absence of genuine competition, European industry (certainly before World War II) shunned innovation. In the most extreme cases—in Latin America, for example —entrepreneurs have not even performed their essential function of providing capital for the expansion of industry; they have exported their capital to other countries.[60] If one marvels at the strong appeal of Communism in Europe and elsewhere, a ready answer may be found in this inventory.

However, even in the United States the unchallenged ascendancy of our merchants and manufacturers resulted in a warped scale of values. Pecuniary incentives were over-emphasized. The rapid rate of industrial expansion stemmed not only from the genius of the system. It was purchased both in England and the United States at the price of brutally exploiting the working population at a time when workers, lacking in labor organization and politically impotent (even though they had suffrage), were incapable of resisting. This was a time when the 60-hour week was common, when women and children were cruelly used under conditions that beggar description, and when all workers were huddled in sunless cities, housed in indescribably squalid slums, and miserably underpaid.

One of the best measures of any society is the condition of its cities. Ours, in glaring contrast to European cities like London, Paris, Zurich, Geneva, Turin, Milan and Vienna, are drab, treeless, lacking in green areas, devoid of fountains and gracious squares, cluttered with billboards and festooned with neon. If the European cities referred to by contrast provide civilized amenities, it must not be thought that this has been the work of their now ascendant entrepreneurial class. Businessmen and industrialists everywhere have been too busy making money to worry seriously about the condition of their cities, except perhaps for an occasional job of face-lifting. What Justice Fortas has called "the driving need for immediate results" has overwhelmed all other needs, including those on which our survival may ultimately depend.

Inscribed in Latin on Wren's tomb in St. Paul's Cathedral are the words, "Reader, if you seek my monument look around you." Surely this may be said as aptly if we seek the monument of a society and its culture. But what do we see as we look around us?

The wealthiest nation in all history has not yet provided for the efficient movement of people through its metropolitan areas—its cities are blighted, the air above them is foul, its streams are polluted, vast numbers of its people are still inadequately housed, and its public services (education, police and probation, public health, etc.) neglected. The indictment is a harsh one, but accurate. It is only in recent years, at the initiative of a government and within the framework of a system responsive to other groups as well as entrepreneurs, that we

---

[60] It is perhaps relevant at this point to note again that (for other reasons) large incomes no longer play their historic role of financing industrial expansion in the United States. Between 1955–1959 inclusive, 70 per cent of the funds invested in the private sector of the economy derived from internal sources—mostly retained earnings.

are becoming concerned about the *quality* of American life as well as the quantity of our output.

The dreary inventory cited above—and it could be extended to include much more—suggests one of the two basic flaws in a society overwhelmingly dominated by an elite of property owners. Such a system inevitably presents a problem in priorities. In such a system, the allocation of resources is invariably biased in favor of the satisfaction of superficial needs (over-sized and over-powered automobiles in annual models, countless gadgets, cosmetics, endless changes in the style of attire, etc.), and the synthesizing of such needs through high-pressure advertising and salesmanship to the neglect of fundamental needs —schools, hospitals, sanitation systems, efficient public transport, libraries, research, and so on. The reasons for this have been brilliantly analyzed by Professor John Kenneth Galbraith in *The Affluent Society* and need not be explored here.[61] The problem of priorities is perhaps best underscored by noting the still large army of prosperous citizens who are somehow able to reconcile an annual expenditure of approximately one billion dollars on new car models (which contain negligible mechanical improvements) with the contention that we cannot afford the increased taxes needed for an adeqate school system, or, for that matter, an adequate sewage disposal system.[62]

The second basic flaw in the rule of an economic elite is that under the guidance of their policies the distribution of income is so biased in their favor that large masses lack the purchasing power with which to buy the output of a now vastly expanded industry. Such an outcome was avoided by Britain in the nineteenth century because its head start in the industrial revolution and its empire gave it a decisive advantage in the markets of the world and made it less dependent on the mass consumer at home. Our vast natural resources, the built-in safety valve provided by our frontier, our freedom from the Balkanization that has plagued Europe, the comparatively early advent of the industrial revolution, all conspired to defer here, as in Britain, the kind of reckoning that finally came in the thirties. There is no reason to believe that a serious depression would not recur if we were to revert—as many prosperous Americans would have us do—to pre-depression policies and practices. We are led to the conclusion that the rapid expansion of the means of production which is made possible in the early stages of a capitalist system by *denying* the masses the means with which to buy consumer goods, can be continued in the later stages only if the masses acquire these means. Committed to what had worked so well for them in the past, understandably immersed in the short-term view, the economically privileged could not understand that the system of which they are the beneficiaries is a set of evolving and not static relationships. Income disparities that once fostered economic

[61] Cf. also, *Evolution of Liberalism*, pp. 238–46, 368–76.

[62] There is a note of fantasy, given the vast sums we spend frivolously, in our failure to spend the $2 billion necessary for adequate sewage disposal after a warning from Arthur S. Flemming, President Eisenhower's Secretary of Health, Education and Welfare, that "we may be confronted by a crisis of such gravity as to jeopardize the further growth and development of many areas of the country. . . ."

growth now frustrate it. The main trend of government policy has been to reckon with such evolution and by a variety of means to provide the masses with purchasing power sufficient—more accurately, nearly sufficient—to keep the economy working.

One of the great questions of our time is whether the propertied classes in under-developed countries have a mission comparable to the historic revolutionary role of the wealthy in Britain and America of rapidly accelerating the normally sluggish expansion of production. So far they have not come forward and, where they have, their role has been reactionary rather than revolutionary. Clearly Communism, in concentrating on the production of capital goods, is playing such a revolutionary role in Russia and probably in China. The hope of our time is that the underdeveloped countries of the world may find a formula less brutal than Communism, and less crude than the plutocratic phase of capitalism, by means of which they can leap across the ages and catch up with the present.

PART TWO

❧

Selected Readings

Democracy

THE SECOND TREATISE

An Essay Concerning the True Original, Extent,
and End of Civil Government

John Locke

1632–1704

✂✁

John Locke and Sir Isaac Newton are justly known as the presiding spirits of the Enlightenment, that period during which Western Europe finally broke with the Middle Ages and modern science came into its own. If Newton's province was the science of physical nature, Locke's central concern was man and society. In the *Essay Concerning Human Understanding* (1687) he dealt with the theoretical problem of the origin and extent of knowledge. The second of his *Two Treatises of Government* (1690) had a more practical orientation; it provided the great apology for England's revolution of 1688. It was that text which inspired our founding fathers, not to mention the French *philosophes*.

If, in England, *The Second Treatise* defended an accomplished fact, in America it was a summons to action. Locke's great work appealed to Americans as to Englishmen because of its essential common sense. Even Locke's ambiguities and inconsistencies were a source of strength (where human affairs are concerned the English have always been content to leave logical rigor to the French).

Locke is justly regarded as one of the great founders of the democratic tradition, although Burke, who is catalogued later in these pages as an elitist, was in fundamental agreement with him. Both Locke and Burke were content with the settlement of 1688. Both were committed to the principle of "mixed" government and both were essentially conservative Englishmen. But historical circumstance has decreed that they play different roles. The reasons are simple. Ideas that were liberal when Locke affirmed them had become conservative a century later. Burke's *Reflections* [1] denounced a great revolution; Locke's *Treatise* defended one. Burke will always be the spokesman for those lost in "the remembrance of things past" while Locke's ideas still inspire men who have found a vision of the future.

John Locke, from *The Second Treatise* (London, 1690), Chapters II, IV, V, VIII, IX, XI, XVIII.
[1] See pp. 231–39 of this volume.

CHAPTER II

OF THE STATE OF NATURE

4. To understand Political Power right, and derive it from its Original, we must consider what State all Men are naturally in, and that is, a *State of perfect Freedom* to order their Actions, and dispose of their Possessions, and Persons as they think fit, within the bounds of the Law of Nature, without asking leave, or depending upon the Will of any other Man.

A *State* also *of Equality*, wherein all the Power and Jurisdiction is recipro-cal, no one having more than another: there being nothing more evident, than that Creatures of the same species and rank promiscuously born to all the same advantages of Nature, and the use of the same faculties, should also be equal one amongst another without Subordination or Subjection, unless the Lord and Mas-ter of them all, should by any manifest Declaration of his Will set one above an-other, and confer on him by an evident and clear appointment an undoubted Right to Dominion and Sovereignty.

. . .

6. But though this be a *State of Liberty*, yet it is *not a State of Licence*, though Man in that State have an uncontroleable Liberty, to dispose of his Per-son or Possessions, yet he has not Liberty to destroy himself, or so much as any Creature in his Possession, but where some nobler use, than its bare Preservation calls for it. The *State of Nature* has a Law of Nature to govern it, which obliges every one: And Reason, which is that Law, teaches all Mankind, who will but consult it, that being all equal and independent, no one ought to harm another in his Life, Health, Liberty, or Possessions. For Men being all the Workmanship of one Omnipotent, and infinitely wise Maker; All the Servants of one Sovereign Master, sent into the World by his order and about his business, they are his Property, whose Workmanship they are, made to last during his, not one anothers Pleasure. And being furnished with like Faculties, sharing all in one Community of Nature, there cannot be supposed any such *Subordination* among us, that may Authorize us to destroy one another, as if we were made for one anothers uses, as the inferior ranks of Creatures are for ours. Every one as he is *bound to preserve himself*, and not to quit his Station wilfully; so by the like reason when his own Preservation comes not in competition, ought he, as much as he can, *to preserve the rest of Mankind*, and may not unless it be to do Justice on an Offender, take away, or impair the life, or what tends to the Preservation of the Life, the Lib-erty, Health, Limb or Goods of another.

7. And that all Men may be restrained from invading others Rights, and from doing hurt to one another, and the Law of Nature be observed, which willeth the Peace and *Preservation of all Mankind*, the *Execution* of the Law of Nature is in that State, put into every Mans hands, whereby every one has a right

to punish the transgressors of that Law to such a Degree, as may hinder its Violation. For the *Law of Nature* would, as all other Laws that concern Men in this World, be in vain, if there were no body that in the State of Nature, had a *Power to Execute* that Law, and thereby preserve the innocent and restrain offenders, and if any one in the State of Nature may punish another, for any evil he has done, every one may do so. For in that *State of perfect Equality*, where naturally there is no superiority or jurisdiction of one, over another, what any may do in Prosecution of that Law, every one must needs have a Right to do.

8. And thus in the State of Nature, *one Man comes by a Power over another*; but yet no Absolute or Arbitrary Power, to use a Criminal when he has got him in his hands, according to the passionate heats, or boundless extravagancy of his own Will, but only to retribute to him, so far as calm reason and conscience dictates, what is proportionate to his Transgression, which is so much as may serve for *Reparation* and *Restraint*. For these two are the only reasons, why one Man may lawfully do harm to another, which is that we call *punishment*. In transgressing the Law of Nature, the Offender declares himself to live by another Rule, than that of *reason* and common Equity, which is that measure God has set to the actions of Men, for their mutual security: and so he becomes dangerous to Mankind, the tye, which is to secure them from injury and violence, being slighted and broken by him. Which being a trespass against the whole Species, and the Peace and Safety of it, provided for by the Law of Nature, every man upon this score, by the Right he hath to preserve Mankind in general, may restrain, or where it is necessary, destroy things noxious to them, and so may bring such evil on any one, who hath transgressed that Law, as may make him repent the doing of it, and thereby deter him, and by his Example others, from doing the like mischief. And in this case, and upon this ground, every *Man hath a Right to punish the Offender, and be Executioner of the Law of Nature*.

. . .

11. From these *two distinct Rights*, the one of *Punishing* the Crime *for restraint*, and preventing the like Offence, which right of punishing is in every body; the other of taking *reparation*, which belongs only to the injured party, comes it to pass that the Magistrate, who by being Magistrate, hath the common right of punishing put into his hands, can often, where the publick good demands not the execution of the Law, *remit* the punishment of Criminal Offences by his own Authority, but yet cannot *remit* the satisfaction due to any private Man, for the damage he has received. . . .

12. By the same reason, may a Man in the State of Nature *punish the lesser breaches* of that Law. It will perhaps be demanded, with death? I answer, Each Transgression may be *punished* to that *degree*, and with so much *Severity* as will suffice to make it an ill bargain to the Offender, give him cause to repent, and terrifie others from doing the like. Every Offence that can be committed in the State of Nature, may in the State of Nature be also punished, equally, and as far forth as it may, in a Common-wealth; for though it would be besides my present

purpose, to enter here into the particulars of the Law of Nature, or its *measures of punishment;* yet, it is certain there is such a Law, and that too, as intelligible and plain to a rational Creature, and a Studier of that Law, as the positive Laws of Common-wealths, nay possibly plainer. . . .

13. To this strange Doctrine, *viz.* That *in the State of Nature, every one has the Executive Power* of the Law of Nature, I doubt not but it will be objected, That it is unreasonable for Men to be Judges in their own Cases, that Self-love will make Men partial to themselves and their Friends. And on the other side, that Ill Nature, Passion and Revenge will carry them too far in punishing others. And hence nothing but Confusion and Disorder will follow, and that therefore God hath certainly appointed Government to restrain the partiality and violence of Men. I easily grant, that *Civil Government* is the proper Remedy for the Inconveniences of the State of Nature, which must certainly be Great, where Men may be Judges in their own Case. . . . I shall desire those who make this Objection, to remember that *Absolute Monarchs* are but Men, and if Government is to be the Remedy of those Evils, which necessarily follow from Mens being Judges in their own Cases, and the State of Nature is therefore not to be endured, I desire to know what kind of Government that is, and how much better it is than the State of Nature, where one Man commanding a multitude, has the Liberty to be Judge in his own Case, and may do to all his Subjects whatever he pleases, without the least liberty to any one to question or controle those who Execute his Pleasure? And in whatsoever he doth, whether led by Reason, Mistake or Passion, must be submitted to? Much better it is in the State of Nature wherein Men are not bound to submit to the unjust will of another: And if he that judges, judges amiss in his own, or any other Case, he is answerable for it to the rest of Mankind.

14. 'Tis often asked as a mighty Objection, *Where are,* or ever were, there any *Men in such a State of Nature?* To which it may suffice as an answer at present; That since all *Princes* and Rulers of *Independent* Governments all through the World, are in a State of Nature, 'tis plain the World never was, nor ever will be, without Numbers of Men in that State. I have named all Governors of *Independent* Communities, whether they are, or are not, in League with others: For 'tis not every Compact that puts an end to the State of Nature between Men, but only this one of agreeing together mutually to enter into one Community, and make one Body Politick; other Promises and Compacts, Men may make one with another, and yet still be in the State of Nature. The Promises and Bargains for Truck, etc., between the two Men in the Desert Island, mentioned by *Garcilasso De la vega,* in his History of *Peru,* or between a *Swiss* and an *Indian,* in the Woods of *America,* are binding to them, though they are perfectly in a State of Nature, in reference to one another. For Truth and keeping of Faith belongs to Men, as Men, and not as Members of Society.

15. To those that say, There were never any Men in the State of Nature; I will . . . affirm, That all Men are naturally in that State, and remain so, till by their own Consents they make themselves Members of some Politick Society; And I doubt not in the Sequel of this Discourse, to make it very clear.

CHAPTER IV
OF SLAVERY

22. The *Natural Liberty* of Man is to be free from any Superior Power on Earth, and not to be under the Will or Legislative Authority of Man, but to have only the Law of Nature for his Rule. The *Liberty of Man, in Society,* is to be under no other Legislative Power, but that established, by consent, in the Common-wealth, nor under the Dominion of any Will, or Restraint of any Law, but what the Legislative shall enact, according to the Trust put in it. *Freedom* then is not what Sir *R. F*[ilmer] tells us, . . . *A Liberty for every one to do what he lists, to live as he pleases, and not to be tyed by any Laws:* But *Freedom of Men under Government,* is, to have a standing Rule to live by, common to every one of that Society, and made by the Legislative Power erected in it; A Liberty to follow my own Will in all things, where the Rule prescribes not; and not to be subject to the inconstant, uncertain, unknown, Arbitrary Will of another Man. As *Freedom of Nature* is to be under no other restraint but the Law of Nature.

23. This *Freedom* from Absolute, Arbitrary Power, is so necessary to, and closely joyned with a Man's Preservation, that he cannot part with it, but by what forfeits his Preservation and Life together. For a Man, not having the Power of his own Life, *cannot,* by Compact, or his own Consent, *enslave himself* to any one, nor put himself under the Absolute, Arbitrary Power of another, to take away his Life, when he pleases. No body can give more Power than he has himself; and he that cannot take away his own Life, cannot give another power over it. . . .

· · ·

CHAPTER V
OF PROPERTY

25. Whether we consider natural *Reason,* which tells us, that Men, being once born, have a right to their Preservation, and consequently to Meat and Drink, and such other things, as Nature affords for their Subsistence: Or *Revela-*

tion, which gives us an account of those Grants God made of the World to *Adam*, and to *Noah*, and his Sons, 'tis very clear, that God, as King *David* says, *Psal.* CXV. xvj. *has given the Earth to the Children of Men*, given it to Mankind in common. But this being supposed, it seems to some a very great difficulty, how any one should ever come to have a *Property* in any thing: I will not content my self to answer, That if it be difficult to make out *Property*, upon a supposition, that God gave the World to *Adam* and his Posterity in common; it is impossible that any Man, but one universal Monarch, should have any *Property*, upon a supposition, that God gave the World to *Adam*, and his Heirs in Succession, exclusive of all the rest of his Posterity. But I shall endeavour to shew, how Men might come to have a *property* in several parts of that which God gave to Mankind in common, and that without any express Compact of all the Commoners.

26. God, who hath given the World to Men in common, hath also given them reason to make use of it to the best advantage of Life, and convenience. The Earth, and all that is therein, is given to Men for the Support and Comfort of their being. And though all the Fruits it naturally produces, and Beasts it feeds, belong to Mankind in common, as they are produced by the spontaneous hand of Nature; and no body has originally a private Dominion, exclusive of the rest of Mankind, in any of them, as they are thus in their natural state: yet being given for the use of Men, there must of necessity be a means *to appropriate* them some way or other before they can be of any use, or at all beneficial to any particular Man. The Fruit, or Venison, which nourishes the wild *Indian*, who knows no Inclosure, and is still a Tenant in common, must be his, and so his, *i.e.* a part of him, that another can no longer have any right to it, before it can do him any good for the support of his Life.

27. Though the Earth, and all inferior Creatures be common to all Men, yet every Man has a *Property* in his own *Person*. This no Body has any Right to but himself. The *Labour* of his Body, and the *Work* of his Hands, we may say, are properly his. Whatsoever then he removes out of the State that Nature hath provided, and left it in, he hath mixed his *Labour* with, and joyned to it something that is his own, and thereby makes it his *Property*. It being by him removed from the common state Nature placed it in, it hath by this *labour* something annexed to it, that excludes the common right of other Men. For this *Labour* being the unquestionable Property of the Labourer, no Man but he can have a right to what that is once joyned to, at least there is enough, and as good left in common for others.

28. He that is nourished by the Acorns he pickt up under an Oak, or the Apples he gathered from the Trees in the Wood, has certainly appropriated them to himself. No Body can deny but the nourishment is his. I ask then, When did they begin to be his? When he digested? Or when he eat? Or when he boiled? Or when he brought them home? Or when he pickt them up? And 'tis plain, if the

first gathering made them not his, nothing else could. That *labour* put a distinction between them and common. That added something to them more than
Nature, the common Mother of all, had done; and so they became his private
right. And will any one say he had no right to those Acorns or Apples he thus
appropriated, because he had not the consent of all Mankind to make them his?
Was it a Robbery thus to assume to himself what belonged to all in Common? If
such a consent as that was necessary, Man had starved, notwithstanding the
Plenty God had given him. We see in *Commons*, which remain so by Compact,
that 'tis the taking any part of what is common, and removing it out of the state
Nature leaves it in, which *begins the Property*; without which the Common is of
no use. And the taking of this or that part, does not depend on the express consent of all the Commoners. Thus the Grass my Horse has bit; the Turfs my Servant has cut; and the Ore I have digg'd in any place where I have a right to them
in common with others, become my *Property*, without the assignation or consent
of any body. The *labour* that was mine, removing them out of that common state
they were in, hath *fixed* my *Property* in them.

29. By making an explicit consent of every Commoner, necessary to any
ones appropriating to himself any part of what is given in common, Children or
Servants could not cut the Meat which their Father or Master had provided for
them in common, without assigning to every one his peculiar part. Though the
Water running in the Fountain be every ones, yet who can doubt, but that in the
Pitcher is his only who drew it out? His *labour* hath taken it out of the hands of
Nature, where it was common, and belong'd equally to all her Children, and *hath*
thereby *appropriated* it to himself.

30. Thus this Law of reason makes the Deer, that *Indian's* who hath killed
it; 'tis allowed to be his goods who hath bestowed his labour upon it, though
before, it was the common right of every one. And amongst those who are
counted the Civiliz'd part of Mankind, who have made and multiplied positive
Laws to determine Property, this original Law of Nature for the *beginning of
Property*, in what was before common, still takes place; and by vertue thereof,
what Fish any one catches in the Ocean, that great and still remaining Common
of Mankind; or what Ambergriese any one takes up here, is *by* the *Labour* that
removes it out of that common state Nature left it in, *made* his *Property* who
takes that pains about it. And even amongst us the Hare that any one is Hunting,
is thought his who pursues her during the Chase. For being a Beast that is still
looked upon as common, and no Man's private Possession; whoever has imploy'd so much *labour* about any of that kind, as to find and pursue her, has
thereby removed her from the state of Nature, wherein she was common, and
hath *begun a Property*.

31. It will perhaps be objected to this, That if gathering the Acorns, or
other Fruits of the Earth, etc. makes a right to them, then any one may *ingross* as
much as he will. To which I Answer, Not so. The same Law of Nature, that does

by this means give us Property, does also *bound* that *Property* too. *God has given us all things richly*, 1 Tim. vi. 17. is the Voice of Reason confirmed by Inspiration. But how far has he given it us? *To enjoy*. As much as any one can make use of to any advantage of life before it spoils; so much he may by his labour fix a Property in. Whatever is beyond this, is more than his share, and belongs to others. Nothing was made by God for Man to spoil or destroy. And thus considering the plenty of natural Provisions there was a long time in the World, and the few spenders, and to how small a part of that provision the industry of one Man could extend it self, and ingross it to the prejudice of others; especially keeping within the *bounds*, set by reason of what might serve for his *use;* there could be then little room for Quarrels or Contentions about Property so establish'd.

32. But the *chief matter of Property* being now not the Fruits of the Earth, and the Beasts that subsist on it, but the *Earth it self;* as that which takes in and carries with it all the rest: I think it is plain, that *Property* in that too is acquired as the former. *As much Land* as a Man Tills, Plants, Improves, Cultivates, and can use the Product of, so much is his *Property*. He by his Labour does, as it were, inclose it from the Common. Nor will it invalidate his right to say, Every body else has an equal Title to it; and therefore he cannot appropriate, he cannot inclose, without the Consent of all his Fellow-Commoners, all Mankind. God, when he gave the World in common to all Mankind, commanded Man also to labour, and the penury of his Condition required it of him. God and his Reason commanded him to subdue the Earth, *i.e.* improve it for the benefit of Life, and therein lay out something upon it that was his own, his labour. He that in Obedience to this Command of God, subdued, tilled and sowed any part of it, thereby annexed to it something that was his *Property*, which another had no Title to, nor could without injury take from him.

33. Nor was this *appropriation* of any parcel of *Land*, by improving it, any prejudice to any other Man, since there was still enough, and as good left; and more than the yet unprovided could use. So that in effect, there was never the less left for others because of his inclosure for himself. For he that leaves as much as another can make use of, does as good as take nothing at all. No Body could think himself injur'd by the drinking of another Man, though he took a good Draught, who had a whole River of the same Water left him to quench his thirst. And the Case of Land and Water, where there is enough of both, is perfectly the same.

34. God gave the World to Men in Common; but since he gave it them for their benefit, and the greatest Conveniences of Life they were capable to draw from it, it cannot be supposed he meant it should always remain common and uncultivated. He gave it to the use of the Industrious and Rational, (and *Labour* was to be *his Title* to it;) not to the Fancy or Covetousness of the Quarrelsom and Contentious. He that had as good left for his Improvement, as was already

taken up, needed not complain, ought not to meddle with what was already im-
proved by another's Labour: If he did, 'tis plain he desired the benefit of another's Pains, which he had no right to, and not the Ground which God had
given him in common with others to labour on, and whereof there was
as good left, as that already possessed, and more than he knew what to do with,
or his Industry could reach to.

35. . . . And hence subduing or cultivating the Earth, and having Dominion, we see are joyned together. The one gave Title to the other. So that God,
by commanding to subdue, gave Authority so far to *appropriate*. And the Condition of Humane Life, which requires Labour and Materials to work on, necessarily introduces *private Possessions*.

36. . . . This I dare boldly affirm, That the same *Rule of Propriety,* (*viz.*)
that every Man should have as much as he could make use of, would hold still in
the World, without straitning any body, since there is Land enough in the World
to suffice double the Inhabitants had not the *Invention of Money*, and the tacit
Agreement of Men to put a value on it, introduced (by Consent) larger Possessions, and a Right to them; which, how it has done, I shall, by and by, shew
more at large.

· · ·

37. . . . Before the Appropriation of Land, he who gathered as much of
the wild Fruit, killed, caught, or tamed, as many of the Beasts as he could; he
that so employed his Pains about any of the spontaneous Products of Nature, as
any way to alter them, from the state which Nature put them in, *by* placing any
of his *Labour* on them, did thereby *acquire a Propriety in them:* But if they
perished, in his Possession, without their due use; if the Fruits rotted, or the
Venison putrified, before he could spend it, he offended against the common Law
of Nature, and was liable to be punished; he invaded his Neighbour's share, for
he had *no Right, farther than his Use* called for any of them, and they might
serve to afford him Conveniencies of Life.

38. The same *measures* governed the *Possession of Land* too: Whatsoever
he tilled and reaped, laid up and made use of, before it spoiled, that was his
peculiar Right; whatsoever he enclosed, and could feed, and make use of, the
Cattle and Product was also his. But if either the Grass of his Inclosure rotted on
the Ground, or the Fruit of his planting perished without gathering, and laying
up, this part of the Earth, notwithstanding his Inclosure, was still to be looked on
as Waste, and might be the Possession of any other. . . .

· · ·

46. . . . Now of those good things which Nature hath provided in common,
every one had a Right (as hath been said) to as much as he could use, and had a
Property in all that he could affect with his Labour: all that his Industry could
extend to, to alter from the State Nature had put it in, was his. He that *gathered*
a Hundred Bushels of Acorns or Apples, had thereby a *Property* in them; they

were his Goods as soon as gathered. He was only to look that he used them before they spoiled; else he took more than his share, and robb'd others. And indeed it was a foolish thing, as well as dishonest, to hoard up more than he could make use of. If he gave away a part to any body else, so that it perished not uselesly in his Possession, these he also made use of. And if he also bartered away Plumbs that would have rotted in a Week, for Nuts that would last good for his eating a whole Year, he did no injury; he wasted not the common Stock; destroyed no part of the portion of Goods that belonged to others, so long as nothing perished uselesly in his hands. Again, if he would give his Nuts for a piece of Metal, pleased with its colour; or exchange his Sheep for Shells, or Wool for a sparkling Pebble or a Diamond, and keep those by him all his Life, he invaded not the Right of others, he might heap up as much of these durable things as he pleased; the *exceeding of the bounds of his* just *Property* not lying in the largeness of his Possession, but the perishing of any thing uselesly in it.

47. And thus *came in the use of Money*, some lasting thing that Men might keep without spoiling, and that by mutual consent Men would take in exchange for the truly useful, but perishable Supports of Life.

48. And as different degrees of Industry were apt to give Men Possessions in different Proportions, so this *Invention of Money* gave them the opportunity to continue and enlarge them. For supposing an Island, separate from all possible Commerce with the rest of the World, wherein there were but a hundred Families, but there were Sheep, Horses and Cows, with other useful Animals, wholsome Fruits, and Land enough for Corn for a hundred thousand times as many, but nothing in the Island, either because of its Commonness, or Perishableness, fit to supply the place of *Money:* What reason could any one have there to enlarge his Possessions beyond the use of his Family, and a plentiful supply to its Consumption, either in what their own Industry produced, or they could barter for like perishable, useful Commodities, with others? Where there is not something both lasting and scarce, and so valuable to be hoarded up, there Men will not be apt to enlarge their *Possessions of Land*, were it never so rich, never so free for them to take. For I ask, What would a Man value Ten Thousand, or an Hundred Thousand Acres of excellent *Land*, ready cultivated, and well stocked too with Cattle, in the middle of the in-land Parts of *America*, where he had no hopes of Commerce with other Parts of the World, to draw *Money* to him by the Sale of the Product? It would not be worth the inclosing, and we should see him give up again to the wild Common of Nature, whatever was more than would supply the Conveniencies of Life to be had there for him and his Family.

49. Thus in the beginning all the World was *America*, and more so than that is now; for no such thing as *Money* was any where known. Find out something that hath the *Use and Value of Money* amongst his Neighbours, you shall see the same Man will begin presently to *enlarge* his *Possessions*.

50. But since Gold and Silver, being little useful to the Life of Man in proportion to Food, Rayment, and Carriage, has its *value* only from the consent of Men, whereof Labour yet makes, in great part, *the measure*, it is plain, that Men have agreed to disproportionate and unequal Possession of the Earth, they having by a tacit and voluntary consent found out a way, how a man may fairly possess more land than he himself can use the product of, by receiving in exchange for the overplus, Gold and Silver, which may be hoarded up without injury to any one, these metalls not spoileing or decaying in the hands of the possessor. This partage of things, in an inequality of private possessions, men have made practicable out of the bounds of Societie, and without compact, only by putting a value on gold and silver and tacitly agreeing in the use of Money. For in Governments the Laws regulate the right of property, and the possession of land is determined by positive constitutions.

·   ·   ·

CHAPTER VIII

OF THE BEGINNING OF POLITICAL SOCIETIES

95. Men being, as has been said, by Nature, all free, equal and independent, no one can be put out of this Estate, and subjected to the Political Power of another, without his own *Consent*. The only way whereby any one devests himself of his Natural Liberty, and *puts on the bonds of Civil Society* is by agreeing with other Men to joyn and unite into a Community, for their comfortable, safe, and peaceable living one amongst another, in a secure Enjoyment of their Properties, and a greater Security against any that are not of it. This any number of Men may do, because it injures not the Freedom of the rest; they are left as they were in the Liberty of the State of Nature. When any number of Men have so *consented to make one Community* or Government, they are thereby presently incorporated, and make *one Body Politick*, wherein the *Majority* have a Right to act and conclude the rest.

96. For when any number of Men have, by the consent of every individual, made a *Community*, they have thereby made that *Community* one Body, with a Power to Act as one Body, which is only by the will and determination of the *majority*. For that which acts any Community, being only the consent of the individuals of it, and it being necessary to that which is one body to move one way; it is necessary the Body should move that way whither the greater force carries it, which is the *consent of the majority*: or else it is impossible it should act or continue one Body, *one Community*, which the consent of every individual that united into it, agreed that it should; and so every one is bound by that consent to be concluded by the *majority*. And therefore we see that in Assemblies

impowered to act by positive Laws where no number is set by that positive Law which impowers them, the *act of the Majority* passes for the act of the whole, and of course determines, as having by the Law of Nature and Reason, the power of the whole.

97. And thus every Man, by consenting with others to make one Body Politick under one Government, puts himself under an Obligation to every one of that Society, to submit to the determination of the *majority*, and to be concluded by it; or else this *original Compact*, whereby he with others incorporates into *one Society*, would signifie nothing, and be no Compact, if he be left free, and under no other ties, than he was in before in the State of Nature. For what appearance would there be of any Compact? What new Engagement if he were no farther tied by any Decrees of the Society, than he himself thought fit, and did actually consent to? This would be still as great a liberty, as he himself had before his Compact, or any one else in the State of Nature hath, who may submit himself and consent to any acts of it if he thinks fit.

98. For if *the consent of the majority* shall not in reason, be received, as *the act of the whole*, and conclude every individual; nothing but the consent of every individual can make any thing to be the act of the whole: But such a consent is next impossible ever to be had . . .

99. . . . And thus that, which begins and actually *constitutes any Political Society*, is nothing but the consent of any number of Freemen capable of a majority to unite and incorporate into such a Society. And this is that, and that only, which did, or could give *beginning* to any *lawful Government* in the World.

•   •   •

CHAPTER IX

OF THE ENDS OF POLITICAL SOCIETY
AND GOVERNMENT

123. If Man in the State of Nature be so free, as has been said; If he be absolute Lord of his own Person and Possessions, equal to the greatest, and subject to no Body, why will he part with his Freedom? Why will he give up this Empire, and subject himself to the Dominion and Controul of any other Power? To which 'tis obvious to Answer, that though in the state of Nature he hath such a right, yet the Enjoyment of it is very uncertain, and constantly exposed to the Invasion of others. For all being Kings as much as he, every Man his Equal, and the greater part no strict Observers of Equity and Justice, the enjoyment of the property he has in this state is very unsafe, very unsecure. This makes him willing to quit a Condition, which however free, is full of fears and continual dangers: And 'tis not without reason, that he seeks out, and is willing to joyn in

Society with others who are already united, or have a mind to unite for the mutual *Preservation* of their Lives, Liberties and Estates, which I call by the general Name, *Property.*

124. The great and *chief end* therefore, of Mens uniting into Commonwealths, and putting themselves under Government, *is the Preservation of their Property.* To which in the state of Nature there are many things wanting.

First, There wants an *establish'd,* settled, known *Law,* received and allowed by common consent to be the Standard of Right and Wrong, and the common measure to decide all Controversies between them. For though the Law of Nature be plain and intelligible to all rational Creatures; yet Men being biassed by their Interest, as well as ignorant for want of study of it, are not apt to allow of it as a Law binding to them in the application of it to their particular Cases.

125. *Secondly,* In the State of Nature there wants a *known and indifferent Judge,* with Authority to determine all differences according to the established Law. For every one in that state being both Judge and Executioner of the Law of Nature, Men being partial to themselves, Passion and Revenge is very apt to carry them too far, and with too much heat, in their own Cases; as well as negligence, and unconcernedness, to make them too remiss, in other Mens.

126. *Thirdly,* In the state of Nature there often wants *Power* to back and support the Sentence when right, and to *give* it due *Execution.* They who by any Injustice offended, will seldom fail, where they are able, by force to make good their Injustice: such resistance many times makes the punishment dangerous, and frequently destructive, to those who attempt it.

. . .

131. But though Men when they enter into Society, give up the Equality, Liberty, and Executive Power they had in the State of Nature, into the hands of the Society, to be so far disposed of by the Legislative, as the good of the Society shall require; yet it being only with an intention in every one the better to preserve himself his Liberty and Property; (For no rational Creature can be supposed to change his condition with an intention to be worse) the power of the Society, or *Legislative* constituted by them, *can never be suppos'd to extend farther than the common good;* but is obliged to secure every ones Property by providing against those three defects above-mentioned, that made the State of Nature so unsafe and uneasie. And so whoever has the Legislative or Supream Power of any Common-wealth, is bound to govern by establish'd *standing Laws,* promulgated and known to the People, and not by Extemporary Decrees; by *indifferent* and upright *Judges,* who are to decide Controversies by those Laws; And to imploy the force of the Community at home, *only in the Execution of such Laws,* or abroad to prevent or redress Foreign Injuries, and secure the Community from Inroads and Invasion. And all this to be directed to no other *end,* but the *Peace, Safety,* and *publick good* of the People.

. . .

CHAPTER XI
OF THE EXTENT OF THE LEGISLATIVE POWER

134. The great end of Mens entring into Society, being the enjoyment of their Properties in Peace and Safety, and the great instrument and means of that being the Laws establish'd in that Society; the *first and fundamental positive Law* of all Commonwealths, *is the establishing of the Legislative* Power; as the *first and fundamental natural Law,* which is to govern even the Legislative it self, is *the preservation of the Society,* and (as far as will consist with the publick good) of every person in it. This *Legislative* is not only *the supream power* of the Commonwealth, but sacred and unalterable in the hands where the Community have once placed it; nor can any Edict of any Body else, in what Form soever conceived, or by what Power soever backed, have the force and obligation of a *Law,* which has not its *Sanction from* that *Legislative,* which the publick has chosen and appointed. For without this the Law could not have that, which is absolutely necessary to its being a *Law, the consent of the Society,* over whom no Body can have a power to make Laws, but by their own consent, and by Authority received from them; and therefore all the *Obedience,* which by the most solemn Ties any one can be obliged to pay, ultimately terminates in this *Supream Power,* and is directed by those Laws which it enacts: nor can any Oaths to any Foreign Power whatsoever, or any Domestick Subordinate Power, discharge any Member of the Society from his *Obedience to the Legislative,* acting pursuant to their trust, nor oblige him to any Obedience contrary to the Laws so enacted, or farther than they do allow; it being ridiculous to imagine one can be tied ultimately to *obey* any *Power* in the Society, which is not *the Supream.*

135. Though the *Legislative,* whether placed in one or more, whether it be always in being, or only by intervals, tho' it be the *Supream* Power in every Common-wealth; yet,

First, It is *not,* nor can possibly be absolutely *Arbitrary* over the Lives and Fortunes of the People. For it being but the joynt power of every Member of the Society given up to that Person, or Assembly, which is Legislator, it can be no more than those persons had in a State of Nature before they enter'd into Society, and gave up to the Community. For no Body can transfer to another more power than he has in himself; and no Body has an absolute Arbitrary Power over himself, or over any other, to destroy his own Life, or take away the Life or Property of another. A Man, as has been proved, cannot subject himself to the Arbitrary Power of another; and having in the State of Nature no Arbitrary Power over the Life, Liberty, or Possession of another, but only so much as the Law of Nature gave him for the preservation of himself, and the rest of Mankind; this is all he doth, or can give up to the Common-wealth, and by it to the

Legislative Power, so that the Legislative can have no more than this. Their Power in the utmost Bounds of it, is *limited to the publick good* of the Society. It is a Power, that hath no other end but preservation, and therefore can never have a right to destroy, enslave, or designedly to impoverish the Subjects. The Obligations of the Law of Nature, cease not in Society, but only in many Cases are drawn closer, and have by Humane Laws known Penalties annexed to them, to inforce their observation. Thus the Law of Nature stands as an Eternal Rule to all Men, *Legislators* as well as others. The *Rules* that they make for other Mens Actions, must, as well as their own and other Mens Actions, be comformable to the Law of Nature, *i.e.* to the Will of God, of which that is a Declaration, and the *fundamental Law of Nature* being *the preservation of Mankind,* no Humane Sanction can be good, or valid against it.

136. *Secondly,* The *Legislative,* or Supream Authority, cannot assume to its self a power to Rule by extemporary Arbitrary Decrees, but *is bound to dispense Justice,* and decide the Rights of the Subject *by promulgated standing Laws, and known Authoris'd Judges.* . . . Men unite into Societies, that they may have the united strength of the whole Society to secure and defend their Properties, and may have *standing Rules* to bound it, by which every one may know what is his. To this end it is that Men give up all their Natural Power to the Society which they enter into, and the Community put the Legislative Power into such hands as they think fit, with this trust, that they shall be govern'd by *declared Laws,* or else their Peace, Quiet, and Property will still be at the same uncertainty, as it was in the state of Nature.

137. Absolute Arbitrary Power, or Governing without *settled standing Laws,* can neither of them consist with the ends of Society and Government, which Men would not quit the freedom of the state of Nature for, and tie themselves up under, were it not to preserve their Lives, Liberties and Fortunes; and by *stated Rules* of Right and Property to secure their Peace and Quiet. . . .

138. *Thirdly,* The *Supream Power cannot take* from any Man any part of his *Property* without his own consent. For the preservation of Property being the end of Government, and that for which Men enter into Society, it necessarily supposes and requires, that the People should *have Property,* without which they must be suppos'd to lose that by entring into Society, which was the end for which they entered into it, too gross an absurdity for any Man to own. . . . Hence it is a mistake to think, that the Supream or *Legislative Power* of any Commonwealth, can do what it will, and dispose of the Estates of the Subject *arbitrarily,* or take any part of them at pleasure. This is not much to be fear'd in Governments where the *Legislative* consists, wholly or in part, in Assemblies which are variable, whose Members upon the Dissolution of the Assembly, are Subjects under the common Laws of their Country, equally with the rest. But in Governments, where the *Legislative* is in one lasting Assembly always in being, or in one Man, as in Absolute Monarchies, there is danger still, that they will

think themselves to have a distinct interest, from the rest of the Community; and so will be apt to increase their own Riches and Power, by taking, what they think fit, from the People. For a Man's *Property* is not at all secure, though there be good and equitable Laws to set the bounds of it, between him and his Fellow Subjects, if he who commands those Subjects, have Power to take from any private Man, what part he pleases of his *Property*, and use and dispose of it as he thinks good.

. . .

140. 'Tis true, Governments cannot be supported without great Charge, and 'tis fit every one who enjoys his share of the Protection, should pay out of his Estate his proportion for the maintenance of it. But still it must be with his own Consent, *i.e.* the Consent of the Majority, giving it either by themselves, or their Representatives chosen by them. For if any one shall claim a *Power to lay* and levy *Taxes* on the People, by his own Authority, and without such consent of the People, he thereby invades the *Fundamental Law of Property*, and subverts the end of Government. For what property have I in that which another may by right take, when he pleases to himself?

141. *Fourthly*, The *Legislative cannot transfer the Power of Making Laws* to any other hands. For it being but a delegated Power from the People, they, who have it, cannot pass it over to others. The People alone can appoint the Form of the Commonwealth, which is by Constituting the Legislative, and appointing in whose hands that shall be. And when the People have said, We will submit to rules, and be govern'd by *Laws* made by such Men, and in such Forms, no Body else can say other Men shall make *Laws* for them; nor can the people be bound by any *Laws* but such as are Enacted by those, whom they have Chosen, and Authorised to make *Laws* for them. . . .

142. These are the *Bounds* which the trust that is put in them by the Society, and the Law of God and Nature, have *set to the Legislative* Power of every Commonwealth, in all Forms of Government.

First, They are to govern by *promulgated establish'd Laws*, not to be varied in particular Cases, but to have one Rule for Rich and Poor, for the Favourite at Court, and the Country Man at Plough.

Secondly, These *Laws* also ought to be designed *for* no other end ultimately but *the good of the People.*

Thirdly, they must *not raise Taxes* on the Property of the People, *without the Consent of the People*, given by themselves, or their Deputies. And this properly concerns only such Governments where the *Legislative* is always in being, or at least where the People have not reserv'd any part of the Legislative to Deputies, to be from time to time chosen by themselves.

Fourthly, the *Legislative* neither must *nor can transfer the Power of making Laws* to any Body else, or place it any where but where the People have.

CHAPTER XVIII
OF TYRANNY

199. As Usurpation is the exercise of Power, which another hath a Right to; so *Tyranny* is *the exercise of Power beyond Right,* which no Body can have a Right to. And this is making use of the Power any one has in his hands; not for the good of those, who are under it, but for his own private separate Advantage. When the Governour, however intituled, makes not the Law, but his Will, the Rule; and his Commands and Actions are not directed to the preservation of the Properties of his People, but the satisfaction of his own Ambition, Revenge, Covetousness, or any other irregular Passion.

200. If one can doubt this to be Truth, or Reason, because it comes from the obscure hand of a Subject, I hope the Authority of a King [*James*] will make it pass with him. . . . Thus that Learned King who well understood the Notions of things, makes the difference betwixt a *King* and a *Tyrant* to consist only in this, That one makes the Laws the Bounds of his Power, and the Good of the Publick, the end of his Government; the other makes all give way to his own Will and Appetite.

201. 'Tis a Mistake to think this Fault is proper only to Monarchies; other Forms of Government are liable to it, as well as that. For where-ever the Power that is put in any hands for the Government of the People, and the Preservation of their Properties, is applied to other ends, and made use of to impoverish, harass, or subdue them to the Arbitrary and Irregular Commands of those that have it: There it presently becomes *Tyranny*, whether those that thus use it are one or many. Thus we read of the Thirty Tyrants at *Athens*, as well as one at *Syracuse;* and the intolerable Dominion of the *Decemviri* at *Rome* was nothing better.

202. *Where-ever Law ends, Tyranny begins,* if the Law be transgressed to another's harm. And whosoever in Authority exceeds the Power given him by the Law, and makes use of the Force he has under his Command, to compass that upon the Subject, which the Law allows not, ceases in that to be a Magistrate, and acting without Authority, may be opposed, as any other Man, who by force invades the Right of another. . . .

203. May the *Commands* then *of a Prince be opposed?* May he be resisted as often as any one shall find himself aggrieved, and but imagine he has not Right done him? This will unhinge and overturn all Polities, and instead of Government and Order leave nothing but Anarchy and Confusion.

204. To this I Answer: That *Force* is to be *opposed* to nothing, but to unjust and unlawful *Force;* whoever makes any opposition in any other Case,

draws on himself a just Condemnation both from God and Man; and so no such Danger or Confusion will follow, as is often suggested. For,

.   .   .

208. . . . [I]f the unlawful acts done by the Magistrate, be maintained (by the Power he has got) and the remedy which is due by Law, be by the same Power obstructed; yet the *Right of resisting,* even in such manifest Acts of Tyranny, *will not* suddenly, or on slight occasions, *disturb the Government.* For if it reach no farther than some private Mens Cases, though they have a right to defend themselves, and to recover by force, what by unlawful force is taken from them; yet the Right to do so, will not easily ingage them in a Contest, wherein they are sure to perish; it being as impossible for one or a few oppressed Men to *disturb the Government,* where the Body of the People do not think themselves concerned in it, as for a raving mad Man, or heady Male-content to overturn a well-settled State; the People being as little apt to follow the one, as the other.

209. But if either these illegal Acts have extended to the Majority of the People; or if the Mischief and Oppression has light only on some few, but in such Cases, as the Precedent, and Consequences seem to threaten all, and they are perswaded in their Consciences, that their Laws, and with them their Estates, Liberties, and Lives are in danger, and perhaps their Religion too, how they will be hindered from resisting illegal force, used against them, I cannot tell. This is an *Inconvenience,* I confess, that *attends all Governments* whatsoever, when the Governours have brought it to this pass, to be generally suspected of their People; the most dangerous state which they can possibly put themselves in: wherein they are the less to be pitied, because it is so easie to be avoided; It being as impossible for a Governor, if he really means the good of his People, and the preservation of them and their Laws together, not to make them see and feel it; as it is for the Father of a Family, not to let his Children see he loves, and takes care of them.

210. But if all the World shall observe Pretences of one kind, and Action's of another; Arts used to elude the Law, and the Trust of Prerogative (which is an Arbitrary Power in some things left in the Prince's hand to do good, not harm to the People) employed contrary to the end, for which it was given: if the People shall find the Ministers, and subordinate Magistrates chosen suitable to such ends, and favoured, or laid by proportionably, as they promote, or oppose them: If they see several Experiments made of Arbitrary Power, and that Religion underhand favoured (though publickly proclaimed against) which is readiest to introduce it, and the Operators in it supported, as much as may be; and when that cannot be done, yet approved still, and liked the better: if a *long Train of Actings shew the Councils* all tending that way, how can a Man any more hinder himself from being perswaded in his own Mind, which way things are going; or from casting about how to save himself. . . .

THE SOCIAL CONTRACT

Jean Jacques Rousseau

1712–1778

❧

Few great figures have been the subject of more controversy and widely divergent interpretation than Jean Jacques Rousseau. The influence of his writings was enormous, not only in terms of their practical political impact, but in their consequences for the history of philosophy and intellectual history.

On one hand, Rousseau became, through no design of his own, the patron-saint of the French Revolution (his was the first statue commissioned by the French National Assembly which regarded itself as the image of the assembly depicted in *The Social Contract*); on the other, he profoundly influenced closeted philosophers like Kant. On one hand, he belongs to the company of *philosophes* who were the architects of the French Enlightenment; on the other, to the romantic idealists of nineteenth-century Germany who rebelled against the Enlightenment.

Born in the Age of Reason, he exalted the feelings, sentiments, and emotions. He has been praised as the prophet of modern democracy and condemned as the precursor of modern totalitarianism. The moderate Jefferson and militant Robespierre both found inspiration in his writings. An unregenerate individualist who sought to free the individual from the tyranny of the state, he often writes like a collectivist who would submerge the individual in the "moral and collective body" born of the social contract. Such are the paradoxes that surround Rousseau and his work.

He is best known for his two *Discourses* (1750, 1773), the *Nouvelle Héloise* (1761), *Emile* (1762), his self-revelatory *Confessions* (translated in 1876) and, above all, for *The Social Contract* (1762). The last, with its key concepts of the "general will" and the "social compact" and its dedication to government based upon the consent of the governed, moves well beyond Locke in the direction of modern democracy.

Jean Jacques Rousseau, from *The Social Contract*, ed. and trans. by Henry J. Tozer (London, 1898), Book I (Chapters I, II, III, V, VI, VII, IX), Book II (Chapter I, II, III, IV, VI, VII, XI), Book III (Chapters I, III, IV, V, VI, X, XIII, XIV, XV, XVI, XVII, XVIII), and Book IV (Chapter I). Certain footnotes which appeared in the original have been deleted.

Rousseau was a Genevan by birth, but was of French descent and lived most of his life in France. His native city-state with its free institutions and small size supplied the idealized model which inspired him as he wrote *The Social Contract*. Inconsistent in his thinking and irregular in his personal life, he no doubt deserved having said to him what he said to his despised adversary, Voltaire: "If there is nothing in you that I can honor but your talents, that is no fault of mine."

BOOK I

CHAPTER I
Subject of the First Book

Man is born free, and everywhere he is in chains. Many a one believes himself the master of others, and yet he is a greater slave than they. How has this change come about? I do not know. What can render it legitimate? I believe that I can settle this question.

If I considered only force and the results that proceed from it, I should say that so long as a people is compelled to obey and does obey, it does well; but that, so soon as it can shake off the yoke and does shake it off, it does better; for, if men recover their freedom by virtue of the same right by which it was taken away, either they are justified in resuming it, or there was no justification for depriving them of it. But the social order is a sacred right which serves as a foundation for all others. This right however, does not come from nature. It is therefore based on conventions. The question is to know what these conventions are. Before coming to that, I must establish what I have just laid down.

CHAPTER II
Primitive Societies

•   •   •

Just as a herdsman is superior in nature to his herd, so chiefs, who are the herdsmen of men, are superior in nature to their people. Thus, according to Philo's account, the Emperor Caligula reasoned, inferring truly enough from this analogy that kings are gods, or that men are brutes.

The reasoning of Caligula is tantamount to that of Hobbes and Grotius. Aristotle, before them all, had likewise said that men are not naturally equal, but that some are born for slavery and others for dominion.

Aristotle was right, but he mistook the effect for the cause. Every man born in slavery is born for slavery; nothing is more certain. Slaves lose everything in their bonds, even the desire to escape from them; they love their servitude as the companions of Ulysses loved their brutishness. If, then, there are slaves by nature, it is because there have been slaves contrary to nature. The first slaves were made such by force; their cowardice kept them in bondage.

· · ·

CHAPTER III
The Right of the Strongest

The strongest man is never strong enough to be always master, unless he transforms his power into right, and obedience into duty. Hence the right of the strongest—a right apparently assumed in irony, and really established in principle. But will this phrase never be explained to us? Force is a physical power; I do not see what morality can result from its effects. To yield to force is an act of necessity, not of will; it is at most an act of prudence. In what sense can it be a duty?

Let us assume for a moment this pretended right. I say that nothing results from it but inexplicable nonsense; for if force constitutes right, the effect changes with the cause, and any force which overcomes the first succeeds to its rights. As soon as men can disobey with impunity, they may do so legitimately; and since the strongest is always in the right, the only thing is to act in such a way that one may be the strongest. But what sort of a right is it that perishes when force ceases? If it is necessary to obey by compulsion, there is no need to obey from duty; and if men are no longer forced to obey, obligation is at an end. We see, then, that this word *right* adds nothing to force; it here means nothing at all.

Obey the powers that be. If that means, Yield to force, the precept is good but superfluous; I reply that it will never be violated. All power comes from God, I admit; but every disease comes from him too; does it follow that we are prohibited from calling in a physician? If a brigand should suprise me in the recesses of a wood, am I bound not only to give up my purse when forced, but am I also morally bound to do so when I might conceal it? For, in effect, the pistol which he holds is a superior force.

Let us agree, then, that might does not make right, and that we are bound to obey none but lawful authorities. Thus my original question ever recurs.

CHAPTER V
That It Is Always Necessary to go Back to a First Convention

If I should concede all that I have so far refuted, those who favour despotism would be no farther advanced. There will always be a great difference between subduing a multitude and ruling a society. When isolated men, however numerous they may be, are subjected one after another to a single person, this seems to me only a case of master and slaves, not of a nation and its chief; they form, if you will, an aggregation, but not an association, for they have neither public property nor a body politic. Such a man, had he enslaved half the world, is never anything but an individual; his interest, separated from that of the rest, is never anything but a private interest. If he dies, his empire after him is left disconnected and disunited, as an oak dissolves and becomes a heap of ashes after the fire has consumed it.

A nation, says Grotius, can give itself to a king. According to Grotius, then, a nation is a nation before it gives itself to a king. This gift itself is a civil act, and presupposes a public resolution. Consequently, before examining the act by which a nation elects a king, it would be proper to examine the act by which a nation becomes a nation; for this act, being necessarily anterior to the other, is the real foundation of the society.

In fact, if there were no anterior convention, where, unless the election were unanimous, would be the obligation upon the minority to submit to the decision of the majority? And whence do the hundred who desire a master derive the right to vote on behalf of ten who do not desire one? The law of the plurality of votes is itself established by convention, and presupposes unanimity once at least.

CHAPTER VI
The Social Pact

I assume that men have reached a point at which the obstacles that endanger their preservation in the state of nature overcome by their resistance the forces which each individual can exert with a view to maintaining himself in that state. Then this primitive condition can no longer subsist, and the human race would perish unless it changed its mode of existence.

Now, as men cannot create any new forces, but only combine and direct those that exist, they have no other means of self-preservation than to form by aggregation a sum of forces which may overcome the resistance, to put them in action by a single motive power, and to make them work in concert.

This sum of forces can be produced only by the combination of many; but the strength and freedom of each man being the chief instruments of his preservation, how can he pledge them without injuring himself, and without neglecting the cares which he owes to himself? This difficulty, applied to my subject, may be expressed in these terms:—

"To find a form of association which may defend and protect with the whole force of the community the person and property of every associate, and by means of which each, coalescing with all, may nevertheless obey only himself, and remain as free as before." Such is the fundamental problem of which the social contract furnishes the solution.

The clauses of this contract are so determined by the nature of the act that the slightest modification would render them vain and ineffectual; so that, although they have never perhaps been formally enunciated, they are everywhere the same, everywhere tacitly admitted and recognised, until, the social pact being violated, each man regains his original rights and recovers his natural liberty, whilst losing the conventional liberty for which he renounced it.

These clauses, rightly understood, are reducible to one only, viz. the total alienation to the whole community of each associate with all his rights; for, in the first place, since each gives himself up entirely, the conditions are equal for all; and, the conditions being equal for all, no one has any interest in making them burdensome to others.

Further, the alienation being made without reserve, the union is as perfect as it can be, and an individual associate can no longer claim anything; for, if any rights were left to individuals, since there would be no common superior who could judge between them and the public, each, being on some point his own judge, would soon claim to be so on all; the state of nature would still subsist, and the association would necessarily become tyrannical or useless.

In short, each giving himself to all, gives himself to nobody; and as there is not one associate over whom we do not acquire the same rights which we concede to him over ourselves, we gain the equivalent of all that we lose, and more power to preserve what we have.

If, then, we set aside what is not of the essence of the social contract, we shall find that it is reducible to the following terms: "Each of us puts in common his person and his whole power under the supreme direction of the general will; and in return we receive every member as an indivisible part of the whole."

Forthwith, instead of the individual personalities of all the contracting parties, this act of association produces a moral and collective body, which is composed of as many members as the assembly has voices, and which receives from this same act its unity, its common self (*moi*), its life, and its will. This public person, which is thus formed by the union of all the individual members, formerly took the name of *city*, and now takes that of *republic* or *body politic*, which is called by its members *State* when it is passive, *sovereign* when it is active, *power* when it is compared to similar bodies. With regard to the associates, they take collectively the name of *people*, and are called individually *citizens*, as participating in the sovereign power, and *subjects*, as subjected to the laws of the State. But these terms are often confused and are mistaken one for another; it is sufficient to know how to distinguish them when they are used with complete precision.

CHAPTER VII
The Sovereign

We see from this formula that the act of association contains a reciprocal engagement between the public and individuals, and that every individual, contracting so to speak with himself, is engaged in a double relation, viz. as a member of the sovereign towards individuals, and as a member of the State towards the sovereign. But we cannot apply here the maxim of civil law that no one is bound by engagements made with himself; for there is a great difference between being bound to oneself and to a whole of which one forms part.

We must further observe that the public resolution which can bind all subjects to the sovereign in consequence of the two different relations under which each of them is regarded cannot, for a contrary reason, bind the sovereign to itself; and that accordingly it is contrary to the nature of the body politic for the sovereign to impose on itself a law which it cannot transgress. As it can only be considered under one and the same relation, it is in the position of an individual contracting with himself; whence we see that there is not, nor can be, any kind of fundamental law binding upon the body of the people, not even the social contract. This does not imply that such a body cannot perfectly well enter into engagements with others in what does not derogate from this contract; for, with regard to foreigners, it becomes a simple being, an individual.

But the body politic or sovereign, deriving its existence only from the sanctity of the contract, can never bind itself, even to others, in anything that derogates from the original act, such as alienation of some portion of itself, or submission to another sovereign. To violate the act by which it exists would be to annihilate itself; and what is nothing produces nothing.

So soon as the multitude is thus united in one body, it is impossible to injure one of the members without attacking the body, still less to injure the body without the members feeling the effects. Thus duty and interest alike oblige the two contracting parties to give mutual assistance; and the men themselves should seek to combine in this twofold relationship all the advantages which are attendant on it.

Now, the sovereign, being formed only of the individuals that compose it, neither has nor can have any interest contrary to theirs; consequently the sovereign power needs no guarantee towards its subjects, because it is impossible that the body should wish to injure all its members; and we shall see hereafter that it can injure no one as an individual. The sovereign, for the simple reason that it is so, is always everything that it ought to be.

But this is not the case as regards the relation of subjects to the sovereign, which, notwithstanding the common interest, would have no security for the performance of their engagements, unless it found means to ensure their fidelity.

Indeed, every individual may, as a man, have a particular will contrary to, or divergent from, the general will which he has as a citizen; his private interest may prompt him quite differently from the common interest; his absolute and naturally independent existence may make him regard what he owes to the common cause as a gratuitous contribution, the loss of which will be less harmful to others than the payment of it will be burdensome to him; and, regarding the moral person that constitutes the State as an imaginary being because it is not a man, he would be willing to enjoy the rights of a citizen without being willing to fulfil the duties of a subject. The progress of such injustice would bring about the ruin of the body politic.

In order, then, that the social pact may not be a vain formulary, it tacitly includes this engagement, which can alone give force to the others,—that whoever refuses to obey the general will shall be constrained to do so by the whole body; which means nothing else than that he shall be forced to be free; for such is the condition which, uniting every citizen to his native land, guarantees him from all personal dependence, a condition that ensures the control and working of the political machine, and alone renders legitimate civil engagements, which, without it, would be absurd and tyrannical, and subject to the most enormous abuses.

CHAPTER IX
Real Property

. . .

I shall close this chapter and this book with a remark which ought to serve as a basis for the whole social system; it is that instead of destroying natural equality, the fundamental pact, on the contrary, substitutes a moral and lawful equality for the physical inequality which nature imposed upon men, so that, although unequal in strength or intellect, they all become equal by convention and legal right.*

BOOK II

CHAPTER I
That Sovereignty Is Inalienable

The first and most important consequence of the principles above established is that the general will alone can direct the forces of the State according to the object of its institution, which is the common good; for if the opposition of private interests has rendered necessary the establishment of societies, the agreement of these same interests has rendered it possible. That which is common to these different interests forms the social bond; and unless there were some point in which all interests agree, no society could exist. Now, it is solely with regard to this common interest that the society should be governed.

I say, then, that sovereignty, being nothing but the exercise of the general will, can never be alienated, and that the sovereign power, which is only a collective being, can be represented by itself alone; power indeed can be transmitted, but not will.

In fact, if it is not impossible that a particular will should agree on some

* Under bad governments this equality is only apparent and illusory; it serves only to keep the poor in their misery and the rich in their usurpation. In fact, laws are always useful to those who possess and injurious to those that have nothing; whence it follows that the social state is advantageous to men only so far as they all have something, and none of them has too much.

point with the general will, it is at least impossible that this agreement should be lasting and constant; for the particular will naturally tends to preferences, and the general will to equality. It is still more impossible to have a security for this agreement; even though it should always exist, it would not be a result of art, but of chance. The sovereign may indeed say: "I will now what a certain man wills, or at least what he says that he wills"; but he cannot say: "What that man wills to-morrow, I shall also will," since it is absurd that the will should bind itself as regards the future, and since it is not incumbent on any will to consent to anything contrary to the welfare of the being that wills. If, then, the nation simply promises to obey, it dissolves itself by that act and loses its character as a people; the moment there is a master, there is no longer a sovereign, and forthwith the body politic is destroyed.

This does not imply that the orders of the chiefs cannot pass for decisions of the general will, so long as the sovereign, free to oppose them, refrains from doing so. In such a case the consent of the people should be inferred from the universal silence. This will be explained at greater length.

CHAPTER II
That Sovereignty Is Indivisible

For the same reason that sovereignty is inalienable it is indivisible; for the will is either general,* or it is not; it is either that of the body of the people, or that of only a portion. In the first case, this declared will is an act of sovereignty and constitutes law; in the second case, it is only a particular will, or an act of magistracy—it is at most a decree.

But our publicists, being unable to divide sovereignty in its principle, divide it in its object. They divide it into force and will, into legislative power and executive power; into rights of taxation, of justice, and of war; into internal administration and power of treating with foreigners—sometimes confounding all these departments, and sometimes separating them. They make the sovereign a fantastic being, formed of connected parts; it is as if they composed a man of several bodies, one with eyes, another with arms, another with feet, and nothing else. The Japanese conjurers, it is said, cut up a child before the eyes of the spectators; then, throwing all its limbs into the air, they make the child come down again alive and whole. Such almost are the jugglers' tricks of our publicists; after dismembering the social body by a deception worthy of the fair, they recombine its parts, nobody knows how.

This error arises from their not having formed exact notions about the sovereign authority, and from their taking as parts of this authority what are only emanations from it. Thus, for example, the acts of declaring war and making peace have been regarded as acts of sovereignty, which is not the case, since neither of them is a law, but only an application of the law, a particular act

---

* That a will may be general, it is not always necessary that it should be unanimous, but it is necessary that all votes should be counted; any formal exclusion destroys the generality.

which determines the case of the law, as will be clearly seen when the idea attached to the word *law* is fixed.

By following out the other divisions in the same way, it would be found that, whenever the sovereignty appears divided, we are mistaken in our supposition; and that the rights which are taken as parts of that sovereignty are all subordinate to it, and always suppose supreme wills of which these rights are merely executive.

. . .

CHAPTER III
Whether the General Will Can Err

It follows from what precedes that the general will is always right and always tends to the public advantage; but it does not follow that the resolutions of the people have always the same rectitude. Men always desire their own good, but do not always discern it; the people are never corrupted, though often deceived, and it is only then that they seem to will what is evil.

There is often a great deal of difference between the will of all and the general will; the latter regards only the common interest, while the former has regard to private interests, and is merely a sum of particular wills; but take away from these same wills the pluses and minuses which cancel one another,* and the general will remains as the sum of the differences.

If the people came to a resolution when adequately informed and without any communication among the citizens, the general will would always result from the great number of slight differences, and the resolution would always be good. But when factions, partial associations, are formed to the detriment of the whole society, the will of each of these associations becomes general with reference to its members, and particular with reference to the State; it may then be said that there are no longer as many voters as there are men, but only as many voters as there are associations. The differences become less numerous and yield a less general result. Lastly, when one of these associations becomes so great that it predominates over all the rest, you no longer have as the result a sum of small differences, but a single difference; there is then no longer a general will, and the opinion which prevails is only a particular opinion.

It is important, then, in order to have a clear declaration of the general will, that there should be no partial association in the State, and that every citizen should express only his own opinion.† Such was the unique and sublime institu-

---

* "Every interest," says the Marquis d'Argenson, "has different principles. The accord of two particular interests is formed by opposition to that of a third." He might have added that the accord of all interests is formed by opposition to that of each. Unless there were different interests, the common interest would scarcely be felt and would never meet with any obstacle; everything would go of itself, and politics would cease to be an art.

† "It is true," says Machiavelli, "that some divisions injure the State, while some are beneficial to it; those are injurious to it which are accompanied by cabals and factions; those assist it which are maintained without cabals, without factions. Since, therefore, no founder of a State can provide against enmities in it, he ought at least to provide that there shall be no cabals" (*History of Florence*, Book VII.).

tion of the great Lycurgus. But if there are partial associations, it is necessary to multiply their number and prevent inequality, as Solon, Numa, and Servius did. These are the only proper precautions for ensuring that the general will may always be enlightened, and that the people may not be deceived.

CHAPTER IV

The Limits of the Sovereign Power

If the State or city is nothing but a moral person, the life of which consists in the union of its members, and if the most important of its cares is that of self-preservation, it needs a universal and compulsive force to move and dispose every part in the manner most expedient for the whole. As nature gives every man an absolute power over all his limbs, the social pact gives the body politic an absolute power over all its members; and it is this same power which, when directed by the general will, bears, as I said, the name of sovereignty.

But besides the public person, we have to consider the private persons who compose it, and whose life and liberty are naturally independent of it. The question, then, is to distinguish clearly between the respective rights of the citizens and of the sovereign as well as between the duties which the former have to fulfil in their capacity as subjects and the natural rights which they ought to enjoy in their character as men.

It is admitted that whatever part of his power, property, and liberty each one alienates by the social compact is only that part of the whole of which the use is important to the community; but we must also admit that the sovereign alone is judge of what is important.

All the services that a citizen can render to the State he owes to it as soon as the sovereign demands them; but the sovereign, on its part, cannot impose on its subjects any burden which is useless to the community; it cannot even wish to do so, for, by the law of reason, just as by the law of nature, nothing is done without a cause.

The engagements which bind us to the social body are obligatory only because they are mutual; and their nature is such that in fulfilling them we cannot work for others without also working for ourselves. Why is the general will always right, and why do all invariably desire the prosperity of each, unless it is because there is no one but appropriates to himself this word *each* and thinks of himself in voting on behalf of all? This proves that equality of rights and the notion of justice that it produces are derived from the preference which each gives to himself, and consequently from man's nature; that the general will, to be truly such, should be so in its object as well as in its essence; that it ought to proceed from all in order to be applicable to all; and that it loses its natural rectitude when it tends to some individual and determinate object, because in that case, judging of what is unknown to us, we have no true principle of equity to guide us.

Indeed, so soon as a particular fact or right is in question with regard to a point which has not been regulated by an anterior general convention, the matter becomes contentious; it is a process in which the private persons interested are one of the parties and the public the other, but in which I perceive neither the law which must be followed, nor the judge who should decide. It would be ridiculous in such a case to wish to refer the matter for an express decision of the general will, which can be nothing but the decision of one of the parties, and which, consequently, is for the other party only a will that is foreign, partial, and inclined on such an occasion to injustice as well as liable to error. Therefore, just as a particular will cannot represent the general will, the general will in turn changes its nature when it has a particular end, and cannot, as general, decide about either a person or a fact. When the people of Athens, for instance, elected or deposed their chiefs, decreed honours to one, imposed penalties on another, and by multitudes of particular decrees exercised indiscriminately all the functions of government, the people no longer had any general will properly so called; they no longer acted as a sovereign power, but as magistrates. This will appear contrary to common ideas, but I must be allowed time to expound my own.

From this we must understand that what generalises the will is not so much the number of voices as the common interest which unites them; for, under this system, each necessarily submits to the conditions which he imposes on others— an admirable union of interest and justice, which gives to the deliberations of the community a spirit of equity that seems to disappear in the discussion of any private affair, for want of a common interest to unite and identify the ruling principle of the judge with that of the party.

By whatever path we return to our principle we always arrive at the same conclusion, viz. that the social compact establishes among the citizens such an equality that they all pledge themselves under the same conditions and ought all to enjoy the same rights. Thus, by the nature of the compact, every act of sovereignty, that is, every authentic act of the general will, binds or favours equally all the citizens; so that the sovereign knows only the body of the nation, and distinguishes none of those that compose it.

What, then, is an act of sovereignty properly so called? It is not an agreement between a superior and an inferior, but an agreement of the body with each of its members; a lawful agreement, because it has the social contract as its foundation; equitable, because it is common to all; useful, because it can have no other object than the general welfare; and stable, because it has the public force and the supreme power as a guarantee. So long as the subjects submit only to such conventions, they obey no one, but simply their own will; and to ask how far the respective rights of the sovereign and citizens extend is to ask up to what point the latter can make engagements among themselves, each with all and all with each.

Thus we see that the sovereign power, wholly absolute, wholly sacred, and wholly inviolable as it is, does not, and cannot, pass the limits of general conventions, and that every man can fully dispose of what is left to him of his property

and liberty by these conventions; so that the sovereign never has a right to burden one subject more than another, because then the matter becomes particular
and his power is no longer competent.

These distinctions once admitted, so untrue is it that in the social contract
there is on the part of individuals any real renunciation, that their situation, as a
result of this contract, is in reality preferable to what it was before, and that,
instead of an alienation, they have only made an advantageous exchange of an
uncertain and precarious mode of existence for a better and more assured one, of
natural independence for liberty, of the power to injure others for their own
safety, and of their strength, which others might overcome, for a right which the
social union renders inviolable. Their lives, also, which they have devoted to the
State, are continually protected by it; and in exposing their lives for its defence,
what do they do but restore what they have received from it? What do they do
but what they would do more frequently and with more risk in the state of nature, when, engaging in inevitable struggles, they would defend at the peril of
their lives their means of preservation? All have to fight for their country in case
of need, it is true; but then no one ever has to fight for himself. Do we not gain,
moreover, by incurring, for what ensures our safety, a part of the risks that we
should have to incur for ourselves individually, as soon as we were deprived of
it?

CHAPTER VI
The Law

By the social compact we have given existence and life to the body politic;
the question now is to endow it with movement and will by legislation. For the
original act by which this body is formed and consolidated determines nothing in
addition as to what it must do for its own preservation.

What is right and conformable to order is such by the nature of things, and
independently of human conventions. All justice comes from God, he alone is the
source of it; but could we receive it direct from so lofty a source, we should need
neither government nor laws. Without doubt there is a universal justice emanat-
ing from reason alone; but this justice, in order to be admitted among us, should
be reciprocal. Regarding things from a human standpoint, the laws of justice are
inoperative among men for want of a natural sanction; they only bring good to
the wicked and evil to the just when the latter observe them with every one, and no
one observes them in return. Conventions and laws, then, are necessary to couple
rights with duties and apply justice to its object. In the state of nature, where
everything is in common, I owe nothing to those to whom I have promised nothing; I recognize as belonging to others only what is useless to me. This is not the
case in the civil state, in which all rights are determined by law.

But then, finally, what is a law? So long as men are content to attach to this
word only metaphysical ideas, they will continue to argue without being understood; and when they have stated what a law of nature is, they will know no
better what a law of the State is.

I have already said that there is no general will with reference to a particular object. In fact, this particular object is either in the State or outside of it. If it is outside the State, a will which is foreign to it is not general in relation to it; and if it is within the State, it forms part of it; then there is formed between the whole and its part a relation which makes of it two separate beings, of which the part is one, and the whole, less this same part, is the other. But the whole less one part is not the whole, and so long as the relation subsists, there is no longer any whole, but two unequal parts; whence it follows that the will of the one is no longer general in relation to the other.

But when the whole people decree concerning the whole people, they consider themselves alone; and if a relation is then constituted, it is between the whole object under one point of view and the whole object under another point of view, without any division at all. Then the matter respecting which they decree is general like the will that decrees. It is this act that I call a law.

When I say that the object of the laws is always general, I mean that the law considers subjects collectively, and actions as abstract, never a man as an individual nor a particular action. Thus the law may indeed decree that there shall be privileges, but cannot confer them on any person by name; the law can create several classes of citizens, and even assign the qualifications which shall entitle them to rank in these classes, but it cannot nominate such and such persons to be admitted to them; it can establish a royal government and a hereditary succession, but cannot elect a king or appoint a royal family; in a word, no function which has reference to an individual object appertains to the legislative power.

From this standpoint we see immediately that it is no longer necessary to ask whose office it is to make laws, since they are acts of the general will; nor whether the prince is above the laws, since he is a member of the State; nor whether the law can be unjust, since no one is unjust to himself; nor how we are free and yet subject to the laws, since the laws are only registers of our wills.

We see, further, that since the law combines the universality of the will with the universality of the object, whatever any man prescribes on his own authority is not a law; and whatever the sovereign itself prescribes respecting a particular object is not a law, but a decree, not an act of sovereignty, but of magistracy.

I therefore call any State a republic which is governed by laws, under whatever form of administration it may be; for then only does the public interest predominate and the commonwealth count for something. Every legitimate government is republican;* I will explain hereafter what government is.

Laws are properly only the conditions of civil association. The people, being subjected to the laws, should be the authors of them; it concerns only the associates to determine the conditions of association. But how will they be determined? Will it be by a common agreement, by a sudden inspiration? Has the body politic an organ for expressing its will? Who will give it the foresight necessary to

---

* I do not mean by this word an aristocracy or democracy only, but in general any government directed by the general will, which is the law. To be legitimate, the government must not be combined with the sovereign power, but must be its minister; then monarchy itself is a republic. . . .

frame its acts and publish them at the outset? Or how shall it declare them in the hour of need? How would a blind multitude, which often knows not what it wishes because it rarely knows what is good for it, execute of itself an enterprise so great, so difficult, as a system of legislation? Of themselves, the people always desire what is good, but do not always discern it. The general will is always right, but the judgment which guides it is not always enlightened. It must be made to see objects as they are, sometimes as they ought to appear; it must be shown the good path that it is seeking, and guarded from the seduction of private interests; it must be made to observe closely times and places, and to balance the attraction of immediate and palpable advantages against the danger of remote and concealed evils. Individuals see the good which they reject; the public desire the good which they do not see. All alike have need of guides. The former must be compelled to conform their wills to their reason; the people must be taught to know what they require. Then from the public enlightenment results the union of the understanding and the will in the social body; and from that the close co-operation of the parts, and, lastly, the maximum power of the whole. Hence arises the need of a legislator.

CHAPTER VII
The Legislator

In order to discover the rules of association that are most suitable to nations, a superior intelligence would be necessary who could see all the passions of men without experiencing any of them; who would have no affinity with our nature and yet know it thoroughly; whose happiness would not depend on us, and who would nevertheless be quite willing to interest himself in ours; and, lastly, one who, storing up for himself with the progress of time a far-off glory in the future, could labour in one age and enjoy in another.* Gods would be necessary to give laws to men.

The same argument that Caligula adduced as to fact, Plato put forward with regard to right, in order to give an idea of the civil or royal man whom he is in quest of in his work the *Statesman*. But if it is true that a great prince is a rare man, what will a great legislator be? The first has only to follow the model which the other has to frame. The latter is the mechanician who invents the machine, the former is only the workman who puts it in readiness and works it. "In the birth of societies," says Montesquieu, "it is the chiefs of the republics who frame the institutions, and afterwards it is the institutions which mould the chiefs of the republics."

He who dares undertake to give institutions to a nation ought to feel himself capable, as it were, of changing human nature; of transforming every individual, who in himself is a complete and independent whole, into part of a greater whole,

---

* A nation becomes famous only when its legislation is beginning to decline. We are ignorant during how many centuries the institutions of Lycurgus conferred happiness on the Spartans before they were known in the rest of Greece.

from which he receives in some manner his life and his being; of altering man's constitution in order to strengthen it; of substituting a social and moral existence for the independent and physical existence which we have all received from nature. In a word, it is necessary to deprive man of his native powers in order to endow him with some which are alien to him, and of which he cannot make use without the aid of other people. The more thoroughly those natural powers are deadened and destroyed, the greater and more durable are the acquired powers, the more solid and perfect also are the institutions; so that if every citizen is nothing, and can be nothing, except in combination with all the rest, and if the force acquired by the whole be equal or superior to the sum of the natural forces of all the individuals, we may say that legislation is at the highest point of perfection which it can attain.

The legislator is in all respects an extraordinary man in the State. If he ought to be so by his genius, he is not less so by his office. It is not magistracy nor sovereignty. This office, which constitutes the republic, does not enter into its constitution; it is a special and superior office, having nothing in common with human government; for, if he who rules men ought not to control legislation, he who controls legislation ought not to rule men; otherwise his laws, being ministers of his passions, would often serve only to perpetuate his acts of injustice; he would never be able to prevent private interests from corrupting the sacredness of his work.

When Lycurgus gave laws to his country, he began by abdicating his royalty. It was the practice of the majority of the Greek towns to entrust to foreigners the framing of their laws. The modern republics of Italy often imitated this usage; that of Geneva did the same and found it advantageous. Rome, at her most glorious epoch, saw all the crimes of tyranny spring up in her bosom, and saw herself on the verge of destruction, through uniting in the same hands legislative authority and sovereign power.

Yet the Decemvirs themselves never arrogated the right to pass any law on their sole authority. Nothing that we propose to you, they said to the people, can pass into law without your consent. Romans, be yourselves the authors of the laws which are to secure your happiness.

He who frames laws, then, has, or ought to have, no legislative right, and the people themselves cannot, even if they wished, divest themselves of this incommunicable right, because, according to the fundamental compact, it is only the general will that binds individuals, and we can never be sure that a particular will is conformable to the general will until it has been submitted to the free votes of the people. I have said this already, but it is not useless to repeat it.

Thus we find simultaneously in the work of legislation two things that seem incompatible—an enterprise surpassing human powers, and, to execute it, an authority that is a mere nothing.

Another difficulty deserves attention. Wise men who want to speak to the vulgar in their own language instead of in a popular way will not be understood. Now, there are a thousand kinds of ideas which it is impossible to translate into the language of the people. Views very general and objects very remote are alike beyond its reach; and each individual, approving of no other plan of government than that which promotes his own interests, does not readily perceive the benefits that he is to derive from the continual deprivations which good laws impose. In order that a newly formed nation might approve sound maxims of politics and observe the fundamental rules of state-policy, it would be necessary that the effect should become the cause; that the social spirit, which should be the work of the institution, should preside over the institution itself, and that men should be, prior to the laws, what they ought to become by means of them. Since, then, the legislator cannot employ either force or reasoning, he must needs have recourse to an authority of a different order, which can compel without violence and per-suade without convincing.

It is this which in all ages has constrained the founders of nations to resort to the intervention of heaven, and to give the gods the credit for their own wis-dom, in order that the nations, subjected to the laws of the State as to those of nature, and recognising the same power in the formation of man and in that of the State, might obey willingly, and bear submissively the yoke of the public wel-fare.

The legislator puts into the mouths of the immortals that sublime reason which soars beyond the reach of common men, in order that he may win over by divine authority those whom human prudence could not move.* But it does not belong to every man to make the gods his oracles, nor to be believed when he proclaims himself their interpreter. The great soul of the legislator is the real miracle which must give proof of his mission. Any man can engrave tables of stone, or bribe an oracle, or pretend secret intercourse with some divinity, or train a bird to speak in his ear, or find some other clumsy means to impose on the people. He who is acquainted with such means only will perchance be able to assemble a crowd of foolish persons; but he will never found an empire, and his extravagant work will speedily perish with him. Empty deceptions form but a transient bond; it is only wisdom that makes it lasting. The Jewish law, which still endures, and that of the child of Ishmael, which for ten centuries has ruled half the world, still bear witness to-day to the great men who dictated them; and whilst proud philosophy or blind party spirit sees in them nothing but fortunate impostors, the true statesman admires in their systems the great and powerful genius which directs durable institutions.

It is not necessary from all this to infer with Warburton that politics and religion have among us a common aim, but only that, in the origin of nations, one serves as an instrument of the other.

---

* "It is true," says Machiavelli, "there never was in a nation any promulgator of extraordinary laws who had not recourse to God, because otherwise they would not have been accepted; for there are many advantages recognised by a wise man which are not so self-evident that they can convince others" (*Discourses on Titus Livius*, Book I. chapter 11).

CHAPTER XI
The Different Systems of Legislation

If we ask precisely wherein consists the greatest good of all, which ought to be the aim of every system of legislation, we shall find that it is summed up in two principal objects, *liberty* and *equality*,—liberty, because any individual dependence is so much force withdrawn from the body of the State; equality, because liberty cannot subsist without it.

I have already said what civil liberty is. With regard to equality, we must not understand by this word that the degrees of power and wealth should be absolutely the same; but that, as to power, it should fall short of all violence, and never be exercised except by virtue of station and of the laws; while, as to wealth, no citizen should be rich enough to be able to buy another, and none poor enough to be forced to sell himself,* which supposes, on the part of the great, moderation in property and influence, and, on the part of ordinary citizens, repression of avarice and covetousness.

It is said that this equality is a chimera of speculation which cannot exist in practical affairs. But if the abuse is inevitable, does it follow that it is unnecessary even to regulate it? It is precisely because the force of circumstances is ever tending to destroy equality that the force of legislation should always tend to maintain it.

· · ·

BOOK III

· · ·

CHAPTER I
Government in General

· · ·

We have seen that the legislative power belongs to the people, and can belong to it alone. On the other hand, it is easy to see from the principles already established, that the executive power cannot belong to the people generally as legislative or sovereign, because that power is exerted only in particular acts, which are not within the province of the law, nor consequently within that of the sovereign, all the acts of which must be laws.

The public force, then, requires a suitable agent to concentrate it and put it

---

* If, then, you wish to give stability to the State, bring the two extremes as near together as possible; tolerate neither rich people nor beggars. These two conditions, naturally inseparable, are equally fatal to the general welfare; from the one class spring tyrants, from the other, the supporters of tyranny; it is always between these that the traffic in public liberty is carried on; the one buys and the other sells.

in action according to the directions of the general will, to serve as a means of communication between the State and the sovereign, to effect in some manner in the public person what the union of soul and body effects in a man. This is, in the State, the function of the government, improperly confounded with the sovereign of which it is only the minister.

What, then, is the government? An intermediate body established between the subjects and the sovereign for their mutual correspondence, charged with the execution of the laws and with the maintenance of liberty both civil and political.

The members of this body are called magistrates or *kings,* that is, *governors;* and the body as a whole bears the name of *Prince.* Those therefore who maintain that the act by which a people submits to its chiefs is not a contract are quite right. It is absolutely nothing but a commission, an employment, in which, as simple officers of the sovereign, they exercise in its name the power of which it has made them depositaries, and which it can limit, modify, and resume when it pleases. The alienation of such a right, being incompatible with the nature of the social body, is contrary to the object of the association.

Consequently, I give the name *government* or supreme administration to the legitimate exercise of the executive power, and that of Prince or magistrate to the man or body charged with that administration.

It is in the government that are found the intermediate powers, the relations of which constitute the relation of the whole to the whole, or of the sovereign to the State. This last relation can be represented by that of the extremes of a continued proportion, of which the mean proportional is the government. The government receives from the sovereign the commands which it gives to the people; and in order that the State may be in stable equilibrium, it is necessary, everything being balanced, that there should be equality between the product or the power of the government taken by itself, and the product or the power of the citizens, who are sovereign in the one aspect and subjects in the other.

Further, we could not alter any of the three terms without at once destroying the proportion. If the sovereign wishes to govern, or if the magistrate wishes to legislate, or if the subjects refuse to obey, disorder succeeds order, force and will no longer act in concert, and the State being dissolved falls into despotism or anarchy. . . .

•   •   •

Let us suppose that the State is composed of ten thousand citizens. The sovereign can only be considered collectively and as a body; but every private person, in his capacity of subject, is considered as an individual; therefore the sovereign is to the subject as ten thousand is to one, that is, each member of the State has as his share only one ten-thousandth part of the sovereign authority, although he is entirely subjected to it.

If the nation consists of a hundred thousand men, the position of the subjects does not change, and each alike is subjected to the whole authority of the laws, whilst his vote, reduced to one hundred-thousandth, has ten times less influence in their enactment. The subject, then, always remaining a unit, the proportional power of the sovereign increases in the ratio of the number of the citizens. Whence it follows that the more the State is enlarged, the more does liberty diminish.

. . .

Now, the less the particular wills correspond with the general will, that is, customs with laws, the more should the repressive power be increased. The government, then, in order to be effective, should be relatively stronger in proportion as the people are more numerous.

On the other hand, as the aggrandisement of the State gives the depositaries of the public authority more temptations and more opportunities to abuse their power, the more force should the government have to restrain the people, and the more should the sovereign have in its turn to restrain the government. I do not speak here of absolute force, but of the relative force of the different parts of the State.

. . .

Without embarrassing ourselves with this multiplication of terms, let us be content to consider the government as a new body in the State, distinct from the people and from the sovereign, and intermediate between the two.

There is this essential difference between those two bodies, that the State exists by itself, while the government exists only through the sovereign. Thus the dominant will of the Prince is, or ought to be, only the general will, or the law; its force is only the public force concentrated in itself; so soon as it wishes to perform of itself some absolute and independent act, the connexion of the whole begins to be relaxed. If, lastly, the Prince should chance to have a particular will more active than that of the sovereign, and if, to enforce obedience to this particular will, it should employ the public force which is in its hands, in such a manner that there would be so to speak two sovereigns, the one *de jure* and the other *de facto*, the social union would immediately disappear, and the body politic would be dissolved.

Further, in order that the body of the government may have an existence, a real life, to distinguish it from the body of the State; in order that all its members may be able to act in concert and fulfil the object for which it is instituted, a particular personality is necessary to it, a feeling common to its members, a force, a will of its own tending to its preservation. This individual existence supposes assemblies, councils, a power of deliberating and resolving, rights, titles, and privileges which belong to the Prince exclusively, and which render the position of the magistrate more honourable in proportion as it is more arduous. The difficulty lies in the method of disposing, within the whole, this subordinate whole, in such a way that it may not weaken the general constitution in strengthening its own; that its particular force, intended for its own preservation, may always be kept distinct from the public force, designed for the preservation of the State; and, in a word, that it may always be ready to sacrifice the government to the people, and not the people to the government.

. . .

CHAPTER III
Classification of Governments

· · ·

The sovereign may, in the first place, commit the charge of the government to the whole people, or to the greater part of the people, in such a way that there may be more citizens who are magistrates than simple individual citizens. We call this form of government a *democracy*.

Or it may confine the government to a small number, so that there may be more ordinary citizens than magistrates; and this form bears the name of *aristocracy*.

Lastly, it may concentrate the whole government in the hands of a single magistrate from whom all the rest derive their power. This third form is the most common, and is called *monarchy*, or royal government.

We should remark that all these forms, or at least the first two, admit of degrees, and may indeed have a considerable range; for democracy may embrace the whole people, or be limited to a half. Aristocracy, in its turn, may restrict itself from a half of the people to the smallest number indeterminately. Royalty even is susceptible of some division. Sparta by its constitution always had two kings; and in the Roman Empire there were as many as eight Emperors at once without its being possible to say that the Empire was divided. Thus there is a point at which each form of government blends with the next; and we see that, under three denominations only, the government is really susceptible of as many different forms as the State has citizens.

· · ·

CHAPTER IV
Democracy

He that makes the law knows better than any one how it should be executed and interpreted. It would seem, then, that there could be no better constitution than one in which the executive power is united with the legislative; but it is that very circumstance which makes a democratic government inadequate in certain respects, because things which ought to be distinguished are not, and because the Prince and the sovereign, being the same person, only form as it were a government without government.

It is not expedient that he who makes the laws should execute them, nor that the body of the people should divert its attention from general considerations in order to bestow it on particular objects. Nothing is more dangerous than the influence of private interests on public affairs; and the abuse of the laws by the government is a less evil than the corruption of the legislator, which is the infallible result of the pursuit of private interests. For when the State is changed in its substance all reform becomes impossible. A people which would never abuse the government would likewise never abuse its independence; a people which always governed well would not need to be governed.

Taking the term in its strict sense, there never has existed, and never will exist, any true democracy. It is contrary to the natural order that the majority should govern and that the minority should be governed. It is impossible to imagine that the people should remain in perpetual assembly to attend to public affairs, and it is easily apparent that commissions could not be established for that purpose without the form of administration being changed.

In fact, I think I can lay down as a principle that when the functions of government are shared among several magistracies, the least numerous acquire, sooner or later, the greatest authority, if only on account of the facility in transacting business which naturally leads them on to that.

Moreover, how many things difficult to combine does not this government presuppose! First, a very small State, in which the people may be readily assembled, and in which every citizen can easily know all the rest; secondly, great simplicity of manners, which prevents a multiplicity of affairs and thorny discussions; next, considerable equality in rank and fortune, without which equality in rights and authority could not long subsist; lastly, little or no luxury, for luxury is either the effect of wealth or renders it necessary; it corrupts both the rich and the poor, the former by possession, the latter by covetousness; it betrays the country to effeminacy and vanity; it deprives the State of all its citizens in order to subject them one to another, and all to opinion.

That is why a famous author has assigned virtue as the principle of a republic, for all these conditions could not subsist without virtue; but, through not making the necessary distinctions, this brilliant genius has often lacked precision and sometimes clearness, and has not seen that the sovereign authority being everywhere the same, the same principle ought to have a place in every well-constituted State, in a greater or less degree, it is true, according to the form of government.

Let us add that there is no government so subject to civil wars and internal agitations as the democratic or popular, because there is none which tends so strongly and so constantly to change its form, none which demands more vigilance and courage to be maintained in its own form. It is especially in this constitution that the citizen should arm himself with strength and steadfastness, and say every day of his life from the bottom of his heart what a virtuous Palatine said in the Diet of Poland: *Malo periculosam libertatem quam quietum servitium.*

If there were a nation of gods, it would be governed democratically. So perfect a government is unsuited to men.

CHAPTER V
Aristocracy

We have here two moral persons quite distinct, viz. the government and the sovereign; and consequently two general wills, the one having reference to all the citizens, the other only to the members of the administration. Thus, although the government can regulate its internal policy as it pleases, it can never speak to the people except in the name of the sovereign, that is, in the name of the people themselves. This must never be forgotten.

The earliest societies were aristocratically governed. The heads of families deliberated among themselves about public affairs. The young men yielded readily to the authority of experience. Hence the names *priests, elders, senate, gerontes.* The savages of North America are still governed in this way at the present time, and are very well governed.

But in proportion as the inequality due to institutions prevailed over natural inequality, wealth or power was preferred to age, and aristocracy became elective. Finally, the power transmitted with the father's property to the children, rendering the families patrician, made the government hereditary, and there were senators only twenty years old.

There are, then, three kinds of aristocracy—natural, elective, and hereditary. The first is only suitable for simple nations; the third is the worst of all governments. The second is the best; it is aristocracy properly so-called.

Besides the advantage of the distinction between the two powers, aristocracy has that of the choice of its members; for in a popular government all the citizens are born magistrates; but this one limits them to a small number, and they become magistrates by election only; * a method by which probity, intelligence, experience, and all other grounds of preference and public esteem are so many fresh guarantees that men will be wisely governed.

Further, assemblies are more easily convoked; affairs are better discussed and are despatched with greater order and diligence; while the credit of the State is better maintained abroad by venerable senators, than by an unknown or despised multitude.

In a word, it is the best and most natural order of things that the wisest should govern the multitude, when we are sure that they will govern it for its advantage and not for their own. We should not uselessly multiply means, nor do with twenty thousand men what a hundred chosen men can do still better. But we must observe that the corporate interest begins here to direct the public force in a less degree according to the rule of the general will, and that another inevitable propensity deprives the laws of a part of the executive power.

With regard to special expediencies, a State must not be so small, nor a people so simple and upright, that the execution of the laws should follow immediately upon the public will, as in a good democracy. Nor again must a nation be so large that the chief men, who are dispersed in order to govern it, can set up as sovereigns, each in his own province, and begin by making themselves independent so as at last to become masters.

But if aristocracy requires a few virtues less than popular government, it

* It is very important to regulate by law the form of election of magistrates; for, in leaving it to the will of the Prince, it is impossible to avoid falling into hereditary aristocracy, as happened in the republics of Venice and Berne. In consequence, the first has long been a decaying State, but the second is maintained by the extreme wisdom of its Senate; it is a very honourable and a very dangerous exception.

requires also others that are peculiarly its own, such as moderation among the rich and contentment among the poor; for a rigorous equality would seem to be out of place in it, and was not even observed in Sparta.

Besides, if this form of government comports with a certain inequality of fortune, it is expedient in general that the administration of public affairs should be entrusted to those that are best able to devote their whole time to it, but not, as Aristotle maintains, that the rich should always be preferred. On the contrary, it is important that an opposite choice should sometimes teach the people that there are, in men's personal merits, reasons for preference more important than wealth.

CHAPTER VI
Monarchy

We have hitherto considered the Prince as a moral and collective person united by the force of the laws, and as the depositary of the executive power in the State. We have now to consider this power concentrated in the hands of a natural person, of a real man, who alone has a right to dispose of it according to the laws. He is what is called a monarch or a king.

Quite the reverse of the other forms of administration, in which a collective being represents an individual, in this one an individual represents a collective being; so that the moral unity that constitutes it is at the same time a physical unity, in which all the powers that the law combines in the other with so much effort are combined naturally.

.   .   .

But if there is no government which has more vigour, there is none in which the particular will has more sway and more easily governs others. Everything works for the same end, it is true; but this end is not the public welfare, and the very power of the administration turns continually to the prejudice of the State.

Kings wish to be absolute, and from afar men cry to them that the best way to become so is to make themselves beloved by their people. This maxim is very fine, and also very true in certain respects; unfortunately it will always be ridiculed in courts. Power which springs from the affections of the people is doubtless the greatest, but it is precarious and conditional; princes will never be satisfied with it. The best kings wish to have the power of being wicked if they please, without ceasing to be masters. A political preacher will tell them in vain that, the strength of the people being their own, it is their greatest interest that the people should be flourishing, numerous, and formidable; they know very well that that is not true. Their personal interest is, in the first place, that the people should be weak and miserable, and should never be able to resist them. Supposing all the subjects always perfectly submissive, I admit that it would then be the prince's interest that the people should be powerful, in order that this power, being his own, might render him formidable to his neighbours; but as this interest is only secondary and subordinate, and as the two suppositions are incompatible, it is natural that princes should always give preference to the maxim which is most immediately useful to them. . . .

.   .   .

One essential and inevitable defect, which will always render a monarchical government inferior to a republican one, is that in the latter the public voice hardly ever raises to the highest posts any but enlightened and capable men, who fill them honourably; whereas those who succeed in monarchies are most frequently only petty mischief-makers, petty knaves, petty intriguers, whose petty talents, which enable them to attain high posts in courts, only serve to show the public their ineptitude as soon as they have attained them. The people are much less mistaken about their choice than the prince is; and a man of real merit is almost as rare in a royal ministry as a fool at the head of a republican government. Therefore, when by some fortunate chance one of these born rulers takes the helm of affairs in a monarchy almost wrecked by such a fine set of ministers, it is quite astonishing what resources he finds, and his accession to power forms an epoch in a country.

In order that a monarchical State might be well governed, it would be necessary that its greatness or extent should be proportioned to the abilities of him that governs. It is easier to conquer than to rule. With a sufficient lever, the world may be moved by a finger; but to support it the shoulders of Hercules are required. . . .

The most obvious inconvenience of the government of a single person is the lack of that uninterrupted succession which forms in the two others a continuous connexion. One king being dead, another is necessary; elections leave dangerous intervals; they are stormy; and unless the citizens are of a disinterestedness, an integrity, which this government hardly admits of, intrigue and corruption intermingle with it. It would be hard for a man to whom the State has been sold not to sell it in his turn, and indemnify himself out of the helpless for the money which the powerful have extorted from him. Sooner or later everything becomes venal under such an administration, and the peace which is then enjoyed under a king is worse than the disorder of an interregnum.

What has been done to prevent these evils? Crowns have been made hereditary in certain families; and an order of succession has been established which prevents any dispute on the demise of kings; that is to say, the inconvenience of regencies being substituted for that of elections, an appearance of tranquillity has been preferred to a wise administration, and men have preferred to risk having as their chiefs children, monsters, and imbeciles, rather than have a dispute about the choice of good kings. They have not considered that in thus exposing themselves to the risk of this alternative, they put almost all the chances against themselves. . . .

.   .   .

CHAPTER X

The Abuse of the Government and Its Tendency to Degenerate

As the particular will acts incessantly against the general will, so the government makes a continual effort against the sovereignty. The more this effort is increased, the more is the constitution altered; and as there is here no other corporate will which, by resisting that of the Prince, may produce equilibrium with it, it must happen sooner or later that the Prince at length oppresses the sovereign and violates the social treaty. Therein is the inherent and inevitable vice which, from the birth of the body politic, tends without intermission to destroy it, just as old age and death at length destroy the human body.

There are two general ways by which a government degenerates, viz. when it contracts, or when the State is dissolved.

The government contracts when it passes from the majority to the minority, that is, from democracy to aristocracy, and from aristocracy to royalty. That is its natural tendency. If it retrograded from the minority to the majority, it might be said to relax; but this inverse progress is impossible.

In reality, the government never changes its form except when its exhausted energy leaves it too weak to preserve itself; and if it becomes still more relaxed as it extends, its force will be annihilated, and it will no longer subsist. We must therefore concentrate the energy as it dwindles; otherwise the State which it sustains will fall into ruin.

The dissolution of the State may occur in two ways.

Firstly, when the Prince no longer administers the State in accordance with the laws and effects a usurpation of the sovereign power. Then a remarkable change takes place—the State, and not the government, contracts; I mean that the State dissolves, and that another is formed within it, which is composed only of the members of the government, and which is to the rest of the people nothing more than their master and their tyrant. So that as soon as the government usurps the sovereignty, the social compact is broken, and all the ordinary citizens, rightfully regaining their natural liberty, are forced, but not morally bound, to obey.

The same thing occurs also when the members of the government usurp separately the power which they ought to exercise only collectively; which is no less a violation of the laws, and occasions still greater disorder. Then there are, so to speak, as many Princes as magistrates; and the State, not less divided than the government, perishes or changes its form.

When the State is broken up, the abuse of the government, whatever it may be, takes the common name of *anarchy*. To distinguish, democracy degenerates into *ochlocracy*, aristocracy into *oligarchy*; I should add that royalty degenerates into *tyranny*; but this last word is equivocal and requires explanation.

In the vulgar sense a tyrant is a king who governs with violence and without regard to justice and the laws. In the strict sense, a tyrant is a private person who arrogates to himself the royal authority without having a right to it. It is in this sense that the Greeks understood the word tyrant; they bestowed it indifferently on good and bad princes whose authority was not legitimate. Thus *tyrant* and *usurper* are two words perfectly synonymous.

To give different names to different things, I call the usurper of royal authority a *tyrant,* and the usurper of sovereign power a *despot.* The tyrant is he who, contrary to the laws, takes upon himself to govern according to the laws; the despot is he who sets himself above the laws themselves. Thus the tyrant cannot be a despot, but the despot is always a tyrant.

CHAPTER XIII
How the Sovereign Authority Is Maintained
(*continued*)

It is not sufficient that the assembled people should have once fixed the constitution of the State by giving their sanction to a body of laws; it is not sufficient that they should have established a perpetual government, or that they should have once for all provided for the election of magistrates. Besides the extraordinary assemblies which unforeseen events may require, it is necessary that there should be fixed and periodical ones which nothing can abolish or prorogue; so that, on the appointed day, the people are rightfully convoked by the law, without needing for that purpose any formal summons.

But, excepting these assemblies which are lawful by their date alone, every assembly of the people that has not been convoked by the magistrates appointed for that duty and according to the prescribed forms, ought to be regarded as unlawful and all that is done in it as invalid, because even the order to assemble ought to emanate from the law.

As for the more or less frequent meetings of the lawful assemblies, they depend on so many considerations that no precise rules can be given about them. Only it may be said generally that the more force a government has, the more frequently should the sovereign display itself.

This, I shall be told, may be good for a single city; but what is to be done when the State comprises many cities? . . .

.   .   .

If, however, the State cannot be reduced to proper limits, one resource still remains; it is not to allow any capital, but to make the government sit alternately in each town, and also to assemble in them by turns the estates of the country.

People the territory uniformly, extend the same rights everywhere, spread everywhere abundance and life; in this way the State will become at once the strongest and the best governed that may be possible. Remember that the walls of the towns are formed solely of the remains of houses in the country. For every palace that I see rising in the capital, I seem to see a whole rural district laid in ruins.

CHAPTER XIV
How the Sovereign Authority Is Maintained
(*continued*)

So soon as the people are lawfully assembled as a sovereign body, the whole jurisdiction of the government ceases, the executive power is suspended, and the person of the meanest citizen is as sacred and inviolable as that of the first magistrate, because where the represented are, there is no longer any representative. . . .

These intervals of suspension, in which the Prince recognizes or ought to recognize the presence of a superior, have always been dreaded by that power; and these assemblies of the people, which are the shield of the body politic and the curb of the government, have in all ages been the terror of the chief men; hence such men are never wanting in solicitude, objections, obstacles, and promises, in the endeavour to make the citizens disgusted with the assemblies. When the latter are avaricious, cowardly, pusillanimous, and more desirous of repose than of freedom, they do not long hold out against the repeated efforts of the government; and thus, as the resisting force constantly increases, the sovereign authority at last disappears, and most of the States decay and perish before their time.

But between the sovereign authority and the arbitrary government there is sometimes introduced an intermediate power of which I must speak.

CHAPTER XV
Deputies or Representatives

So soon as the service of the State ceases to be the principal business of the citizens, and they prefer to render aid with their purses rather than their persons, the State is already on the brink of ruin. Is it necessary to march to battle, they pay troops and remain at home; is it necessary to go to the council, they elect deputies and remain at home. As a result of indolence and wealth, they at length have soldiers to enslave their country and representatives to sell it.

It is the bustle of commerce and of the arts, it is the greedy pursuit of gain, it is effeminacy and love of comforts, that commute personal services for money. Men sacrifice a portion of their profit in order to increase it at their ease. Give money and soon you will have chains. That word *finance* is a slave's word; it is unknown among citizens. In a country that is really free, the citizens do everything with their hands and nothing with money; far from paying for exemption from their duties, they would pay to perform them themselves. I am far removed from ordinary ideas; I believe that statute-labour (*les corvées*) is less repugnant to liberty than taxation is.

The better constituted a State is, the more do public affairs outweigh private ones in the minds of the citizens. There is, indeed, a much smaller number of private affairs, because the amount of the general prosperity furnishes a more considerable portion to that of each individual, and less remains to be sought by individual exertions. In a well-conducted city-state every one hastens to the assemblies; while under a bad government no one cares to move a step in order to attend them, because no one takes an interest in the proceedings, since it is foreseen that the general will will not prevail; and so at last private concerns become all-absorbing. Good laws pave the way for better ones; bad laws lead to worse ones. As soon as any one says of the affairs of the State, "Of what importance are they to me?" we must consider that the State is lost.

The decline of patriotism, the active pursuit of private interests, the vast size of States, conquests, and the abuses of government, have suggested the plan of deputies or representatives of the people in the assemblies of the nation. It is this which in certain countries they dare to call the third estate. Thus the private interest of two orders is put in the first and second rank, the public interest only in the third.

Sovereignty cannot be represented for the same reason that it cannot be alienated; it consists essentially in the general will, and the will cannot be represented; it is the same or it is different; there is no medium. The deputies of the people, then, are not and cannot be its representatives; they are only its commissioners and can conclude nothing definitely. Every law which the people in person have not ratified is invalid; it is not a law. The English nation thinks that it is free, but is greatly mistaken, for it is so only during the election of members of Parliament; as soon as they are elected, it is enslaved and counts for nothing. The use which it makes of the brief moments of freedom renders the loss of liberty well-deserved.

The idea of representatives is modern; it comes to us from feudal government, that absurd and iniquitous government, under which mankind is degraded and the name of man dishonoured. In the republics, and even in the monarchies, of antiquity, the people never had representatives; they did not know the word. It is very singular that in Rome, where the tribunes were so sacred, it was not even imagined that they could usurp the functions of the people, and in the midst of so great a multitude, they never attempted to pass of their own accord a single *plebiscitum*. We may judge, however, of the embarrassment which the crowd sometimes caused from what occurred in the time of the Gracchi, when a part of the citizens gave their votes on the house-tops. But where right and liberty are all in all, inconveniences are nothing. In that wise nation everything was estimated at a true value; it allowed the lictors to do what the tribunes had not dared to do, and was not afraid that the lictors would want to represent it.

To explain, however, in what manner the tribunes sometimes represented it, it is sufficient to understand how the government represents the sovereign. The law being nothing but the declaration of the general will, it is clear that in their legislative capacity the people cannot be represented; but they can and should be represented in the executive power, which is only force applied to law. This shows that very few nations would, upon careful examination, be found to have laws. . . .

. . . .

I do not mean by all this that slaves are necessary and that the right of slavery is lawful, since I have proved the contrary; I only mention the reasons why modern nations who believe themselves free have representatives, and why ancient nations had none. Be that as it may, as soon as a nation appoints representatives, it is no longer free; it no longer exists.

After very careful consideration I do not see that it is possible henceforward for the sovereign to preserve among us the exercise of its rights unless the State is very small. But if it is very small, will it not be subjugated? No; I shall show hereafter how the external power of a great nation can be combined with the convenient polity and good order of a small State.

CHAPTER XVI
That the Institution of the Government Is Not a Contract

The legislative power being once well established, the question is to establish also the executive power; for this latter, which operates only by particular acts, not being of the essence of the other, is naturally separated from it. If it were possible that the sovereign, considered as such, should have the executive power, law and fact would be so confounded that it could no longer be known what is law and what is not; and the body politic, thus perverted, would soon become a prey to the violence against which it was instituted.

The citizens being all equal by the social contract, all can prescribe what all ought to do, while no one has a right to demand that another should do what he will not do himself. Now, it is properly his right, indispensable to make the body politic live and move, which the sovereign gives to the Prince in establishing the government.

Several have pretended that the instrument in this establishment is a contract between the people and the chiefs whom they set over themselves—a contract by which it is stipulated between the two parties on what conditions the one binds itself to rule, the other to obey. It will be agreed, I am sure, that this is a strange method of contracting. But let us see whether such a position is tenable.

First, the supreme authority can no more be modified than alienated; to limit it is to destroy it. It is absurd and contradictory that the sovereign should acknowledge a superior; to bind itself to obey a master is to regain full liberty.

Further, it is evident that this contract of the people with such or such persons is a particular act; whence it follows that the contract cannot be a law nor an act of sovereignty, and that consequently it is unlawful.

Moreover, we see that the contracting parties themselves would be under the law of nature alone, and without any security for the performance of their reciprocal engagements, which is in every way repugnant to the civil state. He who possesses the power being always capable of executing it, we might as well give the name contract to the act of a man who should say to another: "I give you all my property, on condition that you restore me what you please."

There is but one contract in the State—that of association; and this of itself excludes any other. No public contract can be conceived which would not be a violation of the first.

CHAPTER XVII

The Institution of the Government

Under what general notion, then, must be included the act by which the government is instituted? I shall observe first that this act is complex, or composed of two others, viz. the establishment of the law and the execution of the law.

By the first, the sovereign determines that there shall be a governing body established in such or such a form; and it is clear that this act is a law.

By the second, the people nominate the chiefs who will be entrusted with the government when established. Now, this nomination being a particular act, is not a second law, but only a consequence of the first, and a function of the government.

The difficulty is to understand how there can be an act of government before the government exists, and how the people, who are only sovereign or subjects, can, in certain circumstances, become the Prince or the magistrates.

Here, however, is disclosed one of those astonishing properties of the body politic, by which it reconciles operations apparently contradictory; for this is effected by a sudden conversion of sovereignty into democracy in such a manner that, without any perceptible change, and merely by a new relation of all to all, the citizens, having become magistrates, pass from general acts to particular acts, and from the law to the execution of it.

This change of relation is not a subtlety of speculation without example in practice; it occurs every day in the Parliament of England, in which the Lower House on certain occasions resolves itself into Grand Committee in order to discuss business better, and thus becomes a simple commission instead of the sovereign court that it was the moment before. In this way it afterwards reports to itself, as the House of Commons, what it has just decided in Grand Committee.

Such is the advantage peculiar to a democratic government, that it can be established in fact by a simple act of the general will; and after this, the provisional government remains in power, should that be the form adopted, or establishes in the name of the sovereign the government prescribed by the law; and thus everything is according to rule. It is impossible to institute the government in any other way that is legitimate without renouncing the principles heretofore established.

CHAPTER XVIII
Means of Preventing Usurpations of the Government

From these explanations it follows, in confirmation of chapter XVI, that the act which institutes the government is not a contract, but a law; that the depositaries of the executive power are not the masters of the people, but its officers; that the people can appoint them and dismiss them at pleasure; that for them it is not a question of contracting, but of obeying; and that in undertaking the functions which the State imposes on them, they simply fulfil their duty as citizens, without having in any way a right to discuss the conditions.

When, therefore, it happens that the people institute a hereditary government, whether monarchical in a family or aristocratic in one order of citizens, it is not an engagement that they make, but a provisional form which they give to the administration, until they please to regulate it differently.

It is true that such changes are always dangerous, and that the established government must never be touched except when it becomes incompatible with the public good; but this circumspection is a maxim of policy, not a rule of right; and the State is no more bound to leave the civil authority to its chief men than the military authority to its generals.

Moreover, it is true that in such a case all the formalities requisite to distinguish a regular and lawful act from a seditious tumult, and the will of a whole people from the clamours of a faction, cannot be too carefully observed. It is especially in this case that only such concessions should be made as cannot in strict justice be refused; and from this obligation also the Prince derives a great advantage in preserving its power in spite of the people, without their being able to say that it has usurped the power; for while appearing to exercise nothing but its rights, it may very easily extend them, and, under pretext of maintaining the public peace, obstruct the assemblies designed to re-establish good order; so that it takes advantage of a silence which it prevents from being broken, or of irregularities which it causes to be committed, so as to assume in its favour the approbation of those whom fear renders silent and punish those that dare to speak. It is in this way that the Decemvirs, having at first been elected for one year, and then kept in office for another year, attempted to retain their power in perpetuity by no longer permitting the *comitia* to assemble; and it is by this easy method that all the governments in the world, when once invested with the public force, usurp sooner or later the sovereign authority.

The periodical assemblies of which I have spoken before are fitted to prevent or postpone this evil, especially when they need no formal convocation; for then the Prince cannot interfere with them, without openly proclaiming itself a violator of the laws and an enemy of the State.

These assemblies, which have as their object the maintenance of the social treaty, ought always to be opened with two propositions, which no one should be able to suppress, and which should pass separately by vote.

The first: "Whether it pleases the sovereign to maintain the present form of government."

The second: "Whether it pleases the people to leave the administration to those at present entrusted with it."

I presuppose here what I believe that I have proved, viz. that there is in the State no fundamental law which cannot be revoked, not even the social compact; for if all the citizens assembled in order to break this compact by a solemn agreement, no one can doubt that it would be quite legitimately broken. Grotius even thinks that each man can renounce the State of which he is a member, and regain his natural freedom and his property by quitting the country.* Now it would be absurd if all the citizens combined should be unable to do what each of them can do separately.

BOOK IV

CHAPTER I
That the General Will Is Indestructible

So long as a number of men in combination are considered as a single body, they have but one will, which relates to the common preservation and to the general well-being. In such a case all the forces of the State are vigorous and simple, and its principles are clear and luminous; it has no confused and conflicting interests; the common good is everywhere plainly manifest and only good sense is required to perceive it. Peace, union, and equality are foes to political subtleties. Upright and simple-minded men are hard to deceive because of their simplicity; allurements and refined pretexts do not impose upon them; they are not even cunning enough to be dupes. When, in the happiest nation in the world, we see troops of peasants regulating the affairs of the State under an oak and always acting wisely, can we refrain from despising the refinements of other nations, who make themselves illustrious and wretched with so much art and mystery?

A State thus governed needs very few laws; and in so far as it becomes necessary to promulgate new ones, this necessity is universally recognized. The first man to propose them only gives expression to what all have previously felt, and neither factions nor eloquence will be needed to pass into law what every one has already resolved to do, so soon as he is sure that the rest will act as he does.

What deceives reasoners is that, seeing only States that are ill-constituted from the beginning, they are impressed with the impossibility of maintaining such a policy in those States; they laugh to think of all the follies to which a cunning knave, an insinuating speaker, can persuade the people of Paris or Lon-

---

* It must be clearly understood that no one should leave in order to evade his duty and relieve himself from serving his country at a moment when it needs him. Flight in that case would be criminal and punishable; it would no longer be retirement, but desertion.

don. They know not that Cromwell would have been put in irons by the people of Berne, and the Duke of Beaufort imprisoned by the Genevese.

But when the social bond begins to be relaxed and the State weakened, when private interests begin to make themselves felt and small associations to exercise influence on the State, the common interest is injuriously affected and finds adversaries; unanimity no longer reigns in the voting; the general will is no longer the will of all; opposition and disputes arise, and the best counsel does not pass uncontested.

Lastly, when the State, on the verge of ruin, no longer subsists except in a vain and illusory form, when the social bond is broken in all hearts, when the basest interest shelters itself impudently under the sacred name of the public welfare, the general will becomes dumb; all, under the guidance of secret motives, no more express their opinions as citizens than if the State had never existed; and, under the name of laws, they deceitfully pass unjust decrees which have only private interest as their end.

Does it follow from this that the general will is destroyed or corrupted? No; it is always constant, unalterable, and pure; but it is subordinated to others which get the better of it. Each, detaching his own interest from the common interest, sees clearly that he cannot completely separate it; but his share in the injury done to the State appears to him as nothing in comparison with the exclusive advantage which he aims at appropriating to himself. This particular advantage being excepted, he desires the general welfare for his own interests quite as strongly as any other. Even in selling his vote for money, he does not extinguish in himself the general will, but eludes it. The fault that he commits is to change the state of the question, and to answer something different from what he was asked; so that, instead of saying by a vote: "It is beneficial to the State," he says: "It is beneficial to a certain man or a certain party that such or such a motion should pass." Thus the law of public order in assemblies is not so much to maintain in them the general will as to ensure that it shall always be consulted and always respond.

•   •   •

TWO LETTERS

Thomas Jefferson

1743–1826

≥⊱⊰≤

Today the greedy distractions of modern living limit correspondence to the bare communication of routine information. In Thomas Jefferson's day great men often revealed more of themselves in their letters than in their public papers and addresses.

Over many years Jefferson exchanged views with John Adams, his great friend and rival among the Federalists, and Du Pont de Nemours, the Frenchman who founded the American dynasty that still bears his name. De Nemours was one of the ablest of the French Physiocrats who, condemning government interference in French agriculture, gave us the term *"laissez faire, laissez passer."*

Of the brilliant group of men who assisted at the birth of our nation, Jefferson was perhaps the most gifted and most versatile. He was a typical man of the Enlightenment: a humanist and optimist dedicated to improving the lot of man and sublimely confident of man's rationality. Jefferson never referred to himself as a democrat in his speeches or public papers. He sometimes used the word in his voluminous correspondence, but it is clear that when he did he was generally thinking of the New England town meeting and direct government by voters in small communities. It must be remembered that most of the men who framed the Constitution regarded democracy as suspect.

The two letters reprinted here represent a more intimate and informal expression of Jefferson's views on democracy than can be found in most of his public statements. However, the following passage from his *Notes on Virginia*, richly merits quoting:

"Every government degenerates when trusted to the rulers of the people alone. The people themselves therefore are its only depositories. . . . The influence over government must be shared among all the people. If every individual which composes their mass participates of the ultimate authority, the government will be safe; because the corrupting the whole mass will exceed any private resources of wealth: and public ones cannot be provided but by levies on the people. In this case every man would have to pay his own price." [1]

From *The Writings of Thomas Jefferson*, Monticello edition, ed. A. A. Lipscomb (Washington, 1905), XIII, 396–403; XIV, 487–93.

[1] From *Notes on Virginia*, ed. William Peden (Chapel Hill: University of North Carolina Press, 1955), pp. 148–49.

A LETTER TO DU PONT DE NEMOURS

Poplar Forest, Apr. 24, 1816.

I received, my dear friend your letter covering the constitution of your Equinoctial republics, just as I was setting out for this place. I brought it with me, and have read it with great satisfaction. I suppose it well-formed for those for whom it is intended, and the excellence of every government is its adaptation to the state of those to be governed by it. For us it would not do. Distinguishing between the structure of the government and the moral principles on which you prescribe its administration, with the latter we concur cordially, with the former we should not. We of the United States, you know are constitutionally and conscientiously Democrats. We consider society as one of the natural wants with which man has been created; that he has been endowed with faculties and qualities to effect its satisfaction by concurrence of others having the same want; that when by the exercise of these faculties he has procured a state of society, it is one of his acquisitions which he has a right to regulate and controul, jointly indeed with all those who have concurred in the procurement, whom he cannot exclude from its use or direction more than they him. We think experience has proved it safer, for the mass of individuals composing the society, to reserve to themselves personally the exercise of all rightful powers to which they are competent, and to delegate those to which they are not competent to deputies named, and removable for unfaithful conduct, by themselves immediately. Hence with us, the people (by which is meant the mass of individuals composing the society) being competent to judge of facts occurring in ordinary life, they have retained the functions of judges of facts, under the name of jurors; but being unqualified for the management of affairs requiring intelligence above the common level, yet competent judges of human character, they chuse for their management representatives, some by themselves immediately, others by electors chosen by themselves. Thus, our President is chosen by ourselves, directly *in practice,* for we vote for A. as elector only on the condition he will vote for B.; our representatives by ourselves immediately, our Senate and judges of the law through electors chosen by ourselves. And we believe that this proximate choice and power of removal is the best security which experience has sanctioned for ensuring an honest conduct in the functionaries of the society. Your three or four alembications have indeed a seducing appearance. We should conceive prima facie, that the last extract would be the pure alcohol of the substance, three or four times rectified; but in proportion as they are more and more sublimated, they are also farther and farther removed from the controul of society, and human character, we believe, requires in general constant and immediate controul to prevent its being biassed from right by the seductions of self love. Your process produces, therefore, a structure of government from which the fundamental principle of ours is excluded. You first set as zeros all individuals not having lands, which are the greater number in every society of long standing. Those holding lands are permitted to manage in person the small affairs of their commune or corporation, and to elect a deputy for the canton; in which election, too, every one's vote is to be an unit, a plurality, or a fraction, in proportion to his landed possessions. The assemblies of Cantons then elect for the Districts, those of Districts for Circles, and those of Circles for the National assemblies. Some of these highest councils, too, are in a considerable degree self-elected, the regency partially, the judiciary entirely, and some are for life. Whenever, therefore, an esprit de corps, or of party, gets possession of them, which experience shows to be inevitable, there are no means of breaking it up; for they will never elect but those of their own spirit. Juries are allowed in criminal cases only.

I acknowledge myself strong affection for our own form. Yet both of us act and think from the same motive. We both consider the people as our children, and love them with parental affection. But you love them as infants whom you are afraid to trust without nurses, and I as adults, whom I freely leave to self government. And you are right in the case referred to you, my criticism being built on a state of society not under your contemplation. It is, in fact, like a critique on Homer by the laws of the Drama.

But when we come to the moral principles on which the government is to be administered, we come to what is proper for all conditions of society. I meet you there in all the benevolence and rectitude of your native character, and I love myself always most when I concur most with you. Liberty, truth, probity, honor are declared to be the four cardinal principles of your society. I believe with you that morality, compassion, generosity are innate elements of the human construction; that there exists a right independent of force; that a right to property is founded in our natural wants, in the means with which we were endowed to satisfy these wants, and the right to what we acquire by those means without violating the similar rights of other sensible beings; that no one has a right to obstruct another, exercising his faculties innocently for the relief of sensibilities made a part of his nature; that justice is the fundamental law of society; that the majority oppressing an individual, is guilty of crime, abuses its strength, and by acting on the law of the strongest, breaks up the foundations of society; that action by the citizens in person in affairs within their reach and competence, and in all others by representatives, chosen immediately and removable by themselves, constitutes the essence of a republic; that all governments are more or less republican in proportion as this principle enters more or less into their composition; and that a government by representation is capable of extension over a greater surface of country than one of any other form.

These, my friend, are the essentials in which you and I agree; however, in our zeal for their maintenance, we may be perplexed and divaricate, as to the structure of society most likely to secure them.

In the constitution of Spain as proposed by the late Cortes, there was a principle entirely new to me, and not noticed in yours, that no person, born after that day, should ever acquire the rights of citizenship until he could read and write. It is impossible sufficiently to estimate the wisdom of this provision. Of all those which have been thought of for securing fidelity in the administration of the government, constant ralliance to the principles of the constitution, and progressive amendments with the progressive advances of the human mind, or changes in human affairs, it is the most effectual. Enlighten the people generally, and tyranny and oppressions of body and mind will vanish like evil spirits at the dawn of day. Altho' I do not, with some enthusiasts, believe that the human condition will ever advance to such a state of perfection as that there shall no longer be pain or vice in the world, yet I believe it susceptible of much improvement, and, most of all, in matters of government and religion; and that the diffusion of knowledge among the people is to be the instrument by which it is to be effected. The constitution of the Cortes had defects enough; but when I saw in it this amendatory provision I was satisfied all would come right in time, under its salutary operation. No people have more need of a similar provision than those for whom you have felt so much interest. No mortal wishes them more success than I do, but if what I have heard of the ignorance and bigotry of the mass be true, I doubt their capacity to understand and to support a free government, and fear their emancipation from the foreign tyranny of Spain will result in a military despotism at home. Palacios may be great; others may be great; but it is the multitude which possesses force; and wisdom must yield to that. For such a condition of society, the constitution you have devised is probably the best imaginable. It is certainly calculated to elicit the best talents, altho', perhaps, not well-guarded against the egoism of its functionaries, but that egoism will be light in comparison with the pressure of a military despot, and his army of Janissaries. Like Solon to the Athenians, you have given to your Columbians, not the best possible government, but the best they can bear. By-the-bye, I wish you had called them the Columbian republics, to distinguish them from our American republics. Theirs would be the more honorable name, and they best entitled to it; for Columbus discovered their continent, but never saw ours.

To them liberty and happiness; to you the meed of wisdom and goodness in teaching them how to attain them, with the affectionate respect and friendship of Th. J.

From A LETTER TO JOHN ADAMS

Monticello, Oct. 28, 1813.

. . . I agree with you that there is a natural aristocracy among men. The grounds of this are virtue and talents. Formerly, bodily powers gave place among the aristoi. But since the invention of gunpowder has armed the weak as well as the strong with missile death, bodily strength, like beauty, good humor, politeness and other accomplishments, has become but an auxiliary ground for distinction. There is also an artificial aristocracy, founded on wealth and birth, without either virtue or talents; for with these it would belong to the first class. The natural aristocracy I consider as the most precious gift of nature, for the instruction, the trusts, and government of society. And indeed, it would have been inconsistent in creation to have formed man for the social state, and not to have provided virtue and wisdom enough to manage the concerns of the society. May we not even say, that that form of government is the best, which provides the most effectually for a pure selection of these natural aristoi into the offices of government? The artificial aristocracy is a mischievous ingredient in government, and provision should be made to prevent its ascendency. On the question, what is the best provision, you and I differ; but we differ as rational friends, using the free exercise of our own reason, and mutually indulging its errors. You think it best to put the pseudo-aristoi into separate chamber of legislation, where they may be hindered from doing mischief by their co-ordinate branches, and where, also, they may be a protection to wealth against the Agrarian and plundering enterprises of the majority of the people. I think that to give them power in order to prevent them from doing mischief, is arming them for it, and increasing instead of remedying the evil. For if the co-ordinate branches can arrest their action, so may they that of the co-ordinates. Mischief may be done negatively as well as positively. Of this, a cabal in the Senate of the United States has furnished many proofs. Nor do I believe them necessary to protect the wealthy; because enough of these will find their way into every branch of the legislation, to protect themselves. From fifteen to twenty legislatures of our own, in action for thirty years past, have proved that no fears of an equalization of property are to be apprehended from them. I think the best remedy is exactly that provided by all our constitutions, to leave to the citizens the free election and separation of the aristoi from the pseudo-aristoi, of the wheat from the chaff. In general they will elect the really good and wise. In some instances, wealth may corrupt, and birth blind them; but not in sufficient degree to endanger the society.

It is probable that our difference of opinion may, in some measure, be produced by a difference of character in those among whom we live. From what I have seen of Massachusetts and Connecticut myself, and still more from what I have heard, and the character given of the former by yourself, who know them so much better, there seems to be in those two States a traditionary reverence for certain families, which has rendered the offices of the government nearly hereditary in those families. I presume that from an early period of your history, members of those families happening to possess virtue and talents, have honestly exercised them for the good of the people, and by their services have endeared their names to them. . . . But although this hereditary succession to office with you, may, in some degree, be founded in real family merit, yet in a much higher de-

gree, it has proceeded from your strict alliance of Church and State. These families are canonised in the eyes of the people on common principles, "you tickle
me, and I will tickle you." In Virginia we have nothing of this. Our clergy, before the revolution, having been secured against rivalship by fixed salaries, did
not give themselves the trouble of acquiring influence over the people. Of wealth,
there were great accumulations in particular families, handed down from generation to generation, under the English law of entails. But the only object of ambition for the wealthy was a seat in the King's Council. All their court then was
paid to the crown and its creatures; and they Philipised in all collisions between
the King and the people. Hence they were unpopular; and that unpopularity continues attached to their names. A Randolph, a Carter, or a Burwell must have
great personal superiority over a common competitor to be elected by the people
even at this day. At the first session of our legislature after the Declaration of
Independence, we passed a law abolishing entails. And this was followed by one
abolishing the privilege of primogeniture, and dividing the lands of intestates
equally among all their children, or other representatives. These laws, drawn by
myself, laid the ax to the foot of pseudo-aristocracy. And had another which I
prepared been adopted by the legislature, our work would have been complete. It
was a bill for the more general diffusion of learning. This proposed to divide
every county into wards of five or six miles square, like your townships; to establish in each ward a free school for reading, writing and common arithmetic; to
provide for the annual selection of the best subjects from these schools, who
might receive, at the public expense, a higher degree of education at a district
school; and from these district schools to select a certain number of the most
promising subjects to be completed at an University, where all the useful sciences should be taught. Worth and genius would thus have been sought out from
every condition of life, and completely prepared by education for defeating the
competition of wealth and birth for public trusts. My proposition had, for a further object, to impart to these wards those portions of self-government for which
they are best qualified, by confiding to them the care of their poor, their roads,
police, elections, the nomination of jurors, administration of justice in small
cases, elementary exercises of militia; in short, to have made them little republics, with a warden at the head of each, for all those concerns which, being under
their eye, they would better manage than the larger republics of the county or
State. A general call of ward meetings by their wardens on the same day through
the State, would at any time produce the genuine sense of the people on any required point, and would enable the State to act in mass, as your people have so
often done, and with so much effect by their town meetings. The law for religious
freedom, which made a part of this system, having put down the aristocracy of
the clergy, and restored to the citizen the freedom of the mind, and those of entails and descents nurturing an equality of condition among them, this on education would have raised the mass of the people to the high ground of moral re-
spectability necessary to their own safety, and to orderly government; and would
have completed the great object of qualifying them to select the veritable aristoi,

for the trusts of government, to the exclusion of the pseudalists . . . Although this law has not yet been acted on but in a small and inefficient degree, it is still considered as before the legislature, with other bills of the revised code, not yet taken up, and I have great hope that some patriotic spirit will, at a favorable moment, call it up, and make it the key-stone of the arch of our government.

With respect to aristocracy, we should further consider, that before the establishment of the American States, nothing was known to history but the man of the old world, crowned within limits either small or overcharged, and steeped in the vices which that situation generates. A government adapted to such men would be one thing; but a very different one, that for the man of these States. Here every one may have land to labor for himself, if he chooses; or, preferring the exercise of any other industry, may exact for it such compensation as not only to afford a comfortable subsistence, but wherewith to provide for a cessation from labor in old age. Every one, by his property, or by his satisfactory situation, is interested in the support of law and order. And such men may safely and advantageously reserve to themselves a wholesome control over their public affairs, and a degree of freedom, which, in the hands of the *canaille* of the cities of Europe, would be instantly perverted to the demolition and destruction of everything public and private. The history of the last twenty-five years of France, and of the last forty years in America, nay of its last two hundred years, proves the truth of both parts of this observation.

But even in Europe a change has sensibly taken place in the mind of man. Science had liberated the ideas of those who read and reflect, and the American example had kindled feelings of right in the people. An insurrection has consequently begun, of science, talents, and courage, against rank and birth, which have fallen into contempt. It has failed in its first effort, because the mobs of the cities, the instrument used for its accomplishment, debased by ignorance, poverty and vice, could not be restrained to rational action. But the world will recover from the panic of this first catastrophe. Science is progressive, and talents and enterprise on the alert. Resort may be had to the people of the country, a more governable power from their principles and subordination; and rank, and birth, and tinsel-aristocracy will finally shrink into insignificance, even there. This, however, we have no right to meddle with. It suffices for us, if the moral and physical condition of our own citizens qualifies them to select the able and good for the direction of their government, with a recurrence of elections at such short periods as will enable them to displace an unfaithful servant, before the mischief he meditates may be irremediable.

I have thus stated my opinion on a point on which we differ, not with a view to controversy, for we are both too old to change opinions which are the result of a long life of inquiry and reflection; but on the suggestions of a former letter of yours, that we ought not to die before we have explained ourselves to each other. We acted in perfect harmony, through a long and perilous contest for our liberty and independence. A constitution has been acquired, which, though neither of us thinks perfect, yet both consider as competent to render our fellow citizens the happiest and the securest on whom the sun has ever shone. If we do not think exactly alike as to its imperfections, it matters little to our country, which, after devoting to it long lives of disinterested labor, we have delivered over to our successors in life, who will be able to take care of it and of themselves.*

· · ·

* Adams responded: ". . . your distinction between natural and artificial aristocracy, does not appear to me founded. Birth and wealth are conferred upon some men as imperiously by nature as genius, strength, or beauty. . . ." (Letter of November 15, 1813, *Ibid.,* vol. 14, p. 5.) [Ed.]

MAJORITY RULE AND MINORITY RIGHTS

Henry Steele Commager

1902–

❧

Henry Steele Commager is one of this country's ablest historians. He has taught at Columbia, Cambridge and Oxford Universities and is now professor of history at Amherst College. An avowed disciple of Vernon Louis Parrington, his chief interest is American intellectual history. He is perhaps best known for *The American Mind* (1950) which goes beyond Parrington's *Main Currents* and interprets American thought since the 1880's.

Professor Commager's dedication to the principles of democracy permeates most of his work, especially the small volume, based on lectures presented at the University of Virginia, from which the following selection has been taken.

'A grave responsibility confronts this Court,' said Mr. Justice Frankfurter in presenting the majority opinion in the Gobitis case, 'whenever in the course of litigation it must reconcile the conflicting claims of liberty and authority.' [1] That opinion held that 'except where the transgression of constitutional liberty is too plain for argument, personal freedom is best maintained—as long as the remedial channels of the democratic process remain open and unobstructed— where it is ingrained in a people's habits and not enforced against popular policy by the coercion of adjudicated law,' and sustained the constitutionality of the flag-salute requirement by the Minersville School District. Perhaps the most remarkable thing about this opinion was that it was so widely, I might say all but universally, misunderstood.[2] Liberals—or those who regarded themselves as such

Henry Steele Commager, from *Majority Rule and Minority Rights* (New York, 1943), pp. 3–27. Copyright 1943 by Oxford University Press, Inc. Reprinted by permission.

[1] Minersville School District *v.* Gobitis, 310 U.S. 586. See also West Virginia State Board of Education *v.* Barnette, 63 S. Ct. Reporter 1178.

[2] See references in *52 Yale Law Journal* 175, n.

—almost to a man denounced the opinion as illiberal and celebrated the dissenting opinion written by the Chief Justice. The apparent inability of most Americans today to understand the logic and the implications of Mr. Justice Frankfurter's opinion suggests the desirability, indeed the imperative necessity, of a reconsideration of the basic problem it presents: the problem of majority rule *versus* limited government.

This is, to be sure, a very old problem—as old as government itself: it is a universal problem, pressing everywhere for solution. But it is not too much to assert that it is a problem that can best be understood in connection with American experience. For it was in America that the doctrine of majority rule was first successfully asserted and effectuated; it was in America that the principle of limited government was first institutionalized and that machinery for maintaining it was first fashioned.

These statements may require some elaboration. What we have here are two fundamental—perhaps the two most fundamental—principles of American politics: the principle that men make government, and the principle that there are limits to the authority of government. The philosophical origins of the first principle may be found in the natural-rights philosophy of the seventeenth century— in the notion that all rights inhered originally in men and that men, living in a state of nature, came together for mutual self-protection and set up government, and that the governments thus instituted derive all their just powers from the consent of the governed. However sound this may be as a description of an historical process—and Jefferson for one did not question its soundness—it was indubitably a correct description of what had happened in the New World from the time of the Mayflower Compact on to the organization of government along the banks of the Holston and the Watauga and the Tennessee, and of what was to happen, again and again, along the frontier from the Blue Ridge to the Willamette.[3]

The second great basic principle—that governments are limited, that there are things no government may do, rights no government may impair, powers no government may exercise—traces its philosophical origins deep into the past but again derives authority from American experience with Parliamentary and royal pretensions. It held, simply enough, that as government was instituted to secure certain rights, its jurisdiction was strictly limited to the fields assigned to it, and that if it overstepped the bounds of its jurisdiction its acts were not law. In the great words of Samuel Adams, addressed to Shelburne and Rockingham and Camden, 'in all free states the constitution is fixed; it is from thence that the legislative derives its authority; therefore it cannot change the constitution without destroying its own foundations.'[4]

But Americans did more than espouse and formulate these political princi-

[3] See F. J. Turner, 'Western State-making in the Revolutionary Era' in *The Significance of Sections in American History.*
[4] These letters are reproduced in H. S. Commager, *Documents of American History,* no. 44.

ples. The great achievement of the men of the Revolutionary era was that, in the words of old John Adams, 'they realized the doctrines of the wisest writers.' They institutionalized their principles. They fashioned a mechanism for putting into effect the idea that men make government. This was, needless to say, the institution of the constitutional convention that provided a legal and perfectly peaceful method of altering or abolishing governments and creating new ones. It is no exaggeration to say that this institution of the constitutional convention was— with the possible exception of the federal system—the greatest political invention to come out of the New World.[5]

And that same generation, more conscious of the dangers than of the potentialities of government, more concerned with protection against governmental tyranny than with the promotion of majority welfare, devised cunning mechanisms for putting limitations upon government. When we contemplate the ingenuity of the Fathers in setting up their system of checks and balances we are deeply impressed, almost dismayed. That the limits of governmental authority might not be misunderstood, that authority was described—for the first time—in written constitutions, and to these constitutions were added bills of rights. But this was merely elementary. There were, in addition, the checks and balances of the federal system, of the tripartite division of powers, of the bicameral legislatures, of frequent elections, and of impeachment. And atop all this there developed—I would not say there was established—the practice of judicial review.

But in their laudable zeal to give reality to John Dickinson's description of a free people—'Not those over whom government is reasonably and equitably exercised, but those who live under a government so constitutionally checked and controuled, that proper provision is made against its being otherwise exercised' —the framers of our constitutions confused, it would seem, jurisdiction with power, and the confusion has persisted down to our own day. They failed properly to distinguish between the authority government should have, and the manner in which government might exercise that authority which it did have. They set up limits on the jurisdiction of government, enumerating things no government could do; and this was eminently proper and in harmony with the philosophy of the Revolutionary era. But they went farther. So fearful were they of governmental tyranny that even where they granted to government certain necessary powers they put obstacles in the way of the effective exercise of those powers. They set up not only boundaries to government but impediments in government. Thus they not only made it difficult for government to invade fields denied to it, but they made it difficult for government to operate at all. They created a system where deadlock would be the normal character of the American government—a situation from which political parties rescued us.[6]

So here we have two institutions which are—or would appear to be— fundamentally contradictory. We have first the institutionalization of the princi-

---

[5] See, for a penetrating analysis of the significance of this, A. C. McLaughlin, *The Foundations of American Constitutionalism*, ch. iv.

[6] There is a thoughtful discussion of this in C. H. McIlwain, *Constitutionalism.*

ple that men can alter, abolish, and institute governments, can, in short, make government conform to their will. But over against this we have the institutional-ization of the principle that governments are limited—that there are things not even a majority may require government to do because they are outside the jurisdiction of any government. If the majority may use government to do its will, is that not an attack upon the inalienable rights of men over against government? If there are limits upon what government may do, is that not a challenge to or even a denial of the principle of majority rule? Here is a paradox not yet resolved in our political philosophy or our constitutional system.

This paradox is presented in most familiar form in Jefferson's First Inaugural Address: 'All, too, will bear in mind this sacred principle, that though the will of the majority is in all cases to prevail, that will to be rightful must be reasonable; that the minority possess their equal rights which equal law must protect, and to violate would be oppression.' And throughout our history runs this theme of majority will and minority rights. Jefferson, as we shall see, emphasized majority will, and so did Jefferson's successors, Jackson and Lincoln—Jackson, who brushed aside judicial interposition,[7] Lincoln, who reminded us that

A majority . . . is the only true sovereign of a free people. Whoever rejects it does, of necessity, fly into anarchy or to despotism. Unanimity is impossible; the rule of a minority, as a permanent arrangement, is wholly inadmissable; so that, rejecting the majority principle anarchy or despotism in some form is all that is left.[8]

But the emphasis since the Civil War has been increasingly on minority rights—an emphasis so marked, between Reconstruction and the New Deal, that it is no great exaggeration to say that tenderness for the minority became the distinguishing characteristic of the American constitutional system.

Underlying this distinction are, of course, the assumptions that majority will and minority rights are antithetical, that majority rule constantly threatens minority rights, and that the principal function of our constitutional system is to protect minority rights against infringement.

So plausible are these assumptions that there has developed, in course of time, the theory of the 'tyranny of the majority'—a theory which derived much support abroad as well as here from the misleading observations of Tocqueville.

[7] See, for example, Jackson's veto of the recharter of the Second Bank of the United States: 'If the opinion of the Supreme Court covered the whole ground of this act, it ought not to control the coordinate authorities of the Government. The Congress, the Executive, and the Court must each for itself be guided by its own opinion of the Constitution . . . The opinion of the judges has no more authority over Congress than the opinion of Congress has over the judges, and on that point the President is independent of both. The authority of the Supreme Court must not, therefore, be permitted to control the Congress or the Executive when acting in their legislative capacities, but to have only such influence as the force of the reasoning may deserve.' Quoted in Commager, *Documents of American History*, no. 147.

[8] *The Works of Abraham Lincoln*, ii, 5.

Tocqueville, who leaned heavily for material and authority on that pillar of conservatism, Joseph Story,[9] confessed that 'the very essence of democratic government consists in the absolute sovereignty of the majority,' and concluded from this that the prospects for American democracy were bleak indeed.[10] His analysis of the consequences that flow from the tyranny of the majority has given comfort, ever since, to those who fear democracy. So persuasive is this theory of the tyranny of the majority that many Americans have come to believe that our constitutional system is not, in fact, based upon the principle of majority rule. And they have found support and consolation in the curious notion that ours is a 'republican' form of government, and that a republic is the very opposite of a democracy.

The fear of the tyranny of the majority has haunted many of the most distinguished and respectable American statesmen and jurists since the days of the founding of the Republic; it persists today, after a century and a half of experience. It was first formulated, in elaborate and coherent fashion, by John Adams in his famous *Defense of the Constitutions of Government of the United States of America* (1786). The people, Adams urges, are not to be trusted, nor are their representatives, without an adequate system of checks and balances:

> If it is meant by the people . . . a representative assembly, . . . they are not the best keepers of the people's liberties or their own, if you give them all the power, legislative, executive and judicial. They would invade the liberties of the people, at least the majority of them would invade the liberties of the minority, sooner and oftener than any absolute monarch.

Anticipating the arguments to be used again and again in the next century, Adams appealed to the experience of the past and conjured up hypothetical dangers in the future:

> The experience of all ages has proved, that they [the people] constantly give away their liberties into the hands of grandees, or kings, idols of their own creation. The management of the executive and judicial powers together always corrupts them, and throws the whole power into the hands of the most profligate and abandoned among them.

And if the majority were to control all branches of the government:

> Debts would be abolished first; taxes laid heavy on the rich, and not at all on the others; and at last a downright equal division of everything be demanded and voted. The idle, the vicious, the intemperate, would rush into the utmost extravagance of debauchery, sell and

[9] George Pierson, *Tocqueville and Beaumont in America,* 726 ff.

[10] A. de Tocqueville, *Democracy in America,* ed. John Bigelow, I, 271. See the whole of chapters 15 and 16 for Tocqueville's animadversions on the tyranny of the majority.

spend all their share, and then demand a new division of those who purchased from them. The moment the idea is admitted into society, that property is not as sacred as the laws of God, and that there is not a force of law and public justice to protect it, anarchy and tyranny commence.[11]

That other great apostle of conservatism, Alexander Hamilton, approached the subject of majority rule in far more circumspect fashion.

It was a thing hardly to be expected [he wrote in No. 26 of the *Federalist*] that in a popular revolution the minds of men should stop at that happy mean which marks the salutary boundary between POWER and PRIVILEGE, and combines the energy of government with the security of private rights. A failure in this delicate and important point is the great source of the inconveniences we experience, and if we are not cautious to avoid a repetition of the error, in our future attempts to rectify and ameliorate our system, we may travel from one chimerical project to another . . .

And, in No. 51, he warned his countrymen that

It is of great importance in a republic not only to guard the society against the oppression of its rulers, but to guard one part of the society against the injustice of the other part. Different interests necessarily exist in different classes of citizens. If a majority be united by a common interest, the rights of the minority will be insecure . . . Justice is the end of government. It is the end of civil society . . . In a society under the forms of which the stronger faction can readily unite and oppress the weaker, anarchy may as truly be said to reign as in a state of nature where the weaker individual is not secured against the violence of the stronger.

In the privacy of the Federal Convention Hamilton has been even more candid. 'The voice of the people,' he said in his famous diatribe against the Virginia and New Jersey plans,

has been said to be the voice of God; and however generally this maxim has been quoted and believed, it is not true to fact. The people are turbulent and changing, they seldom judge or determine right. Give therefore to the [rich] a distinct, permanent share in the government. They will check the unsteadiness of the second . . . Can a democratic Assembly, who annually revolve in the mass of the people, be supposed steadily to pursue the public good? Nothing but a permanent body can check the imprudence of democracy. Their turbulent and uncontrolling disposition requires checks.[12]

[11] *The Works of John Adams*, ed. by Charles Francis Adams, VI, 7, 64, 9.
[12] *The Works of Alexander Hamilton*, ed. by H. C. Lodge, I, 401.

Later publicists were to ring the changes on this theme again and again: the majority would surrender its power to a despot—or a boss—; it would plunder the rich; it would oppress minorities; it would destroy the liberties of men. Thus doughty old Chancellor Kent, resisting the proposal for broadening the suffrage in New York State:

> By the report before us we propose to annihilate, at one stroke, all those property distinctions and to bow before the idol of universal suffrage. That extreme democratic principle, when applied to the legislative and executive departments of government, has been regarded with terror, by the wise men of every age, because in every European republic, ancient and modern, in which it has been tried, it has terminated disastrously, and been productive of corruption, injustice, violence, and tyranny. And dare we flatter ourselves that we are a peculiar people, who can run the career of history, exempted from the passions which have disturbed and corrupted the rest of mankind? [13]

So, too, the learned Justice Story threw the great weight of his prestige against the proposal that a majority had a right to alter their form of government.[14] So Calhoun dedicated his splendid talents to the formulation of an ingenious system designed to arrest the exercise of the tyranny of the majority against the peculiar institution,[15] and his great opponent, Daniel Webster, was no less zealous to protect the inherited rights of well-entrenched minorities against majority interference.[16] By mid-century the anti-majority theory was fully formulated, and it is pertinent to recall why and by whom it was formulated. It was formulated in defense of property interests allegedly threatened by majority greed by those who put property rights above human rights. It was formulated by those who already had political privileges and were determined that the common man should not share them. It was formulated in defense of slavery in the just fear that slavery and majority rule were ultimately incompatible. It was formulated, in short, by those who proved themselves completely out of harmony with the fundamental tendencies of American society and who have been rejected by the American people.

The latter-day representatives of the minority-rights doctrine—a motley group—have been neither as distinguished nor as plausible as their predecessors. In Theodore Woolsey, William Graham Sumner, John W. Burgess, Henry Cabot Lodge, James M. Beck, Henry L. Mencken, Ralph Adams Cram, Walter Lippmann, Dorothy Thompson, and Isabel Patterson, in the learned jurists Cooley and Field and Brewer and Sutherland and McReynolds, the argument is less

---

[13] N. H. Carter and W. L. Stone, *Reports of the Proceedings and Debates of the Convention of 1821*, pp. 219 ff.

[14] See Rachel Luther *v.* Luther Borden and W. W. Story, *Life and Letters of Joseph Story*, II, 415.

[15] See 'A Disquisition on Government,' in *Works* (Cralle ed.), I, *passim*.

[16] See Webster's argument in the case of Luther *v.* Borden, *Works* (1851 ed.), VI, 217 ff.

assured, the logic less coherent, the shrill note more frequent. And the contemporary presentation is almost completely lacking in the dignity and in the muscular intellectual toughness that characterized the argument of Adams and Calhoun and Webster. For our edification it is conveniently epitomized and assembled in the six volumes of the *Hearings of the Senate Judiciary Committee* on the court reform bill of 1937—where we may consult it, though whether either with pleasure or with profit is a matter of opinion.[17]

Confronted by these different interpretations of the American constitutional system, of democracy and of republicanism, we may turn with some confidence to Thomas Jefferson. On these questions he is, indubitably, our leading authority. He helped to create and to establish the new political systems in America, and he furnished them with a good part of their political philosophy. He never wrote a formal treatise on the subject (as did his old friend John Adams), but in his public papers and his private letters we can find the most comprehensive and consistent statement of the nature of American democracy that has come down to us from the generation of the founders.

And it must be observed, first, that Jefferson was by no means unaware of the dangers inherent in majority rule. He had had experience with recalcitrant assemblies in Virginia; he had watched, on the whole with approval, but not without misgivings, the course of rule by succeeding—and ever more radical—assemblies in France; he had rallied the forces of liberalism against legislative tyranny as represented in the Alien and Sedition Acts. His proposed constitution for Virginia provided a complicated system of checks and balances; [18] his *Notes on Virginia* counted it 'precisely the definition of despotic government' that 'all powers of government, legislative, executive, and judiciary, result to the legislative body.' [19] Writing to his friend James Madison, in 1789, he had counselled against the 'tyranny of legislatures' as 'the most formidable dread,' [20] and the following year he had reaffirmed, to Noah Webster, his conviction that there were rights beyond the jurisdiction of 'ordinary' government.[21] The Kentucky Resolutions, which he drafted, contained an eloquent expression of the doctrine that the majority of the national legislature might not violate the terms of the compact the states had made, and the first annual message to the Congress—in its original form—repudiated legislative omnipotence where personal liberties were concerned.

Yet none of these things implies distrust of majority rule, for majority rule is neither anarchy nor absolutism, but government within self-imposed restraints. And we search in vain through the voluminous writings of Jefferson for any ex-

[17] See 'Reorganization of the Federal Judiciary,' U.S. 75th Cong. 1st Sess. *Sen. Comm. on the Judiciary, Hearings on*, 1392, 6 parts.

[18] It is printed in *The Writings of Thomas Jefferson*, ed. by Paul Leicester Ford, II, 7 ff. (hereafter cited as Ford).

[19] *Ibid.* III, 223.

[20] 15 March 1789. *Ibid.* 223.

[21] 4 Dec. 1790. *The Writings of Thomas Jefferson*, ed. by A. E. Lipscomb and A. E. Bergh, VII, 112 (hereafter cited as Memorial ed.)

pression of distrust of the virtue or the wisdom of the people. What we do find, on the contrary, from the beginning to the end of Jefferson's career, is an unterrified and unflinching faith in majority rule.

'I am not among those who fear the people,' he wrote to Kercheval in 1816; 'they and not the rich, are our dependence for continued freedom.' [22] It was the reiteration of an argument that the author of the Declaration of Independence found it necessary to make with increasing frequency. Back in 1787 he had had to reassure many of his friends, who were stampeded by the Shays' rebellion into a reaction against democracy. Writing to Madison from Paris he pointed out the true solution of the problem which that uprising presented:

> Educate and inform the whole mass of the people. Enable them to see that it is their interest to preserve peace and order, and they will preserve them. And it requires no very high degree of education to convince them of this. They are the only sure reliance for the preservation of our liberty. After all, it is my principle that the will of the majority should prevail. [23]

And to another Virginia friend, Colonel Carrington, went the same reassurance:

> The tumults in America I expected would have produced in Europe an unfavorable opinion of our political state. But it has not. On the contrary, the small effect of these tumults seems to have given more confidence in the firmness of our governments. The interposition of the people themselves on the side of government has had a great effect on the opinion here. I am persuaded myself that the good sense of the people will always be found to be the best army. They may be led astray for a moment, but will soon correct themselves. The people are the only censors of their governors; and even their errors will tend to keep these to the true principles of their institution. [24]

That the people, if led astray, would 'soon correct themselves' was a fixed conviction and one which, *mirabile dictu*, found confirmation in their tenacious support of his own administration. Thus to John Tyler in 1804:

> No experiment can be more interesting than that we are now trying, and which we trust will end in establishing the fact that man may be governed by reason and truth . . . The firmness with which the people have withstood the late abuses of the press, the discernment that they have manifested between truth and falsehood, show that they may safely be trusted to hear everything true and false, and to form correct judgment between them . . . [25]

[22] 12 July 1816. *Ibid.* xv, 39.
[23] 20 Dec. 1787. *Ibid.* vi, 392.
[24] 16 Jan. 1787. *Ibid.* vi, 57.
[25] 28 June 1804. *Ibid.* xi, 33.

This was the consistent note—that the people may—and must—be trusted. 'No government can continue good,' he assured John Adams, 'but under the control of the people'; [26] and again, to that doughty opponent of judicial pretensions, Spencer Roane, 'Independence can be trusted nowhere but with the people in the mass. They are inherently independent of all but the moral law.' [27] 'I know of no safe depository of the ultimate powers of the society,' he told William Jarvis, 'but the people themselves; and if we think them not enlightened enough to exercise their control with a wholesome discretion, the remedy is not to take it from them, but to inform their discretion by education.' [28] And recalling Hume's argument that 'all history and experience' confounded the notion that 'the people are the origin of all just power,' Jefferson burst out with uncharacteristic violence: 'And where else will this degenerate son of science, this traitor to his fellow men, find the origin of just powers, if not in the majority of the society? Will it be in the minority? Or in an individual of that minority?' [29] And we hear an echo of that question which the First Inaugural submits to the contemporary world: 'Sometimes it is said that man can not be trusted with the government of himself. Can he, then, be trusted with the government of others? Or have we found angels in the form of kings to govern him? Let history answer this question.' For himself, Jefferson knew the answer. His devotion to the people was not that of the benevolent despot, the party boss, or the dictator, but of a good citizen, and his whole career is a monument to the sincerity of his confession to Du Pont de Nemours.

. . .

To all of this many of Jefferson's contemporaries could have subscribed without reservation: he, assuredly, had no monopoly on faith in popular government. 'We of the United States,' as he explained simply, 'are constitutionally and conscientiously democrats.' [31] But in one respect Jefferson went farther than most of his contemporaries, went so far, indeed, that his argument sounds bizarre and almost alien to our ears. That was his advocacy of what we may call the doctrine of the continuing majority. It was easy enough for most Americans to subscribe to the compact theory of government—the compact made, of course, by the original majority—just as it is easy for us to subscribe, now, to the doctrine that we are, all of us, bound by the compact made at Philadelphia in 1787 and ratified by the majority of that time. And just as we have invested that Constitution with sacrosanctity, [32] so—in England, in France, in America of the eighteenth century—there was a tendency to regard the original compact, the product of the Golden Age of the past, with reverence and to invest it with a peculiar sanctity. Such an attitude was foreign to Jefferson. His conviction, how-

---

[26] 10 Dec. 1819. *Ibid.* xv, 234.
[27] 6 Sept. 1819. *Ibid.* xv, 213–14.
[28] 28 Sept. 1820. *Ibid.* xv, 278.
[29] To Major John Cartwright, 5 June 1824. *Ibid.* xvi, 44–5.
[31] *Ibid.* xiv, 487.
[32] See E. S. Corwin, 'The Constitution as Instrument and as Symbol,' 30 *Am. Pol. Sci. Rev.*; and Max Lerner, 'Constitution and Court as Symbols,' in *Ideas for the Ice Age,* pp. 232 ff.

ever, that each new majority must write its own fundamental law has sometimes been regarded as merely an amusing exaggeration, a whimsey to be indulged along with the whimsey that a little rebellion, now and then, is an excellent thing. But there can be no doubt of Jefferson's sincerity in the matter, nor of his persuasion that the issue was one of fundamental importance.

This problem is more fundamental, and more complex, than might appear at first glance—this problem of the original *versus* the continuing majority. All of us seem to agree that we are bound by the original majority—by the majority of 1787, or that which decreed our state constitutions. But what if the will of the present majority conflicts with that of the original majority? Is majority will valid only for some past generation? The easy answer is that the present majority can, if it chooses, change the original compact by constitutional amendment or by substituting an entirely new constitution. But it takes more than a majority to amend a constitution or to write a new one, and under our present system a determined minority can, if it will, effectively veto any change in the federal document and in most state documents. . . .

· · ·

Jefferson, as we know, entertained no reverence for the constitutional dogmas of the past. His attitude, set forth in the famous letter to Samuel Kercheval, of July 1816, is too familiar to justify quotation in full:

> Let us [not] weakly believe that one generation is not as capable as another of taking care of itself, and of ordering its own affairs. Let us . . . avail ourselves of our reason and experience, to correct the crude essays of our first and unexperienced, although wise, virtuous and well-meaning counsels. And lastly, let us provide in our Constitution for its revision at stated periods. What these periods should be, nature herself indicates . . . Each generation is as independent of the one preceding, as that was of all which had gone before. It has, then, like them, a right to choose for itself the form of government it believes most promotive of its own happiness . . . and it is for the peace and good of mankind that a solemn opportunity of doing this every nineteen or twenty years should be provided by the Constitution.[35]

This was no fleeting notion, inspired by dissatisfaction with the Virginia constitution and the proposal to call a new constitutional convention, but a settled conviction. Back in France, it would appear, he had discussed this principle with LaFayette and his friends when they were preparing the Declaration of the Rights of Man,[36] and at the same time he had written to Madison that he supposed it 'self-evident'

> that the earth belongs in usufruct to the living; that the dead have neither power nor rights over it . . . No society can make a perpet-

[35] 12 July 1816. Memorial ed. xv, 41-2.
[36] *Letters of LaFayette and Jefferson*, G. Chinard, ed., 80-1.

ual constitution, or even a perpetual law. The earth belongs always to the living generation; they may manage it, then, and what proceeds from it, as they please, during the usufruct . . . Every constitution, then, and every law, naturally expires at the end of thirty-four years. If it be enforced longer, it is an act of force and not of right.

And he added, with reference to repeals of amendments:

It may be said, that the succeeding generation, exercising, in fact, the power of repeal, this leaves them as free as if the constitution or law had been expressly limited to thirty-four years only. In the first place this objection admits the right, in proposing an equivalent. But the power of repeal is not an equivalent. It might be, indeed, if every form of government were so perfectly contrived that the will of the majority could always be obtained, fairly and without impediment. But this is true of no form . . . A law of limited duration is much more manageable than one which needs a repeal.[37]

Again and again Jefferson returned to this proposition. . . . The controversy over the reorganization of Dartmouth College evoked a letter to Governor Plumer which, when compared with the opinions of Marshall and Story in the Dartmouth College case, suggests strikingly the difference between the doctrines of the original and the continuing majority.

The idea that institutions established for the use of the nation cannot be touched or modified, even to make them answer their end, because of rights gratuitously supposed in those employed to manage them in trust for the public, may perhaps be a salutary provision against the abuses of a monarch, but is most absurd against the nation itself. Yet our lawyers and priests generally inculcate this doctrine, and suppose that preceding generations held the earth more freely than we do; had a right to impose laws on us, unalterable by ourselves, and that we, in like manner, can make laws and impose burdens on future generations, which they will have no right to alter; in fine, that the earth belongs to the dead and not the living.[39]

We can dispose more briefly of Jefferson's conception of the nature and meaning of republicanism; were it not for recent and widely publicized misinterpretations [41] of the term, the matter would scarcely merit our attention. The term 'republican'—as a legal rather than a political one—has always presented certain difficulties of precise definition, but it has remained for the undismayed conservatives of our own generation to make the curious discovery that *res*

[37] 6 Sept. 1789. Memorial ed. VII, 454 ff.
[39] 16 July 1816. *Ibid.* xv, 46–7.
[41] See, for example, John Corbin, *Two Frontiers of Freedom,* and Isabel Paterson, *The God of the Machine,* ch. 12.

publica—the common thing—is the very antithesis of democracy! [42] Jefferson, who has some claim to have fathered both republicanism and democracy in the United States, was happily unaware of this antithesis, and it is suggestive, at least, that his political party was called successively the Republican, the Republican-Democratic, and the Democratic. On a number of occasions he essayed a definition of the term 'republican.' In 1792 he confided to the *Anas* that he 'took the occasion' to 'lay down the catholic principle of republicanism, to wit, that every people may establish what form of government they please, and change it as they please, the will of the nation being the only thing essential.' [43] Writing to Isaac Tiffany about Aristotle's *Politics* he calls 'a democracy the only pure republic' and urges that 'the republican element of popular control' be 'pushed to the maximum of its practicable exercise.' [44] . . . The 'mother principle' of republicanism, he told Kercheval, was 'that governments are republican in proportion as they embody the will of their people, and execute it.' [46] And finally, not to belabor a point sufficiently obvious, we may note Jefferson's attempt clearly to define the term.

> Were I to assign to this term a precise and definite idea [he wrote John Taylor], I would say, purely and simply, it means a government by its citizens in mass, acting directly and personally, according to rules established by the majority; and that every other government is more or less republican in proportion as it has in its composition more or less of this ingredient of the direct action of its citizens.[47]

It is suggestive that most of these observations on the nature of democracy and of republicanism were inspired by the pretensions of the courts to act as the singular interpreters of the Constitution and to interpret the constitutional document (with some aid from the unwritten 'higher law,' useful ever since when the constitutional document appears inadequate) [48] as a limitation on majority will. For it is the courts alone who have formulated a clear-cut and dogmatic answer to the problem we posed at the beginning of our investigation—the problem of majority will and minority rights. That answer has the inestimable advantages of both plausibility and clarity. It has never been more lucidly or succinctly put than by Jefferson's great opponent, Hamilton—from whose argument Marshall draws so freely:

> There is no position which depends on clearer principles than that every act of a delegated authority, contrary to the tenor of the com-

[42] Jefferson himself usually used the word 'republican' rather than 'democrat,' but it is reasonably clear that he thought they meant the same thing. See C. A. Beard, *Thomas Jefferson*. Address at the University of Virginia, 13 April 1943.

[43] *The Anas*. 30 Dec. 1792. Memorial ed. I, 330.

[44] 26 August 1816. *Ibid*. xv, 66.

[46] 12 July 1816. *Ibid*. xv, 33.

[47] 28 May 1816. *Ibid*. xv, 19.

[48] See H. S. Commager, 'Constitutional History and the Higher Law,' in Conyers Read, ed. *The Constitution Reconsidered*.

mission under which it is excerised, is void. No legislative act, therefore, contrary to the Constitution can be valid. To deny this would be
to affirm that the deputy is greater than his principal . . .

If it be said that the legislative body are themselves the constitutional
judges of their own powers, and that the construction they put upon
them is conclusive upon the other departments, it may be answered
that this cannot be the natural presumption where it is not to be col-
lected from any particular provisions in the Constitution. It is not
otherwise to be supposed that the Constitution could intend to enable
the representatives of the people to substitute their *will* to that of
their constituents. It is far more rational to suppose that the courts
were designed to be an intermediate body between the people and the
legislature, in order, among other things, to keep the latter within the
limits assigned to their authority. The interpretation of the laws is the
proper and peculiar province of the courts. A constitution is, in fact,
and must be regarded by the judges, as a fundamental law. It therefore belongs to them to ascertain its meaning, as well as the meaning
of any particular act proceeding from the legislative body. If there
should happen to be an irreconcilable variance between the two, that
which has the superior obligation and validity ought, of course, to be
preferred . . .[49]

What Hamilton has reference to—as what Marshall had reference to in his comparable statement in Marbury *v.* Madison [50]—is the review of congressional legislation by federal courts. The same logic would apply to the review of state legislation by state courts. In both of these operations the function of judicial review
is to confine majority will to constitutional bounds. . . .

The argument supporting judicial review, as here set forth by Hamilton, is
pat, simple, and by now deeply rooted in our constitutional system and deeply
ingrained in our political thinking. It is sometimes forgotten that Jefferson rejected it *in toto*. . . .

[49] *The Federalist*, No. 78. But see no. 81 for some important qualifications of the principle here announced.
[50] i Cranch 137 (1803).

THE PEOPLE AND
THE VOTERS

Walter Lippmann

1889–

⊰≪

Dean of American commentators, erudite, perceptive and judicious, Walter Lippmann occupies a special place among those who write about public affairs. Almost uniquely, he can comment with the assurance that what he says will be read by presidents and by many, both in and out of government, who are responsible for formulating and guiding policy. Among his many books are *The Coming Tests with Russia* (1961), *The Cold War* (1947), *The Good Society* (1938), *A Preface to Morals* (1929) and *Public Opinion* (1922).

Lippmann describes himself as a liberal democrat. *Essays in the Public Philosophy,* from which the following selection is taken, provides good insight into his personal political beliefs. Written at a time of great pessimism concerning the capacity of democracy to cope with the tensions of the twentieth century, this book is a prescription for democracy's ills by one who cherishes democracy very much.

· · ·

. . . When we speak of popular sovereignty, we must know whether we are talking about The People, as voters, or about *The People,* as a community of the entire living population, with their predecessors and successors.

It is often assumed, but without warrant, that the opinions of The People as voters can be treated as the expression of the interests of *The People* as an historic community. The crucial problem of modern democracy arises from the fact that this assumption is false. The voters cannot be relied upon to represent *The People*. The opinions of voters in elections are not to be accepted unquestioningly as true judgments of the vital interests of the community.

To whom, for example, did the Preamble of the Constitution refer when it said that "We, the People of the United States . . . ordain and establish this Constitution"? On September 17, 1787, about forty members signed the draft on which they had been working since May 25, for one hundred and sixteen days. In Article VII of their text they stipulated that if and when conventions in nine states had ratified it, then for those nine states The People of the United States would have ordained and established the Constitution. In this context a majority of the delegates elected to nine state conventions were deemed to be entitled to act as The People of the United States.

The inhabitants of the United States who were qualified to vote for these delegates were not a large number. They included no slaves, no women and, except in New York, only such adult males as could pass property and other highly restrictive tests. We do not have accurate figures. But according to the census of 1790 the population was 3,929,782. Of these, 3,200,000 were free persons and the adult males among them who were entitled to vote are estimated to have been less than 500,000. Using the Massachusetts figures as a statistical sample, it may be assumed that less than 160,000 actually voted for delegates to all the ratifying conventions; and of those voting, perhaps 100,000 favored the adoption of the Constitution.[3]

The exact figures do not matter. The point is that the voters were not—and we may add that they have never been and can never be—more than a fraction of the total population. They were less than 5 per cent when the Constitution was ordained. They were not yet 40 per cent in 1952 when, except under the special conditions in the South, we had universal adult suffrage. Manifestly, the voters can never be equal to the whole population, even to the whole living adult population.

Because of the discrepancy between The People as voters and *The People* as the corporate nation, the voters have no title to consider themselves the proprietors of the commonwealth and to claim that their interests are identical with the public interest. A prevailing plurality of the voters are not *The People*. The claim that they are is a bogus title invoked to justify the usurpation of the executive power by representative assemblies and the intimidation of public men by demagogic politicians. In fact demagoguery can be described as the sleight of hand by which a faction of The People as voters are invested with the authority of *The People*. That is why so many crimes are committed in the people's name.

There are eminent political philosophers who reject this analytical distinction. Those who are strongly nominalist in their cast of mind, which modern men

[3] These figures are from a memorandum prepared for me by my friend, Prof. Allan Nevins. In his covering letter, January 24, 1952, he says:
"Anyone who writes about election figures in our early national history treads upon very unsafe ground. Trustworthy data—the statistics and the general information—are too scanty for any explicit statement of detailed conclusions for the country as a whole. As you will see, I have found figures for various states and localities, but we have no warrant for generalizing them to apply to the country in its entirety. *What we can say with absolute certainty, I think, is that in these early elections the vote was under 5 per cent of the whole population.*"

tend to be, look upon the abstract concept of a corporate people as mere words
and rather like conjuring up spooks. Thus, according to that resolute nominalist,
Jeremy Bentham, "the community is a fictitious *body,* composed of the individual persons who are considered as constituting as it were its *members.* The interest of the community then is, what?—The sum of the interests of the several
members who compose it." [4]

There is an apparent toughness and empirical matter-of-factness in this
statement. But the hard ice is thin. For Bentham has forgotten that "the several
members who compose" the community are never identically the same members
from one hour to another. If a community were what he says it is, then in theory
it should be possible to make a directory of its members, each with his address.
But no such list could ever be compiled. While it was being compiled, new members would be being born and old members would be dying. That is why it makes
no sense to describe "The People of the United States" who ordained and established the Constitution as the inhabitants of the United States on that particular
June 21, 1788, when the Constitution was established and ordained. Between
sunrise and sunset of that historic day the persons composing *The People* had
changed. In thirty years they had changed greatly; and in a hundred years, entirely.

The people, then, is not only, as Bentham assumed, the aggregate of living
persons. The people is also the stream of individuals, the connected generations
of changing persons, that Burke was talking about when he invoked the partnership "not only between those who are living" but also with "those who are dead,
and those who are to be born." *The People* are a corporation, an entity, that is to
say, which lives on while individuals come into it and go out of it.

For this reason Bentham cannot have been right when he said that the interests of the community are no more than the sum of the interests of the several
members who happen to compose it at any particular instant of time. He cannot
have been right when he said that "the happiness of the individuals, of whom a
community is composed, that is their pleasures and their security, is the end and
the sole end which the legislator ought to have in view." [5]

For besides the happiness and the security of the individuals of whom a
community is at any moment composed, there are also the happiness and the security of the individuals of whom generation after generation it will be composed. If we think of it in terms of individual persons, the corporate body of *The
People* is for the most part invisible and inaudible. Indeed as a whole it is nonexistent, in that so many are dead and so many are not yet born. Yet this corporate
being, though so insubstantial to our senses, binds, in Burke's words, a man to
his country with "ties which though light as air, are as strong as links of iron." [6]
That is why young men die in battle for their country's sake and why old men
plant trees they will never sit under.

[4] Jeremy Bentham, *The Principles of Morals and Legislation,* Ch. I, Sec. IV.
[5] *Ibid.,* Ch. III, Sec. I.
[6] Edmund Burke's speech on *Conciliation with America* (1775).

This invisible, inaudible, and so largely nonexistent community gives rational meaning to the necessary objectives of government. If we deny it, identifying the people with the prevailing pluralities who vote in order to serve, as Bentham has it, "their pleasures and their security," where and what is the nation, and whose duty and business is it to defend the public interest? Bentham leaves us with the state as an arena in which factions contend for their immediate advantage in the struggle for survival and domination. Without the invisible and transcendent community to bind them, why should they care for posterity? And why should posterity care about them, and about their treaties and their contracts, their commitments and their promises? Yet without these engagements to the future, they could not live and work; without these engagements the fabric of society is unraveled and shredded.

·   ·   ·

CAPITALISM, SOCIALISM AND DEMOCRACY

Joseph A. Schumpeter

1883–1950

☙❧

Joseph A. Schumpeter was one of the most distinguished economists of his time. He was born in Moravia (now Czechoslovakia) and served as Austrian Minister of Finance in the years immediately following World War I. Before coming to Harvard University as a professor in 1932, he taught at the University of Bonn. During his years at Harvard he served as president of the American Economic Association and the Econometric Society.

His best known works are *The Theory of Economic Development* (English translation, 1934), *Business Cycles* (1939), and the widely read *Capitalism, Socialism and Democracy,* from which the following selection is taken.

THE CLASSICAL DOCTRINE OF DEMOCRACY

I. The Common Good and the Will of the People

The eighteenth-century philosophy of democracy may be couched in the following definition: the democratic method is that institutional arrangement for arriving at political decisions which realizes the common good by making the people itself decide issues through the election of individuals who are to assemble in order to carry out its will. Let us develop the implications of this.

It is held, then, that there exists a Common Good, the obvious beacon light of policy, which is always simple to define and which every normal person can be made to see by means of rational argument. There is hence no excuse for not seeing it and in fact no explanation for the presence of people who do not see it except ignorance—which can be removed—stupidity and anti-social interest. Moreover, this common good implies definite answers to all questions so that every social fact and every measure taken or to be taken can unequivocally be classed as "good" or "bad." All people having therefore to agree, in principle at least, there is also a Common Will of the people (= will of all reasonable individuals) that is exactly coterminous with the common good or interest or welfare or happiness. The only thing, barring stupidity and sinister interests, that can possibly bring in disagreement and account for the presence of an opposition is a difference of opinion as to the speed with which the goal, itself common to nearly all, is to be approached. Thus every member of the community, conscious of that goal, knowing his or her mind, discerning what is good and what is bad, takes part, actively and responsibly, in furthering the former and fighting the latter and all the members taken together control their public affairs.

It is true that the management of some of these affairs requires special aptitudes and techniques and will therefore have to be entrusted to specialists who have them. This does not affect the principle, however, because these specialists simply act in order to carry out the will of the people exactly as a doctor acts in order to carry out the will of the patient to get well. It is also true that in a community of any size, especially if it displays the phenomenon of division of labor, it would be highly inconvenient for every individual citizen to have to get into contact with all the other citizens on every issue in order to do his part in ruling or governing. It will be more convenient to reserve only the most important decisions for the individual citizens to pronounce upon—say by referendum—and to deal with the rest through a committee appointed by them—an assembly or parliament whose members will be elected by popular vote. This committee or body of delegates, as we have seen, will not represent the people in a legal sense but it will do so in a less technical one—it will voice, reflect or represent the will of the electorate. Again as a matter of convenience, this committee, being large, may resolve itself into smaller ones for the various departments of public affairs. Finally, among these smaller committees there will be a general-purpose committee, mainly for dealing with current administration, called cabinet or government, possibly with a general secretary or scapegoat at its head, a so-called prime minister.

As soon as we accept all the assumptions that are being made by this theory of the polity—or implied by it—democracy indeed acquires a perfectly unambiguous meaning and there is no problem in connection with it except how to bring it about. Moreover we need only forget a few logical qualms in order to be able to add that in this case the democratic arrangement would not only be the best of all conceivable ones, but that few people would care to consider any other. It is no less obvious however that these assumptions are so many statements of fact every one of which would have to be proved if we are to arrive at that conclusion. And it is much easier to disprove them.

There is, first, no such thing as a uniquely determined common good that all people could agree on or be made to agree on by the force of rational argument. This is due not primarily to the fact that some people may want things other than the common good but to the much more fundamental fact that to different individuals and groups the common good is bound to mean different things. . . .

Secondly, even if a sufficiently definite common good—such as for instance the utilitarian's maximum of economic satisfaction—proved acceptable to all, this would not imply equally definite answers to individual issues. Opinions on these might differ to an extent important enough to produce most of the effects of "fundamental" dissension about ends themselves. The problems centering in the evaluation of present versus future satisfactions, even the case of socialism versus capitalism, would be left still open, for instance, after the conversion of every individual citizen to utilitarianism. . . .

.   .   .

But, third, as a consequence of both preceding propositions, the particular concept of the will of the people or the *volonté générale* that the utilitarians made their own vanishes into thin air. For that concept presupposes the existence of a uniquely determined common good discernible to all. Unlike the romanticists the utilitarians had no notion of that semi-mystic entity endowed with a will of its own—that "soul of the people" which the historical school of jurisprudence made so much of. They frankly derived their will of the people from the wills of individuals. And unless there is a center, the common good, toward which, in the long run at least, *all* individual wills gravitate, we shall not get that particular type of "natural" *volonté générale*. The utilitarian center of gravity, on the one hand, unifies individual wills, tends to weld them by means of rational discussion into the will of the people and, on the other hand, confers upon the latter the exclusive ethical dignity claimed by the classic democratic creed. *This creed does not consist simply in worshiping the will of the people as such* but rests on certain assumptions about the "natural" object of that will which object is sanctioned by utilitarian reason. Both the existence and the dignity of this kind of *volonté générale* are gone as soon as the idea of the common good fails us. And both the pillars of the classical doctrine inevitably crumble into dust.

II. The Will of the People and Individual Volition

Of course, however conclusively those arguments may tell against this particular conception of the will of the people, they do not debar us from trying to build up another and more realistic one. . . .

.   .   .

. . . I will . . . repeat that even if the opinions and desires of individual citizens were perfectly definite and independent data for the democratic process to work with, and if everyone acted on them with ideal rationality and promptitude, it would not necessarily follow that the political decisions produced by that process from the raw material of those individual volitions would represent anything that could in any convincing sense be called the will of the people. It is not only conceivable but, whenever individual wills are much divided, very likely that the political decisions produced will not conform to "what people really want." Nor can it be replied that, if not exactly what they want, they will get a "fair compromise." This may be so. The chances for this to happen are greatest with those issues which are quantitative in nature or admit of gradation, such as the question how much is to be spent on unemployment relief provided everybody favors some expenditure for that purpose. But with qualitative issues, such as the question whether to persecute heretics or to enter upon a war, the result attained may well, though for different reasons, be equally distasteful to all the people whereas the decision imposed by a non-democratic agency might prove much more acceptable to them.

· · ·

ANOTHER THEORY OF DEMOCRACY

I. Competition for Political Leadership

I think that most students of politics have by now come to accept the criticisms leveled at the classical doctrine of democracy. . . . I also think that most of them agree, or will agree before long, in accepting another theory which is much truer to life and at the same time salvages much of what sponsors of the democratic method really mean by this term. Like the classical theory, it may be put into the nutshell of a definition.

It will be remembered that our chief troubles about the classical theory centered in the proposition that "the people" hold a definite and rational opinion about every individual question and that they give effect to this opinion—in a democracy—by choosing "representatives" who will see to it that that opinion is carried out. Thus the selection of the representatives is made secondary to the primary purpose of the democratic arrangement which is to vest the power of deciding political issues in the electorate. Suppose we reverse the roles of these two elements and make the deciding of issues by the electorate secondary to the election of the men who are to do the deciding. To put it differently, we now take the view that the role of the people is to produce a government, or else an intermediate body which in turn will produce a national executive or government. And we define: the democratic method is that institutional arangement for arriving at political decisions in which individuals acquire the power to decide by means of a competitive struggle for the people's vote.

Defense and explanation of this idea will speedily show that, as to both plausibility of assumptions and tenability of propositions, it greatly improves the theory of the democratic process.

First of all, we are provided with a reasonably efficient criterion by which to distinguish democratic governments from others. We have seen that the classical theory meets with difficulties on that score because both the will and the good of the people may be, and in many historical instances have been, served just as well or better by governments that cannot be described as democratic according to any accepted usage of the term. Now we are in a somewhat better position partly because we are resolved to stress a *modus procedendi* the presence or absence of which it is in most cases easy to verify.

For instance, a parliamentary monarchy like the English one fulfills the requirements of the democratic method because the monarch is practically constrained to appoint to cabinet office the same people as parliament would elect. A "constitutional" monarchy does not qualify to be called democratic because electorates and parliaments, while having all the other rights that electorates and parliaments have in parliamentary monarchies, lack the power to impose their choice as to the governing committee: the cabinet ministers are in this case servants of the monarch, in substance as well as in name, and can in principle be dismissed as well as appointed by him. Such an arrangement may satisfy the people. The electorate may reaffirm this fact by voting against any proposal for change. The monarch may be so popular as to be able to defeat any competition for the supreme office. But since no machinery is provided for making this competition effective the case does not come within our definition.

Second, the theory embodied in this definition leaves all the room we may wish to have for a proper recognition of the vital fact of leadership. The classical theory did not do this but, as we have seen, attributed to the electorate an altogether unrealistic degree of initiative which practically amounted to ignoring leadership. But collectives act almost exclusively by accepting leadership—this is the dominant mechanism of practically any collective action which is more than a reflex. Propositions about the working and the results of the democratic method that take account of this are bound to be infinitely more realistic than propositions which do not. They will not stop at the execution of a *volonté générale* but will go some way toward showing how it emerges or how it is substituted or faked. What we have termed Manufactured Will is no longer outside the theory, an aberration for the absence of which we piously pray; it enters on the ground floor as it should.

Third, however, so far as there are genuine group-wise volitions at all—for instance the will of the unemployed to receive unemployment benefit or the will of other groups to help—our theory does not neglect them. On the contrary we are now able to insert them in exactly the role they actually play. Such volitions do not as a rule assert themselves directly. Even if strong and definite they remain latent, often for decades, until they are called to life by some political leader who turns them into political factors. This he does, or else his agents do it for him, by organizing these volitions, by working them up and by including eventually appropriate items in his competitive offering. The interaction between sectional interests and public opinion and the way in which they produce the pattern we call the political situation appear from this angle in a new and much clearer light.

Fourth, our theory is of course no more definite than is the concept of competition for leadership. This concept presents similar difficulties as the concept of competition in the economic sphere, with which it may be usefully compared. In economic life competition is never completely lacking, but hardly ever is it perfect. Similarly, in political life there is always some competition, though perhaps only a potential one, for the allegiance of the people. To simplify matters we have restricted the kind of competition for leadership which is to define democracy, to free competition for a free vote. The justification for this is that democracy seems to imply a recognized method by which to conduct the competitive struggle, and that the electoral method is practically the only one available for communities of any size. But though this excludes many ways of securing leadership which should be excluded, such as competition by military insurrection, it does not exclude the cases that are strikingly analogous to the economic phenomena we label "unfair" or "fraudulent" competition or restraint of competition. And we cannot exclude them because if we did we should be left with a completely unrealistic ideal. Between this ideal case which does not exist and the cases in which all competition with the established leader is prevented by force, there is a continuous range of variation within which the democratic method of government shades off into the autocratic one by imperceptible steps. But if we wish to understand and not to philosophize, this is as it should be. The value of our criterion is not seriously impaired thereby.

Fifth, our theory seems to clarify the relation that subsists between democracy and individual freedom. If by the latter we mean the existence of a sphere of individual self-government the boundaries of which are historically variable—*no* society tolerates absolute freedom even of conscience and of speech, *no* society reduces that sphere to zero—the question clearly becomes a matter of degree. We have seen that the democratic method does not necessarily guarantee a greater amount of individual freedom than another political method would permit in similar circumstances. It may well be the other way round. But there is still a relation between the two. If, on principle at least, everyone is free to compete for political leadership by presenting himself to the electorate, this will in most cases though not in all mean a considerable amount of freedom of discussion *for all*. In particular it will normally mean a considerable amount of freedom of the press. This relation between democracy and freedom is not absolutely stringent and can be tampered with. But, from the standpoint of the intellectual, it is nevertheless very important. At the same time, it is all there is to that relation.

Sixth, it should be observed that in making it the primary function of the electorate to produce a government (directly or through an intermediate body) I intended to include in this phrase also the function of evicting it. The one means simply the acceptance of a leader or a group of leaders, the other means simply the withdrawal of this acceptance. This takes care of an element the reader may have missed. He may have thought that the electorate controls as well as installs. But since electorates normally do not control their political leaders in any way except by refusing to reelect them or the parliamentary majorities that support them, it seems well to reduce our ideas about this control in the way indicated by our definition. Occasionally, spontaneous revulsions occur which upset a government or an individual minister directly or else enforce a certain course of action. But they are not only exceptional, they are, as we shall see, contrary to the spirit of the democratic method.

Seventh, our theory sheds much-needed light on an old controversy. Whoever accepts the classical doctrine of democracy and in consequence believes that the democratic method is to guarantee that issues be decided and policies framed according to the will of the people must be struck by the fact that, even if that will were undeniably real and definite, decision by simple majorities would in many cases distort it rather than give effect to it. Evidently the will of the majority is the will of the majority and not the will of "the people." The latter is a mosaic that the former completely fails to "represent." To equate both by definition is not to solve the problem. Attempts at real solutions have however been made by the authors of the various plans for Proportional Representation.

These plans have met with adverse criticism on practical grounds. It is in fact obvious not only that proportional representation will offer opportunities for all sorts of idiosyncrasies to assert themselves but also that it may prevent democracy from producing efficient governments and thus prove a danger in times of stress. But before concluding that democracy becomes unworkable if its principle is carried out consistently, it is just as well to ask ourselves whether this principle really implies proportional representation. As a matter of fact it does not. If acceptance of leadership is the true function of the electorate's vote, the case for proportional representation collapses because its premises are no longer binding. The principle of democracy then merely means that the reins of government should be handed to those who command more support than do any of the competing individuals or teams. And this in turn seems to assure the standing of the majority system within the logic of the democratic method, although we might still condemn it on grounds that lie outside of that logic.

· · ·

THE INFERENCE

I. Some Implications of the Preceding Analysis

The theory of competitive leadership has proved a satisfactory interpretation of the facts of the democratic process. So we shall naturally use it in our attempt to unravel the relation between democracy and a socialist order of things. As has been stated before, socialists claim not only compatibility; they claim that democracy implies socialism and that there cannot be true democracy except in socialism. On the other hand, the reader cannot but be familiar with at least some of the numerous pamphlets that have been published in this country during the last few years in order to prove that a planned economy, let alone full-fledged socialism, is completely incompatible with democracy. Both standpoints are of course easy to understand from the psychological background of the contest and from the natural wish of both parties to it to secure the support of a people the great majority of whom fervently believes in democracy. But suppose we ask: where lies the truth?

Our analysis in this and preceding parts of this book readily yields an answer. Between socialism as we defined it and democracy as we defined it there is no necessary relation: the one can exist without the other. At the same time there is no incompatibility: in appropriate states of the social environment the socialist engine can be run on democratic principles.

But observe that these simple statements depend upon our view about what socialism and democracy are. Therefore they mean not only less than, but also something different from, what either party to the contest has in mind. For this reason and also because behind the question of mere compatibility there inevitably arises the further question whether the democratic method will work more or less effectively in a socialist as compared with a capitalist regime, we have still a lot of explaining to do. In particular we must try to formulate the conditions under which the democratic method can be expected to give satisfaction. . . .

.   .   .

II. *Conditions for the Success of the Democratic Method*

If a physicist observes that the same mechanism works differently at different times and in different places, he concludes that its functioning depends upon conditions extraneous to it. We cannot but arrive at the same conclusion. . . .

. . . The conditions which I hold must be fulfilled for the democratic method to be a success—in societies in which it is possible for it to work at all—I shall group under four headings; and I shall confine myself to the great industrial nations of the modern type.

The first condition is that the human material of politics—the people who man the party machines, are elected to serve in parliament, rise to cabinet office —should be of sufficiently high quality. This means more than that individuals of adequate ability and moral character must exist in sufficient numbers. As has been pointed out before, the democratic method selects not simply from the population but only from those elements of the population that are available for the political vocation or, more precisely, that offer themselves for election. All methods of selection do this of course. All of them therefore may, according to the degree to which a given vocation attracts talent and character, produce in it a level of performance that is above or below the national average. But the competitive struggle for responsible office is, on the one hand, wasteful of personnel and energy. On the other hand, the democratic process may easily create conditions in the political sector that, once established, will repel most of the men who can make a success at anything else. For both these reasons, adequacy of material is particularly important for the success of democratic government. It is not true that in a democracy people always have the kind and quality of government they want or merit.

There may be many ways in which politicians of sufficiently good quality can be secured. Thus far however, experience seems to suggest that the only effective guarantee is in the existence of a social stratum, itself a product of a severely selective process, that takes to politics as a matter of course. If such a stratum be neither too exclusive nor too easily accessible for the outsider and if it be strong enough to assimilate most of the elements it currently absorbs, it not only will present for the political career products of stocks that have successfully passed many tests in other fields—served, as it were, an apprenticeship in private affairs—but it will also increase their fitness by endowing them with traditions that embody experience, with a professional code and with a common fund of views.

. . .

The second condition for the success of democracy is that the effective range of political decision should not be extended too far. How far it can be extended depends not only on the general limitations of the democratic method which follow from the analysis presented in the preceding section but also on the particular circumstances of each individual case. To put this more concretely: the range does not only depend, for instance, on the kind and quantity of matters that can be successfully handled by a government subject to the strain of an incessant struggle for its political life; it also depends, at any given time and place, on the quality of the men who form that government and on the type of political machine and the pattern of public opinion they have to work with. From the standpoint of our theory of democracy it is not necessary to require, as it would be from the standpoint of the classical theory, that only such matters should be dealt with by the political apparatus which the people at large can fully understand and have a serious opinion about. But a less exacting requirement of the same nature still imposes itself. It calls for additional comment.

Of course there cannot be any legal limits to what a parliament, led by the prime minister, might subject to its decision, if need be, by means of a constitutional amendment. But, so Edmund Burke argued in discussing the behavior of the English government and Parliament with respect to the American colonies, in order to function properly that all-powerful parliament must impose limits upon itself. Similarly we may argue that, even within the range of matters that have to be submitted to parliamentary vote, it is often necessary for government and parliament to pass measures on which their decision is purely formal or, at most, of a purely supervisory nature. Otherwise the democratic method may turn out legislative freaks. Take for instance the case of so bulky and so technical a measure as a criminal code. The democratic method will apply to the question whether or not a country is to have such a codification at all. It will also apply to certain "issues" that the government may choose to select for political decision which is more than formal—for instance, whether certain practices of labor or employers' associations should or should not be considered criminal. But for the rest, government and parliament will have to accept the specialists' advice whatever they may think themselves. For crime is a complex phenomenon. The term in fact covers many phenomena that have very little in common. Popular slogans about it are almost invariably wrong. And a rational treatment of it requires that legislation in this matter should be protected from both the fits of vindictiveness and the fits of sentimentality in which the laymen in the government and in the parliament are alternatingly prone to indulge. This is what I meant to convey by stressing the limitations upon the *effective* range of political decision—the range within which politicians decide in truth as well as in form.

Again, the condition in question can indeed be fulfilled by a corresponding limitation of the activities of the state. But it would be a serious misunderstanding if the reader thought that such a limitation is necessarily implied. Democracy does not require that every function of the state be subject to its political method. For instance, in most democratic countries a large measure of independence from political agencies is granted to the judges. Another instance is the position held by the Bank of England until 1914. Some of its functions were in fact of a public nature. Nevertheless these functions were vested with what legally was just a business corporation that was sufficiently independent of the political sector to have a policy of its own. Certain federal agencies in this country are other cases in point. The Interstate Commerce Commission embodies an attempt to extend the sphere of public authority without extending the sphere of political decision. Or, to present still another example, certain of our states finance state universities "without any strings," that is to say, without interfering with what in some cases amounts to practically complete autonomy.

Thus, almost any type of human affairs may conceivably be made to enter the sphere of the state without becoming part of the material of the competitive struggle for political leadership beyond what is implied in passing the measure that grants the power and sets up the agency to wield it and the contact that is implied in the government's role of general supervisor. It is of course true that this supervision may degenerate into vitiating influence. The politician's power to appoint the personnel of non-political public agencies, if remorselessly used, will often suffice in itself to corrupt them. But that does not affect the principle in question.

As a third condition, democratic government in modern industrial society must be able to command, for all purposes the sphere of public activity is to include—no matter whether this be much or little—the services of a well-trained bureaucracy of good standing and tradition, endowed with a strong sense of duty and a no less strong *esprit de corps*. Such a bureaucracy is the main answer to the argument about government by amateurs. Potentially it is the only answer to the question so often heard in this country: democratic politics has proved itself unable to produce decent city government; how can we expect the nation to fare if everything, eventually including the whole of the productive process, is to be handed over to it? And finally, it is also the principal answer to the question about how our second condition can be fulfilled whenever the sphere of public control is wide.

It is not enough that the bureaucracy should be efficient in current administration and competent to give advice. It must also be strong enough to guide and, if need be, to instruct the politicians who head the ministries. In order to be able to do this it must be in a position to evolve principles of its own and sufficiently independent to assert them. It must be a power in its own right. This amounts to saying that in fact though not in form appointment, tenure and promotion must depend largely—within civil service rules that politicians hesitate to violate—on its own corporate opinion in spite of all the clamor that is sure to arise whenever politicians or the public find themselves crossed by it as they frequently must.

Again, as in the case of the personnel of politics, the question of the available human material is all-important. Training though essential is quite secondary to this. And again, both requisite material and the traditional code necessary for the functioning of an official class of this kind can be most easily secured if there is a social stratum of adequate quality and corresponding prestige that can be drawn upon for recruits—not too rich, not too poor, not too exclusive, not too accessible. The bureaucracies of Europe, in spite of the fact that they have drawn enough hostile criticism to blur their records, exemplify very well what I am trying to convey. They are the product of a long development that started with the *ministeriales* of medieval magnates (originally serfs selected for administrative and military purposes who thereby acquired the status of petty nobles) and went on through the centuries until the powerful engine emerged which we behold today. It cannot be created in a hurry. It cannot be "hired" with money. But it grows everywhere, whatever the political method a nation may adopt. Its expansion is the one certain thing about our future.

The fourth set of conditions may be summed up in the phrase Democratic Self-control. Everybody will of course agree that the democratic method cannot work smoothly unless all the groups that count in a nation are willing to accept any legislative measure as long as it is on the statute book and all executive orders issued by legally competent authorities. But democratic self-control implies much more than this.

Above all, electorates and parliaments must be on an intellectual and moral level high enough to be proof against the offerings of the crook and the crank, or else men who are neither will be driven into the ways of both. Moreover, miscarriages that will discredit democracy and undermine allegiance to it may also occur if measures are passed without regard to the claims of others or to the national situation. The individual proposals for legislative reform or executive action must, as it were, be content to stand in an orderly breadline; they must not attempt to rush the shop. Recalling what has been said in the preceding chapter about the *modus operandi* of the democratic method, the reader will realize that this involves a lot of voluntary subordination.

In particular, politicians in parliament must resist the temptation to upset or embarrass the government each time they could do so. No successful policy is possible if they do this. This means that the supporters of the government must accept its lead and allow it to frame and act upon a program and that the opposition should accept the lead of the "shadow cabinet" as its head and allow it to keep political warfare within certain rules. Fulfillment of this requirement, habitual violation of which spells the beginning of the end of a democracy, will be seen to call for just the right amount—not too much, not too little—of traditionalism. To protect this traditionalism is in fact one of the purposes for which rules of parliamentary procedure and etiquette exist.

The voters outside of parliament must respect the division of labor between themselves and the politicians they elect. They must not withdraw confidence too easily between elections and they must understand that, once they have elected an individual, political action is his business and not theirs. This means that they must refrain from instructing him about what he is to do—a principle that has indeed been universally recognized by constitutions and political theory ever since Edmund Burke's time. But its implications are not generally understood. On the one hand, few people realize that this principle clashes with the classical doctrine of democracy and really spells its abandonment. For if the people are to rule in the sense of deciding individual issues, what could be more natural for them to do than to issue instructions to their representatives as the voters for the French States-General did in and before 1789? On the other hand, it is still less recognized that if the principle be accepted, not only instructions as formal as those French *cahiers* but also less formal attempts at restricting the freedom of action of members of parliament—the practice of bombarding them with letters and telegrams for instance—ought to come under the same ban.

We cannot enter into the various delicate problems which this raises concerning the true nature of democracy as defined by us. All that matters here is that successful democratic practice in great and complicated societies has invariably been hostile to political back-seat driving—to the point of resorting to secret diplomacy and lying about intentions and commitments—and that it takes a lot of self-control on the part of the citizen to refrain from it.

Finally, effective competition for leadership requires a large measure of tolerance for difference of opinion. It has been pointed out before that this tolerance never is and never can be absolute. But it must be possible for every would-be leader who is not lawfully excluded to present his case without producing disorder. And this may imply that people stand by patiently while somebody is attacking their most vital interests or offending their most cherished ideals—or as an alternative, that the would-be leader who holds such views restrains himself correspondingly. Neither is possible without genuine respect for the opinions of one's fellow citizens amounting to a willingness to subordinate one's own opinions.

Every system can stand deviating practice to a certain extent. But even the necessary minimum of democratic self-control evidently requires a national character and national habits of a certain type which have not everywhere had the opportunity to evolve and which the democratic method itself cannot be relied on to produce. And nowhere will that self-control stand tests beyond a varying degree of severity. In fact the reader need only review our conditions in order to satisfy himself that democratic government will work to full advantage only if all the interests that matter are practically unanimous not only in their allegiance to the country but also in their allegiance to the structural principles of the existing society. Whenever these principles are called in question and issues arise that rend a nation into two hostile camps, democracy works at a disadvantage. And it may cease to work at all as soon as interests and ideals are involved on which people refuse to compromise.

This may be generalized to read that the democratic method will be at a disadvantage in troubled times. In fact, democracies of all types recognize with practical unanimity that there are situations in which it is reasonable to abandon competitive and to adopt monopolistic leadership. In ancient Rome a non-elective office conferring such a monopoly of leadership in emergencies was provided for by the constitution. The incumbent was called *magister populi* or *dictator*. Similar provisions are known to practically all constitutions, our own included: the President of the United States acquires in certain conditions a power that makes him to all intents and purposes a dictator in the Roman sense, however great the differences are both in legal construction and in practical details. If the monopoly is effectively limited either to a definite time (as it originally was in Rome) or to the duration of a definite short-run emergency, the democratic principle of competitive leadership is merely suspended. If the monopoly, either in law or in fact, is not limited as to time—and if not limited as to time it will of course tend to become unlimited as to everything else—the democratic principle is abrogated and we have the case of dictatorship in the present-day sense.

III. Democracy in the Socialist Order

1. In setting forth our conclusions we had better begin with the relation between democracy and the capitalist order of things.

This ideology of democracy as reflected by the classical doctrine rests on a rationalist scheme of human action and of the values of life. By virtue of a previous argument (Chapter XI) this fact would in itself suffice to suggest that it is of bourgeois origin. History clearly confirms this suggestion: historically, the modern democracy rose along with capitalism, and in casual connection with it. But the same holds true for democratic practice: democracy in the sense of our theory of competitive leadership presided over the process of political and institutional change by which the bourgeoisie reshaped, and from its own point of view rationalized, the social and political structure that preceded its ascendancy: the democratic method was the political tool of that reconstruction. We have seen

that the democratic method works, particularly well, also in certain extra- and
pre-capitalist societies. But modern democracy is a product of the capitalist
process.

Whether or not democracy is one of those products of capitalism which are
to die out with it is of course another question. And still another is how well or
ill capitalist society qualifies for the task of working the democratic method it
evolved.

As regards the latter question, it is clear that capitalist society qualifies well
in one respect. The bourgeoisie has a solution that is peculiar to it for the problem of how the sphere of political decision can be reduced to those proportions
which are manageable by means of the method of competitive leadership. The
bourgeois scheme of things limits the sphere of politics by limiting the sphere of
public authority; its solution is in the ideal of the parsimonious state that exists
primarily in order to guarantee bourgeois legality and to provide a firm frame
for autonomous individual endeavor in all fields. If, moreover, account be taken
of the pacific—at any rate, anti-militarist—and free-trade tendencies we have
found to be inherent in bourgeois society, it will be seen that the importance of
the role of political decision in the bourgeois state can, in principle at least, be
scaled down to almost any extent that the disabilities of the political sector may
require.

Now this kind of state has no doubt ceased to appeal to us. Bourgeois
democracy is certainly a very special historical case and any claims that may be
made on behalf of it are obviously contingent upon acceptance of standards
which are no longer ours. But it is absurd to deny that this solution which we
dislike is a solution and that bourgeois democracy is democracy. On the contrary, as its colors fade it is all the more important to recognize how colorful it
was in the time of its vitality; how wide *and equal* the opportunities it offered to
the families (if not to the individuals); how large the personal freedom it
granted to those who passed its tests (or to their children). It is also important
to recognize how well it stood, for some decades at least, the strain of uncon-
genial conditions and how well it functioned, when faced by demands that were
outside of and hostile to the bourgeois interests.

Also in another respect capitalist society in its meridian qualified well for
the task of making democracy a success. It is easier for a class whose interests
are best served by being left alone to practice democratic self-restraint than it is
for classes that naturally try to live on the state. The bourgeois who is primarily
absorbed in his private concerns is in general—as long as these concerns are not
seriously threatened—much more likely to display tolerance of political differences and respect for opinions he does not share than any other type of human
being. . . . [I]n many cases practices that failed to conform to the spirit of the
democratic method have become important enough to distort its *modus operandi*.
That there "cannot" be true democracy in the capitalist order is nevertheless an
obvious over-statement.

In both respects however capitalism is rapidly losing the advantages it used to possess. Bourgeois democracy which is wedded to that ideal of the state has for some time been working with increasing friction. In part this was due to the fact that, as we have seen before, the democratic method never works at its best when nations are much divided on fundamental questions of social structure. And this difficulty in turn proved particularly serious, because bourgeois society signally failed to fulfill another condition for making the democratic method function. The bourgeoisie produced individuals who made a success at political leadership upon entering a political class of non-bourgeois origin, but it did not produce a successful political stratum of its own although, so one should think, the third generations of the industrial families had all the opportunity to form one. Why this was so has been fully explained in Part II. All these facts together seem to suggest a pessimistic prognosis for this type of democracy. They also suggest an explanation of the apparent ease with which in some cases it surrendered to dictatorship.

2. The ideology of classical socialism is the offspring of bourgeois ideology. In particular, it fully shares the latter's rationalist and utilitarian background and many of the ideas and ideals that entered the classical doctrine of democracy. So far as this goes, socialists in fact experienced no difficulty whatever in appropriating this part of the bourgeois inheritance and in making out a case for the proposition that those elements of the classical doctrine which socialism is unable to absorb—the emphasis on protection of private property for instance —are really at variance with its fundamental principles. Creeds of this kind could survive even in entirely non-democratic forms of socialism and we may trust the scribes and pharisees to bridge by suitable phrases any gap there may be between creed and practice. But it is the practice that interests us—the fate of democratic practice as interpreted by the doctrine of competitive leadership. And so, since we have seen that non-democratic socialism is perfectly possible, the real question is again how well or ill socialism qualifies for the task of making the democratic method function should it attempt to do so.

The essential point to grasp is this. No responsible person can view with equanimity the consequences of extending the democratic method, that is to say the sphere of "politics," to all economic affairs. Believing that democratic socialism means precisely this, such a person will naturally conclude that democratic socialism must fail. But this does not necessarily follow. As has been pointed out before, extension of the range of public management does not imply corresponding extension of the range of political management. Conceivably, the former may be extended so as to absorb a nation's economic affairs while the latter still remains within the boundaries set by the limitations of the democratic method.

It does follow however that in socialist society these limitations will raise a much more serious problem. For socialist society lacks the automatic restrictions imposed upon the political sphere by the bourgeois scheme of things. Moreover, in socialist society it will no longer be possible to find comfort in the thought that the inefficiencies of political procedure are after all a guarantee of freedom. Lack of efficient management will spell lack of bread. However, the agencies that are to operate the economic engine—the Central Board we met in Part III as well as the subordinate bodies entrusted with the management of individual industries or concerns—may be so organized and manned as to be sufficiently exempt in the fulfillment of their current duties from interference by politicians or, for that matter, by fussing citizens' committees or by their workmen. That is to say, they may be sufficiently removed from the atmosphere of political strife as to display no inefficiencies other than those associated with the term Bureaucracy. And even these *can* be much reduced by an appropriate concentration of responsibility on individuals and by a system of well-chosen incentives and penalties, of which the methods of appointment and promotion are the most important part.

Serious socialists, when off the stump and in a responsible mood, have always been aware of this problem and also of the fact that "democracy" is no answer to it. . . .

. . . [W]e are now in a position to link up this conclusion with an answer to the problem of democracy in socialism. In a sense, of course, the present-day forms and organs of democratic procedure are as much the outgrowth of the structure and the issues of the bourgeois world as is the fundamental principle of democracy itself. But this is no reason why they should have to disappear along with capitalism. General elections, parties, parliaments, cabinets and prime ministers may still prove to be the most convenient instruments for dealing with the agenda that the socialist order may reserve for political decision. The list of these agenda will be relieved of all those items that at present arise from the clash of private interests and from the necessity of regulating them. Instead there will be new ones. There will be such questions to decide as what the volume of investment should be or how existing rules for the distribution of the social product should be amended and so on. General debates about efficiency, investigation committees of the type of the English Royal Commissions would continue to fulfill their present functions.

Thus the politicians in the cabinet, and in particular the politician at the head of the Ministry of Production, would no doubt assert the influence of the political element, both by their legislative measures concerning the general principles of running the economic engine and by their power to appoint which could not be entirely absent or entirely formal. But they need not do so to an extent incompatible with efficiency. And the Minister of Production need not interfere more with the internal working of individual industries than English Ministers of Health or of War interfere with the internal working of their respective departments.

3. It goes without saying that operating socialist democracy in the way indicated would be a perfectly hopeless task except in the case of a society that fulfills all the requirements of "maturity" listed in Part III, including, in particular, the ability to establish the socialist order in a democratic way and the existence of a bureaucracy of adequate standing and experience. But a society that

does fulfill these requirements—I shall not deal with any other—would first of all command an advantage of possibly decisive importance.

I have emphasized that democracy cannot be expected to function satisfactorily unless the vast majority of the people in all classes are resolved to abide by the rules of the democratic game and that this in turn implies that they are substantially agreed on the fundamentals of their institutional structure. At present the latter condition fails to be fulfilled. So many people have renounced, and so many more are going to renounce, allegiance to the standards of capitalist society that on this ground alone democracy is bound to work with increasing friction. At the stage visualized however, socialism may remove the rift. It may reestablish agreement as to the tectonic principles of the social fabric. If it does, then the remaining antagonisms will be exactly of the kind with which the democratic method is well able to cope.

. . . [R]emaining antagonisms will be further decreased in number and importance by the elimination of clashing capitalist interests. The relations between agriculture and industry, small-scale and large-scale industry, steel-producing and steel-consuming industries, protectionist and export industries will—or may—cease to be political questions to be settled by the relative weights of pressure groups and become technical questions to which technicians would be able to give unemotional and unequivocal answers. Though it may be utopian to expect that there would be no distinct economic interests or conflicts between them, and still more utopian to expect that there would be no non-economic issues to disagree about, a good case may be made out for expecting that the sum total of controversial matter would be decreased even as compared with what it was in intact capitalism. There would, for instance, be no silver men. Political life would be purified.

On the face of it, socialism has no obvious solution to offer for the problem solved in other forms of society by the presence of a political class of stable traditions. I have said before that there will be a political profession. There may evolve a political set, about the quality of which it is idle to speculate.

Thus far socialism scores. It might still be argued that this score can be easily balanced by the importance and likelihood of possible deviations. To some extent we have provided for this by insisting on economic maturity which among other things implies that no great sacrifices need be required of one generation for the benefit of a later one. But even if there is no necessity for sweating the people by means of a Gosplan, the task of keeping the democratic course may prove to be extremely delicate. Circumstances in which the individuals at the helm would normally succeed in solving it are perhaps no easier to imagine than circumstances in which, faced by a spectacle of paralysis spreading from the political sector all over the nation's economy, they might be driven into a course of action which must always have some temptation for men beholding the tremendous power over the people inherent in the socialist organization. After all, effective management of the socialist economy means dictatorship not *of* but *over* the proletariat in the factory. The men who are there so strictly disciplined would, it is true, be sovereign at the elections. But just as they may use this sovereignty in order to relax the discipline of the factory, so governments—precisely the governments which have the future of the nation at heart—may avail themselves of this discipline in order to restrict this sovereignty. As a matter of practical necessity, socialist democracy may eventually turn out to be more of a sham than capitalist democracy ever was.

In any case, that democracy will not mean increased personal freedom. And, once more, it will mean no closer approximation to the ideals enshrined in the classical doctrine.

REYNOLDS *v.* SIMS

卐

Three issues are involved in the historic Supreme Court reapportionment decisions that began with *Baker* v. *Carr* in 1962. The first concerns the court's jurisdiction which the late Justice Felix Frankfurter
questioned when, in a famous dissent, he argued "There is not under
our Constitution a judicial remedy for every political mischief . . .";[1]
the second, the applicability of the Equal Protection Clause of the Fourteenth Amendment on which the Court subsequently relied in ordering
nonconforming states to reapportion; and the third, the meaning of
democracy. The first two questions belong to discussions of constitutional law. In connection with the third, the majority of the Supreme
Court sought to restate the meaning of democracy in a new and crucial
context. The excerpts which follow are selected for their bearing on
the third issue.

   The record of the Warren Court in protecting the rights of individuals, whether of impecunious defendants, security suspects or segregated minority groups is by this time celebrated. In this instance it
turned its attention to individuals partly deprived of their right to vote
for state legislators and in some cases for congressmen by virtue of
their residence in urban areas.

   Chief Justice Earl Warren delivered the opinion of the Court.

. . .

   . . . Undoubtedly, the right of suffrage is a fundamental matter in a free
and democratic society. Especially since the right to exercise the franchise in a
free and unimpaired manner is preservative of other basic civil and political
rights, any alleged infringement of the right of citizens to vote must be carefully
and meticulously scrutinized. . . .

   Legislators represent people, not trees or acres. Legislators are elected by
voters, not farms or cities or economic interests. As long as ours is a representative form of government, and our legislatures are those instruments of government elected directly by and directly representative of the people, the right to
elect legislators in a free and unimpaired fashion is a bedrock of our political
system. It could hardly be gainsaid that a constitutional claim had been asserted
by an allegation that certain otherwise qualified voters had been entirely prohibited from voting for members of their state legislature. And, if a State should

From *Reynolds* v. *Sims*, 377 U.S. 533, 561–68, 571–77 (1964). Certain footnotes which
appeared in the original have been deleted.
[1] 369 U.S. 270 (1962).

provide that the votes of citizens in one part of the State should be given two times, or five times, or 10 times the weight of votes of citizens in another part of the State, it could hardly be contended that the right to vote of those residing in the disfavored areas had not been effectively diluted. It would appear extraordinary to suggest that a state could be constitutionally permitted to enact a law providing that certain of the state's voters could vote two, five, or 10 times for their legislative representatives, while voters living elsewhere could vote only once. And it is inconceivable that a state law to the effect that, in counting votes for legislators, the votes of citizens in one part of the State would be multiplied by two, five, or 10, while the votes of persons in another area would be counted only at face value, could be constitutionally sustainable. Of course, the effect of state legislative districting schemes which give the same number of representatives to unequal numbers of constituents is identical. Overweighting and overvaluation of the votes of those living here has the certain effect of dilution and undervaluation of the votes of those living there. The resulting discrimination against those individual voters living in disfavored areas is easily demonstrable mathematically. Their right to vote is simply not the same right to vote as that of those living in a favored part of the State. Two, five, or 10 of them must vote before the effect of their voting is equivalent to that of their favored neighbor. Weighting the votes of citizens differently, by any method or means, merely because of where they happen to reside, hardly seems justifiable. One must be ever aware that the Constitution forbids "sophisticated as well as simple-minded modes of discrimination." *Lane* v. *Wilson,* 307 U.S. 268, 275, *Gomillion* v. *Lightfoot,* 364 U.S. 339, 342. As we stated in *Wesberry* v. *Sanders, supra:*

> "We do not believe that the Framers of the Constitution intended to permit the same vote-diluting discrimination to be accomplished through the device of districts containing widely varied numbers of inhabitants. To say that a vote is worth more in one district than in another would . . . run counter to our fundamental ideas of democratic government. . . ." [41]

State legislatures are, historically, the fountainhead of representative government in this country. A number of them have their roots in colonial times, and substantially antedate the creation of our Nation and our Federal Government. In fact, the first formal stirrings of American political independence are to be found, in large part, in the views and actions of several of the colonial legislative bodies. With the birth of our National Government, and the adoption and ratification of the Federal Constitution, state legislatures retained a most important place in our Nation's governmental structure. But representative government is in essence self-government through the medium of elected representatives of the people, and each and every citizen has an inalienable right to full and effective participation in the political processes of his State's legislative bodies. Most citizens can achieve this participation only as qualified voters through the elec-

[41] 376 U.S., at 8.

tion of legislators to represent them. Full and effective participation by all citizens in state government requires, therefore, that each citizen has an equally effective voice in the election of members of his state legislature. Modern and viable state government needs, and the Constitution demands, no less.

Logically, in a society ostensibly grounded on representative government, it would seem reasonable that a majority of the people of a State could elect a majority of that State's legislators. To conclude differently, and to sanction minority control of state legislative bodies, would appear to deny majority rights in a way that far surpasses any possible denial of minority rights that might otherwise be thought to result. Since legislatures are responsible for enacting laws by which all citizens are to be governed, they should be bodies which are collectively responsive to the popular will. And the concept of equal protection has been traditionally viewed as requiring the uniform treatment of persons standing in the same relation to the governmental action questioned or challenged. With respect to the allocation of legislative representation, all voters, as citizens of a State, stand in the same relation regardless of where they live. Any suggested criteria for the differentiation of citizens are insufficient to justify any discrimination, as to the weight of their votes, unless relevant to the permissible purposes of legislative apportionment. Since the achieving of fair and effective representation for all citizens is concededly the basic aim of legislative apportionment, we conclude that the Equal Protection Clause guarantees the opportunity for equal participation by all voters in the election of state legislators. Diluting the weight of votes because of place of residence impairs basic constitutional rights under the Fourteenth Amendment just as much as invidious discriminations based upon factors such as race, *Brown* v. *Board of Education,* 347 U.S. 483, or economic status, *Griffin* v. *Illinois,* 351 U.S. 12, *Douglas* v. *California,* 372 U.S. 353. Our constitutional system amply provides for the protection of minorities by means other than giving them majority control of state legislatures. And the democratic ideals of equality and majority rule, which have served this Nation so well in the past, are hardly of any less significance for the present and the future.

We are told that the matter of apportioning representation in a state legislature is a complex and many-faceted one. We are advised that States can rationally consider factors other than population in apportioning legislative representation. We are admonished not to restrict the power of the States to impose differing views as to political philosophy on their citizens. We are cautioned about the dangers of entering into political thickets and mathematical quagmires. Our answer is this: a denial of constitutionally protected rights demands judicial protection; our oath and our office require no less of us. As stated in *Gomillion* v. *Lightfoot, supra:*

> "When a State excercises power wholly within the domain of state interest, it is insulated from federal judicial review. But such

insulation is not carried over when state power is used as an instrument for circumventing a federally protected right."

To the extent that a citizen's right to vote is debased, he is that much less a citizen. The fact that an individual lives here or there is not a legitimate reason for overweighting or diluting the efficacy of his vote. The complexions of societies and civilizations change, often with amazing rapidity. A nation once primarily rural in character becomes predominantly urban.[43] Representation schemes once fair and equitable become archaic and outdated. But the basic principle of representative government remains, and must remain, unchanged—the weight of a citizen's vote cannot be made to depend on where he lives. Population is, of necessity, the starting point for consideration and the controlling criterion for judgment in legislative apportionment controversies.[44] A citizen, a qualified voter, is no more nor no less so because he lives in the city or on the farm. This is the clear and strong command of our Constitution's Equal Protection Clause. This is an essential part of the concept of a government of laws and not men. This is at the heart of Lincoln's vision of "government of the people, by the people, [and] for the people." The Equal Protection Clause demands no less than substantially equal state legislative representation for all citizens, of all places as well as of all races.

. . .

Much has been written since our decision in *Baker* v. *Carr* about the applicability of the so-called federal analogy to state legislative apportionment arrangements. . . . We . . . find the federal analogy inapposite and irrelevant to state legislative districting schemes. Attempted reliance on the federal analogy appears often to be little more than an after-the-fact rationalization offered in defense of maladjusted state apportionment arrangements. The original constitu-

[43] Although legislative apportionment controversies are generally viewed as involving urban-rural conflicts, much evidence indicates that presently it is the fast-growing suburban areas which are probably the most seriously underrepresented in many of our state legislatures. And, while currently the thrust of state legislative malapportionment results, in most States, in underrepresentation of urban and suburban areas, in earlier times cities were in fact overrepresented in a number of States. In the early 19th century, certain of the seaboard cities in some of the Eastern and Southern States possessed and struggled to retain legislative representation disproportionate to population, and bitterly opposed according additional representation to the growing inland areas. Conceivably, in some future time, urban areas might again be in a situation of attempting to acquire or retain legislative representation in excess of that to which, on a population basis, they are entitled. Malapportionment can, and has historically, run in various directions. However and whenever it does, it is constitutionally impermissible under the Equal Protection Clause.

[44] The British experience in eradicating "rotten boroughs" is interesting and enlightening. Parliamentary representation is now based on districts of substantially equal population, and periodic reapportionment is accomplished through independent Boundary Commissions. For a discussion of the experience and difficulties in Great Britain in achieving fair legislative representation, see Edwards, "Theoretical and Comparative Aspects of Reapportionment and Redistricting: With Reference to Baker v. Carr," 15 Vand. L. Rev. 1265, 1275 (1962). See also the discussion in *Baker* v. *Carr*, 369 U.S., at 302–307. (Frankfurter, J., dissenting.)

tions of 36 of our States provided that representation in both houses of the state legislatures would be based completely, or predominantly, on population. And the Founding Fathers clearly had no intention of establishing a pattern or model for the apportionment of seats in state legislatures when the system of representation in the Federal Congress was adopted.[53] Demonstrative of this is the fact that the Northwest Ordinance, adopted in the same year, 1787, as the Federal Constitution, provided for the apportionment of seats in territorial legislatures solely on the basis of population.

The system of representation in the two Houses of the Federal Congress is one ingrained in our Constitution, as part of the law of the land. It is one conceived out of compromise and concession indispensable to the establishment of our federal republic. Arising from unique historical circumstances, it is based on the consideration that in establishing our type of federalism a group of formerly independent States bound themselves together under one national government. Admittedly, the original 13 States surrendered some of their sovereignty in agreeing to join together "to form a more perfect Union." But at the heart of our constitutional system remains the concept of separate and distinct governmental entities which have delegated some, but not all, of their formerly held powers to the single national government. The fact that almost three-fourths of our present States were never in fact independently sovereign does not detract from our view that the so-called federal analogy is inapplicable as a sustaining precedent for state legislative apportionments. The developing history and growth of our republic cannot cloud the fact that, at the time of the inception of the system of representation in the Federal Congress, a compromise between the larger and smaller States on this matter averted a deadlock in the constitutional convention which had threatened to abort the birth of our Nation. In rejecting an asserted analogy to the federal electoral college in *Gray* v. *Sanders, supra,* we stated:

> "We think the analogies to the electoral college, to districting and redistricting, and to other phases of the problems of representation in state or federal legislatures or conventions are inapposite. The inclusion of the electoral college in the Constitution, as the result of specific historical concerns, validated the collegiate principle despite its inherent numerical inequality, but implied nothing about the use of an analogous system by a State in a statewide election. No such spe-

---

[53] Thomas Jefferson repeatedly denounced the inequality of representation provided for under the 1776 Virginia Constitution and frequently proposed changing the State Constitution to provide that both houses be apportioned on the basis of population. In 1816 he wrote that "a government is republican in proportion as every member composing it has his equal voice in the direction of its concerns . . . by representatives chosen by himself . . . ." Letter to Samuel Kercheval, 10 Writings of Thomas Jefferson (Ford ed. 1899), 38. And a few years later, in 1819, he stated: "Equal representation is so fundamental a principle in a true republic that no prejudice can justify its violation because the prejudices themselves cannot be justified." Letter to William King, Jefferson Papers, Library of Congress, Vol. 216, p. 38616.

cific accommodation of the latter was ever undertaken, and therefore no validation of its numerical inequality ensured."

Political subdivisions of States—countries, cities, or whatever—never were and never have been considered as sovereign entities. Rather, they have been traditionally regarded as subordinate governmental instrumentalities created by the State to assist in the carrying out of state governmental functions. As stated by the Court in *Hunter* v. *City of Pittsburgh*, 207 U.S. 161, 178, these governmental units are "created as convenient agencies for exercising such as the governmental powers of the State as may be entrusted to them," and the "number, nature and duration of the powers conferred upon [them] . . . and the territory over which they shall be exercised rests in the absolute discretion of the State." The relationship of the States to the Federal Government could hardly be less analogous.

. . .

Since we find the so-called federal analogy inapposite to a consideration of the constitutional validity of state legislative apportionment schemes, we necessarily hold that the Equal Protection Clause requires both houses of a state legislature to be apportioned on a population basis. The right of a citizen to equal representation and to have his vote weighted equally with those of all other citizens in the election of members of one house of a bicameral state legislature would amount to little if States could effectively submerge the equal-population principle in the apportionment of seats in the other house. If such a scheme were permissible, an individual citizen's ability to exercise an effective voice in the only instrument of state government directly representative of the people might be almost as effectively thwarted as if neither house were apportioned on a population basis. Deadlock between the two bodies might result in compromise and concession on some issues. But in all too many cases the more probable result would be frustration of the majority will through minority veto in the house not apportioned on a population basis, stemming directly from the failure to accord adequate overall legislative representation to all of the State's citizens on a nondiscriminatory basis. In summary, we can perceive no constitutional difference, with respect to the geographical distribution of state legislative representation, between the two houses of a bicameral state legislature.

We do not believe that the concept of bicameralism is rendered anachronistic and meaningless when the predominant basis of representation in the two state legislative bodies is required to be the same—population. A prime reason for bicameralism, modernly considered, is to insure mature and deliberate consideration of, and to prevent precipitate action on, proposed legislative measures. Simply because the controlling criterion for apportioning representation is required to be the same in both houses does not mean that there will be no differences in the composition and complexion of the two bodies. Different constituencies can be represented in the two houses. One body could be composed of single-member districts while the other could have at least some multimember districts. The length of terms of the legislators in the separate bodies could differ. The numerical size of the two bodies could be made to differ, even significantly, and the geographical size of districts from which legislators are elected could also be made to differ. And apportionment in one house could be arranged so as to balance off minor inequities in the representation of certain areas in the other house. In summary, these and other factors could be, and are presently in many States, utilized to engender differing complexions and collective attitudes in the two bodies of a state legislature, although both are apportioned substantially on a population basis.

Elitism

THE REPUBLIC

Plato

427–347 B.C.

Plato's political philosophy is set forth in the *Republic*, the *Statesman*, and the *Laws*. The *Republic* and the *Laws* are his two longest works and, of these, the *Republic* is by far the greater. It is safe to say that, in the history of western culture, no other work, apart from the *Bible*, has been as widely read and studied through the centuries or as influential.

The *Republic* is much more than a political treatise. In it, Plato presents his views on ethics and metaphysics, on art, on education, and on the many ramifications of his entire philosophy. Not only is it endlessly rich in insight, it ranks as a literary masterpiece. The passages which follow have been selected because they bear directly on his social and political philosophy.

The basic difference between the *Laws* and the *Republic* is that in the *Republic* Plato sets out to define the ideal state without reference to time and place or the possibility of its realization; in the *Laws* he describes the best possible kind of state under the conditions prevalent in Greece as he knew it. Neither the *Laws* nor the *Statesman* declare that a society is best governed when it is under the rule of an intellectual elite. This is the thesis of the *Republic*.

Plato was born into a distinguished and prosperous Athenian family. He had an aristocrat's natural distaste for democracy. His experience with democracy was limited to Athenian democracy during the period following Athens' defeat in the disastrous Peloponnesian Wars, hardly a time in which any form of government could function to best advantage. His revered master, Socrates, had been tried and condemned by this same democracy. This helps us understand Plato's contempt for democracy and his preference for the alternative described in the following selections. Because of the unique place of the *Republic* in the literature of the humanities, this selection is by far the most extensive in this volume. The whole dialogue is recited by Socrates on the day after it took place to a small group of friends. Its avowed purpose, which leads to a description of the ideal state, is to define the meaning of justice.

BOOK II

. . .

A State, I said, arises, as I conceive, out of the needs of mankind; no one is self-sufficing, but all of us have many wants. Can any other origin of a State be imagined?

There can be no other.

Then, as we have many wants, and many persons are needed to supply them, one takes a helper for one purpose and another for another; and when these partners and helpers are gathered together in one habitation the body of inhabitants is termed a State.

True, he said.

And they exchange with one another, and one gives, and another receives, under the idea that the exchange will be for their good.

Very true.

Then, I said, let us begin and create in idea a State; and yet the true creator is necessity, who is the mother of our invention.

Of course, he replied.

Now the first and greatest of necessities is food, which is the condition of life and existence.

Certainly.

The second is a dwelling, and the third clothing and the like.

True.

And now let us see how our city will be able to supply this great demand: We may suppose that one man is a husbandman, another a builder, some one else a weaver—shall we add to them a shoemaker, or perhaps some other purveyor to our bodily wants?

Quite right.

The barest notion of a State must include four or five men.

Clearly.

And how will they proceed? Will each bring the result of his labours into a common stock?—the individual husbandman, for example, producing for four, and labouring four times as long and as much as he need in the provision of food with which he supplies others as well as himself; or will he have nothing to do with others and not be at the trouble of producing for them, but provide for himself alone a fourth of the food in a fourth of the time, and in the remaining three-

Plato, from *The Republic*, trans. Benjamin Jowett (London, 1894), Books II, III, IV. V, VI, and VIII.

fourths of his time be employed in making a house or a coat or a pair of shoes, having no partnership with others, but supplying himself all his own wants?

Adeimantus thought that he should aim at producing food only and not at producing everything.

Probably, I replied, that would be the better way; and when I hear you say this, I am myself reminded that we are not all alike; there are diversities of natures among us which are adapted to different occupations.

Very true.

And will you have a work better done when the workman has many occupations, or when he has only one?

When he has only one.

Further, there can be no doubt that a work is spoilt when not done at the right time?

No doubt.

For business is not disposed to wait until the doer of the business is at leisure; but the doer must follow up what he is doing, and make the business his first object.

He must.

And if so, we must infer that all things are produced more plentifully and easily and of a better quality when one man does one thing which is natural to him and does it at the right time, and leaves other things.

Undoubtedly.

Then more than four citizens will be required; for the husbandman will not make his own plough or mattock, or other implements of agriculture, if they are to be good for anything. Neither will the builder make his tools—and he too needs many; and in like manner the weaver and shoemaker.

Not to mention the importers and exporters, who are called merchants?

Yes.

Then we shall want merchants?

We shall.

And if merchandise is to be carried over the sea, skilful sailors will also be needed, and in considerable numbers?

Yes, in considerable numbers.

Suppose now that a husbandman, or an artisan, brings some production to market, and he comes at a time when there is no one to exchange with him,—is he to leave his calling and sit idle in the market-place?

Not at all; he will find people there who, seeing the want, undertake the office of salesmen. In well-ordered States they are commonly those who are the weakest in bodily strength, and therefore of little use for any other purpose; their duty is to be in the market, and to give money in exchange for goods to those who desire to sell and to take money from those who desire to buy.

This want, then, creates a class of retail-traders in our State. Is not 'retailer' the term which is applied to those who sit in the market-place engaged in buying and selling, while those who wander from one city to another are called merchants?

Yes, he said.

And there is another class of servants, who are intellectually hardly on the level of companionship; still they have plenty of bodily strength for labour, which accordingly they sell, and are called, if I do not mistake, hirelings, hire being the name which is given to the price of their labour.

True.

.   .   .

And our State must once more enlarge; and this time the enlargement will be nothing short of a whole army, which will have to go out and fight with the invaders for all that we have, as well as for the things and persons whom we were describing above.

Why? he said; are they not capable of defending themselves?

No, I said; not if we were right in the principle which was acknowledged by all of us when we were framing the State: The principle, as you will remember, was that one man cannot practise many arts with success.

.   .   .

Then we have found the desired natures; and now that we have found them, how are they to be reared and educated? Is not this an enquiry which may be expected to throw light on the greater enquiry which is our final end—How do justice and injustice grow up in States? for we do not want either to omit what is to the point or to draw out the argument to an inconvenient length.

Adeimantus thought that the enquiry would be of great service to us.

Then, I said, my dear friend, the task must not be given up, even if somewhat long.

Certainly not.

Come then, and let us pass a leisure hour in storytelling, and our story shall be the education of our heroes.

By all means.

And what shall be their education? Can we find a better than the traditional sort?—and this has two divisions, gymnastic for the body, and music for the soul.

True.

Shall we begin education with music, and go on to gymnastic afterwards?

By all means.

And when you speak of music, do you include literature or not?

I do.

And literature may be either true or false?

Yes.

And the young shall be trained in both kinds, and we begin with the false?

I do not understand your meaning, he said.

You know, I said, that we begin by telling children stories which, though not wholly destitute of truth, are in the main fictitious; and these stories are told them when they are not of an age to learn gymnastics.

Very true.

That was my meaning when I said that we must teach music before gymnastics.

Quite right, he said.

You know also that the beginning is the most important part of any work, especially in the case of a young and tender thing; for that is the time at which the character is being formed and the desired impression is more readily taken.

Quite true.

And shall we just carelessly allow children to hear any casual tales which may be devised by casual persons, and to receive into their minds ideas for the most part the very opposite of those which we should wish them to have when they are grown up?

We cannot.

Then the first thing will be to establish a censorship of the writers of fiction, and let the censors receive any tale of fiction which is good, and reject the bad; and we will desire mothers and nurses to tell their children the authorized ones only. Let them fashion the mind with such tales, even more fondly than they mould the body with their hands; but most of those which are now in use must be discarded.

． ． ．

BOOK III

． ． ．

But shall our superintendence go no further, and are the poets only to be required by us to express the image of the good in their works, on pain, if they do anything else, of expulsion from our State? Or is the same control to be extended to other artists, and are they also to be prohibited from exhibiting the opposite forms of vice and intemperance and meanness and indecency in sculpture and building and the other creative arts; and is he who cannot conform to this rule of ours to be prevented from practising his art in our State, lest the taste of our citizens be corrupted by him? We would not have our guardians grow up amid images of moral deformity, as in some noxious pasture, and there browse and feed upon many a baneful herb and flower day by day, little by little, until they silently gather a festering mass of corruption in their own soul. Let our artists rather be those who are gifted to discern the true nature of the beautiful and graceful; then will our youth dwell in a land of health, amid fair sights and sounds, and receive the good in everything; and beauty, the effluence of fair

works, shall flow into the eye and ear, like a health-giving breeze from a purer
region, and insensibly draw the soul from earliest years into likeness and sympathy with the beauty of reason.

There can be no nobler training than that, he replied.

And therefore, I said, Glaucon, musical training is a more potent instrument
than any other, because rhythm and harmony find their way into the inward
places of the soul, on which they mightily fasten, imparting grace, and making
the soul of him who is rightly educated graceful, or of him who is ill-educated
ungraceful; and also because he who has received this true education of the inner
being will most shrewdly perceive omissions or faults in art and nature, and with
a true taste, while he praises and rejoices over and receives into his soul the
good, and becomes noble and good, he will justly blame and hate the bad, now in
the days of his youth, even before he is able to know the reason why; and when
reason comes he will recognize and salute the friend with whom his education
has made him long familiar.

Yes, he said, I quite agree with you in thinking that our youth should be
trained in music and on the grounds which you mention.

And as there are two principles of human nature, one the spirited and the
other the philosophical, some God, as I should say, has given mankind two arts
answering to them (and only indirectly to the soul and body), in order that these
two principles (like the strings of an instrument) may be relaxed or drawn
tighter until they are duly harmonized.

That appears to be the intention.

And he who mingles music with gymnastic in the fairest proportions, and
best attempers them to the soul, may be rightly called the true musician and
harmonist in a far higher sense than the tuner of the strings.

You are quite right, Socrates.

And such a presiding genius will be always required in our State if the
government is to last.

Yes, he will be absolutely necessary.

Such, then, are our principles of nurture and education: Where would be
the use of going into further details about the dances of our citizens, or about
their hunting and coursing, their gymnastic and equestrian contests? For these
all follow the general principle, and having found that, we shall have no difficulty
in discovering them.

I dare say that there will be no difficulty.

Very good, I said; then what is the next question? Must we not ask who are
to be rulers and who subjects?

Certainly.

There can be no doubt that the elder must rule the younger.

Clearly.

And that the best of these must rule.

That is also clear.

Now, are not the best husbandmen those who are most devoted to husbandry?

Yes.

And as we are to have the best of guardians for our city, must they not be those who have most the character of guardians?

Yes.

And to this end they ought to be wise and efficient, and to have a special care of the State?

True.

And a man will be most likely to care about that which he loves?

To be sure.

And he will be most likely to love that which he regards as having the same interests with himself, and that of which the good or evil fortune is supposed by him at any time most to affect his own?

Very true, he replied.

Then there must be a selection. Let us note among the guardians those who in their whole life show the greatest eagerness to do what is for the good of their country, and the greatest repugnance to do what is against her interests.

Those are the right men.

And they will have to be watched at every stage, in order that we may see whether they preserve their resolution, and never, under the influence either of force or enchantment, forget or cast off their sense of duty to the State.

. . .

Therefore, as I was just now saying, we must inquire who are the best guardians of their own conviction that what they think the interest of the State is to be the rule of their lives. We must watch them from their youth upwards, and make them perform actions in which they are most likely to forget or to be deceived, and he who remembers and is not deceived is to be selected, and he who fails in the trial is to be rejected. That will be the way?

Yes.

And there should also be toils and pains and conflicts prescribed for them, in which they will be made to give further proof of the same qualities.

Very right, he replied.

And then, I said, we must try them with enchantments—that is the third sort of test—and see what will be their behaviour: like those who take colts amid noise and tumult to see if they are of a timid nature, so must we take our youth amid terrors of some kind, and again pass them into pleasures, and prove them more thoroughly than gold is proved in the furnace, that we may discover whether they are armed against all enchantments, and of a noble bearing always, good guardians of themselves and of the music which they have learned, and retaining under all circumstances a rhythmical and harmonious nature, such as will be most serviceable to the individual and to the State. And he who at every age, as boy and youth and in mature life, has come out of the trial victorious and pure, shall be appointed a ruler and guardian of the State; he shall be honoured

in life and death, and shall receive sepulture and other memorials of honour, the
greatest that we have to give. But him who fails, we must reject. I am inclined to
think that this is the sort of way in which our rulers and guardians should be
chosen and appointed. I speak generally, and not with any pretension to exact-
ness.

And speaking generally, I agree with you, he said.

And perhaps the word 'guardian' in the fullest sense ought to be applied to
this higher class only who preserve us against foreign enemies and maintain
peace among our citizens at home, that the one may not have the will, or the
others the power, to harm us. The young men whom we before called guardians
may be more properly designated auxiliaries and supporters of the principles of
the rulers.

I agree with you, he said.

How then may we devise one of those needful falsehoods of which we lately
spoke—just one royal lie which may deceive the rulers, if that be possible, and at
any rate the rest of the city?

What sort of lie? he said.

Nothing new, I replied; only an old Phoenician tale of what has often occurred before now in other places, (as the poets say, and have made the world
believe,) though not in our time, and I do not know whether such an event could
ever happen again, or could now even be made probable, if it did.

How your words seem to hesitate on your lips!

You will not wonder, I replied, at my hesitation when you have heard.

Speak, he said, and fear not.

Well, then, I will speak, although I really know not how to look you in the
face, or in what words to utter the audacious fiction, which I propose to commu-
nicate gradually, first to the rulers, then to the soldiers, and lastly to the people.
They are to be told that their youth was a dream, and the education and training
which they received from us, an appearance only; in reality during all that time
they were being formed and fed in the womb of the earth, where they themselves
and their arms and appurtenances were manufactured; when they were completed, the earth, their mother, sent them up; and so, their country being their
mother and also their nurse, they are bound to advise for her good, and to defend her against attacks, and her citizens they are to regard as children of the
earth and their own brothers.

You had good reason, he said, to be ashamed of the lie which you were
going to tell.

True, I replied, but there is more coming; I have only told you half. Citizens, we shall say to them in our tale, you are brothers, yet God has framed you
differently. Some of you have the power of command, and in the composition of
these he has mingled gold, wherefore also they have the greatest honour; others
he has made of silver, to be auxiliaries; others again who are to be husbandmen
and craftsmen he has composed of brass and iron; and the species will generally
be preserved in the children. But as all are of the same original stock, a golden

parent will sometimes have a silver son, or a silver parent a golden son. And God proclaims as a first principle to the rulers, and above all else, that there is nothing which they should so anxiously guard, or of which they are to be such good guardians, as of the purity of the race. They should observe what elements mingle in their offspring; for if the son of a golden or silver parent has an admixture of brass and iron, then nature orders a transposition of ranks, and the eye of the ruler must not be pitiful towards the child because he has to descend in the scale and become a husbandman or artisan, just as there may be sons of artisans who having an admixture of gold or silver in them are raised to honour, and become guardians or auxiliaries. For an oracle says that when a man of brass or iron guards the State, it will be destroyed. Such is the tale; is there any possibility of making our citizens believe in it?

Not in the present generation, he replied; there is no way of accomplishing this; but their sons may be made to believe in the tale, and their sons' sons, and posterity after them.

I see the difficulty, I replied; yet the fostering of such a belief will make them care more for the city and for one another. Enough, however, of the fiction, which may now fly abroad upon the wings of rumour, while we arm our earth-born heroes, and lead them forth under the command of their rulers. Let them look round and select a spot whence they can best suppress insurrection, if any prove refractory within, and also defend themselves against enemies, who like wolves may come down on the fold from without; there let them encamp, and when they have encamped, let them sacrifice to the proper Gods and prepare their dwellings.

Just so, he said.

And their dwellings must be such as will shield them against the cold of winter and the heat of summer.

I suppose that you mean houses, he replied.

Yes, I said; but they must be the houses of soldiers, and not of shop-keepers.

What is the difference? he said.

That I will endeavour to explain, I replied. To keep watch-dogs, who, from want of discipline or hunger, or some evil habit or other, would turn upon the sheep and worry them, and behave not like dogs but wolves, would be a foul and monstrous thing in a shepherd?

Truly monstrous, he said.

And therefore every care must be taken that our auxiliaries, being stronger than our citizens, may not grow to be too much for them and become savage tyrants instead of friends and allies?

Yes, great care should be taken.

And would not a really good education furnish the best safeguard?

But they are well-educated already, he replied.

I cannot be so confident, my dear Glaucon, I said; I am much more certain that they ought to be, and that true education, whatever that may be, will have the greatest tendency to civilize and humanize them in their relations to one another, and to those who are under their protection.

Very true, he replied.

And not only their education, but their habitations, and all that belongs to them, should be such as will neither impair their virtue as guardian, nor tempt them to prey upon the other citizens. Any man of sense must acknowledge that.

He must.

Then now let us consider what will be their way of life, if they are to realize our idea of them. In the first place, none of them should have any property of his own beyond what is absolutely necessary; neither should they have a private house or store closed against any one who has a mind to enter; their provisions should be only such as are required by trained warriors, who are men of temperance and courage; they should agree to receive from the citizens a fixed rate of pay, enough to meet the expenses of the year and no more; and they will go to mess and live together like soldiers in a camp. Gold and silver we will tell them that they have from God; the diviner metal is within them, and they have therefore no need of the dross which is current among men, and ought not to pollute the divine by any such earthly admixture; for that commoner metal has been the source of many unholy deeds, but their own is undefiled. And they alone of all the citizens may not touch or handle silver or gold, or be under the same roof with them, or wear them, or drink from them. And this will be their salvation, and they will be the saviours of the State. But should they ever acquire homes or lands or moneys of their own, they will become housekeepers and husbandmen instead of guardians, enemies and tyrants instead of allies of the other citizens; hating and being hated, plotting and being plotted against, they will pass their whole life in much greater terror of internal than of external enemies, and the hour of ruin, both to themselves and to the rest of the State, will be at hand. For all which reasons may we not say that thus all our State be ordered, and that these shall be the regulations appointed by us for our guardians concerning their houses and all other matters?

Yes, said Glaucon.

BOOK IV

Here Adeimantus interposed a question: How would you answer, Socrates, said he, if a person were to say that you are making these people miserable, and that they are the cause of their own unhappiness; the city in fact belongs to them, but they are none the better for it; whereas other men acquire lands, and build large and handsome houses, and have everything handsome about them, offering sacrifices to the gods on their own account, and practising hospitality; moreover, as you were saying just now, they have gold and silver, and all that is usual

among the favourites of fortune; but our poor citizens are no better than mercenaries who are quartered in the city and are always mounting guard?

Yes, I said; and you may add that they are only fed, and not paid in addition to their food, like other men; and therefore they cannot, if they would, take
a journey of pleasure; they have no money to spend on a mistress or any other
luxurious fancy, which, as the world goes, is thought to be happiness; and many
other accusations of the same nature might be added.

But, said he, let us suppose all this to be included in the charge.

You mean to ask, I said, what will be our answer?

Yes.

If we proceed along the old path, my belief, I said, is that we shall find the
answer. And our answer will be that, even as they are, our guardians may very
likely be the happiest of men; but that our aim in founding the State was not the
disproportionate happiness of any one class, but the greatest happiness of the
whole; we thought that in a State which is ordered with a view to the good of the
whole we should be most likely to find justice, and in the ill-ordered State injustice: and, having found them, we might then decide which of the two is the happier. At present, I take it, we are fashioning the happy State, not piecemeal, or
with a view of making a few happy citizens, but as a whole; and by and by we
will proceed to view the opposite kind of State. Suppose that we were painting a
statue, and some one came up to us and said, Why do you not put the most beautiful colours on the most beautiful parts of the body—the eyes ought to be purple,
but you have made them black—to him we might fairly answer, Sir, you would
not surely have us beautify the eyes to such a degree that they are no longer
eyes; consider rather whether, by giving this and the other features their due
proportion, we make the whole beautiful. And so I say to you, do not compel us
to assign to the guardians a sort of happiness which will make them anything but
guardians; for we too can clothe our husbandmen in royal apparel, and set
crowns of gold on their heads, and bid them till the ground as much as they like,
and no more. Our potters also might be allowed to repose on couches, and feast
by the fireside, passing round the winecup, while their wheel is conveniently at
hand, and working at pottery only as much as they like; in this way we might
make every class happy—and then, as you imagine, the whole State would be
happy. But do not put this idea into our heads; for, if we listen to you, the
husbandman will be no longer a husbandman, the potter will cease to be a
potter, and no one will have the character of any distinct class in the State.
Now that is not of much consequence where the corruption of society, and
pretension to be what you are not, is confined to cobblers; but when the guardians of the laws and of the government are only seeming and not real guardians, then see how they turn the State upside down; and on the other hand
they alone have the power of giving order and happiness to the State. We mean
our guardians to be true saviours and not the destroyers of the State, whereas
our opponent is thinking of peasants at a festival, who are enjoying a life of
revelry, not of citizens who are doing their duty to the State. But if so, we mean

different things, and he is speaking of something which is not a State. And therefore we must consider whether in appointing our guardians we would look to
their greatest happiness individually, or whether this principle of happiness does
not rather reside in the State as a whole. But if the latter be the truth, then the
guardians and auxiliaries, and all others equally with them, must be compelled or
induced to do their own work in the best way. And thus the whole State will grow
up in a noble order, and the several classes will receive the proportion of happiness which nature assigns to them.

I think that you are quite right.

I wonder whether you will agree with another remark which occurs to me.

What may that be?

There seem to be two causes of the deterioration of the arts.

What are they?

Wealth, I said, and poverty.

How do they act?

The process is as follows: When a potter becomes rich, will he, think you,
any longer take the same pains with his art?

Certainly not.

He will grow more and more indolent and careless?

Very true.

And the result will be that he becomes a worse potter?

Yes; he greatly deteriorates.

But, on the other hand, if he has no money, and cannot provide himself with
tools or instruments, he will not work equally well himself, nor will he teach his
sons or apprentices to work equally well.

Certainly not.

Then, under the influence either of poverty or of wealth, workmen and their
work are equally liable to degenerate?

That is evident.

Here, then, is a discovery of new evils, I said, against which the guardians
will have to watch, or they will creep into the city unobserved.

What evils?

Wealth, I said, and poverty; the one is the parent of luxury and indolence,
and the other of meanness and viciousness, and both of discontent.

.   .   .

The time then has arrived, Glaucon, when, like huntsmen, we should surround the cover, and look sharp that justice does not steal away, and pass out of
sight and escape us; for beyond a doubt she is somewhere in this country: watch
therefore and strive to catch a sight of her, and if you see her first, let me know.

Would that I could! but you should regard me rather as a follower who has
just eyes enough to see what you show him—that is about as much as I am good
for.

Offer up a prayer with me and follow.

I will, but you must show me the way.

Here is no path, I said, and the wood is dark and perplexing; still we must push on.

Let us push on.

Here I saw something: Halloo! I said, I begin to perceive a track, and I believe that the quarry will not escape.

Good news, he said.

Truly, I said, we are stupid fellows.

Why so?

Why, my good sir, at the beginning of our inquiry, ages ago, there was justice tumbling out at our feet, and we never saw her; nothing could be more ridiculous. Like people who go about looking for what they have in their hands—that was the way with us—we looked not at what we were seeking, but at what was far off in the distance; and therefore, I suppose, we missed her.

What do you mean?

I mean to say that in reality for a long time past we have been talking of justice, and have failed to recognize her.

I grow impatient at the length of your exordium.

Well then, tell me, I said, whether I am right or not: You remember the original principle which we were always laying down at the foundation of the State, that one man should practise one thing only, the thing to which his nature was best adapted;—now justice is this principle or a part of it.

Yes, we often said that one man should do one thing only.

Further, we affirmed that justice was doing one's own business, and not being a busybody; we said so again and again, and many others have said the same to us.

Yes, we said so.

Then to do one's own business in a certain way may be assumed to be justice. Can you tell me whence I derive this inference?

I cannot, but I should like to be told.

Because I think that this is the only virtue which remains in the State when the other virtues of temperance and courage and wisdom are abstracted; and, that this is the ultimate cause and condition of the existence of all of them, and while remaining in them is also their preservative; and we were saying that if the three were discovered by us, justice would be the fourth or remaining one.

That follows of necessity.

If we are asked to determine which of these four qualities by its presence contributes most to the excellence of the State, whether the agreement of rulers and subjects, or the preservation in the soldiers of the opinion which the law ordains about the true nature of dangers, or wisdom and watchfulness in the rulers, or whether this other which I am mentioning, and which is found in children and women, slave and freeman, artisan, ruler, subject,—the quality, I mean, of every one doing his own work, and not being a busybody, would claim the palm—the question is not so easily answered.

Certainly, he replied, there would be a difficulty in saying which.

Then the power of each individual in the State to do his own work appears to compete with the other political virtues, wisdom, temperance, courage.

Yes, he said.

And the virtue which enters into this competition is justice?

Exactly.

Let us look at the question from another point of view: Are not the rulers in a State those to whom you would entrust the office of determining suits at law?

Certainly.

And are suits decided on any other ground but that a man may neither take what is another's, nor be deprived of what is his own?

Yes; that is their principle.

Which is a just principle?

Yes.

Then on this view also justice will be admitted to be the having and doing what is a man's own, and belongs to him?

Very true.

Think, now, and say whether you agree with me or not. Suppose a carpenter to be doing the business of a cobbler, or a cobbler of a carpenter; and suppose them to exchange their implements or their duties, or the same person to be doing the work of both, or whatever be the change; do you think that any great harm would result to the State?

Not much.

But when the cobbler or any other man whom nature designed to be a trader, having his heart lifted up by wealth or strength or the number of his followers, or any like advantage, attempts to force his way into the class of warriors, or a warrior into that of legislators and guardians, for which he is unfitted, and either to take the implements or the duties of the other; or when one man is trader, legislator, and warrior all in one, then I think you will agree with me in saying that this interchange and this meddling of one with another is the ruin of the State.

Most true.

Seeing then, I said, that there are three distinct classes, any meddling of one with another, or the change of one into another, is the greatest harm to the State, and may be most justly termed evil-doing?

Precisely.

And the greatest degree of evil-doing to one's own city would be termed by you injustice?

Certainly.

This then is injustice; and on the other hand when the trader, the auxiliary, and the guardian each do their own business, that is justice, and will make the city just.

I agree with you.

BOOK V

. . .

. . . I suppose that I must retrace my steps and say what I perhaps ought to have said before in the proper place. The part of the men has been played out, and now properly enough comes the turn of the women. Of them I will proceed to speak, and the more readily since I am invited by you.

For men born and educated like our citizens, the only way, in my opinion, of arriving at a right conclusion about the possession and use of women and children is to follow the path on which we originally started, when we said that the men were to be the guardians and watchdogs of the herd.

True.

Let us further suppose the birth and education of our women to be subject to similar or nearly similar regulations; then we shall see whether the result accords with our design.

What do you mean?

What I mean may be put into the form of a question, I said: Are dogs divided into hes and shes, or do they both share equally in hunting and in keeping watch and in the other duties of dogs? or do we entrust to the males the entire and exclusive care of the flocks, while we leave the females at home, under the idea that the bearing and suckling their puppies is labour enough for them?

No, he said, they share alike; the only difference between them is that the males are stronger and the females weaker.

But can you use different animals for the same purpose, unless they are bred and fed in the same way?

You cannot.

Then, if women are to have the same duties as men, they must have the same nurture and education?

Yes.

The education which was assigned to the men was music and gymnastic.

Yes.

Then women must be taught music and gymnastic and also the art of war, which they must practise like the men?

That is the inference, I suppose.

. . .

And if . . . the male and the female sex appear to differ in their fitness for any art or pursuit, we should say that such pursuit or art ought to be assigned to one or the other of them; but if the difference consists only in women bearing and men begetting children, this does not amount to a proof that a woman differs from a man in respect of the sort of education she should receive; and we shall therefore continue to maintain that our guardians and their wives ought to have the same pursuits.

Very true, he said.

• • •

One woman has a gift of healing, another not; one is a musician, and another has no music in her nature?

Very true.

And one woman has a turn for gymnastic and military exercises, and another is unwarlike and hates gymnastics?

Certainly.

And one woman is a philosopher, and another is an enemy of philosophy; one has spirit, and another is without spirit?

That is also true.

Then one woman will have the temper of a guardian, and another not. Was not the selection of the male guardians determined by differences of this sort?

Yes.

Men and women alike possess the qualities which make a guardian; they differ only in their comparative strength or weakness.

Obviously.

And those women who have such qualities are to be selected as the companions and colleagues of men who have similar qualities and whom they resemble in capacity and in character?

Very true.

And ought not the same natures to have the same pursuits?

They ought.

Then, as we were saying before, there is nothing unnatural in assigning music and gymnastic to the wives of the guardians—to that point we come round again.

• • •

Yes, that was a mighty wave which you have escaped.

Yes, I said, but a greater is coming; you will not think much of this when you see the next.

Go on; let me see.

The law, I said, which is the sequel of this and of all that has preceded, is to the following effect,—'that the wives of our guardians are to be common, and their children are to be common, and no parent is to know his own child, nor any child his parent.'

Yes, he said, that is a much greater wave than the other; and the possibility as well as the utility of such a law are far more questionable.

I do not think, I said, that there can be any dispute about the very great utility of having wives and children in common; the possibility is quite another matter, and will be very much disputed.

• • •

. . . I think that if our rulers and their auxiliaries are to be worthy of the name which they bear, there must be willingness to obey in the one and the power of command in the other; the guardians must themselves obey the laws, and they must also imitate the spirit of them in any details which are entrusted to their care.

That is right, he said.

You, I said, who are their legislator, having selected the men, will now select the women and give them to them;—they must be as far as possible of like natures with them; and they must live in common houses and meet at common meals. None of them will have anything specially his or her own; they will be together, and will be brought up together, and will associate at gymnastic exercises. And so they will be drawn by a necessity of their natures to have intercourse with each other—necessity is not too strong a word, I think?

Yes, he said;—necessity, not geometrical, but another sort of necessity which lovers know, and which is far more convincing and constraining to the mass of mankind.

True, I said; and this, Glaucon, like all the rest, must proceed after an orderly fashion; in a city of the blessed, licentiousness is an unholy thing which the rulers will forbid.

Yes, he said, and it ought not to be permitted.

Then clearly the next thing will be to make matrimony sacred in the highest degree, and what is most beneficial will be deemed sacred?

Exactly.

And how can marriages be made most beneficial?—that is a question which I put to you, because I see in your house dogs for hunting, and of the nobler sort of birds not a few. Now, I beseech you, do tell me, have you ever attended to their pairing and breeding?

In what particulars?

Why, in the first place, although they are all of a good sort, are not some better than others?

True.

And do you breed from them all indifferently, or do you take care to breed from the best only?

From the best.

And do you take the oldest or the youngest, or only those of ripe age?

I choose only those of ripe age.

And if care was not taken in the breeding, your dogs and birds would greatly deteriorate?

Certainly.

And the same of horses and of animals in general?

Undoubtedly.

Good heavens! my dear friend, I said, what consummate skill will our rulers need if the same principle holds of the human species!

Certainly, the same principle holds; but why does this involve any particular skill?

Because, I said, our rulers will often have to practise upon the body corporate with medicines. Now you know that when patients do not require medicines, but have only to be put under a regimen, the inferior sort of practitioner is deemed to be good enough; but when medicine has to be given, then the doctor should be more of a man.

That is quite true, he said; but to what are you alluding?

I mean, I replied, that our rulers will find a considerable dose of falsehood and deceit necessary for the good of their subjects: we were saying that the use of all these things regarded as medicines might be of advantage.

And we were very right.

And this lawful use of them seems likely to be often needed in the regulations of marriages and births.

How so?

Why, I said, the principle has been already laid down that the best of either sex should be united with the best as often, and the inferior with the inferior, as seldom as possible; and that they should rear the offspring of the one sort of union, but not of the other if the flock is to be maintained in first-rate condition. Now these goings-on must be a secret which the rulers only know, or there will be a further danger of our herd, as the guardians may be termed, breaking out into rebellion.

Very true.

Had we not better appoint certain festivals at which we will bring together the brides and bridegrooms, and sacrifices will be offered and suitable hymeneal songs composed by our poets: the number of weddings is a matter which must be left to the discretion of the rulers, whose aim will be to preserve the average of population? There are many other things which they will have to consider, such as the effects of wars and diseases and any similar agencies, in order as far as this is possible to prevent the State from becoming either too large or too small.

Certainly, he replied.

We shall have to invent some ingenious kind of lots which the less worthy may draw on each occasion of our bringing them together, and then they will accuse their own ill-luck and not the rulers.

To be sure, he said.

And I think that our braver and better youth, besides their other honours and rewards, might have greater facilities of intercourse with women given them; their bravery will be a reason, and such fathers ought to have as many sons as possible.

True.

And the proper officers, whether male or female or both, for offices are to be held by women as well as by men—

Yes—

The proper officers will take the offspring of the good parents to the pen or fold, and there they will deposit them with certain nurses who dwell in a separate quarter; but the offspring of the inferior, or of the better when they chance to be deformed, will be put away in some mysterious, unknown place, as they should be.

Yes, he said, that must be done if the breed of the guardians is to be kept pure.

They will provide for their nurture, and will bring the mothers to the fold when they are full of milk, taking the greatest possible care that no mother recognizes her own child; and other wet-nurses may be engaged if more are required. Care will also be taken that the process of suckling shall not be protracted too long; and the mothers will have no getting up at night or other trouble, but will hand over all this sort of thing to the nurses and attendants.

You suppose the wives of our guardians to have a fine easy time of it when they are having children.

.   .   .

Did you ever know an example in any other State of a ruler who would speak of one of his colleagues as his friend and of another as not being his friend?

Yes, very often.

And the friend he regards and describes as one in whom he has an interest, and the other as a stranger in whom he has no interest?

Exactly.

But would any of your guardians think or speak of any other guardian as a stranger?

Certainly he would not; for every one whom they meet will be regarded by them either as a brother or sister, or father or mother, or son or daughter, or as the child or parent of those who are thus connected with him.

Capital, I said; but let me ask you once more: Shall they be a family in name only; or shall they in all their actions be true to the name? For example, in the use of the word 'father', would the care of a father be implied and the filial reverence and duty and obedience to him which the law commands; and is the violator of these duties to be regarded as an impious and unrighteous person who is not likely to receive much good either at the hands of God or of man? Are these to be or not to be the strains which the children will hear repeated in their ears by all the citizens about those who are intimated to them to be their parents and the rest of their kinsfolk?

These, he said, and none other; for what can be more ridiculous than for them to utter the names of family ties with the lips only and not to act in the spirit of them?

Then in our city the language of harmony and concord will be more often heard than in any other. As I was describing before, when any one is well or ill, the universal word will be 'with me it is well' or 'it is ill'.

Most true.

And agreeably to this mode of thinking and speaking, were we not saying that they will have their pleasures and pains in common?

Yes, and so they will.

And they will have a common interest in the same thing which they will alike call 'my own', and having this common interest they will have a common feeling of pleasure and pain?

Yes, far more so than in other States.

And the reason of this, over and above the general constitution of the State, will be that the guardians will have a community of women and children?

That will be the chief reason.

And this unity of feeling we admitted to be the greatest good, as was implied in our own comparison of a well-ordered State to the relation of the body and the members, when affected by pleasure or pain?

That we acknowledged, and very rightly.

Then the community of wives and children among our citizens is clearly the source of the greatest good to the State?

Certainly.

And this agrees with the other principle which we were affirming,—that the guardians were not to have houses or lands or any other property; their pay was to be their food, which they were to receive from the other citizens, and they were to have no private expenses; for we intended them to preserve their true character of guardians.

Right, he replied.

Both the community of property and the community of families, as I am saying, tend to make them more truly guardians; they will not tear the city in pieces by differing about 'mine' and 'not mine'; each man dragging any acquisition which he has made into a separate house of his own, where he has a separate wife and children and private pleasures and pains; but all will be affected as far as may be by the same pleasures and pains because they are all of one opinion about what is near and dear to them, and therefore they all tend towards a common end.

Certainly, he replied.

And as they have nothing but their persons which they can call their own, suits and complaints will have no existence among them; they will be delivered from all those quarrels of which money or children or relations are the occasion.

.   .   .

You agree then, I said, that men and women are to have a common way of life such as we have described—common education, common children; and they are to watch over the citizens in common whether abiding in the city or going out to war; they are to keep watch together, and to hunt together like dogs; and always and in all things, as far as they are able, women are to share with the men? And in so doing they will do what is best, and will not violate, but preserve the natural relation of the sexes.

.   .   .

Now then, I said, I go to meet that which I liken to the greatest of the waves; yet shall the word be spoken, even though the wave break and drown me in laughter and dishonour; and do you mark my words.

Proceed.

I said: *Until philosophers are kings, or the kings and princes of this world have the spirit and power of philosophy, and political greatness and wisdom meet in one, and those commoner natures who pursue either to the exclusion of the other are compelled to stand aside, cities will never have rest from their evils,—no, nor the human race, as I believe,—and then only will this our State have a possibility of life and behold the light of day.* Such was the thought, my dear Glaucon, which I would fain have uttered if it had not seemed too extravagant; for to be convinced that in no other State can there be happiness private or public is indeed a hard thing.

.   .   .

Then now for a definition, he said.

Follow me, I said, and I hope that I may in some way or other be able to give you a satisfactory explanation.

Proceed.

.   .   .

. . . [M]ay we not say of the philosopher that he is a lover, not of a part of wisdom only, but of the whole?

Yes, of the whole.

And he who dislikes learning, especially in youth, when he has no power of judging what is good and what is not, such an one we maintain not to be a philosopher or a lover of knowledge, just as he who refuses his food is not hungry, and may be said to have a bad appetite and not a good one?

Very true, he said.

Whereas he who has a taste for every sort of knowledge and who is curious to learn and is never satisfied, may be justly termed a philosopher? Am I not right?

Glaucon said: If curiosity makes a philosopher, you will find many a strange being will have a title to the name. All the lovers of sights have a delight in learning, and must therefore be included. Musical amateurs, too, are a folk strangely out of place among philosophers, for they are the last persons in the world who would come to anything like a philosophical discussion, if they could help, while they run about at the Dionysiac festivals as if they had let out their ears to hear every chorus; whether the performance is in town or country—that makes no difference—they are there. Now are we to maintain that all these and any who have similar tastes, as well as the professors of quite minor arts, are philosophers?

Certainly not, I replied; they are only an imitation.

He said: Who then are the true philosophers?

Those, I said, who are lovers of the vision of truth.

That is also good, he said; but I should like to know what you mean?

To another, I replied, I might have a difficulty in explaining; but I am sure that you will admit a proposition which I am about to make.

What is the proposition?

That since beauty is the opposite of ugliness, they are two?

Certainly.

And inasmuch as they are two, each of them is one?

True again.

And of just and unjust, good and evil, and of every other class, the same remark holds: taken singly, each of them is one; but from the various combinations of them with actions and things and with one another, they are seen in all sorts of lights and appear many?

Very true.

And this is the distinction which I draw between the sight-loving, art-loving, practical class and those of whom I am speaking, and who are alone worthy of the name of philosophers.

How do you distinguish them? he said.

The lovers of sounds and sights, I replied, are, as I conceive, fond of fine tones and colours and forms and all the artificial products that are made out of them, but their mind is incapable of seeing or loving absolute beauty.

True, he replied.

Few are they who are able to attain to the sight of this.

Very true.

And he who, having a sense of beautiful things has no sense of absolute beauty, or who, if another lead him to a knowledge of that beauty is unable to follow—of such a one I ask, Is he awake or in a dream only? Reflect: is not the dreamer, sleeping or waking, one who likens dissimilar things, who puts the copy in the place of the real object?

I should certainly say that such an one was dreaming.

But take the case of the other, who recognizes the existence of absolute beauty and is able to distinguish the idea from the objects which participate in the idea, neither putting the objects in the place of the idea nor the idea in the place of the objects—is he a dreamer, or is he awake?

He is wide awake.

And may we not say that the mind of the one who knows has knowledge, and that the mind of the other, who opines only, has opinion?

Certainly.

.   .   .

Then those who see the many beautiful, and who yet neither see absolute beauty, nor can follow any guide who points the way thither; who see the many just, and not absolute justice, and the like,—such persons may be said to have opinion but not knowledge?

That is certain.

But those who see the absolute and eternal and immutable may be said to know, and not to have opinion only?

Neither can that be denied.

The one love and embrace the subjects of knowledge, the other those of opinion? The latter are the same, as I dare say you will remember, who listened to sweet sounds and gazed upon fair colours, but would not tolerate the existence of absolute beauty.

Yes, I remember.

Shall we then be guilty of any impropriety in calling them lovers of opinion rather than lovers of wisdom, and will they be very angry with us for thus describing them?

I shall tell them not to be angry; no man should be angry at what is true.

But those who love the truth in each thing are to be called lovers of wisdom and not lovers of opinion.

Assuredly.

BOOK VI

. . .

And what is the next question? he asked.

Surely, I said, the one which follows next in order. Inasmuch as philosophers only are able to grasp the eternal and unchangeable, and those who wander in the region of the many and variable are not philosophers, I must ask you which of the two classes should be the rulers of our State?

And how can we rightly answer that question?

Whichever of the two are best able to guard the laws and institutions of our State—let them be our guardians.

Very good.

Neither, I said, can there be any question that the guardian who is to keep anything should have eyes rather than no eyes?

There can be no question of that.

And are not those who are verily and indeed wanting in the knowledge of the true being of each thing, and who have in their souls no clear pattern, and are unable as with a painter's eye to look at the absolute truth and to that original to repair, and having perfect vision of the other world to order the laws about beauty, goodness, justice in this, if not already ordered, and to guard and preserve the order of them—are not such persons, I ask, simply blind?

Truly, he replied, they are much in that condition.

And shall they be our guardians when there are others who, besides being their equals in experience and falling short of them in no particular of virtue, also know the very truth of each thing?

There can be no reason, he said, for rejecting those who have this greatest of all great qualities; they must always have the first place unless they fail in some other respect.

Suppose then, I said, that we determine how far they can unite this and the other excellences.

By all means.

In the first place, as we began by observing, the nature of the philospher has to be ascertained. We must come to an understanding about him, and, when we have done so, then, if I am not mistaken, we shall also acknowledge that such a union of qualities is possible, and that those in whom they are united, and those only, should be rulers in the State.

What do you mean?

Let us suppose that philosophical minds always love knowledge of a sort which shows them the eternal nature not varying from generation and corruption.

Agreed.

And further, I said, let us agree that they are lovers of all true being; there is no part whether greater or less, or more or less honourable, which they are willing to renounce; as we said before of the lover and the man of ambition.

True.

And if they are to be what we were describing, is there not another quality which they should also possess?

What quality?

Truthfulness: they will never intentionally receive into their mind falsehood, which is their detestation, and they will love the truth.

Yes, that may be safely affirmed of them.

'May be,' my friend, I replied, is not the word; say rather, 'must be affirmed': for he whose nature is amorous of anything cannot help loving all that belongs or is akin to the object of his affections.

Right, he said.

And is there anything more akin to wisdom than truth?

How can there be?

Can the same nature be a lover of wisdom and a lover of falsehood?

Never.

The true lover of learning then must from his earliest youth, as far as in him lies, desire all truth?

Assuredly.

But then again, as we know by experience, he whose desires are strong in one direction will have them weaker in others; they will be like a stream which has been drawn off into another channel.

True.

He whose desires are drawn towards knowledge in every form will be absorbed in the pleasures of the soul, and will hardly feel bodily pleasure—I mean, if he be a true philosopher and not a sham one.

That is most certain.

Such a one is sure to be temperate and the reverse of covetous; for the motives which make another man desirous of having and spending, have no place in his character.

Very true.

Another criterion of the philosophical nature has also to be considered.

What is that?

There should be no secret corner of illiberality; nothing can be more antagonistic than meanness to a soul which is ever longing after the whole of things both divine and human.

Most true, he replied.

Then how can he who has magnificence of mind and is the spectator of all time and all existence, think much of human life?

He cannot.

Or can such a one account death fearful?

No indeed.

Then the cowardly and mean nature has no part in true philosophy?

Certainly not.

Or again: can he who is harmoniously constituted, who is not covetous or mean, or a boaster, or a coward—can he, I say, ever be unjust or hard in his dealings?

Impossible.

Then you will soon observe whether a man is just and gentle, or rude and unsociable; these are the signs which distinguish even in youth the philosophical nature from the unphilosophical.

True.

There is another point which should be remarked.

What point?

Whether he has or has not a pleasure in learning; for no one will love that which gives him pain, and in which after much toil he makes little progress.

Certainly not.

And again, if he is forgetful and retains nothing of what he learns, will he not be an empty vessel?

That is certain.

Labouring in vain, he must end in hating himself and his fruitless occupation?

Yes.

Then a soul which forgets cannot be ranked among genuine philosophic natures; we must insist that the philosopher should have a good memory?

Certainly.

And once more, the inharmonious and unseemly nature can only tend to disproportion?

Undoubtedly.

And do you consider truth to be akin to proportion or to disproportion?

To proportion.

Then, besides other qualities, we must try to find a naturally well-proportioned and gracious mind, which will move spontaneously towards the true being of everything.

Certainly.

Well, and do not all these qualities, which we have been enumerating, go together, and are they not, in a manner, necessary to a soul, which is to have a full and perfect participation of being?

They are absolutely necessary, he replied.

And must not that be a blameless study which he only can pursue who has the gift of a good memory, and is quick to learn,—noble, gracious, the friend of truth, justice, courage, temperance, who are his kindred?

The god of jealousy himself, he said, could find no fault with such a study.

And to men like him, I said, when perfected by years and education, and to these only you will entrust the State.

Here Adeimantus interposed and said: To these statements, Socrates, no one can offer a reply; but when you talk in this way, a strange feeling passes over the minds of your hearers: They fancy that they are led astray a little at each step in the argument, owing to their own want of skill in asking and answering questions; these littles accumulate, and at the end of the discussion they are found to have sustained a mighty overthrow and all their former notions appear to be turned upside down. And as unskilful players of draughts are at last shut up by their more skilful adversaries and have no piece to move, so they too find themselves shut up at last; for they have nothing to say in this new game of which words are the counters; and yet all the time they are in the right. The observation is suggested to me by what is now occurring. For any one of us might say, that although in words he is not able to meet you at each step of the argument, he sees as a fact that the votaries of philosophy, when they carry on the study, not only in youth as a part of education, but as the pursuit of their maturer years, most of them become strange monsters, not to say utter rogues, and that those who may be considered the best of them are made useless to the world by the very study which you extol.

Well, and do you think that those who say so are wrong?

I cannot tell, he replied; but I should like to know what is your opinion.

Hear my answer; I am of opinion that they are quite right.

Then how can you be justified in saying that cities will not cease from evil until philosophers rule in them, when philosophers are acknowledged by us to be of no use to them?

You ask a question, I said, to which a reply can only be given in a parable.

Yes, Socrates; and that is a way of speaking to which you are not at all accustomed, I suppose.

I perceive, I said, that you are vastly amused at having plunged me into such a hopeless discussion; but now hear the parable, and then you will be still more amused at the meagreness of my imagination: for the manner in which the best men are treated in their own States is so grievous that no single thing on earth is comparable to it; and therefore, if I am to plead their cause, I must have recourse to fiction, and put together a figure made up of many things, like the fabulous unions of goats and stags which are found in pictures. Imagine then a fleet or a ship in which there is a captain who is taller and stronger than any of the crew, but he is a little deaf and has a similar infirmity in sight, and his knowledge of navigation is not much better. The sailors are quarrelling with one another about the steering—every one is of opinion that he has a right to steer, though he has never learned the art of navigation and cannot tell who taught him or when he learned, and will further assert that it cannot be taught, and they are ready to cut in pieces any one who says the contrary. They throng about the captain, begging and praying him to commit the helm to them; and if at any time they do not prevail, but others are preferred to them, they kill the others or throw them overboard, and having first chained up the noble captain's senses with drink or some narcotic drug, they mutiny and take possession of the ship and make free with the stores; thus, eating and drinking, they proceed on their voyage in such manner as might be expected of them. Him who is their partisan and cleverly aids them in their plot for getting the ship out of the captain's hands into their own whether by force or persuasion, they compliment with the name of sailor, pilot, able seaman, and abuse the other sort of man, whom they call a good-for-nothing; but that the true pilot must pay attention to the year and seasons and sky and stars and winds, and whatever else belongs to his art, if he intends to be really qualified for the command of a ship, and that he must and will be the steerer, whether other people like or not—the possibility of this union of authority with the steerer's art has never seriously entered into their thoughts or been made part of their calling. Now in vessels which are in a state of mutiny and by sailors who are mutineers, how will the true pilot be regarded? Will he not be called by them a prater, a star-gazer, a good-for-nothing?

Of course, said Adeimantus.

Then you will hardly need, I said, to hear the interpretation of the figure, which describes the true philosopher in his relation to the State; for you understand already.

Certainly.

Then suppose you now take this parable to the gentleman who is surprised at finding that philosophers have no honour in their cities; explain it to him and try to convince him that their having honour would be far more extraordinary.

I will.

Say to him, that, in deeming the best votaries of philosophy to be useless to the rest of the world, he is right; but also tell him to attribute their uselessness to the fault of those who will not use them, and not to themselves. The pilot should not humbly beg the sailors to be commanded by him—that is not the order of nature; neither are 'the wise to go to the doors of the rich'—the ingenious author of this saying told a lie—but the truth is, that, when a man is ill, whether he be rich or poor, to the physician he must go, and he who wants to be governed, to him who is able to govern. The ruler who is good for anything ought not to beg his subjects to be ruled by him; although the present governors of mankind are of a different stamp; they may be justly compared to the mutinous sailors, and the true helmsmen to those who are called by them good-for-nothings and star-gazers.

Precisely so, he said.

•   •   •

And this was what we foresaw, and this was the reason why truth forced us to admit, not without fear and hesitation, that neither cities nor States nor individuals will ever attain perfection until the small class of philosophers whom we termed useless but not corrupt are providentially compelled, whether they will or not, to take care of the State, and until a like necessity be laid on the State to obey them; or until kings, or if not kings, the sons of kings or princes, are divinely inspired with a true love of true philosophy. That either or both of these alternatives are impossible, I see no reason to affirm: if they were so, we might indeed be justly ridiculed as dreamers and visionaries. Am I not right?

Quite right.

If then, in the countless ages of the past, or at the present hour in some foreign clime which is far away and beyond our ken, the perfected philosopher is or has been or hereafter shall be compelled by a superior power to have the charge of the State, we are ready to assert to the death, that this our constitution has been, and is—yea, and will be whenever the Muse of Philosophy is queen. There is no impossibility in all this; that there is a difficulty, we acknowledge ourselves.

•   •   •

BOOK VIII

And so, Glaucon, we have arrived at the conclusion that in the perfect State wives and children are to be in common; and that all education and the pursuits of war and peace are also to be common, and the best philosophers and the braves warriors are to be their kings?

That, replied Glaucon, has been acknowledged.

Yes, I said; and we have further acknowledged that the governors, when appointed themselves, will take their soldiers and place them in houses such as we were describing, which are common to all, and contain nothing private, or individual; and about their property, you remember what we agreed?

Yes, I remember that no one was to have any of the ordinary possessions of mankind; they were to be warrior athletes and guardians, receiving from the other citizens, in lieu of annual payment, only their maintenance, and they were to take care of themselves and of the whole State.

True, I said; and now that this division of our task is concluded, let us find the point at which we digressed, that we may return into the old path.

There is no difficulty in returning; you implied, then as now, that you had finished the description of the State: you said that such a State was good, and that the man was good who answered to it, although, as now appears, you had more excellent things to relate both of State and man. And you said further, that if this was the true form, then the others were false; and of the false forms, you said, as I remember, that there were four principal ones, and that their defects, and the defects of the individuals corresponding to them, were worth examining. When we had seen all the individuals, and finally agreed as to who was the best and who was the worst of them, we were to consider whether the best was not also the happiest, and the worst the most miserable.

.   .   .

I shall particularly wish to hear what were the four constitutions of which you were speaking.

That question, I said, is easily answered: the four governments of which I spoke, so far as they have distinct names, are, first, those of Crete and Sparta, which are generally applauded; what is termed oligarchy comes next; this is not equally approved, and is a form of government which teems with evils: thirdly, democracy, which naturally follows oligarchy, although very different: and lastly comes tyranny, great and famous, which differs from them all, and is the fourth and worst disorder of a State. I do not know, do you? of any other constitution which can be said to have a distinct character. There are lordships and principalities which are bought and sold, and some other intermediate forms of government. But these are nondescripts and may be found equally among Hellenes and among barbarians.

Yes, he replied, we certainly hear of many curious forms of government which exist among them.

Do you know, I said, that governments vary as the dispositions of men vary, and that there must be as many of the one as there are of the other? For we cannot suppose that States are made of 'oak and rock', and not out of the human natures which are in them, and which in a figure turn the scale and draw other things after them?

Yes, he said, the States are as the men are; they grow out of human characters.

Then if the constitutions of States are five, the dispositions of individual minds will also be five?

Certainly.

Him who answers to aristocracy, and whom we rightly call just and good, we have already described.

We have.

Then let us now proceed to describe the inferior sort of natures, being the contentious and ambitious, who answer to the Spartan policy; also the oligarchical, democratical, and tyrannical. Let us place the most just by the side of the most unjust, and when we see them we shall be able to compare the relative happiness or unhappiness of him who leads a life of pure justice or pure injustice.

The inquiry will then be completed. And we shall know whether we ought to pursue injustice, as Thrasymachus advises, or in accordance with the conclusions of the argument to prefer justice.

Certainly, he replied, we must do as you say.

Shall we follow our old plan, which we adopted with a view to clearness, of taking the State first and then proceeding to the individual, and begin with the government of honours?—I know of no name for such a government other than timocracy, or perhaps timarchy. We will compare with this the like character in the individual; and, after that, consider oligarchy and the oligarchical man; and then again we will turn our attention to democracy and the democratical man; and lastly, we will go and view the city of tyranny, and once more take a look into the tyrant's soul, and try to arrive at a satisfactory decision.

That way of viewing and judging of the matter will be very suitable.

First, then, let us inquire how timocracy (the government of honour) arises out of aristocracy (the government of the best). Clearly, all political changes originate in divisions of the actual governing power; a government which is united, however small, cannot be moved.

Very true, he said.

In what way, then, will our city be moved, and in what manner will the two classes of auxiliaries and rulers disagree among themselves or with one another? Shall we, after the manner of Homer, pray the Muses to tell us 'how discord first arose'? Shall we imagine them in solemn mockery, to play and jest with us as if we were children, and to address us in a lofty tragic vein, making believe to be in earnest?

How would they address us?

After this manner:—A city which is thus constituted can hardly be shaken; but, seeing that everything which has a beginning has also an end, even a constitution such as yours will not last for ever, but will in time be dissolved. And this is the dissolution:—In plants that grow in the earth, as well as in animals that move on the earth's surface, fertility and sterility of soul and body occur when the circumferences of the circles of each are completed, which in short-lived existences pass over a short space, and in long-lived ones over a long space. But to the knowledge of human fecundity and sterility all the wisdom and education of your rulers will not attain; the laws which regulate them will not be discovered by an intelligence which is alloyed with sense, but will escape them, and they will bring children into the world when they ought not.

. . .

. . . For when your guardians are ignorant of the law of births, and unite bride and bridegroom out of season, the children will not be goodly or fortunate. And though only the best of them will be appointed by their predecessors, still they will be unworthy to hold their fathers' places, and when they come into power as guardians, they will soon be found to fail in taking care of us, the Muses, first by undervaluing music; which neglect will soon extend to gymnastic; and hence the young men of your State will be less cultivated. In the succeed-

ing generation rulers will be appointed who have lost the guardian power of test-
ing the metal of your different races, which, like Hesiod's, are of gold and silver
and brass and iron. And so iron will be mingled with silver, and brass with gold,
and hence there will arise dissimilarity and inequality and irregularity, which always and in all places are causes of hatred and war. This the Muses affirm to be
the stock from which discord has sprung, wherever arising; and this is their answer to us.

Yes, and we may assume that they answer truly.

Why, yes, I said, of course they answer truly; how can the Muses speak
falsely?

And what do the Muses say next?

When discord arose, then the two races were drawn different ways: the iron
and brass fell to acquiring money and land and houses and gold and silver; but
the gold and silver races, not wanting money but having the true riches in their
own nature, inclined towards virtue and the ancient order of things. There was a
battle between them, and at last they agreed to distribute their land and houses
among individual owners; and they enslaved their friends and maintainers,
whom they had formerly protected in the condition of freemen, and made of
them subjects and servants; and they themselves were engaged in war and in
keeping a watch against them.

I believe that you have rightly conceived the origin of the change.

And the new government which thus arises will be of a form intermediate
between oligarchy and aristocracy?

Very true.

Such will be the change, and after the change has been made, how will they
proceed? Clearly, the new State, being in a mean between oligarchy and the perfect State, will partly follow one and partly the other, and will also have some
peculiarities.

True, he said.

In the honour given to rulers, in the abstinence of the warrior class from
agriculture, handicrafts, and trade in general, in the institution of common
meals, and in the attention paid to gymnastics and military training—in all these
respects this State will resemble the former.

True.

But in the fear of admitting philosophers to power, because they are no
longer to be had simple and earnest, but are made up of mixed elements; and in
turning from them to passionate and less complex characters, who are by nature
fitted out for war rather than peace; and in the value set by them upon military
stratagems and contrivances, and in the waging of everlasting wars—this State
will be for the most part peculiar.

Yes.

Yes, I said; and men of this stamp will be covetous of money, like those
who live in oligarchies; they will have a fierce secret longing after gold and silver, which they will hoard in dark places, having magazines and treasuries of

their own for the deposit and concealment of them; also castles which are just nests for their eggs, and in which they will spend large sums on their wives, or on any others whom they please.

That is most true, he said.

And they are miserly because they have no means of openly acquiring the money which they prize; they will spend that which is another man's on the gratification of their desires, stealing their pleasures and running away like chil-dren from the law, their father: they have been schooled not by gentle influences but by force, for they have neglected her who is the true Muse, the companion of reason and philosophy, and have honoured gymnastic more than music.

Undoubtedly, he said, the form of government which you describe is a mix-ture of good and evil.

Why, there is a mixture, I said; but one thing, and one thing only, is pre-dominantly seen,—the spirit of contention and ambition; and these are due to the prevalence of the passionate or spirited element.

Assuredly, he said.

Such is the origin and such the character of this State, which has been de-scribed in outline only; the more perfect execution was not required, for a sketch is enough to show the type of the most perfectly just and most perfectly unjust; and to go through all the States and all the characters of men, omitting none of them, would be an interminable labour.

Very true, he replied.

Now what man answers to this form of government—how did he come into being, and what is he like?

I think, said Adeimantus, that in the spirit of contention which characterizes him, he is not unlike our friend Glaucon.

Perhaps, I said, he may be like him in that one point; but there are other respects in which he is very different.

In what respects?

He should have more of self-assertion and be less cultivated, and yet a friend of culture; and he should be a good listener, but no speaker. Such a person is apt to be rough with slaves, unlike the educated man, who is too proud for that; and he will also be courteous to freemen, and remarkably obedient to authority; he is a lover of power and a lover of honour; claiming to be a ruler, not because he is eloquent, or on any ground of that sort, but because he is a soldier and has performed feats of arms; he is also a lover of gymnastic exercises and of the chase.

Yes, that is the type of character which answers to timocracy.

Such a one will despise riches only when he is young; but as he gets older he will be more and more attracted to them, because he has a piece of the avari-cious nature in him, and is not single-minded towards virtue, having lost his best guardian.

Who was that? said Adeimantus.

Philosophy, I said, tempered with music, who comes and takes up her abode in a man, and is the only saviour of his virtue throughout life.

Good, he said.

Such, I said, is the timocratical youth, and he is like the timocratical State.

Exactly.

His origin is as follows:—He is often the young son of a brave father, who dwells in an ill-governed city, of which he declines the honours and offices, and will not go to law, or exert himself in any way, but is ready to waive his rights in order that he may escape trouble.

And how does the son come into being?

The character of the son begins to develop when he hears his mother complaining that her husband has no place in the government, of which the consequence is that she has no precedence among other women. Further, when she sees her husband not very eager about money, and instead of battling and railing in the law courts or assembly, taking whatever happens to him quietly; and when she observes that his thoughts always centre in himself, while he treats her with very considerable indifference, she is annoyed, and says to her son that his father is only half a man and far too easy-going: adding all the other complaints about her own ill-treatment which women are so fond of rehearsing.

Yes, said Adeimantus, they give us plenty of them, and their complaints are so like themselves.

And you know, I said, that the old servants also, who are supposed to be attached to the family, from time to time talk privately in the same strain to the son; and if they see any one who owes money to his father, or is wronging him in any way, and he fails to prosecute them, they tell the youth that when he grows up he must retaliate upon people of this sort, and be more of a man than his father. He has only to talk abroad and he hears and sees the same sort of thing: those who do their own business in the city are called simpletons, and held in no esteem, while the busy-bodies are honoured and applauded. The result is that the young man, hearing and seeing all these things—hearing, too, the words of his father, and having a nearer view of his way of life, and making comparisons of him and others—is drawn opposite ways: while his father is watering and nourishing the rational principle in his soul, the others are encouraging the passionate and appetitive; and he being not originally of a bad nature, but having kept bad company, is at last brought by their joint influence to a middle point, and gives up the kingdom which is within him to the middle principle of contentiousness and passion, and becomes arrogant and ambitious.

You seem to me to have described his origin perfectly.

Then we have now, I said, the second form of government and the second type of character?

We have.

Next, let us look at another man who, as Aeschylus says,

'Is set over against another State;'

or rather, as our plan requires, begin with the State.

By all means.

I believe that oligarchy follows next in order.

And what manner of government do you term oligarchy?

A government resting on a valuation of property, in which the rich have power and the poor man is deprived of it.

I understand, he replied.

Ought I not begin by describing how the change from timocracy to oligarchy arises?

Yes.

Well, I said, no eyes are required in order to see how the one passes into the other.

How?

The accumulation of gold in the treasury of private individuals is the ruin of timoracy; they invent illegal modes of expenditure; for what do they or their wives care about the law?

Yes, indeed.

And then one, seeing another grow rich, seeks to rival him, and thus the great mass of the citizens become lovers of money.

Likely enough.

And so they grow richer and richer, and the more they think of making a fortune the less they think of virtue; for when riches and virtue are placed together in the scales of the balance, the one always rises as the other falls.

True.

And in proportion as riches and rich men are honoured in the State, virtue and the virtuous are dishonoured.

Clearly.

And what is honoured is cultivated, and that which has no honour is neglected.

That is obvious.

And so at last, instead of loving contention and glory, men become lovers of trade and money; they honour and look up to the rich man, and make a ruler of him, and dishonour the poor man.

They do so.

They next proceed to make a law which fixes a sum of money as the qualification of citizenship; the sum is higher in one place and lower in another, as the oligarchy is more or less exclusive; and they allow no one whose property falls below the amount fixed to have any share in the government. These changes in the constitution they effect by force of arms, if intimidation has not already done their work.

Very true.

And this, speaking generally, is the way in which oligarchy is established.

Yes, he said; but what are the characteristics of this form of government, and what are the defects of which we were speaking?

First of all, I said, consider the nature of the qualification. Just think what would happen if pilots were to be chosen according to their property, and a poor man were refused permission to steer, even though he were a better pilot?

You mean that they would shipwreck?

Yes; and is not this true of the government of anything?

I should imagine so.

Except a city?—or would you include a city?

Nay, he said, the case of a city is the strongest of all, inasmuch as the rule of a city is the greatest and most difficult of all.

This, then, will be the first great defect of oligarchy?

Clearly.

And here is another defect which is quite as bad.

What defect?

The inevitable division: such a State is not one, but two States, the one of poor, the other of rich men; and they are living on the same spot and always conspiring against one another.

That, surely, is at least as bad.

Another discreditable feature is, that, for a like reason, they are incapable of carrying on any war. Either they arm the multitude, and then they are more afraid of them than of the enemy; or, if they do not call them out in the hour of battle, they are oligarchs, indeed, few to fight as they are few to rule. And at the same time their fondness for money makes them unwilling to pay taxes.

How discreditable!

And, as we said before, under such a constitution the same persons have too many callings—they are husbandmen, tradesmen, warriors, all in one. Does that look well?

Anything but well.

There is another evil which is, perhaps, the greatest of all, and to which this State first begins to be liable.

What evil?

A man may sell all that he has, and another may acquire his property; yet after the sale he may dwell in the city of which he is no longer a part, being neither trader, nor artisan, nor horseman, nor hoplite, but only a poor, helpless creature.

Yes, that is an evil which also first begins in this State.

The evil is certainly not prevented there; for oligarchies have both the extremes of great wealth and utter poverty.

True.

But think again: In his wealthy days, while he was spending his money, was a man of this sort a whit more good to the State for the purposes of citizenship? Or did he only seem to be a member of the ruling body, although in truth he was neither ruler nor subject, but just a spendthrift?

As you say, he seemed to be a ruler, but was only a spendthrift.

May we not say that this is the drone in the house who is like the drone in the honeycomb, and that the one is the plague of the city as the other is of the hive?

Just so, Socrates.

And God has made the flying drones, Adeimantus, all without stings, whereas of the walking drones he has made some without stings but others have dreadful stings; of the stingless class are those who in their old age end as paupers; of the stingers come all the criminal class, as they are termed.

Most true, he said.

Clearly then, whenever you see paupers in a State, somewhere in that neighbourhood there are hidden away thieves and cut-purses and robbers of temples, and all sorts of malefactors.

Clearly.

Well, I said, and in oligarchical States do you not find paupers?

Yes, he said; nearly everybody is a pauper who is not a ruler.

And may we be so bold as to affirm that there are also many criminals to be found in them, rogues who have stings, and whom the authorities are careful to restrain by force?

Certainly, we may be so bold.

The existence of such persons is to be attributed to want of education, ill-training, and an evil constitution of the State?

True.

Such, then, is the form and such are the evils of oligarchy; and there may be many other evils.

Very likely.

Then oligarchy, or the form of government in which the rulers are elected for their wealth, may now be dismissed. Let us next proceed to consider the nature and origin of the individual who answers to this State.

By all means.

Does not the timocratical man change into the oligarchical on this wise?

How?

A time arrives when the representative of timocracy has a son: at first he begins by emulating his father and walking in his footsteps, but presently he sees him of a sudden foundering against the State as upon a sunken reef, and he and all that he has is lost; he may have been a general or some other high officer who is brought to trial under a prejudice raised by informers, and either put to death, or exiled, or deprived of the privileges of a citizen, and all his property taken from him.

Nothing more likely.

And the son has seen and known all this—he is a ruined man, and his fear has taught him to knock ambition and passion headforemost from his bosom's throne; humbled by poverty he takes to money-making and by mean and miserly savings and hard work gets a fortune together. Is not such a one likely to seat the concupiscent and covetous element on the vacant throne and to suffer it to play the great king within him, girt with tiara and chain and scimitar?

Most true, he replied.

And when he has made reason and spirit sit down on the ground obediently on either side of their sovereign, and taught them to know their place, he compels the one to think only of how lesser sums may be turned into larger ones, and will not allow the other to worship and admire anything but riches and rich men, or to be ambitious of anything so much as the acquisition of wealth and the means of acquiring it.

Of all changes, he said, there is none so speedy or so sure as the conversion of the ambitious youth into the avaricious one.

And the avaricious, I said, is the oligarchical youth?

Yes, he said; at any rate the individual out of whom he came is like the State out of which oligarchy came.

Let us then consider whether there is any likeness between them.

Very good.

First, then, they resemble one another in the value which they set upon wealth?

Certainly.

Also in their penurious, laborious character; the individual only satisfies his necessary appetites, and confines his expenditure to them; his other desires he subdues, under the idea that they are unprofitable.

True.

He is a shabby fellow, who saves something out of everything and makes a purse for himself; and this is the sort of man whom the vulgar applaud. Is he not a true image of the State which he represents?

He appears to me to be so; at any rate money is highly valued by him as well as by the State.

You see that he is not a man of cultivation, I said.

I imagine not, he said; had he been educated he would never have made a blind god director of his chorus, or given him chief honour.

Excellent! I said. Yet consider: Must we not further admit that owing to this want of cultivation there will be found in him dronelike desires as of pauper and rogue, which are forcibly kept down by his general habit of life?

True.

Do you know where you will have to look if you want to discover his rogueries?

Where must I look?

You should see him where he has some great opportunity of acting dishonestly, as in the guardianship of an orphan.

Aye.

It will be clear enough then that in his ordinary dealings which give him a reputation for honesty he coerces his bad passions by an enforced virtue; not making them see that they are wrong, or taming them by reason, but by necessity and fear constraining them, and because he trembles for his possessions.

To be sure.

Yes, indeed, my dear friend, but you will find that the natural desires of the drone commonly exist in him all the same whenever he has to spend what is not his own.

Yes, and they will be strong in him too.

The man, then, will be at war with himself; he will be two men, and not one; but, in general, his better desires will be found to prevail over his inferior ones.

True.

For these reasons such a one will be more respectable than most people; yet the true virtue of a unanimous and harmonious soul will flee far away and never come near him.

I should expect so.

And surely, the miser individually will be an ignoble competitor in a State for any prize of victory, or other object of honourable ambition; he will not spend his money in the contest for glory; so afraid is he of awakening his expensive appetites and inviting them to help and join in the struggle; in true oligarchical fashion he fights with a small part only of his resources, and the result commonly is that he loses the prize and saves his money.

Very true.

Can we any longer doubt, then, that the miser and money-maker answers to the oligarchical State?

There can be no doubt.

Next comes democracy; of this the origin and nature have still to be considered by us; and then we will inquire into the ways of the democratic man, and bring him up for judgement.

That, he said, is our method.

Well, I said, and how does the change from oligarchy into democracy arise? Is it not on this wise?—The good at which such a State aims is to become as rich as possible, a desire which is insatiable?

What then?

The rulers, being aware that their power rests upon their wealth, refuse to curtail by law the extravagance of the spendthrift youth because they gain by their ruin; they take interest from them and buy up their estates and thus increase their own wealth and importance?

To be sure.

There can be no doubt that the love of wealth and the spirit of moderation cannot exist together in citizens of the same state to any considerable extent; one or the other will be disregarded.

That is tolerably clear.

And in oligarchical States, from the general spread of carelessness and extravagance, men of good family have often been reduced to beggary?

Yes, often.

And still they remain in the city; there they are, ready to sting and fully armed, and some of them owe money, some have forfeited their citizenship; a third class are in both predicaments; and they hate and conspire against those who have got their property, and against everybody else, and are eager for revolution.

That is true.

On the other hand, the men of business, stooping as they walk, and pretending not even to see those whom they have already ruined, insert their sting—that is, their money—into some one else who is not on his guard against them, and recover the parent sum many times over multiplied into a family of children: and so they make drone and pauper to abound in the State.

Yes, he said, there are plenty of them—that is certain.

The evil blazes up like a fire; and they will not extinguish it, either by restricting a man's use of his own property, or by another remedy:

What other?

One which is the next best, and has the advantage of compelling the citizens to look to their characters:—Let there be a general rule that every one shall enter into voluntary contracts at his own risk, and there will be less of this scandalous money-making, and the evils of which we were speaking will be greatly lessened in the State.

Yes, they will be greatly lessened.

At present the governors, induced by the motives which I have named, treat their subjects badly; while they and their adherents, especially the young men of the governing class, are habituated to lead a life of luxury and idleness both of body and mind; they do nothing, and are incapable of resisting either pleasure or pain.

Very true.

They themselves care only for making money, and are as indifferent as the pauper to the cultivation of virtue.

Yes, quite as indifferent.

Such is the state of affairs which prevails among them. And often rulers and their subjects may come in one another's way, whether on a journey or on some other occasion of meeting, on a pilgrimage or a march, as fellow-soldiers or fellow-sailors; aye and they may observe the behaviour of each other in the very moment of danger—for where danger is, there is no fear that the poor will be despised by the rich—and very likely the wiry sunburnt poor man may be placed in battle at the side of a wealthy one who has never spoilt his complexion and has plenty of superfluous flesh—when he sees such a one puffing and at his wits' end, how can he avoid drawing the conclusion that men like him are only rich because no one has the courage to despoil them? And when they meet in private will not people be saying to one another, 'Our warriors are not good for much'?

Yes, he said, I am quite aware that this is their way of talking.

And, as in a body which is diseased the addition of a touch from without may bring on illness, and sometimes even when there is no external provocation a commotion may arise within—in the same way wherever there is weakness in the State there is also likely to be illness, of which the occasion may be very slight, the one party introducing from without their oligarchical, the other their democratical allies, and then the State falls sick, and is at war with herself; and may be at times distracted, even when there is no external cause.

Yes, surely.

And then democracy comes into being after the poor have conquered their opponents, slaughtering some and banishing some, while to the remainder they give an equal share of freedom and power; and this is the form of government in which the magistrates are commonly elected by lot.

Yes, he said, that is the nature of democracy, whether the revolution has been effected by arms, or whether fear has caused the opposite party to withdraw.

And now what is their manner of life, and what sort of a government have they? for as the government is, such will be the man.

Clearly, he said.

In the first place, are they not free; and is not the city full of freedom and frankness—a man may say and do what he likes?

'Tis said so, he replied.

And where freedom is, the individual is clearly able to order for himself his own life as he pleases?

Clearly.

Then in this kind of State there will be the greatest variety of human natures?

There will.

This, then, seems likely to be the fairest of States, being like an embroidered robe which is spangled with every sort of flower. And just as women and children think a variety of colours to be all things most charming, so there are many men to whom this State, which is spangled with the manners and characters of mankind, will appear to be the fairest of States.

Yes.

Yes, my good Sir, and there will be no better in which to look for a government.

Why?

Because of the liberty which reigns there—they have a complete assortment of constitutions; and he who has a mind to establish a State, as we have been doing, must go to a democracy as he would to a bazaar at which they sell them, and pick out the one that suits him; then, when he has made his choice, he may found his State.

He will be sure to have patterns enough.

And there being no necessity, I said, for you to govern in this State, even if you have the capacity, or to be governed, unless you like, or to go to war when the rest go to war, or to be at peace when others are at peace, unless you are so disposed—there being no necessity also, because some law forbids you to hold office or be a dicast, that you should not hold office or be a dicast, if you have a fancy—is not this a way of life which for the moment is supremely delightful?

For the moment, yes.

And is not their humanity to the condemned in some cases quite charming? Have you not observed how, in a democracy, many persons, although they have been sentenced to death or exile, just stay where they are and walk about the world—the gentleman parades like a hero, and nobody sees or cares?

Yes, he replied, many and many a one.

See too, I said, the forgiving spirit of democracy, and the 'don't care' about trifles, and the disregard which she shows of all the fine principles which we solemnly laid down at the foundation of the city—as when we said that, except in the case of some rarely gifted nature, there never will be a good man who has not from his childhood been used to play amid things of beauty and make of them a joy and a study—how grandly does she trample all these fine notions of ours under her feet never giving a thought to the pursuits which make a statesman, and prompting to honour any one who professes to be the people's friend.

Yes, she is of a noble spirit.

These and other kindred characteristics are proper to democracy, which is a charming form of government, full of variety and disorder, and dispensing a sort of equality to equals and unequals alike.

We know her well.

Consider now, I said, what manner of man the individual is, or rather consider, as in the case of the State, how he comes into being.

Very good, he said.

Is not this the way—he is the son of the miserly and oligarchical father who has trained him in his own habits?

Exactly.

And, like his father, he keeps under by force the pleasures which are of the spending and not of the getting sort, being those which are called unnecessary?

Obviously.

Would you like, for the sake of clearness, to distinguish which are the necessary and which are the unnecessary pleasures?

I should.

Are not necessary pleasures those of which we cannot get rid, and of which the satisfaction is a benefit to us? And they are rightly called so, because we are framed by nature to desire both what is beneficial and what is necessary, and cannot help it.

True.

We are not wrong therefore in calling them necessary?

We are not.

And the desires of which a man may get rid, if he takes pains from his youth upwards—of which the presence, moreover, does no good, and in some cases the reverse of good—shall we not be right in saying that all these are unnecessary?

Yes, certainly.

Suppose we select an example of either kind, in order that we may have a general notion of them?

Very good.

Will not the desire of eating, that is, of simple food and condiments, in so far as they are required for health and strength, be of the necessary class?

That is what I should suppose.

The pleasure of eating is necessary in two ways; it does us good and it is essential to the continuance of life?

Yes.

But the condiments are only necessary in so far as they are good for health?

Certainly.

And the desire which goes beyond this, of more delicate food, or other luxuries, which might generally be got rid of, if controlled and trained in youth, and is hurtful to the body, and hurtful to the soul in the pursuit of wisdom and virtue, may be rightly called unnecessary?

Very true.

May we not say that these desires spend, and that the others make money because they conduce to production?

Certainly.

And of the pleasures of love, and all other pleasures, the same holds good?

True.

And the drone of whom we spoke was he who was surfeited in pleasures and desires of this sort, and was the slave of the unnecessary desires, whereas he who was subject to the necessary only was miserly and oligarchical?

Very true.

Again, let us see how the democratical man grows out of the oligarchical: the following, as I suspect, is commonly the process.

What is the process?

When a young man who has been brought up as we were just now describing, in a vulgar and miserly way has tasted drones' honey and has come to associate with fierce and crafty natures who are able to provide for him all sorts of refinements and varieties of pleasure—then, as you may imagine, the change will begin of the oligarchical principle within him into the democratical?

Inevitably.

And as in the city like was helping like, and the change was effected by an alliance from without assisting one division of the citizens, so too the young man is changed by a class of desires coming from without to assist the desires within him, that which is akin and alike again helping that which is akin and alike?

Certainly.

And if there be any ally which aids the oligarchical principle within him, whether the influence of a father or of kindred, advising or rebuking him, then there arises in his soul a faction and an opposite faction, and he goes to war with himself.

It must be so.

And there are times when the democratical principle gives way to the oligarchical, and some of his desires die, and others are banished; a spirit of reverence enters into the young man's soul and order is restored.

Yes, he said, that sometimes happens.

And then, again, after the old desires have been driven out, fresh ones spring up, which are akin to them, and because he their father does not know how to educate them, wax fierce and numerous.

Yes, he said, that is apt to be the way.

They draw him to his old associates, and holding secret intercourse with them, breed and multiply in him.

Very true.

At length they seize upon the citadel of the young man's soul, which they perceive to be void of all accomplishments and fair pursuits and true words, which make their abode in the minds of men who are dear to the gods, and are their best guardians and sentinels.

None better.

False and boastful conceits and phrases mount upwards and take their place.

They are certain to do so.

And so the young man returns into the country of the lotus-eaters, and takes up his dwelling there in the face of all men; and if any help be sent by his friends to the oligarchical part of him, the aforesaid vain conceits shut the gate of the king's fastness; and they will neither allow the embassy itself to enter, nor if private advisers offer the fatherly counsel of the aged will they listen to them or receive them. There is a battle and they gain the day, and then modesty, which they call silliness, is ignominiously thrust into exile by them, and temperance, which they nickname unmanliness, is trampled in the mire and cast forth; they persuade men that moderation and orderly expenditure are vulgarity and meanness, and so, by the help of a rabble of evil appetites, they drive them beyond the border.

Yes, with a will.

And when they have emptied and swept clean the soul of him who is now in their power and who is being initiated by them in great mysteries, the next thing is to bring back to their house insolence and anarchy and waste and impudence in bright array having garlands on their heads, and a great company with them, hymning their praises and calling them by sweet names; insolence they term breeding, and anarchy liberty, and waste magnificence, and impudence courage. And so the young man passes out of his original nature, which was trained in the school of necessity, into the freedom and libertinism of useless and unnecessary pleasures.

Yes, he said, the change in him is visible enough.

After this he lives on, spending his money and labour and time on unnecessary pleasures quite as much as on necessary ones; but if he be fortunate, and is not too much disordered in his wits, when years have elapsed, and the heyday of passion is over—supposing that he then re-admits into the city some part of the exiled virtues, and does not wholly give himself up to their successors—in that case he balances his pleasures and lives in a sort of equilibrium, putting the government of himself into the hands of the one which comes first and wins the turn; and when he has had enough of that, then into the hands of another; he despises none of them but encourages them all equally.

Very true, he said.

Neither does he receive or let pass into the fortress any true word of advice; if any one says to him that some pleasures are the satisfactions of good and noble desires, and others of evil desires, and that he ought to use and honour some and chastise and master the others—whenever this is repeated to him he shakes his head and says that they are all alike, and that one is as good as another.

Yes, he said; that is the way with him.

Yes, I said, he lives from day to day indulging the appetite of the hour; and sometimes he is lapped in drink and strains of the flute; then he becomes a water-drinker, and tries to get thin; then he takes a turn at gymnastics; sometimes idling and neglecting everything, then once more living the life of a philosopher; often he is busy with politics, and starts to his feet and says and does whatever comes into his head; and, if he is emulous of any one who is a warrior, off he is in that direction, or of men of business, once more in that. His life has neither law nor order; and the distracted existence he terms joy and bliss and freedom; and so he goes on.

Yes, he replied, he is all liberty and equality.

Yes, I said; his life is motley and manifold and an epitome of the lives of many;—he answers to the State which we described as fair and spangled. And many a man and many a woman will take him for their pattern, and many a constitution and many an example of manners is contained in him.

Just so.

Let him then be set over against democracy; he may truly be called the democratic man.

Let that be his place, he said.

Last of all comes the most beautiful of all, man and State alike, tyranny and the tyrant; these we have now to consider.

Quite true, he said.

Say, then, my friend, In what manner does tyranny arise?—that it has a democratic origin is evident.

Clearly.

And does not tyranny spring from democracy in the same manner as democracy from oligarchy—I mean, after a sort?

How?

The good which oligarchy proposed to itself and the means by which it was maintained was excess of wealth—am I not right?

Yes.

And the insatiable desire of wealth and the neglect of all other things for the sake of money-getting was also the ruin of oligarchy?

True.

And democracy has her own good, of which the insatiable desire brings her to dissolution?

What good?

Freedom, I replied; which, as they tell you in a democracy, is the glory of the State—and that therefore in a democracy alone will the freeman of nature deign to dwell.

Yes; the saying is in everybody's mouth.

I was going to observe, that the insatiable desire of this and the neglect of other things introduces the change in democracy, which occasions a demand for tyranny.

How so?

When a democracy which is thirsting for freedom has evil cup-bearers presiding over the feast, and has drunk too deeply of the strong wine of freedom, then, unless her rulers are very amenable and give a plentiful draught, she calls them to account and punishes them, and says that they are cursed oligarchs.

Yes, he replied, a very common occurrence.

Yes, I said; and loyal citizens are insultingly termed by her slaves who hug their chains and men of naught; she would have subjects who are like rulers, and rulers who are like subjects: these are men after her own heart, whom she praises and honours both in private and public. Now, in such a State, can liberty have any limit?

Certainly not.

By degrees the anarchy finds a way into private houses, and ends by getting among the animals and infecting them.

How do you mean?

I mean that the father grows accustomed to descend to the level of his sons and to fear them, and the son is on a level with his father, he having no respect or reverence for either of his parents; and this is his freedom, and the metic is equal with the citizen and the citizen with the metic, and the stranger is quite as good as either.

Yes, he said, that is the way.

And these are not the only evils, I said—there are several lesser ones: In such a state of society the master fears and flatters his scholars, and the scholars despise their masters and tutors; young and old are all alike; and the young man is on a level with the old, and is ready to compete with him in word or deed; and old men condescend to the young and are full of pleasantry and gaiety; they are loth to be thought morose and authoritative, and therefore they adopt the manners of the young.

Quite true, he said.

The last extreme of popular liberty, is when the slave bought with money, whether male or female, is just as free as his or her purchaser; nor must I forget to tell of the liberty and equality of the two sexes in relation to each other.

Why not, as Aeschylus says, utter the word which rises to our lips?

That is what I am doing, I replied; and I must add that no one who does not know would believe, how much greater is the liberty which the animals who are under the dominion of man have in a democracy than in any other State: for truly, the she-dogs, as the proverb says, are as good as their she-mistresses, and the horses and asses have a way of marching along with all the rights and dignities of freemen; and they will run at anybody who comes in their way if he does not leave the road clear for them: and all things are just ready to burst with liberty.

When I take a country walk, he said, I often experience what you describe. You and I have dreamed the same thing.

And above all, I said, and as the result of all, see how sensitive the citizens become; they chafe impatiently at the least touch of authority, and at length, as you know, they cease to care even for the laws, written or unwritten; they will have no one over them.

Yes, he said, I know it too well.

Such, my friend, I said, is the fair and glorious beginning out of which springs tyranny.

Glorious indeed, he said. But what is the next step?

The ruin of oligarchy is the ruin of democracy; the same disease magnified and intensified by liberty overmasters democracy—the truth being that the excessive increase of anything often causes a reaction in the opposite direction; and this is the case not only in the seasons and in vegetable and animal life, but above all in forms of government.

True.

The excess of liberty, whether in States or individuals, seems only to pass into excess of slavery.

Yes, the natural order.

And so tyranny naturally arises out of democracy, and the most aggravated form of tyranny and slavery out of the most extreme form of liberty?

As we might expect.

That, however, was not, as I believe, your question—you rather desired to know what is that disorder which is generated alike in oligarchy and democracy, and is the ruin of both?

Just so, he replied.

Well, I said, I meant to refer to the class of idle spendthrifts, of whom the more courageous are the leaders and the more timid the followers, the same whom we were comparing to drones, some stingless, and others having stings.

A very just comparison.

These two classes are the plagues of every city in which they are generated, being what phlegm and bile are to the body. And the good physician and lawgiver of the State ought, like the wise bee-master, to keep them at a distance and prevent, if possible, their ever coming in; and if they have anyhow found a way in, then he should have them and their cells cut out as speedily as possible.

Yes, by all means, he said.

Then, in order that we may see clearly what we are doing, let us imagine democracy to be divided, as indeed it is, into three classes; for in the first place freedom creates rather more drones in the democratic than there were in the oligarchical State.

That is true.

And in the democracy they are certainly more intensified.

How so?

Because in the oligarchical State they are disqualified and driven from office, and therefore they cannot train or gather strength; whereas in a democracy they are almost the entire ruling power, and while the keener sort speak and act, the rest keep buzzing about the bema and do not suffer a word to be said on the other side; hence in democracies almost everything is managed by the drones.

Very true, he said.

Then there is another class which is always being severed from the mass.

What is that?

They are the orderly class, which in a nation of traders is sure to be the richest.

Naturally so.

They are the most squeezable persons and yield the largest amount of honey to the drones.

Why, he said, there is little to be squeezed out of people who have little.

And this is called the wealthy class, and the drones feed upon them.

That is pretty much the case, he said.

The people are a third class, consisting of those who work with their own hands; they are not politicians, and have not much to live upon. This, when assembled, is the largest and most powerful class in a democracy.

True, he said; but then the multitude is seldom willing to congregate unless they get a little honey.

And do they not share? I said. Do not their leaders deprive the rich of their estates and distribute them among the people; at the same time taking care to reserve the larger part for themselves?

Why, yes, he said, to that extent the people do share.

And the persons whose property is taken from them are compelled to defend themselves before the people as they best can?

What else can they do?

And then, although they may have no desire of change, the others charge them with plotting against the people and being friends of oligarchy?

True.

And the end is that when they see the people, not of their own accord, but through ignorance, and because they are deceived by informers, seeking to do them wrong, then at last they are forced to become oligarchs in reality; they do not wish to be, but the sting of the drones torments them and breeds revolution in them.

That is exactly the truth.

Then come impeachments and judgements and trials of one another.

True.

The people have always some champion whom they set over them and nurse into greatness.

Yes, that is their way.

This and no other is the root from which a tyrant springs; when he first appears above ground he is a protector.

Yes, that is quite clear.

How then does a protector begin to change into a tyrant? Clearly when he does what the man is said to do in the tale of the Arcadian temple of Lycaean Zeus.

What tale?

The tale is that he who has tasted the entrails of a single human victim minced up with the entrails of other victims is destined to become a wolf. Did you never hear it?

Oh yes.

And the protector of the people is like him; having a mob entirely at his disposal, he is not restrained from shedding the blood of kinsmen; by the favourite method of false accusation he brings them into court and murders them, making the life of man to disappear, and with unholy tongue and lips tasting the blood of his fellow citizens; some he kills and others he banishes, at the same time hinting at the abolition of debts and partition of lands: and after this, what will be his destiny? Must he not either perish at the hands of his enemies, or from being a man become a wolf—that is, a tyrant?

Inevitably.

This, I said, is he who begins to make a party against the rich?

The same.

After a while he is driven out, but comes back, in spite of his enemies, a tyrant full grown.

That is clear.

And if they are unable to expel him, or to get him condemned to death by a public accusation, they conspire to assassinate him.

Yes, he said, that is their usual way.

Then comes the famous request for a body-guard; which is the device of all those who have got thus far in their tyrannical career—'Let not the people's friend,' as they say, 'be lost to them.'

Exactly.

The people readily assent; all their fears are for him—they have none for themselves.

Very true.

And when a man who is wealthy and is also accused of being an enemy of the people sees this, then, my friend, as the oracle said to Croesus,

'By pebbly Hermus' shore he flees and rests not, and is not ashamed to be a coward.'

And quite right too, said he, for if he were, he would never be ashamed again.

But if he is caught he dies.

Of course.

And he, the protector of whom we spoke, is to be seen, not 'larding the plain' with his bulk, but himself the overthrower of many, standing up in the chariot of State with the reins in his hand, no longer protector, but tyrant absolute.

No doubt, he said.

And now let us consider the happiness of the man, and also of the State in which a creature like him is generated.

Yes, he said, let us consider that.

At first, in the early days of his power, he is full of smiles, and he salutes every one whom he meets;—he to be called a tyrant, who is making promises in public and also in private! liberating debtors, and distributing land to the people and his followers, and wanting to be so kind and good to every one!

Of course, he said.

But when he has disposed of foreign enemies by conquest or treaty, and there is nothing to fear from them, then he is always stirring up some war or other, in order that the people may require a leader.

To be sure.

Has he not also another object, which is that they may be impoverished by payment of taxes, and thus compelled to devote themselves to their daily wants and therefore less likely to conspire against him?

Clearly.

And if any of them are suspected by him of having notions of freedom, and of resistance to his authority, he will have a good pretext for destroying them by placing them at the mercy of the enemy; and for all these reasons the tyrant must be always getting up a war.

He must.

Now he begins to grow unpopular.

A necessary result.

Then some of those who joined in setting him up, and who are in power, speak their minds to him and to one another, and the more courageous of them cast in his teeth what is being done.

Yes, that may be expected.

And the tyrant, if he means to rule, must get rid of them; he cannot stop while he has a friend or an enemy who is good for anything.

He cannot.

And therefore he must look about him and see who is valiant, who is high-minded, who is wise, who is wealthy; happy man, he is the enemy of them all, and must seek occasion against them whether he will or no, until he has made a purgation of the State.

Yes, he said, and a rare purgation.

Yes, I said, not the sort of purgation which the physicians make of the body; for they take away the worse and leave the better part, but he does the reverse.

If he is to rule, I suppose that he cannot help himself.

What a blessed alternative, I said:—to be compelled to dwell only with the many bad, and to be by them hated, or not to live at all!

Yes, that is the alternative.

And the more detestable his actions are to the citizens the more satellites and the greater devotion in them will he require?

Certainly.

And who are the devoted band, and where will he procure them?

They will flock to him, he said, of their own accord, if he pays them.

By the dog! I said, here are more drones, of every sort and from every land.

Yes, he said, there are.

But will he not desire to get them on the spot?

How do you mean?

He will rob the citizens of their slaves; he will then set them free and enrol them in his body-guard.

To be sure, he said; and he will be able to trust them best of all.

What a blessed creature, I said, must this tyrant be; he has put to death the others and has these for his trusted friends.

Yes, he said; they are quite of his sort.

Yes, I said, and these are the new citizens whom he has called into existence, who admire him and are his companions, while the good hate and avoid him.

Of course.

Verily, then, tragedy is a wise thing and Euripides a great tragedian.

Why so?

Why, because he is the author of the pregnant saying,

'Tyrants are wise by living with the wise;'

and he clearly meant to say that they are the wise whom the tyrant makes his companions.

Yes, he said, and he also praises tyranny as godlike; and many other things of the same kind are said by him and by the other poets.

And therefore, I said, the tragic poets being wise men will forgive us and any others who live after our manner if we do not receive them into our State, because they are the eulogists of tyranny.

Yes, he said, those who have the wit will doubtless forgive us.

But they will continue to go to other cities and attract mobs, and hire voices fair and loud and persuasive, and draw the cities over to tyrannies and democracies.

Very true.

Moreover, they are paid for this and receive honour—the greatest honour, as might be expected, from tyrants, and the next greatest from democracies; but the higher they ascend our constitution hill, the more their reputation fails, and seems unable from shortness of breath to proceed further.

True.

But we are wandering from the subject: Let us therefore return and inquire how the tyrant will maintain that fair and numerous and various and ever-changing army of his.

If, he said, there are sacred treasures in the city, he will confiscate and spend them; and in so far as the fortunes of attainted persons may suffice, he will be able to diminish the taxes which he would otherwise have to impose upon the people.

And when these fail?

Why, clearly, he said, then he and his boon companions, whether male or female, will be maintained out of his father's estate.

You mean to say that the people, from whom he has derived his being, will maintain him and his companions?

Yes, he said; they cannot help themselves.

But what if the people fly into a passion, and aver that a grown-up son ought not to be supported by his father, but that the father should be supported by the son? The father did not bring him into being, or settle him in life, in order that when his son became a man he should himself be the servant of his own servants and should support him and his rabble of slaves and companions; but that his son should protect him, and that by his help he might be emancipated from the government of the rich and aristocratic, as they are termed. And so he bids him and his companions depart, just as any other father might drive out of the house a riotous son and his undesirable associates.

By heavens, he said, then the parent will discover what a monster he has been fostering in his bosom; and, when he wants to drive him out, he will find that he is weak and his son strong.

Why, you do not mean to say that the tyrant will use violence? What! beat his father if he opposes him?

Yes, he will, having first disarmed him.

Then he is a parricide, and a cruel guardian of an aged parent; and this is a real tyranny, about which there can be no longer a mistake: as the saying is, the people who would escape the smoke which is the slavery of freemen, has fallen into the fire which is the tyranny of slaves. Thus liberty, getting out of all order and reason, passes into the harshest and bitterest form of slavery.

True, he said.

Very well; and may we not rightly say that we have sufficiently discussed the nature of tyranny, and the manner of the transition from democracy to tyranny?

Yes, quite enough, he said.

POLITICA

Aristotle

384–322 B.C.

☙❧

The philosopher, as medieval schoolmen called Aristotle, was probably the most encyclopedic thinker of all time. Among philosophers no one, with the possible exception of his teacher, Plato, exceeds his influence. Politics was only one of his many interests which embraced all the natural sciences of his day, as well as logic, ethics, art, rhetoric, and metaphysics. Such divergent contemporary philosophies as naturalism and neo-Thomism still draw inspiration from Aristotle, although in contrast to Plato his style is dry and pedantic.

Aristotle was born in Thrace, studied at Plato's Academy in Athens, later tutored young prince Alexander of Macedon, and eventually opened his own school in Athens in 335. His death marked the close of the Golden Age of Greek philosophy.

Most of Aristotle's works on politics are lost, although we know enough about them, especially his description of the constitutions of 158 Greek cities, to know they reflect his interest—manifest most of all in the field of biology—in careful empirical investigation. The *Politics*, an early milestone in the history of political theory, reflects this descriptive interest as well as a deep preoccupation with moral principles.

The *Politics* is not a finished or well organized work—even the sequence of the eight books composing it is under dispute —and is more suggestive of loosely knit lectures than of a work intended for publication. Excerpting it therefore presents special difficulties.

Unlike Plato, Aristotle is explicit about constitutional rule. Whatever form government may take, a rule of law is preferable to a rule of men. Also, he is less critical of democracy than Plato. However, his views concerning slavery and his exclusion of artisans from citizenship in the ideal state on the grounds that they lack the leisure to cultivate virtue place him in the elitist tradition. It must not be forgotten that in all their political writings both Plato and Aristotle were thinking in terms of the small Greek city-state.

From "Politica" in *The Works of Aristotle*, trans. Benjamin Jowett, ed. W. D. Ross (Oxford, 1921), X, Books I, II, III, IV, VII. Footnotes which appeared in the original have been deleted.

BOOK I

· · ·

5   . . . [I]s there any one . . . intended by nature to be a slave, and for whom such a condition is expedient and right, or rather is not all slavery a violation of nature?

There is no difficulty in answering this question, on grounds both of reason and of fact. For that some should rule and others be ruled is a thing not only necessary, but expedient; from the hour of their birth, some are marked out for subjection, others for rule.

And there are many kinds both of rulers and subjects (and that rule is the better which is exercised over better subjects—for example, to rule over men is better than to rule over wild beasts; for the work is better which is executed by better workmen, and where one man rules and another is ruled, they may be said to have a work) ; for in all things which form a composite whole and which are made up of parts, whether continuous or discrete, a distinction between the ruling and the subject element comes to light. Such a duality exists in living creatures, but not in them only; it originates in the constitution of the universe; even in things which have no life there is a ruling principle, as in a musical mode. But we are wandering from the subject. We will therefore restrict ourselves to the living creature, which, in the first place, consists of soul and body: and of these two, the one is by nature the ruler, and the other the subject. But then we must look for the intentions of nature in things which retain their nature, and not in things which are corrupted. And therefore we must study the man who is in the most perfect state both of body and soul, for in him we shall see the true relation of the two; although in bad or corrupted natures the body will often appear to rule over the soul, because they are in an evil and unnatural condition. At all events we may firstly observe in living creatures both a despotical and a constitutional rule; for the soul rules the body with a despotical rule, whereas the intellect rules the appetites with a constitutional and royal rule. And it is clear that the rule of the soul over the body, and of the mind and the rational element over the passionate, is natural and expedient; whereas the equality of the two or the rule of the inferior is always hurtful. The same holds good of animals in relation to men; for tame animals have a better nature than wild, and all tame animals are better off when they are ruled by man; for then they are preserved. Again the male is by nature superior, and the female inferior; and the one rules, and the other is ruled; this principle, of necessity, extends to all mankind. Where then there is such a difference as that between soul and body, or between men and animals (as in the case of those whose business is to use their body, and who can do nothing better), the lower sort are by nature slaves, and it is better for them as for all inferiors that they should be under the rule of a master. For he who can be, and therefore is, another's, and he who participates in rational principle enough to apprehend, but not to have, such a principle, is a slave by nature. Whereas the lower animals cannot even apprehend a principle; they obey their instincts. And indeed the use made of slaves and of tame animals is not very different; for both with their bodies minister to the needs of life. Nature would like to distinguish between the bodies of freemen and slaves, making the one strong for servile labour, the other upright, and although useless for such services, useful for political life in the arts both of war and peace. But the opposite often happens—that some have the souls and others have the bodies of freemen. And doubtless if men differed from one another in the mere forms of their bodies as much as the statues of the Gods do from men, all would acknowledge that the inferior class should be slaves of the superior. And if this is true of the body, how much more just that a similar distinction should exist in the soul? but the beauty of the body is seen, whereas the beauty of the soul is not seen. It is clear, then, that some men are by nature free, and others slaves, and that for these latter slavery is both expedient and right.

6   But that those who take the opposite view have in a certain way right on their side, may be easily seen. For the words slavery and slave are used in two senses. There is a slave or slavery by law as well as by nature. The law of which I speak is a sort of convention—the law by which whatever is taken in war is supposed to belong to the victors. But this right many jurists impeach, as they would an orator who brought forward an unconstitutional measure: they detest the notion that, because one man has the power of doing violence and is superior in brute strength, another shall be his slave and subject. Even among philosophers there is a difference of opinion. The origin of the dispute, and what makes the views invade each other's territory, is as follows: in some sense virtue, when furnished with means, has actually the greatest power of exercising force: and as superior power is only found where there is superior excellence of some kind, power seems to imply virtue, and the dispute to be simply one about justice (for it is due to one party identifying justice with goodwill, while the other identifies it with the mere rule of the stronger). If these views are thus set out separately, the other views have no force or plausibility against the view that the superior in virtue ought to rule, or be master. Others, clinging, as they think, simply to a principle of justice (for law and custom are a sort of justice), assume that slavery in accordance with the custom of war is justified by law, but at the same moment they deny this. For what if the cause of the war be unjust? And again, no one would ever say that he is a slave who is unworthy to be a slave. Were this the case, men of the highest rank would be slaves and the children of slaves if they or their parents chance to have been taken captive and sold. Wherefore Hellenes do not like to call Hellenes slaves, but confine the term to barbarians. Yet, in using this language, they really mean the natural slave of whom we spoke

at first; for it must be admitted that some are slaves everywhere, others nowhere. The same principle applies to nobility. Hellenes regard themselves as noble everywhere, and not only in their own country, but they deem the barbarians noble only when at home, thereby implying that there are two sorts of nobility and freedom, the one absolute, the other relative. . . . What does this mean but that they distinguish freedom and slavery, noble and humble birth, by the two principles of good and evil? They think that as men and animals beget men and animals, so from good men a good man springs. But this is what nature, though she may intend it, cannot always accomplish.

We see then that there is some foundation for this difference of opinion, and that all are not either slaves by nature or freemen by nature, and also that there is in some cases a marked distinction between the two classes, rendering it expedient and right for the one to be slaves and the others to be masters: the one practising obedience, the others exercising the authority and lordship which nature intended them to have. The abuse of this authority is injurious to both; for the interests of part and whole, of body and soul, are the same, and the slave is a part of the master, a living but separated part of his bodily frame. Hence, where the relation of master and slave between them is natural they are friends and have a common interest, but where it rests merely on law and force the reverse is true.

. . . .

13   . . . A question may indeed be raised, whether there is any excellence at all in a slave beyond and higher than merely instrumental and ministerial qualities —whether he can have the virtues of temperance, courage, justice, and the like; or whether slaves possess only bodily and ministerial qualities. And, whichever way we answer the question, a difficulty arises; for, if they have virtue, in what will they differ from freemen? On the other hand, since they are men and share in rational principle, it seems absurd to say that they have no virtue. A similar question may be raised about women and children, whether they too have virtues: ought a woman to be temperate and brave and just, and is a child to be called temperate, and intemperate, or not? So in general we may ask about the natural ruler, and the natural subject, whether they have the same or different virtues. For if a noble nature is equally required in both, why should one of them always rule, and the other always be ruled? Nor can we say that this is a question of degree, for the difference between ruler and subject is a difference of kind, which the difference of more and less never is. Yet how strange is the supposition that the one ought, and that the other ought not, to have virtue! For if the ruler is intemperate and unjust, how can he rule well? if the subject, how can he obey well? If he be licentious and cowardly, he will certainly not do his duty. It is evident, therefore, that both of them must have a share of virtue, but varying as natural subjects also vary among themselves. Here the very constitution of the soul has shown us the way; in it one part naturally rules, and the other is subject, and the virtue of the ruler we maintain to be different from that of the

subject;—the one being the virtue of the rational, and the other of the irrational part. Now, it is obvious that the same principle applies generally, and therefore almost all things rule and are ruled according to nature. But the kind of rule differs;—the freeman rules over the slave after another manner from that in which the male rules over the female, or the man over the child; although the parts of the soul are present in all of them, they are present in different degrees. For the slave has no deliberative faculty at all; the woman has, but it is without authority and the child has, but it is immature. So it must necessarily be supposed to be with the moral virtues also; all should partake of them, but only in such manner and degree as is required by each for the fulfilment of his duty. Hence the ruler ought to have moral virtue in perfection, for his function, taken absolutely, demands a master artificer, and rational principle is such an artificer; the subjects, on the other hand, require only that measure of virtue which is proper to each of them. Clearly, then, moral virtue belongs to all of them; but the temperance of a man and of a woman, or the courage and justice of a man and of a woman, are not, as Socrates maintained, the same; the courage of a man is shown in commanding, of a woman in obeying. And this holds of all other virtues, as will be more clearly seen if we look at them in detail, for those who say generally that virtue consists in a good disposition of the soul, or in doing rightly, or the like, only deceive themselves. Far better than such definitions is their mode of speaking, who, like Gorgias, enumerate the virtues. All classes must be deemed to have their special attributes; as the poet [Plato] says of women,

'Silence is a woman's glory',

but this is not equally the glory of man. The child is imperfect, and therefore obviously his virtue is not relative to himself alone, but to the perfect man and to his teacher, and in like manner the virtue of the slave is relative to a master. Now we determined that a slave is useful for the wants of life, and therefore he will obviously require only so much virtue as will prevent him from failing in his duty through cowardice or lack of self-control. Some one will ask whether, if what we are saying is true, virtue will not be required also in the artisans, for they often fail in their work through the lack of self-control? But is there not a great difference in the two cases? For the slave shares in his master's life; the artisan is less closely connected with him, and only attains excellence in proportion as he becomes a slave. The meaner sort of mechanic has a special and separate slavery; and whereas the slave exists by nature, not so the shoemaker or other artisan. It is manifest, then, that the master ought to be the source of such excellence in the slave, and not a mere possessor of the art of mastership which trains the slave in his duties. Wherefore they are mistaken who forbid us to converse with slaves and say that we should employ command only, for slaves stand even more in need of admonition than children.

.   .   .

BOOK II

1   Our purpose is to consider what form of political community is best of all for those who are most able to realize their ideal of life. We must therefore examine not only this but other constitutions, both such as actually exist in well-governed states, and any theoretical forms which are held in esteem; that what is good and useful may be brought to light. . . .

We will begin with the natural beginning of the subject. Three alternatives are conceivable: The members of a state must either have (1) all things or (2) nothing in common, or (3) some things in common and some not. That they should have nothing in common is clearly impossible, for the constitution is a community, and must at any rate have a common place—one city will be in one place, and the citizens are those who share in that one city. But should a well-ordered state have all things, as far as may be, in common, or some only and not others? For the citizens might conceivably have wives and children and property in common, as Socrates proposes in the *Republic* of Plato. Which is better, our present condition, or the proposed new order of society?

. . . I am speaking of the premiss from which the argument of Socrates proceeds, 'that the greater the unity of the state the better'. Is it not obvious that a state may at length attain such a degree of unity as to be no longer a state?—since the nature of a state is to be a plurality, and in tending to greater unity, from being a state, it becomes a family, and from being a family, an individual; for the family may be said to be more one than the state, and the individual than the family. So that we ought not to attain this greatest unity even if we could, for it would be the destruction of the state. . . .

3   But, even supposing that it were best for the community to have the greatest degree of unity, this unity is by no means proved to follow from the fact 'of all men saying "mine" and "not mine" at the same instant of time,' which, according to Socrates, is the sign of perfect unity in a state.

. . . .

BOOK III

. . . .

. . . [L]et us consider what is the purpose of a state, and how many forms of government there are by which human society is regulated. We have already said . . . that man is by nature a political animal. And therefore, men, even when they do not require one another's help, desire to live together; not but that they are also brought together by their common interests in proportion as they severally attain to any measure of well-being. This is certainly the chief end, both of individuals and of states. And also for the sake of mere life (in which there is possibly some noble element so long as the evils of existence do not greatly over-balance the good) mankind meet together and maintain the political community. And we all see that men cling to life even at the cost of enduring great misfortune, seeming to find in life a natural sweetness and happiness.

.   .   .

7   Having determined these points, we have next to consider how many forms of government there are, and what they are; and in the first place what are the true forms, for when they are determined the perversions of them will at once be apparent. The words constitution and government have the same meaning, and the government, which is the supreme authority in states, must be in the hands of one, or of a few, or of the many. The true forms of government, therefore, are those in which the one, or the few, or the many, govern with a view to the common interest; but governments which rule with a view to the private interest, whether of the one, or of the few, or of the many, are perversions. For the members of a state, if they are truly citizens, ought to participate in its advantages. Of forms of government in which one rules, we call that which regards the common interests, kingship or royalty; that in which more than one, but not many, rule, aristocracy; and it is so called, either because the rulers are the best men, or because they have at heart the best interests of the state and of the citizens. But when the citizens at large administer the state for the common interest, the government is called by the generic name,—a constitution. . . .

Of the above-mentioned forms, the perversions are as follows:—of royalty, tyranny; of aristocracy, oligarchy; of constitutional government, democracy. For tyranny is a kind of monarchy which has in view the interest of the monarch only; oligarchy has in view the interest of the wealthy; democracy, of the needy: none of them the common good of all.

8   . . . Tyranny, as I was saying, is monarchy exercising the rule of a master over the political society; oligarchy is when men of property have the government in their hands; democracy, the opposite, when the indigent, and not the men of property, are the rulers. . . .

.   .   .

. . . [W]hether in oligarchies or in democracies, the number of the governing body, whether the greater number, as in a democracy, or the smaller number, as in an oligarchy, is an accident due to the fact that the rich everywhere are few, and the poor numerous. But if so, there is a misapprehension of the causes of the difference between them. For the real difference between democracy and oligarchy is poverty and wealth. Wherever men rule by reason of their wealth, whether they be few or many, that is an oligarchy, and where the poor rule, that is a democracy. But as a fact the rich are few and the poor many; for few are well-to-do, whereas freedom is enjoyed by all, and wealth and freedom are the grounds on which the oligarchical and democratical parties respectively claim power in the state.

. . . . .

10   There is . . . a doubt as to what is to be the supreme power in the state:— Is it the multitude? Or the wealthy? Or the good? Or the one best man? Or a tyrant? Any of these alternatives seems to involve disagreeable consequences. If the poor, for example, because they are more in number, divide among themselves the property of the rich,—is not this unjust? No, by heaven (will be the reply), for the supreme authority justly willed it. But if this is not injustice, pray what is? Again, when in the first division all has been taken, and the majority divide anew the property of the minority, is it not evident, if this goes on, that they will ruin the state? Yet surely, virtue is not the ruin of those who possess her, nor is justice destructive of a state; and therefore this law of confiscation clearly cannot be just. If it were, all the acts of a tyrant must of necessity be just; for he only coerces other men by superior power, just as the multitude coerce the rich. But is it just then that the few and the wealthy should be the rulers? And what if they, in like manner, rob and plunder the people,—is this just? If so, the other case will likewise be just. But there can be no doubt that all these things are wrong and unjust.

Then ought the good to rule and have supreme power? But in that case everybody else, being excluded from power, will be dishonoured. For the offices of a state are posts of honour; and if one set of men always hold them, the rest must be deprived of them. Then will it be well that the one best man should rule? Nay, that is still more oligarchical, for the number of those who are dishonoured is thereby increased. Some one may say that it is bad in any case for a man, subject as he is to all the accidents of human passion, to have the supreme power, rather than the law. But what if the law itself be democratical or oligarchical, how will that help us out of our difficulties? Not at all; the same consequences will follow.

11   . . . The principle that the multitude ought to be supreme rather than the few best is one that is maintained, and, though not free from difficulty, yet seems to contain an element of truth. For the many, of whom each individual is but an ordinary person, when they meet together may very likely be better than the few good, if regarded not individually but collectively, just as a feast to which many contribute is better than a dinner provided out of a single purse. For each individual among the many has a share of virtue and prudence, and when they meet together, they become in a manner one man, who has many feet, and hands, and senses . . . Whether this principle can apply to every democracy, and to all bodies of men, is not clear. Or rather, by heaven, in some cases it is impossible of application; for the argument would equally hold about brutes; and wherein, it will be asked, do some men differ from brutes? But there may be bodies of men about whom our statement is nevertheless true. And if so, the difficulty which has been already raised, and also another which is akin to it—viz. what power should

be assigned to the mass of freemen and citizens, who are not rich and have no personal merit—are both solved. There is still a danger in allowing them to share the great offices of state, for their folly will lead them into error, and their dishonesty into crime. But there is a danger also in not letting them share, for a state in which many poor men are excluded from office will necessarily be full of enemies. The only way of escape is to assign to them some deliberative and judicial functions. For this reason Solon and certain other legislators give them the power of electing to offices, and of calling the magistrates to account, but they do not allow them to hold office singly. When they meet together their perceptions are quite good enough, and combined with the better class they are useful to the state. . . , but each individual, left to himself, forms an imperfect judgement. On the other hand, the popular form of government involves certain difficulties. In the first place, it might be objected that he who can judge of the healing of a sick man would be one who could himself heal his disease, and make him whole —that is, in other words, the physician; and so in all professions and arts. As, then, the physician ought to be called to account by physicians, so ought men in general to be called to account by their peers. . . . Secondly, does not the same principle apply to elections? For a right election can only be made by those who have knowledge; those who know geometry, for example, will choose a geometrician rightly, and those who know how to steer, a pilot; and, even if there be some occupations and arts in which private persons share in the ability to choose, they certainly cannot choose better than those who know. So that, according to this argument, neither the election of magistrates, nor the calling of them to account, should be entrusted to the many. Yet possibly these objections are to a great extent met by our old answer, that if the people are not utterly degraded, although individually they may be worse judges than those who have special knowledge— as a body they are as good or better. Moreover, there are some arts whose products are not judged of solely, or best, by the artists themselves, namely those arts whose products are recognized even by those who do not possess the art; for example, the knowledge of the house is not limited to the builder only; the user, or, in other words, the master, of the house will even be a better judge than the builder, just as the pilot will judge better of a rudder than the carpenter, and the guest will judge better of a feast than the cook.

. . .

13   . . . [W]hat if the good, the rich, the noble, and the other classes who make up a state, are all living together in the same city, will there, or will there not, be any doubt who shall rule?—No doubt at all in determining who ought to rule in each of the above-mentioned forms of government. For states are characterized by differences in their governing bodies—one of them has a government of the rich, another of the virtuous, and so on. But a difficulty arises when all these elements coexist. How are we to decide? Suppose the virtuous to be very few in number: may we consider their numbers in relation to their duties, and ask whether they are enough to administer the state, or so many as will make up a state? Objections may be urged against all the aspirants to political power. For those who found their claims on wealth or family might be thought to have no

basis of justice; on this principle, if any one person were richer than all the rest, it is clear that he ought to be ruler of them. In like manner he who is very distinguished by his birth ought to have the superiority over all those who claim on the ground that they are freeborn. In an aristocracy, or government of the best, a like difficulty occurs about virtue; for if one citizen be better than the other members of the government, however good they may be, he too, upon the same principle of justice, should rule over them. And if the people are to be supreme because they are stronger than the few, then if one man, or more than one, but not a majority, is stronger than the many, they ought to rule, and not the many.

All these considerations appear to show that none of the principles on which men claim to rule and to hold all other men in subjection to them are strictly right. . . .

If, however, there be some one person, or more than one, although not enough to make up the full complement of a state, whose virtue is so pre-eminent that the virtues or the political capacity of all the rest admit of no comparison with his or theirs, he or they can be no longer regarded as part of a state; for justice will not be done to the superior, if he is reckoned only as the equal of those who are so far inferior to him in virtue and in political capacity. Such an one may truly be deemed a God among men. Hence we see that legislation is necessarily concerned only with those who are equal in birth and in capacity; and that for men of pre-eminent virtue there is no law—they are themselves a law. Any one would be ridiculous who attempted to make laws for them. . . . And for this reason democratic states have instituted ostracism; equality is above all things their aim, and therefore they ostracized and banished from the city for a time those who seemed to predominate too much through their wealth, or the number of their friends, or through any other political influence. . . .

. . . In the perfect state there would be great doubts about the use of [ostracism] not when applied to excess in strength, wealth, popularity, or the like, but when used against some one who is pre-eminent in virtue,—what is to be done with him? Mankind will not say that such an one is to be expelled and exiled; on the other hand, he ought not to be a subject—that would be as if mankind should claim to rule over Zeus, dividing his offices among them. The only alternative is that all should joyfully obey such a ruler, according to what seems to be the order of nature, and that men like him should be kings in their state for life.

14   The preceding discussion, by a natural transition, leads to the consideration of royalty, which we admit to be one of the true forms of government. Let us see whether in order to be well governed a state or country should be under the rule of a king or under some other form of government; and whether monarchy, although good for some, may not be bad for others. . . .

.   .   .

15   . . . [I]s it well that a single man should have the supreme power in all things?

.   .   .

. . . If we call the rule of many men, who are all of them good, aristocracy, and the rule of one man royalty, then aristocracy will be better for states than royalty, whether the government is supported by force or not provided only that a number of men equal in virtue can be found.

BOOK IV

· · ·

2   In our original discussion about governments we divided them into three true forms: kingly rule, aristocracy, and constitutional government, and three corresponding perversions—tyranny, oligarchy, and democracy. Of kingly rule and of aristocracy we have already spoken. . . . In what follows we have to describe . . . the other forms, tyranny, oligarchy, and democracy.

It is obvious which of the three perversions is the worst, and which is the next in badness. That which is the perversion of the first and most divine is necessarily the worst. And just as a royal rule, if not a mere name, must exist by virtue of some great personal superiority in the king, so tyranny, which is the worst of governments, is necessarily the farthest removed from a well-constituted form; oligarchy is little better, for it is a long way from aristocracy, and democracy is the most tolerable of the three.

A writer [Plato] who preceded me has already made these distinctions, but his point of view is not the same as mine. . . .

4   . . . [T]he form of government is a democracy when the free, who are also poor and the majority, govern, and an oligarchy when the rich and the noble govern, they being at the same time few in number.

. . . [T]here are different forms both of democracy and oligarchy. . . .

Of forms of democracy first comes that which is said to be based strictly on equality. In such a democracy the law says that it is just for the poor to have no more advantage than the rich and that neither should be masters, but both equal. For if liberty and equality, as is thought by some, are chiefly to be found in democracy, they will be best attained when all persons alike share in the government to the utmost. And since the people are the majority, and the opinion of the majority is decisive, such a government must necessarily be a democracy. Here then is one sort of democracy. There is another in which the magistrates are elected according to a certain property qualification, but a low one; he who has the required amount of property has a share in the government, but he who loses his property loses his rights. Another kind is that in which all the citizens who are under no disqualification share in the government, but still the law is supreme. In another, everybody, if he be only a citizen, is admitted to the government, but the law is supreme as before. A fifth form of democracy, in other respects the same, is that in which, not the law, but the multitude, have the supreme power, and supersede the law by their decrees. This is a state of affairs brought about by the demagogues. For in democracies which are subject to the law the best citizens hold the first place, and there are no demagogues; but where the laws are not supreme, there demagogues spring up. For the people becomes a monarch, and is many in one; and the many have the power in their hands, not as individuals, but collectively. Homer says that 'it is not good to have a rule of many,' but whether he means this corporate rule, or the rule of many individuals, is uncertain. At all events this sort of democracy, which is now a monarch, and no longer under the control of law, seeks to exercise monarchical sway, and grows into a despot; the flatterer is held in honour; this sort of democracy being relatively to other democracies what tyranny is to other forms of monarchy. The spirit of both is the same, and they alike exercise a despotic rule over the better citizens. The decrees of the demos correspond to the edicts of the tyrant; and the demagogue is to the one what the flatterer is to the other. Both have great power;—the flatterer with the tyrant, the demagogue with democracies of the kind which we are describing. The demagogues make the decrees of the people override the laws, by referring all things to the popular assembly. And therefore they grow great, because the people have all things in their hands, and they hold in their hands the votes of the people, who are too ready to listen to them. Further, those who have any complaint to bring against the magistrates say, 'let the people be judges'; the people are too happy to accept the invitation; and so the authority of every office is undermined. Such a democracy is fairly open to the objection that it is not a constitution at all; for where the laws have no authority, there is no constitution. The law ought to be supreme over all, and the magistracies should judge of particulars, and only this should be considered a constitution. So that if democracy be a real form of government, the sort of system in which all things are regulated by decrees is clearly not even a democracy in the true sense of the word, for decrees relate only to particulars.

These then are the different kinds of democracy.

5   Of oligarchies, too, there are different kinds:—one where the property qualification for office is such that the poor, although they form the majority, have no share in the government, yet he who acquires a qualification may obtain a share. Another sort is when there is a qualification for office, but a high one, and the vacancies in the governing body are filled by co-optation. If the election is made out of all the qualified persons, a constitution of this kind inclines to an aristocracy, if out of a privileged class, to an oligarchy. Another sort of oligarchy is when the son succeeds the father. There is a fourth form, likewise hereditary, in which the magistrates are supreme and not the law. Among oligarchies this is what tyranny is among monarchies, and the last-mentioned

form of democracy among democracies; and in fact this sort of oligarchy receives the name of a dynasty (or rule of powerful families).

.   .   .

8   . . . I will proceed to consider constitutional government; of which the nature will be clearer now that oligarchy and democracy have been defined. For polity or constitutional government may be described generally as a fusion of oligarchy and democracy; but the term is usually applied to those forms of government which incline towards democracy, and the term aristocracy to those which incline towards oligarchy, because birth and education are commonly the accompaniments of wealth. Moreover, the rich already possess the external advantages the want of which is a temptation to crime, and hence they are called noblemen and gentlemen. And inasmuch as aristocracy seeks to give predominance to the best of the citizens, people say also of oligarchies that they are composed of noblemen and gentlemen. Now it appears to be an impossible thing that the state which is governed not by the best citizens but by the worst should be well-governed, and equally impossible that the state which is ill-governed should be governed by the best. But we must remember that good laws, if they are not obeyed, do not constitute good government. Hence there are two parts of good government; one is the actual obedience of citizens to the laws, the other part is the goodness of the laws which they obey; they may obey bad laws as well as good. And there may be a further subdivision; they may obey either the best laws which are attainable to them, or the best absolutely.

        The distribution of offices according to merit is a special characteristic of aristocracy, for the principle of an aristocracy is virtue, as wealth is of an oligarchy, and freedom of a democracy. In all of them there of course exists the right of the majority, and whatever seems good to the majority of those who share in the government has authority. Now in most states the form called polity exists, for the fusion goes no further than the attempt to unite the freedom of the poor and the wealth of the rich, who commonly take the place of the noble. But as there are three grounds on which men claim an equal share in the government, freedom, wealth, and virtue (for the fourth or good birth is the result of the two last, being only ancient wealth and virtue), it is clear that the admixture of the two elements, that is to say, of the rich and poor, is to be called a polity or constitutional government; and the union of the three is to be called aristocracy or the government of the best, and more than any other form of government, except the true and ideal, has a right to this name.

.   .   .

11   We have now to inquire what is the best constitution for most states, and the best life for most men, neither assuming a standard of virtue which is above ordinary persons, nor an education which is exceptionally favoured by nature and circumstances, nor yet an ideal state which is an aspiration only, but having regard to the life in which the majority are able to share, and to the form of government which states in general can attain. . . . For if what was said in the *Ethics* is true, that the happy life is the life according to virtue lived without

impediment, and that virtue is a mean, then the life which is in a mean, and in a mean attainable by every one, must be the best. And the same principles of virtue and vice are characteristic of cities and of constitutions; for the constitution is in a figure the life of the city.

Now in all states there are three elements: one class is very rich, another very poor, and a third in a mean. If is admitted that moderation and the mean are best, and therefore it will clearly be best to possess the gifts of fortune in moderation; for in that condition of life men are most ready to follow rational principle. But he who greatly excels in beauty, strength, birth, or wealth, or on the other hand who is very poor, or very weak, or very much disgraced, finds it difficult to follow rational principle. Of these two the one sort grow into violent and great criminals, the others into rogues and petty rascals. And two sorts of offences correspond to them, the one committed from violence, the other from roguery. Again, the middle class is least likely to shrink from rule, or to be over-ambitious for it; both of which are injuries to the state. Again, those who have too much of the goods of fortune, strength, wealth, friends, and the like, are neither willing nor able to submit to authority. The evil begins at home; for when they are boys, by reason of the luxury in which they are brought up, they never learn, even at school, the habit of obedience. On the other hand, the very poor, who are in the opposite extreme, are too degraded. So that the one class cannot obey, and can only rule despotically; the other knows not how to command and must be ruled like slaves. Thus arises a city, not of freemen, but of masters and slaves, the one despising, the other envying; and nothing can be more fatal to friendship and good fellowship in states than this: for good fellowship springs from friendship; when men are at enmity with one another, they would rather not even share the same path. But a city ought to be composed, as far as possible, of equals and similars; and these are generally the middle classes. Wherefore the city which is composed of middle-class citizens is necessarily best constituted in respect of the elements of which we say the fabric of the state naturally consists. And this is the class of citizens which is most secure in a state, for they do not, like the poor, covet their neighbours' goods; nor do others covet theirs, as the poor covet the goods of the rich; and as they neither plot against others, nor are themselves plotted against, they pass through life safely. Wisely then did Phocylides pray—'Many things are best in the mean; I desire to be of a middle condition in my city.'

Thus it is manifest that the best political community is formed by citizens of the middle class, and that those states are likely to be well-administered, in which the middle class is large, and stronger if possible than both the other classes, or at any rate than either singly; for the addition of the middle class turns the scale, and prevents either of the extremes from being dominant. Great then is the good fortune of a state in which the citizens have a moderate and sufficient property; for where some possess much, and the others nothing, there may arise an extreme democracy, or a pure oligarchy; or a tyranny may grow out of either extreme, —either out of the most rampant democracy, or out of an oligarchy; but it is not so likely to arise out of the middle constitutions and those akin to them. . . . The mean condition of states is clearly best, for no other is free from faction; and where the middle class is large, there are least likely to be factions and dissensions. . . . [D]emocracies are safer and more permanent than oligarchies, because they have a middle class which is more numerous and has a greater share in the government; for when there is no middle class, and the poor greatly exceed in number, troubles arise, and the state soon comes to an end. . . .

These considerations will help us to understand why most governments are either democratical or oligarchical. The reason is that the middle class is seldom numerous in them, and which ever party, whether the rich or the common people, transgresses the mean and predominates, draws the constitution its own way, and thus arises either oligarchy or democracy. There is another reason—the poor and the rich quarrel with one another, and whichever side gets the better, instead of establishing a just or popular government, regards political supremacy as the prize of victory, and the one party sets up a democracy and the other an oligarchy. . . .

What then is the best form of government, and what makes it the best, is evident; and of other constitutions, since we say that there are many kinds of democracy and many of oligarchy, it is not difficult to see which has the first and which the second or any other place in the order of excellence, now that we have determined which is the best. For that which is nearest to the best must of necessity be better, and that which is furthest from it worse, if we are judging absolutely and not relatively to given conditions: I say 'relatively to given conditions,' since a particular government may be preferable, but another form may be better for some people.

· · ·

12   The legislator should always include the middle class in his government; if he makes his laws oligarchical, to the middle class let him look; if he makes them democratical, he should equally by his laws try to attach this class to the state. There only can the government ever be stable where the middle class exceeds one or both of the others, and in that case there will be no fear that the rich will unite with the poor against the rulers. For neither of them will ever be willing to serve the other, and if they look for some form of government more suitable to both, they will find none better than this, for the rich and the poor will never consent to rule in turn, because they mistrust one another. The arbiter is always the one trusted, and he who is in the middle is an arbiter. The more perfect the admixture of the political elements, the more lasting will be the constitution. Many even of those who desire to form aristocratical governments make a mistake, not only in giving too much power to the rich, but in attempting to overreach the people. There comes a time when out of a false good there arises a true evil, since the encroachments of the rich are more destructive to the constitution than those of the people.

· · ·

BOOK VII

. . .

14   Since every political society is composed of rulers and subjects, let us consider whether the relations of one to the other should interchange or be permanent. For the education of the citizens will necessarily vary with the answer given to this question. Now, if some men excelled others in the same degree in which gods and heroes are supposed to excel mankind in general (having in the first place a great advantage even in their bodies, and secondly in their minds), so that the superiority of the governors was undisputed and patent to their subjects, it would clearly be better that once for all the one class should rule and the others serve. But since this is unattainable, and kings have no marked superiority over their subjects, such as Scylax affirms to be found among the Indians, it is obviously necessary on many grounds that all the citizens alike should take their turn of governing and being governed. Equality consists in the same treatment of similar persons, and no government can stand which is not founded upon justice. . . .

REFLECTIONS ON THE REVOLUTION IN FRANCE

Edmund Burke

1729–1797

✂

Edmund Burke is justly celebrated as the father of modern conservatism, although he would no doubt feel uneasy among those who today
style themselves as "new" conservatives. Few men have had his gift
for stirring rhetoric and few could match him for stinging invective.
Both fill the pages of *Reflections on the Revolution in France* (1790) in
which, provoked by the French cataclysm of 1789, he set forth in general terms a creed which has provided texts for conservatives ever since.

Burke denounced the revolution as a "strange chaos of levity
and ferocity." In his *Appeal from the New to the Old Whigs* he reaffirmed this verdict by calling the revolution "a foul, impious, monstrous thing, wholly out of the course of moral nature, generated in
treachery, fraud, falsehood, hypocrisy, and unprovoked murder."[1]
Burke appealed instead to tradition, to the principle of historical continuity and to "the wisdom of our ancestors." He challenged the right
of any single generation to upset the verdict of centuries. The multitude
can be foolish, but the species is wise, he said. One wants no giddy
choices of the day but the "deliberate election of the ages and of
generations."[2]

Content with the English allotment of 1688, Burke opposed reform
of a House of Commons in which a single "rotten borough" had more
representation than the industrial city of Birmingham. Never has more
eloquence been summoned to defend limited monarchy, the church,
aristocracy and private property. The rich he regarded as at worst, "the
ballast in the vessel of the commonwealth"[3] and aristocracy, even the

---

Edmund Burke, from "Reflections on the Revolution in France" in *The Writings and
Speeches of Edmund Burke*, III, Beaconsfield ed. (London, 1901), 240–41, 249, 251–52, 256–
57, 266–67, 269, 272, 274–75, 277, 296–99, 306, 335, 356–57, 395–98, 415–16. Footnotes which
appeared in the original have been deleted.
[1] *Writings and Speeches of Edmund Burke*, IV, p. 71.
[2] "Reform of Representation in the House of Commons (1782)," *Ibid.*, VII, p. 95.
[3] "Reflections," *Ibid.*, III, p. 299.

decadent French aristocracy, as the "Corinthian capital of polished society." [4]

On the other hand, Burke urged that "in all disputes between the people and their rulers, the presumption is at least upon a par in favour of the people" and he reminded his readers "an irregular, convulsive movement may be necessary to throw off an irregular, convulsive disease." [5] When he called democracy "the most shameless thing in the world," [6] he meant "pure" democracy and he had in mind exercises of uninhibited will by instant majorities such as those depicted by Rousseau and exemplified by the French national assembly. But his basic impulse was to regard people as unfit for self-government. They were "rabble, miserable sheep," the "swinish multitude."

Burke had no hereditary title. He served in the House of Commons on the fickle sufferance of a handful of Bristol merchants and later on the patronage of the Duke of Newcastle. Burke's ferocious attack on the French Revolution broke up lifelong friendships and lost him his standing in his own party. But conservatives have venerated him ever since and liberals have much to learn from him.

. . .

I flatter myself that I love a manly, moral, regulated liberty as well as any . . . ; and perhaps I have given . . . good proofs of my attachment to that cause, in the whole course of my public conduct. . . . But I cannot stand forward, and give praise or blame to anything which relates to human actions and human concerns on a simple view of the object, as it stands stripped of every relation, in all the nakedness and solitude of metaphysical abstraction. Circumstances (which with some gentlemen pass for nothing) give in reality to every political principle its distinguishing color and discriminating effect. The circumstances are what render every civil and political scheme beneficial or noxious to mankind. Abstractedly speaking, government, as well as liberty, is good; yet could I, in common sense, ten years ago, have felicitated France on her enjoyment of a government, (for she then had a government,) without inquiry what the nature of that government was, or how it was administered? Can I now congratulate the same nation upon its freedom? Is it because liberty in the abstract may be classed amongst the blessings of mankind, that I am seriously to felicitate a madman who has escaped from the protecting restraint and wholesome darkness of his cell on his restoration to the enjoyment of light and liberty? Am I to congratulate a highway man and murderer who has broke prison upon the recovery of his natural rights? . . .

. . . . .

. . . According to this spiritual doctor of politics [Dr. Richard Price], if his Majesty does not owe his crown to the choice of his people, he is no *lawful* king. Now nothing can be more untrue than that the crown of this kingdom is so held by his Majesty. Therefore, if you follow their rule, the king of Great Britain, who most certainly does not owe his high office to any form of popular election,

---

[4] *Ibid.*, p. 416.
[5] *Ibid.*, p. 263.
[6] *Ibid.*, p. 355.

is in no respect better than the rest of the gang of usurpers, who reign, or rather rob, all over the face of this our miserable world, without any sort of right or title to the allegiance of their people. . . .

· · ·

Whatever may be the success of evasion in explaining away the gross error of *fact*, which supposes that his Majesty (though he holds it in concurrence with the wishes) owes his crown to the choice of his people, yet nothing can evade their full, explicit declaration concerning the principle of a right in the people to choose,—which right is directly maintained, and tenaciously adhered to. All the oblique insinuations concerning election bottom in this proposition, and are referable to it. Lest the foundation of the king's exclusive legal title should pass for a mere rant of adulatory freedom, the political divine proceeds dogmatically to assert, that, by the principles of the Revolution, the people of England have acquired three fundamental rights, all of which, with him, compose one system, and lie together in one short sentence: namely, that we have acquired a right

1. "To choose our own governors."
2. "To cashier them for misconduct."
3. "To frame a government for ourselves."

This new, and hitherto unheard-of bill of rights, though made in the name of the whole people, belongs to those gentlemen and their faction only. The body of the people of England have no share in it. They utterly disclaim it. They will resist the practical assertion of it with their lives and fortunes. They are bound to do so by the laws of their country, made at the time of that very Revolution which is appealed to in favor of the fictitious rights claimed by the society [the Revolution Society addressed by Dr. Price] which abuses its name.

· · ·

So far is it from being true that we acquired a right by the Revolution to elect our kings, that, if we had possessed it before, the English nation did at that time most solemnly renounce and abdicate it, for themselves, and for all their posterity forever. . . .

· · ·

The second claim of the Revolution Society is "a right of cashiering their governors for *misconduct.*" . . .

No government could stand a moment, if it could be blown down with anything so loose and indefinite as an opinion of *"misconduct."* They who led at the Revolution grounded their virtual abdication of King James upon no such light and uncertain principle. They charged him with nothing less than a design, confirmed by a multitude of illegal overt acts, to *subvert the Protestant Church and State,* and their *fundamental,* unquestionable laws and liberties: they charged him with having broken the *original contract* between king and people. This was more than *misconduct.* A grave and overruling necessity obliged them to take the step they took, and took with infinite reluctance, as under that most rigorous of all laws. Their trust for the future preservation of the Constitution was not in future revolutions. The grand policy of all their regulations was to render it al-

most impracticable for any future sovereign to compel the states of the kingdom
to have again recourse to those violent remedies. . . .

•   •   •

Kings, in one sense, are undoubtedly the servants of the people, because
their power has no other rational end than that of the general advantage; but it
is not true that they are, in the ordinary sense, (by our Constitution, at least,)
anything like servants,—the essence of whose situation is to obey the commands
of some other, and to be removable at pleasure. But the king of Great Britain
obeys no other person; all other persons are individually, and collectively too,
under him, and owe to him a legal obedience. . . .

•   •

. . . Such a claim is as ill-suited to our temper and wishes as it is unsup-
ported by any appearance of authority. The very idea of the fabrication of a new
government is enough to fill us with disgust and horror. We wished at the period
of the Revolution, and do now wish, to derive all we possess as *an inheritance
from our forefathers*. Upon that body and stock of inheritance we have taken
care not to inoculate any scion alien to the nature of the original plant. All the
reformations we have hitherto made have proceeded upon the principle of reference to antiquity; and I hope, nay, I am persuaded, that all those which possibly
may be made hereafter will be carefully formed upon analogical precedent, authority, and example.

•   •   •

You * will observe, that, from Magna Charta to the Declaration of Right, it
has been the uniform policy of our Constitution to claim and assert our liberties
as an *entailed inheritance* derived to us from our forefathers, and to be transmitted to our posterity,—as an estate specially belonging to the people of this
kingdom, without any reference whatever to any other more general or prior
right. By this means our Constitution preserves an unity in so great a diversity of
its parts. We have an inheritable crown, an inheritable peerage, and a House of
Commons and a people inheriting privileges, franchises, and liberties from a long
line of ancestors.

This policy appears to me to be the result of profound reflection,—or rather
the happy effect of following Nature, which is wisdom without reflection, and
above it. A spirit of innovation is generally the result of a selfish temper and
confined views. People will not look forward to posterity, who never look backward to their ancestors. Besides, the people of England well know that the idea of
inheritance furnishes a sure principle of conservation, and a sure principle of
transmission, without at all excluding a principle of improvement. It leaves
acquisition free; but it secures what it acquires. Whatever advantages are obtained by a state proceeding on these maxims are locked fast as in a sort of family settlement, grasped as in a kind of mortmain forever. By a constitutional
policy working after the pattern of Nature, we receive, we hold, we transmit our

* The *Reflections* were first cast in the form of a letter to a young Frenchman and
Burke retained the form in his later, and fuller, statement. [Ed.]

government and our privileges, in the same manner in which we enjoy and transmit our property and our lives. The institutions of policy, the goods of fortune,
the gifts of Providence, are handed down to us, and from us, in the same course
and order. Our political system is placed in a just correspondence and symmetry
with the order of the world, and with the mode of existence decreed to a permanent body composed of transitory parts,—wherein, by the disposition of a stu-
pendous wisdom, moulding together the great mysterious incorporation of the
human race, the whole, at one time, is never old or middle-aged or young, but, in
a condition of unchangeable constancy, moves on through the varied tenor of
perpetual decay, fall, renovation, and progression. Thus, by preserving the
method of Nature in the conduct of the state, in what we improve we are never
wholly new, in what we retain we are never wholly obsolete. By adhering in this
manner and on those principles to our forefathers, we are guided, not by the
superstition of antiquarians, but by the spirit of philosophic analogy. In this
choice of inheritance we have given to our frame of polity the image of a relation
in blood: binding up the Constitution of our country with our dearest domestic
ties; adopting our fundamental laws into the bosom of our family affections;
keeping inseparable, and cherishing with the warmth of all their combined and
mutually reflected charities, our state, our hearths, our sepulchres, and our altars.

. . . [Y]ou had all that combination and all that opposition of interests,
you had that action and counteraction, which, in the natural and in the political
world, from the reciprocal struggle of discordant powers draws out the harmony
of the universe. These opposed and conflicting interests, which you considered as
so great a blemish in your old and in our present Constitution, interpose a salutary check to all precipitate resolutions. They render deliberation a matter, not of
choice, but of necessity; they make all change a subject of *compromise,* which
naturally begets moderation; they produce *temperaments,* preventing the sore evil
of harsh, crude, unqualified reformations, and rendering all the headlong exertions of arbitrary power, in the few or in the many, forever impracticable. . . .

The Chancellor of France, at the opening of the States, said, in a tone of
oratorial flourish, that all occupations were honorable. If he meant only that no
honest employment was disgraceful, he would not have gone beyond the truth.
But in asserting that anything is honorable, we imply some distinction in its
favor. The occupation of a hair-dresser, or of a working tallow-chandler, cannot
be a matter of honor to any person,—to say nothing of a number of other more
servile employments. Such descriptions of men ought not to suffer oppression
from the state; but the state suffers oppression, if such as they, either individually or collectively, are permitted to rule. In this you think you are combating
prejudice, but you are at war with Nature.

. . . [D]o not imagine that I wish to confine power, authority, and distinction to blood and names and titles. No, Sir. There is no qualification for government but virtue and wisdom, actual or presumptive. Wherever they are actually

found, they have, in whatever state, condition, profession, or trade, the passport of Heaven to human place and honor. Woe to the country which would madly and impiously reject the service of the talents and virtues, civil, military, or religious, that are given to grace and to serve it; and would condemn to obscurity everything formed to diffuse lustre and glory around a state! Woe to that country, too, that, passing into the opposite extreme, considers a low education, a mean, contracted view of things, a sordid, mercenary occupation, as a preferable title to command! Everything ought to be open,—but not indifferently to every man. . . . I do not hesitate to say that the road to eminence and power, from obscure condition, ought not to be made too easy, nor a thing too much of course. If rare merit be the rarest of all rare things, it ought to pass through some sort of probation. The temple of honor ought to be seated on an eminence. If it be opened through virtue, let it be remembered, too, that virtue is never tried but by some difficulty and some struggle.

Nothing is a due and adequate representation of a state, that does not represent its ability, as well as its property. But as ability is a vigorous and active principle, and as property is sluggish, inert, and timid, it never can be safe from the invasions of ability, unless it be, out of all proportion, predominant in the representation. It must be represented, too, in great masses of accumulation, or it is not rightly protected. The characteristic essence of property, formed out of the combined principles of its acquisition and conservation, is to be *unequal*. The great masses, therefore, which excite envy, and tempt rapacity, must be put out of the possibility of danger. Then they form a natural rampart about the lesser properties in all their gradations. The same quantity of property which is by the natural course of things divided among many has not the same operation. Its defensive power is weakened as it is diffused. In this diffusion each man's portion is less than what, in the eagerness of his desires, he may flatter himself to obtain by dissipating the accumulations of others. The plunder of the few would, indeed, give but a share inconceivably small in the distribution to the many. But the many are not capable of making this calculation; and those who lead them to rapine never intend this distribution.

The power of perpetuating our property in our families is one of the most valuable and interesting circumstances belonging to it, and that which tends the most to the perpetuation of society itself. It makes our weakness subservient to our virtue; it grafts benevolence even upon avarice. The possessors of family wealth, and of the distinction which attends hereditary possession, (as most concerned in it,) are the natural securities for this transmission. With us the House of Peers is formed upon this principle. It is wholly composed of hereditary property and hereditary distinction, and made, therefore, the third of the legislature, and, in the last event, the sole judge of all property in all its subdivisions. The House of Commons, too, though not necessarily, yet in fact, is always so composed, in the far greater part. Let those large proprietors be what they will, (and they have their chance of being amongst the best,) they are, at the very worst, the ballast in the vessel of the commonwealth. For though hereditary wealth, and the rank which goes with it, are too much idolized by creeping sycophants, and the blind, abject admirers of power, they are too rashly slighted in shallow speculations of the petulant, assuming, short-sighted coxcombs of philosophy. Some decent, regulated preëminence, some preference (not exclusive appropriation) given to birth, is neither unnatural, nor unjust, nor impolitic.

It is said that twenty-four millions ought to prevail over two hundred thousand. True; if the constitution of a kingdom be a problem of arithmetic. This sort of discourse does well enough with the lamp-post for its second: to men who *may* reason calmly it is ridiculous. The will of the many, and their interest, must very often differ; and great will be the difference when they make an evil choice. A government of five hundred country attorneys and obscure curates is not good for twenty-four millions of men, though it were chosen by eight-and-forty millions; nor is it better for being guided by a dozen of persons of quality who have betrayed their trust in order to obtain that power.* . . .

. . . [I]f popular representation, or choice, is necesary to the *legitimacy* of all government, the House of Lords is, at one stroke, bastardized and corrupted in blood. That House is no representative of the people at all, even in "semblance" or "in form." . . .

We are but too apt to consider things in the state in which we find them, without sufficiently adverting to the causes by which they have been produced, and possibly may be upheld. Nothing is more certain than that our manners, our civilization, and all the good things which are connected with manners and with civilization, have, in this European world of ours, depended for ages upon two principles, and were, indeed, the result of both combined: I mean the spirit of a gentleman, and the spirit of religion. The nobility and the clergy, the one by profession, and the other by patronage, kept learning in existence, even in the midst of arms and confusions, and whilst governments were rather in their causes than formed. Learning paid back what it received to nobility and to priesthood, and paid it with usury, by enlarging their ideas, and by furnishing their minds. Happy, if they had all continued to know their indissoluble union, and their proper place! Happy, if learning, not debauched by ambition, had been satisfied to continue the instructor, and not aspired to be the master! Along with its natural protectors and guardians, learning will be cast into the mire and trodden down under the hoofs of a swinish multitude.

But one of the first and most leading principles on which the commonwealth and the laws are consecrated is lest the temporary possessors and life-renters in it, unmindful of what they have received from their ancestors, or of what is due to their posterity, should act as if they were the entire masters; that they should

* Such was the composition of the Third Estate, as Burke had earlier described it. [Ed.]

not think it amongst their rights to cut off the entail or commit waste on the inheritance, by destroying at their pleasure the whole original fabric of their society: hazarding to leave to those who come after them a ruin instead of an habitation,—and teaching these successors as little to respect their contrivances as they had themselves respected the institutions of their forefathers. By this unprincipled facility of changing the state as often and as much and in as many ways as there are floating fancies or fashions, the whole chain and continuity of the commonwealth would be broken; no one generation could link with the other; men would become little better than the flies of a summer.

When all the frauds, impostures, violences, rapines, burnings, murders, confiscations, compulsory paper currencies, and every description of tyranny and cruelty employed to bring about and to uphold this Revolution have their natural effect, that is, to shock the moral sentiments of all virtuous and sober minds, the abettors of this philosophic system immediately strain their throats in a declamation against the old monarchical government of France. When they have rendered that deposed power sufficiently black, they then proceed in argument, as if all those who disapprove of their new abuses must of course be partisans of the old,—that those who reprobate their crude and violent schemes of liberty ought to be treated as advocates for servitude. I admit that their necessities do compel them to this base and contemptible fraud. Nothing can reconcile men to their proceedings and projects but the supposition that there is no third option between them and some tyranny as odious as can be furnished by the records of history or by the invention of poets. This prattling of theirs hardly deserves the name of sophistry. It is nothing but plain impudence. Have these gentlemen never heard, in the whole circle of the worlds of theory and practice, of anything between the despotism of the monarch and the despotism of the multitude? Have they never heard of a monarchy directed by laws, controlled and balanced by the great hereditary wealth and hereditary dignity of a nation, and both again controlled by a judicious check from the reason and feeling of the people at large, acting by a suitable and permanent organ? Is it, then, impossible that a man may be found who, without criminal ill intention or pitiable absurdity, shall prefer such a mixed and tempered government to either of the extremes,—and who may repute that nation to be destitute of all wisdom and of all virtue, which, having in its choice to obtain such a government with ease, *or rather to confirm it when actually possessed,* thought proper to commit a thousand crimes, and to subject their country to a thousand evils, in order to avoid it? Is it, then, a truth so universally acknowledged, that a pure democracy is the only tolerable form into which human society can be thrown, that a man is not permitted to hesitate about its merits, without the suspicion of being a friend to tyranny, that is, of being a foe to mankind?

I do not know under what description to class the present ruling authority in France. It affects to be a pure democracy, though I think it in a direct train of becoming shortly a mischievous and ignoble oligarchy. But for the present I admit it to be a contrivance of the nature and effect of what it pretends to. I reprobate no form of government merely upon abstract principles. There may be situations in which the purely democratic form will become necessary. There may be some (very few, and very particularly circumstanced) where it would be clearly desirable. This I do not take to be the case of France, or of any other great country. Until now, we have seen no examples of considerable democracies. The ancients were better acquainted with them. Not being wholly unread in the authors who had seen the most of those constitutions, and who best understood them, I cannot help concurring with their opinion, that an absolute democracy no more than absolute monarchy is to be reckoned among the legitimate forms of government. They think it rather the corruption and degeneracy than the sound constitution of a republic. If I recollect rightly, Aristotle observes, that a democracy has many striking points of resemblance with a tyranny. Of this I am certain, that in a democracy the majority of the citizens is capable of exercising the most cruel oppressions upon the minority, whenever strong divisions prevail in that kind of polity, as they often must,—and that oppression of the minority will extend to far greater numbers, and will be carried on with much greater fury, than can almost ever be apprehended from the dominion of a single sceptre. In such a popular persecution, individual sufferers are in a much more deplorable condition than in any other. Under a cruel prince they have the balmy compassion of mankind to assuage the smart of their wounds, they have the plaudits of the people to animate their generous constancy under their sufferings: but those who are subjected to wrong under multitudes are deprived of all external consolation; they seem deserted by mankind, overpowered by a conspiracy of their whole species.

But admitting democracy not to have that inevitable tendency to party tyranny which I suppose it to have, and admitting it to possess as much good in it when unmixed as I am sure it possesses when compounded with other forms; does monarchy, on its part, contain nothing at all to recommend it? . . .

.   .   .

All this violent cry against the nobility I take to be a mere work of art. To be honored and even privileged by the laws, opinions, and inveterate usages of our country, growing out of the prejudice of ages, has nothing to provoke horror and indignation in any man. Even to be too tenacious of those privileges is not absolutely a crime. The strong struggle in every individual to preserve possession of what he has found to belong to him, and to distinguish him, is one of the securities against injustice and despotism implanted in our nature. It operates as an instinct to secure property, and to preserve communities in a settled state. What is there to shock in this? Nobility is a graceful ornament to the civil order. It is the Corinthian capital of polished society. . . . It is, indeed, one sign of a liberal and benevolent mind to incline to it with some sort of partial propensity. He feels no ennobling principle in his own heart, who wishes to level all the artificial institutions which have been adopted for giving a body to opinion and permanence to fugitive esteem. It is a sour, malignant, envious disposition, without taste for the reality, or for any image or representation of virtue, that sees with joy the unmerited fall of what had long flourished in splendor and in honor. I do not like to see anything destroyed, any void produced in society, any ruin on the face of the land. . . .

∙ ∙ ∙

A DISQUISITION ON GOVERNMENT

John C. Calhoun

1782–1850

❧

John C. Calhoun served as Secretary of War in President James Monroe's cabinet and as vice president under both John Quincy Adams and Andrew Jackson, resigning from the vice presidency after the nullification crisis of 1832. Thereafter, he represented South Carolina in the U.S. Senate where, to protect the South from the rapidly growing economic power of the North, he opposed all tendencies to centralize power in the federal government as well as the admission of new states that would tip the scales even more in favor of the North. Advocate of a lost cause, he combined a profound insight into problems of political philosophy with passionate sectionalism and a vigorous defense of slavery. It was this grasp of theoretical issues, no doubt, that prompted Henry Clay to refer sarcastically to his "metaphysician's brain," thereby provoking Calhoun to the following response:

> *I cannot retort on the Senator the charge of being metaphysical. I cannot accuse him of possessing the powers of analysis and generalization, those higher faculties of the mind (called metaphysical by those who do not possess them) which decompose and resolve into their elements the complex masses of ideas that exist in the world of mind . . . and without which those deep and hidden causes which are in constant action, and producing such mighty changes in the condition of society, would operate unseen and undetected. The absence of these higher qualities of mind is conspicuous throughout the whole course of the Senator's public life. To this may be traced that he prefers the specious to the solid, and the plausible to the true.*[1]

Calhoun's *A Disquisition on Government*, written shortly before his death, while it may not, as he thought, lay a new foundation for political science, is an acute exposition of the conservative position.

John C. Calhoun, from *A Disquisition on Government and a Discourse on the Constitution of the United States*, ed. R. K. Cralle, published under the direction of the General Assembly of the State of South Carolina (Columbia, S.C., 1851), pp. 34–39, 43–51, 57–58.

[1] Cited by John M. Anderson in *Calhoun, Basic Documents* (State College, Pa.: Bald Eagle Press, 1952), p. 14.

. . .

. . . How can those who are invested with the powers of government be prevented from employing them, as the means of aggrandizing themselves, instead of using them to protect and preserve society? It cannot be done by instituting a higher power to control the government, and those who administer it. This would be but to change the seat of authority, and to make this higher power, in reality, the government; with the same tendency, on the part of those who might control its powers, to pervert them into instruments of aggrandizement. Nor can it be done by limiting the powers of government, so as to make it too feeble to be made an instrument of abuse; for, passing by the difficulty of so limiting its powers, without creating a power higher than the government itself to enforce the observance of the limitations, it is a sufficient objection that it would, if practicable, defeat the end for which government is ordained, by making it too feeble to protect and preserve society. The powers necessary for this purpose will ever prove sufficient to aggrandize those who control it, at the expense of the rest of the community.

In estimating what amount of power would be requisite to secure the objects of government, we must take into the reckoning, what would be necessary to defend the community against external, as well as internal dangers. Government must be able to repel assaults from abroad, as well as to repress violence and disorders within. It must not be overlooked, that the human race is not comprehended in a single society or community. The limited reason and faculties of man, the great diversity of language, customs, pursuits, situation and complexion, and the difficulty of intercourse, with various other causes, have, by their operation, formed a great many separate communities, acting independently of each other. Between these there is the same tendency to conflict,—and from the same constitution of our nature,—as between men individually; and even stronger,—because the sympathetic or social feelings are not so strong between different communities, as between individuals of the same community. So powerful, indeed, is this tendency, that it has led to almost incessant wars between contiguous communities for plunder and conquest, or to avenge injuries, real or supposed.

So long as this state of things continues, exigencies will occur, in which the entire powers and resources of the community will be needed to defend its existence. When this is at stake, every other consideration must yield to it. Self-preservation is the supreme law, as well with communities as individuals. And hence the danger of withholding from government the full command of the power and resources of the state; and the great difficulty of limiting its powers consistently with the protection and preservation of the community. And hence the question recurs,—By what means can government, without being divested of the full command of the resources of the community, be prevented from abusing its powers?

The question involves difficulties which, from the earliest ages, wise and good men have attempted to overcome;—but hitherto with but partial success.

For this purpose many devices have been resorted to, suited to the various stages of intelligence and civilization through which our race has passed, and to the different forms of government to which they have been applied. The aid of superstition, ceremonies, education, religion, organic arrangements, both of the government and the community, has been, from time to time, appealed to. Some of the most remarkable of these devices, whether regarded in reference to their wisdom and the skill displayed in their application, or to the permanency of their effects, are to be found in the early dawn of civilization;—in the institutions of the Egyptians, the Hindoos, the Chinese, and the Jews. The only materials which that early age afforded for the construction of constitutions, when intelligence was so partially diffused, were applied with consummate wisdom and skill. To their successful application may be fairly traced the subsequent advance of our race in civilization and intelligence, of which we now enjoy the benefits. For, without a constitution,—something to counteract the strong tendency of government to disorder and abuse, and to give stability to political institutions,—there can be little progress or permanent improvement.

In answering the important question under consideration, it is not necessary to enter into an examination of the various contrivances adopted by these celebrated governments to counteract this tendency to disorder and abuse, nor to undertake to treat of constitution in its most comprehensive sense. What I propose is far more limited,—to explain on what principles government must be formed, in order to resist, by its own interior structure,—or, to use a single term, *organism,*—the tendency to abuse of power. This structure, or organism, is what is meant by constitution, in its strict and more usual sense; and it is this which distinguishes, what are called, constitutional governments from absolute. It is in this strict and more usual sense that I propose to use the term hereafter.

How government, then, must be constructed, in order to counteract, through its organism, this tendency on the part of those who make and execute the laws to oppress those subject to their operation, is the next question which claims attention.

There is but one way in which this can possibly be done, and that is, by such an organism as will furnish the ruled with the means of resisting successfully this tendency on the part of the rulers to oppression and abuse. Power can only be resisted by power,—and tendency by tendency. Those who exercise power and those subject to its exercise,—the rulers and the ruled,—stand in antagonistic relations to each other. The same constitution of our nature which leads rulers to oppress the ruled,—regardless of the object for which government is ordained, —will, with equal strength, lead the ruled to resist, when possessed of the means of making peaceable and effective resistance. Such an organism, then, as will furnish the means by which resistance may be systematically and peaceably made on the part of the ruled, to oppression and abuse of power on the part of the rulers, is the first and indispensable step towards *forming* a constitutional government. And as this can only be effected by or through the right of suffrage,—(the right on the part of the ruled to choose their rulers at proper intervals, and to hold them thereby responsible for their conduct,)—the responsibility of the rulers to the ruled, through the right of suffrage, is the indispensable and primary principle in the *foundation* of a constitutional government. When this right is properly guarded, and the people sufficiently enlightened to understand their own rights and the interests of the community, and duly to appreciate the motives and conduct of those appointed to make and execute the laws, it is all-sufficient to give to those who elect, effective control over those they have elected.

I call the right of suffrage the indispensable and primary principle; for it would be a great and dangerous mistake to suppose, as many do, that it is, of itself, sufficient to form constitutional governments. To this erroneous opinion may be traced one of the causes, why so few attempts to form constitutional governments have succeeded; and why, of the few which have, so small a number have had durable existence. It has led, not only to mistakes in the attempts to form such governments, but to their overthrow, when they have, by some good fortune, been correctly formed. So far from being, of itself, sufficient,—however well guarded it might be, and however enlightened the people,—it would, unaided by other provisions, leave the government as absolute, as it would be in the hands of irresponsible rulers; and with a tendency, at least as strong, towards oppression and abuse of its powers; as I shall next proceed to explain.

The right of suffrage, of itself, can do no more than give complete control to those who elect, over the conduct of those they have elected. In doing this, it accomplishes all it possibly can accomplish. This is its aim,—and when this is attained, its end is fulfilled. It can do no more, however enlightened the people, or however widely extended or well guarded the right may be. The sum total, then, of its effects, when most successful, is, to make those elected, the true and faithful representatives of those who elected them,—instead of irresponsible rulers,—as they would be without it; and thus, by converting it into an agency, and the rulers into agents, to divest government of all claims to sovereignty, and to retain it unimpaired to the community. But it is manifest that the right of suffrage, in making these changes, transfers, in reality, the actual control over the government, from those who make and execute the laws, to the body of the community; and, thereby, places the powers of the government as fully in the mass of the community, as they would be if they, in fact, had assembled, made, and executed the laws themselves, without the intervention of representatives or agents. The more perfectly it does this, the more perfectly it accomplishes its ends; but in doing so, it only changes the seat of authority, without counteracting, in the least, the tendency of the government to oppression and abuse of its powers.

If the whole community had the same interests, so that the interests of each and every portion would be so affected by the action of the government, that the laws which oppressed or impoverished one portion, would necessarily oppress and impoverish all others,—or the reverse,—then the right of suffrage, of itself, would be all-sufficient to counteract the tendency of the government to oppression and abuse of its powers; and, of course, would form, of itself, a perfect constitutional government. The interest of all being the same, by supposition, as far as the action of the government was concerned, all would have like interests as to what laws should be made, and how they should be executed. All strife and struggle would cease as to who should be elected to make and execute them. The only question would be, who was most fit; who the wisest and most capable of understanding the common interest of the whole. This decided, the election would pass off quietly, and without party discord; as no one portion could advance its own peculiar interest without regard to the rest, by electing a favorite candidate.

But such is not the case. On the contrary, nothing is more difficult than to equalize the action of the government, in reference to the various and diversified interests of the community; and nothing more easy than to pervert its powers into instruments to aggrandize and enrich one or more interests by oppressing and impoverishing the others; and this too, under the operation of laws, couched in general terms;—and which, on their face, appear fair and equal. Nor is this the case in some particular communities only. It is so in all; the small and the great,—the poor and the rich,—irrespective of pursuits, productions, or degrees of civilization;—with, however, this difference, that the more extensive and populous the country, the more diversified the condition and pursuits of its population, and the richer, more luxurious, and dissimilar the people, the more difficult it is to equalize the action of the government,—and the more easy for one portion of the community to pervert its powers to oppress, and plunder the other.

Such being the case, it necessarily results, that the right of suffrage, by placing the control of the government in the community must, from the same constitution of our nature which makes government necessary to preserve society, lead to conflict among its different interests,—each striving to obtain possession of its powers, as the means of protecting itself against the others;—or of advancing its respective interests, regardless of the interests of others. For this purpose, a struggle will take place between the various interests to obtain a majority, in order to control the government. If no one interest be strong enough, of itself, to obtain it, a combination will be formed between those whose interests are most alike;—each conceding something to the others, until a sufficient number is obtained to make a majority. The process may be slow, and much time may be required before a compact, organized majority can be thus formed; but formed it will be in time, even without preconcert or design, by the sure workings of that principle or constitution of our nature in which government itself originates. When once formed, the community will be divided into two great parties,—a major and minor,—between which there will be incessant struggles on the one side to retain, and on the other to obtain the majority,—and, thereby, the control of the government and the advantages it confers.

So deeply seated, indeed, is this tendency to conflict between the different interests or portions of the community, that it would result from the action of the government itself, even though it were possible to find a community, where the people were all of the same pursuits, placed in the same condition of life, and in every respect, so situated, as to be without inequality of condition or diversity of interests. The advantages of possessing the control of the powers of the government, and, thereby, of its honors and emoluments, are, of themselves, exclusive of all other considerations, ample to divide even such a community into two great hostile parties.

. . .

Nor is it less certain, from the operation of all these causes, that the dominant majority, for the time, would have the same tendency to oppression and abuse of power, which, without the right of suffrage, irresponsible rulers would have. No reason, indeed, can be assigned, why the latter would abuse their power, which would not apply, with equal force, to the former. The dominant majority, for the time, would, in reality, through the right of suffrage, be the rulers—the controlling, governing, and irresponsible power; and those who make and execute the laws would, for the time, be, in reality, but *their* representatives and agents.

Nor would the fact that the former would constitute a majority of the community, counteract a tendency originating in the constitution of man; and which, as such, cannot depend on the number by whom the powers of the government may be wielded. Be it greater or smaller, a majority or minority, it must equally partake of an attribute inherent in each individual composing it; and, as in each the individual is stronger than the social feelings, the one would have the same tendency as the other to oppression and abuse of power. The reason applies to government in all its forms,—whether it be that of the one, the few, or the many. In each there must, of necessity, be a governing and governed,—a ruling and a subject portion. The one implies the other; and in all, the two bear the same relation to each other;—and have, on the part of the governing portion, the same tendency to oppression and abuse of power. Where the majority is that portion, it matters not how its powers may be exercised;—whether directly by themselves, or indirectly, through representatives or agents. Be it which it may, the minority, for the time, will be as much the governed or subject portion, as are the people in an aristocracy, or the subjects in a monarchy. The only difference in this respect is, that in the government of a majority, the minority may become the majority, and the majority the minority, through the right of suffrage; and thereby change their relative positions, without the intervention of force and revolution. But the duration, or uncertainty of the tenure, by which power is held, cannot, of itself, counteract the tendency inherent in government to oppression and abuse of power. On the contrary, the very uncertainty of the tenure, combined with the violent party warfare which must ever precede a change of parties under such governments, would rather tend to increase than diminish the tendency to oppression.

As, then, the right of suffrage, without some other provision, cannot counteract this tendency of government, the next question for consideration is— What is that other provision? This demands the most serious consideration; for of all the questions embraced in the science of government, it involves a principle, the most important, and the least understood; and when understood, the most difficult of application in practice. It is, indeed, emphatically, that principle which *makes* the constitution, in its strict and limited sense.

From what has been said, it is manifest, that this provision must be of a character calculated to prevent any one interest, or combination of interests, from using the powers of government to aggrandize itself at the expense of the others. Here lies the evil: and just in proportion as it shall prevent, or fail to prevent it, in the same degree it will effect, or fail to effect the end intended to be accomplished. There is but one certain mode in which this result can be secured; and that is, by the adoption of some restriction or limitation, which shall so effectually prevent any one interest, or combination of interests, from obtaining the exclusive control of the government, as to render hopeless all attempts directed to that end. There is, again, but one mode in which this can be effected; and that is, by taking the sense of each interest or portion of the community, which may be unequally and injuriously affected by the action of the government, separately, through its own majority, or in some other way by which its voice may be fairly expressed; and to require the consent of each interest, either to put or to keep the government in action. This, too, can be accomplished only in one way,—and that is, by such an organism of the government,—and, if necessary for the purpose, of the community also,—as will, by dividing and distributing the powers of government, give to each division or interest, through its appropriate organ, either a concurrent voice in making and executing the laws, or a veto on their execution. It is only by such an organism, that the assent of each can be made necessary to put the government in motion; or the power made effectual to arrest its action, when put in motion;—and it is only by the one or the other that the different interests, orders, classes, or portions, into which the community may be divided, can be protected, and all conflict and struggle between them prevented,—by rendering it impossible to put or to keep it in action, without the concurrent consent of all.

Such an organism as this, combined with the right of suffrage, constitutes, in fact, the elements of constitutional government. The one, by rendering those who make and execute the laws responsible to those on whom they operate, prevents the rulers from oppressing the ruled; and the other, by making it impossible for any one interest or combination of interests or class, or order, or portion of the community, to obtain exclusive control, prevents any one of them from oppressing the other. It is clear, that oppression and abuse of power must come, if at all, from the one or the other quarter. From no other can they come. It follows, that the two, suffrage and proper organism combined, are sufficient to counteract the tendency of government to oppression and abuse of power; and to restrict it to the fulfilment of the great ends for which it is ordained.

In coming to this conclusion, I have assumed the organism to be perfect, and the different interests, portions, or classes of the community, to be sufficiently enlightened to understand its character and object, and to exercise, with due intelligence, the right of suffrage. To the extent that either may be defective, to the same extent the government would fall short of fulfilling its end. But this does not impeach the truth of the principles on which it rests. In reducing them to proper form, in applying them to practical uses, all elementary principles are liable to difficulties; but they are not, on this account, the less true, or valuable. Where the organism is perfect, every interest will be truly and fully represented, and of course the whole community must be so. It may be difficult, or even impossible, to make a perfect organism,—but, although this be true, yet even when, instead of the sense of each and of all, it takes that of a few great and prominent interests only, it would still, in a great measure, if not altogether, fulfil the end intended by a constitution. For, in such case, it would require so large a portion of the community, compared with the whole, to concur, or acquiesce in the action of the government, that the number to be plundered would be too few, and the number to be aggrandized too many, to afford adequate motives to oppression and the abuse of its powers. Indeed, however imperfect the organism, it must have more or less effect in diminishing such tendency.

It may be readily inferred, from what has been stated, that the effect of organism is neither to supersede nor diminish the importance of the right of suffrage; but to aid and perfect it. The object of the latter is, to collect the sense of the community. The more fully and perfectly it accomplishes this, the more fully and perfectly it fulfils its end. But the most it can do, of itself, is to collect the sense of the greater number; that is, of the stronger interests, or combination of interests; and to assume this to be the sense of the community. It is only when aided by a proper organism, that it can collect the sense of the entire community, —of each and all its interests; of each, through its appropriate organ, and of the whole, through all of them united. This would truly be the sense of the entire community; for whatever diversity each interest might have within itself,—as all would have the same interest in reference to the action of the government, the individuals composing each would be fully and truly represented by its own majority or appropriate organ, regarded in reference to the other interests. In brief, every individual of every interest might trust, with confidence, its majority or appropriate organ, against that of every other interest.

It results, from what has been said, that there are two different modes in which the sense of the community may be taken; one, simply by the right of suffrage, unaided; the other, by the right through a proper organism. Each collects the sense of the majority. But one regards numbers only, and considers the whole community as a unit, having but one common interest throughout; and collects the sense of the greater number of the whole, as that of the community. The other, on the contrary, regards interests as well as numbers;—considering the community as made up of different and conflicting interests, as far as the action of the government is concerned; and takes the sense of each, through its majority or appropriate organ, and the united sense of all, as the sense of the entire community. The former of these I shall call the numerical, or absolute majority; and the latter, the concurrent, or constitutional majority. I call it the constitutional majority, because it is an essential element in every constitutional government,—be its form what it may. So great is the difference, politically speaking, between the two majorities, that they cannot be confounded, without leading to great and fatal errors; and yet the distinction between them has been so entirely overlooked, that when the term *majority* is used in political discussions, it is applied exclusively to designate the numerical,—as if there were no other. Until this distinction is recognized, and better understood, there will continue to be great liability to error in properly constructing constitutional governments, especially of the popular form, and of preserving them when properly constructed. Until then, the latter will have a strong tendency to slide, first, into the government of the numerical majority, and, finally, into absolute government of some other form. To show that such must be the case, and at the same time to mark more strongly the difference between the two, in order to guard against the danger of overlooking it, I propose to consider the subject more at length.

The first and leading error which naturally arises from overlooking the distinction referred to, is, to confound the numerical majority with the people; and this so completely as to regard them as identical. This is a consequence that necessarily results from considering the numerical as the only majority. All admit, that a popular government, or democracy, is the government of the people; for the terms imply this. A perfect government of the kind would be one which would embrace the consent of every citizen or member of the community; but as this is impracticable, in the opinion of those who regard the numerical as the only majority, and who can perceive no other way by which the sense of the people can be taken,—they are compelled to adopt this as the only true basis of popular government, in contradistinction to governments of the aristocratical or monarchical form. Being thus constrained, they are, in the next place, forced to regard the numerical majority, as, in effect, the entire people; that is, the greater part as the whole; and the government of the greater part as the government of the whole. It is thus the two come to be confounded, and a part made identical with the whole. And it is thus, also, that all the rights, powers, and immunities of the whole people come to be attributed to the numerical majority; and, among others, the supreme, sovereign authority of establishing and abolishing governments at pleasure.

This radical error, the consequence of confounding the two, and of regarding the numerical as the only majority, has contributed more than any other cause, to prevent the formation of popular constitutional governments,—and to destroy them even when they have been formed. It leads to the conclusion that, in their formation and establishment nothing more is necessary than the right of suffrage,—and the allotment to each division of the community a representation in the government, in proportion to numbers. If the numerical majority were really the people; and if, to take its sense truly, were to take the sense of the people truly, a government so constituted would be a true and perfect model of a popular constitutional government; and every departure from it would detract from its excellence. But, as such is not the case,—as the numerical majority, instead of being the people, is only a portion of them,—such a government, instead of being a true and perfect model of the people's government, that is, a people self-governed, is but the government of a part, over a part,—the major over the minor portion.

But this misconception of the true elements of constitutional government does not stop here. It leads to others equally false and fatal, in reference to the best means of preserving and perpetuating them, when, from some fortunate combination of circumstances, they are correctly formed. For they who fall into these errors regard the restrictions which organism imposes on the will of the numerical majority as restrictions on the will of the people, and, therefore, as not only useless, but wrongful and mischievous. And hence they endeavor to destroy organism, under the delusive hope of making government more democratic.

Such are some of the consequences of confounding the two, and of regarding the numerical as the only majority. And in this may be found the reason why so few popular governments have been properly constructed, and why, of these few, so small a number have proved durable. Such must continue to be the result, so long as these errors continue to be prevalent.

There is another error, of a kindred character, whose influence contributes much to the same results: I refer to the prevalent opinion, that a written constitution, containing suitable restrictions on the powers of government, is sufficient, of itself, without the aid of any organism,—except such as is necessary to separate its several departments, and render them independent of each other,—to counteract the tendency of the numerical majority to oppression and the abuse of power.

A written constitution certainly has many and considerable advantages; but it is a great mistake to suppose, that the mere insertion of provisions to restrict and limit the powers of the government, without investing those for whose protection they are inserted with the means of enforcing their observance, will be sufficient to prevent the major and dominant party from abusing its powers. Being the party in possession of the government, they will, from the same constitution of man which makes government necessary to protect society, be in favor of the powers granted by the constitution, and opposed to the restrictions intended to limit them. As the major and dominant party, they will have no need of these restrictions for their protection. The ballot-box, of itself, would be ample protection to them. Needing no other, they would come, in time, to regard these limitations as unnecessary and improper restraints;—and endeavor to elude them, with the view of increasing their power and influence.

The minor, or weaker party, on the contrary, would take the opposite direction;—and regard them as essential to their protection against the dominant party. And, hence, they would endeavor to defend and enlarge the restrictions, and to limit and contract the powers. But where there are no means by which they could compel the major party to observe the restrictions, the only resort left them would be, a strict construction of the constitution,—that is, a construction which would confine these powers to the narrowest limits which the meaning of the words used in the grant would admit.

To this the major party would oppose a liberal construction,—one which would give to the words of the grant the broadest meaning of which they were susceptible. It would then be construction against construction; the one to contract, and the other to enlarge the powers of the government to the utmost. But of what possible avail could the strict construction of the minor party be, against the liberal interpretation of the major, when the one would have all the powers of the government to carry its construction into effect,—and the other be deprived of all means of enforcing its construction? In a contest so unequal, the result would not be doubtful. The party in favor of the restrictions would be over-powered. At first, they might command some respect, and do something to stay the march of encroachment; but they would, in the progress of the contest, be regarded as mere abstractionists; and, indeed, deservedly, if they should indulge the folly of supposing that the party in possession of the ballot-box and the physical force of the country, could be successfully resisted by an appeal to reason, truth, justice, or the obligations imposed by the constitution. For when these, of themselves, shall exert sufficient influence to stay the hand of power, then government will be no longer necessary to protect society, nor constitutions needed to prevent government from abusing its powers. The end of the contest would be the subversion of the constitution, either by the undermining process of construction,—where its meaning would admit of possible doubt,—or by substituting in practice what is called party-usage, in place of its provisions;—or, finally, when no other contrivance would subserve the purpose, by openly and boldly setting them aside. By the one or the other, the restrictions would ultimately be annulled, and the government be converted into one of unlimited powers.

Nor would the division of government into separate, and, as it regards each other, independent departments, prevent this result. Such a division may do much to facilitate its operations, and to secure to its administration greater caution and deliberation; but as each and all the departments, and, of course, the entire government,—would be under the control of the numerical majority, it is too clear to require explanation, that a mere distribution of its powers among its agents or representatives, could do little or nothing to counteract its tendency to oppression and abuse of power. To effect this, it would be necessary to go one step further, and make the several departments the organs of the distinct interests or portions of the community; and to clothe each with a negative on the others. But the effect of this would be to change the government from the numerical into the concurrent majority.

Having now explained the reasons why it is so difficult to form and preserve popular constitutional government, so long as the distinction between the two majorities is overlooked, and the opinion prevails that a written constitution, with suitable restrictions and a proper division of its powers, is sufficient to counteract the tendency of the numerical majority to the abuse of its power,—I shall next proceed to explain, more fully, why the concurrent majority is an indispensable element in forming constitutional governments; and why the numerical majority, of itself, must, in all cases, make governments absolute.

The necessary consequence of taking the sense of the community by the concurrent majority is, as has been explained, to give to each interest or portion of the community a negative on the others. It is this mutual negative among its

various conflicting interests, which invests each with the power of protecting itself;—and places the rights and safety of each, where only they can be securely
placed, under its own guardianship. Without this there can be no systematic,
peaceful, or effective resistance to the natural tendency of each to come into conflict with the others: and without this there can be no constitution. It is this negative power,—the power of preventing or arresting the action of the government,
—be it called by what term it may,—veto, interposition, nullification, check, or
balance of power,—which, in fact, forms the constitution. They are all but different names for the negative power. In all its forms, and under all its names, it
results from the concurrent majority. Without this there can be no negative; and,
without a negative, no constitution. The assertion is true in reference to all constitutional governments, be their forms what they may. It is, indeed, the negative
power which makes the constitution,—and the positive which makes the government. The one is the power of acting;—and the other the power of preventing or
arresting action. The two, combined, make constitutional governments.

But, as there can be no constitution without the negative power, and no
negative power without the concurrent majority;—it follows, necessarily, that
where the numerical majority has the sole control of the government, there can
be no constitution; as constitution implies limitation or restriction,—and, of
course, is inconsistent with the idea of sole or exclusive power. And hence, the
numerical, unmixed with the concurrent majority, necessarily forms, in all cases,
absolute government.

.   .   .

A broader position may, indeed, be taken; viz., that there is a tendency, in
constitutional governments of every form, to degenerate into their respective
absolute forms; and, in all absolute governments, into that of the monarchical
form. But the tendency is much stronger in constitutional governments of the
democratic form to degenerate into their respective absolute forms, than in either
of the others; because, among other reasons, the distinction between the constitutional and absolute forms of aristocratical and monarchical governments, is far
more strongly marked than in democratic governments. The effect of this is, to
make the different orders or classes in an aristocracy, or monarchy, far more
jealous and watchful of encroachment on their respective rights; and more resolute and persevering in resisting attempts to concentrate power in any one class
or order. On the contrary, the line between the two forms, in popular governments, is so imperfectly understood, that honest and sincere friends of the constitutional form not unfrequently, instead of jealously watching and arresting their
tendency to degenerate into their absolute forms, not only regard it with approbation, but employ all their powers to add to its strength and to increase its
impetus, in the vain hope of making the government more perfect and popular.
The numerical majority, perhaps, should usually be one of the elements of a constitutional democracy; but to make it the sole element, in order to perfect the
constitution and make the government more popular, is one of the greatest and
most fatal of political errors.

Among the other advantages which governments of the concurrent have over those of the numerical majority,—and which strongly illustrates their more popular character, is,—that they admit, with safety, a much greater extension of the right of suffrage. It may be safely extended in such governments to universal suffrage: that is,—to every male citizen of mature age, with few ordinary exceptions; but it cannot be so far extended in those of the numerical majority, without placing them ultimately under the control of the more ignorant and dependent portions of the community. For, as the community becomes populous, wealthy, refined, and highly civilized, the difference between the rich and the poor will become more strongly marked; and the number of the ignorant and dependent greater in proportion to the rest of the community. With the increase of this difference, the tendency to conflict between them will become stronger; and, as the poor and dependent become more numerous in proportion, there will be, in governments of the numerical majority, no want of leaders among the wealthy and ambitious, to excite and direct them in their efforts to obtain the control.

The case is different in governments of the concurrent majority. There, mere numbers have not the absolute control; and the wealthy and intelligent being identified in interest with the poor and ignorant of their respective portions or interests of the community, become their leaders and protectors. And hence, as the latter would have neither hope nor inducement to rally the former in order to obtain the control, the right of suffrage, under such a government, may be safely enlarged to the extent stated, without incurring the hazard to which such enlargement would expose governments of the numerical majority. . . .

THUS SPOKE ZARATHUSTRA
and
THE ANTICHRIST

Friedrich Nietzsche

1844–1900

❧

Friedrich Nietzsche was a "literary" rather than a systematic philosopher. He is now being revived as one of the precursors of present-day existentialism, the mood and tenor of which are suggested by his lonely and frustrated life and reflected in iconoclastic writings drenched in what we have come to know as existentialist anguish and despair. He was the alienated man *par excellence* and, in the now established existentialist key, his writings are hostile to traditional philosophy, impetuously categorical and engaged in a quest for "authenticity" which often suggests a kind of intellectual disrobing with intent to shock.

Nietzsche's work has occasioned fierce controversy. Innumerable passages can be cited to confirm the charge that he was a proto-Nazi. Thus one finds in them a contempt for the "rabble," an apothesis of the superman, and a denunciation of the Jews and of Christianity as an offshoot of Judaism. Here, too, is the usual totalitarian scorn of truth ("The falseness of an opinion is not for us any objection to it. . ."),[1] praise of war ("War and courage have accomplished more great things than love of the neighbor."[2]), contempt for humanitarianism and egalitarianism, and scorn for all the "small" virtues prized by the "mob."

On the other hand, Nietzsche's *Übermensch* bears no resemblance to the strutting, jack-booted, would-be supermen who nearly overwhelmed Europe in World War II. He despised German nationalism, and even his vituperations against the Jews are not in the spirit of the

From "Thus Spoke Zarathustra" and "The Antichrist" in *The Portable Nietzsche*, selected and trans. Walter Kaufmann (New York, 1954), pp. 208–14, 398–400, 570–74, 618–20, 644–48. Copyright 1954 by The Viking Press, Inc. Reprinted by permission of The Viking Press, Inc.

[1] "Beyond Good and Evil," *Complete Works*, XII, ed. Oscar Levy, trans. Helen Zimmerman (New York: Russell and Russell, 1964), p. 8. Cf. "The Genealogy of Morals," *Ibid.*, XIII, 179.

[2] "Thus Spoke Zarathustra," p. 159.

conventional anti-Semitism propagated by the Nazis and their precursors.[3]

Thus Spake Zarathustra (1883–92) is by far Nietzsche's most widely read work. *The Antichrist* (1888) is the only essay which he completed of a projected four-part volume to have been called *Revaluation of All Values*. Both works are histrionic, sententious, petulant, and wildly intemperate, strangely mingling adolescent rebellion with brilliant insight and somehow suggesting the truth of his aphorism in *Zarathustra* that "one must . . . have chaos in oneself to give birth to a dancing star."

Born and educated in Germany, Nietzsche became a Swiss subject and taught at the University of Basel, which he left in 1879 claiming ill health. The remainder of his years were lived in pain, loneliness and desolation culminating in insanity. His writings, however, won him increasing notoriety so that at the time of his death he was world-famous.

THUS SPOKE ZARATHUSTRA: SECOND PART

. . .

On the Rabble

Life is a well of joy; but where the rabble drinks too, all wells are poisoned. I am fond of all that is clean, but I have no wish to see the grinning snouts and the thirst of the unclean. They cast their eye into the well: now their revolting smile shines up out of the well. They have poisoned the holy water with their lustfulness; and when they called their dirty dreams "pleasure," they poisoned the language too. The flame is vexed when their moist hearts come near the fire; the spirit itself seethes and smokes where the rabble steps near the fire. In their hands all fruit grows sweetish and overmellow; their glance makes the fruit tree a prey of the wind and withers its crown.

And some who turned away from life only turned away from the rabble: they did not want to share well and flame and fruit with the rabble.

And some who went into the wilderness and suffered thirst with the beasts of prey merely did not want to sit around the cistern with filthy camel drivers.

And some who came along like annihilators and like a hailstorm to all orchards merely wanted to put a foot into the gaping jaws of the rabble to plug up its throat.

The bite on which I gagged the most is not the knowledge that life itself requires hostility and death and torture-crosses—but once I asked, and I was almost choked by my question: What? does life require even the rabble? Are

[3] The Jews are blamed, for example, for the typical Jew, Jesus of Nazareth, who is condemned because he brought salvation and victory to the poor, the sick, and the sinful. Their "decadent slave" morality made possible the feminist, pacifist and labor movements of the nineteenth century, etc. Clearly, these are charges to which many Jews would happily plead guilty. Cf. "The Genealogy of Morals," pp. 30 ff, pp. 50 ff.

poisoned wells required, and stinking fires and soiled dreams and maggots in the bread of life?

Not my hatred but my nausea gnawed hungrily at my life. Alas, I often grew weary of the spirit when I found that even the rabble had *esprit*. And I turned my back on those who rule when I saw what they now call ruling: higgling and haggling for power—with the rabble. I have lived with closed ears among people with foreign tongues: would that the tongue of their higgling and their haggling for power might remain foreign to me. And, holding my nose, I walked disgruntled through all of yesterday and today: verily, all of yesterday and today smells foul of the writing rabble.

Like a cripple who has become deaf and blind and dumb: thus have I lived for many years lest I live with the power-, writing- and pleasure-rabble. Laboriously and cautiously my spirit climbed steps; alms of pleasure were its refreshment; and life crept along for the blind as on a cane.

What was it that happened to me? How did I redeem myself from nausea? Who rejuvenated my sight? How did I fly to the height where no more rabble sits by the well? Was it my nausea itself which created wings for me and water-divining powers? Verily, I had to fly to the highest spheres that I might find the fount of pleasure again.

Oh, I found it, my brothers! Here, in the highest spheres, the fount of pleasure wells up for me! And here is a life of which the rabble does not drink.

You flow for me almost too violently, fountain of pleasure. And often you empty the cup again by wanting to fill it. And I must still learn to approach you more modestly: all-too-violently my heart still flows toward you—my heart, upon which my summer burns, short, hot, melancholy, overblissful: how my summer-heart craves your coolness!

Gone is the hesitant gloom of my spring! Gone the malice of my snowflakes in June! Summer have I become entirely, and summer noon! A summer in the highest spheres with cold wells and blissful silence: oh, come, my friends, that the silence may become still more blissful!

For this is *our* height and our home: we live here too high and steep for all the unclean and their thirst. Cast your pure eyes into the well of my pleasure, friends! How should that make it muddy? It shall laugh back at you in its own purity.

On the tree, Future, we build our nest; and in our solitude eagles shall bring us nourishment in their beaks. Verily, no nourishment which the unclean might share: they would think they were devouring fire and they would burn their mouths. Verily, we keep no homes here for the unclean: our pleasure would be an ice cave to their bodies and their spirits.

And we want to live over them like strong winds, neighbors of the eagles, neighbors of the snow, neighbors of the sun: thus live strong winds. And like a wind I yet want to blow among them one day, and with my spirit take the breath of their spirit: thus my future wills it.

Verily, a strong wind is Zarathustra for all who are low; and this counsel he gives to all his enemies and all who spit and spew: "Beware of spitting *against* the wind!"

Thus spoke Zarathustra.

On the Tarantulas

Behold, this is the hole of the tarantula. Do you want to see the tarantula itself? Here hangs its web; touch it, that it tremble!

There it comes willingly: welcome, tarantula! Your triangle and symbol sits black on your back; and I also know what sits in your soul. Revenge sits in your soul: wherever you bite, black scabs grow; your poison makes the soul whirl with revenge.

Thus I speak to you in a parable—you who make souls whirl, you preachers of *equality*. To me you are tarantulas, and secretly vengeful. But I shall bring your secrets to light; therefore I laugh in your faces with my laughter of the heights. Therefore I tear at your webs, that your rage may lure you out of your lie-holes and your revenge may leap out from behind your word justice. For *that man be delivered from revenge,* that is for me the bridge to the highest hope, and a rainbow after long storms.

The tarantulas, of course, would have it otherwise. "What justice means to us is precisely that the world be filled with the storms of our revenge"—thus they speak to each other. "We shall wreak vengeance and abuse on all whose equals we are not"—thus do the tarantula-hearts vow. "And 'will to equality' shall henceforth be the name for virtue; and against all that has power we want to raise our clamor!"

You preachers of equality, the tyrannomania of impotence clamors thus out of you for equality: your most secret ambitions to be tyrants thus shroud themselves in words of virtue. Aggrieved conceit, repressed envy—perhaps the conceit and envy of your fathers—erupt from you as a flame and as the frenzy of revenge.

. . . Mistrust all who talk much of their justice! Verily, their souls lack more than honey. And when they call themselves the good and the just, do not forget that they would be pharisees, if only they had—power.

My friends, I do not want to be mixed up and confused with others. Some preach my doctrine of life and are at the same time preachers of equality and tarantulas. Although they are sitting in their holes, these poisonous spiders, with their backs turned on life, they speak in favor of life, but only because they wish to hurt. They wish to hurt those who now have power . . .

I do not wish to be mixed up and confused with these preachers of equality. For, to *me* justice speaks thus: "Men are not equal." Nor shall they become equal! What would my love of the overman be if I spoke otherwise?

And behold, my friends: here where the tarantula has its hole, the ruins of an ancient temple rise; behold it with enlightened eyes! Verily, the man who once piled his thoughts to the sky in these stones—he, like the wisest, knew the secret of all life. That struggle and inequality are present even in beauty, and also war for power and more power: that is what he teaches us here in the plainest parable. How divinely vault and arches break through each other in a wrestling match; how they strive against each other with light and shade, the godlike strivers—with such assurance and beauty let us be enemies too, my friends! Let us strive against one another like gods.

Thus spoke Zarathustra.

.   .   .   .

THUS SPOKE ZARATHUSTRA: FOURTH AND LAST PART

.   .   .   .

On the Higher Man

1

The first time I came to men I committed the folly of hermits, the great folly: I stood in the market place. And as I spoke to all, I spoke to none. But in the evening, tightrope walkers and corpses were my companions; and I myself was almost a corpse. But with the new morning a new truth came to me: I learned to say, "Of what concern to me are market and mob and mob noise and long mob ears?"

You higher men, learn this from me: in the market place nobody believes in higher men. And if you want to speak there, very well! But the mob blinks: "We are all equal."

"You higher men"—thus blinks the mob—"there are no higher men, we are all equal, man is man; before God we are all equal."

Before God! But now this god has died. And before the mob we do not want to be equal. You higher men, go away from the market place!

2

Before God! But now this god has died. You higher men, this god was your greatest danger. It is only since he lies in his tomb that you have been resurrected. Only now the great noon comes; only now the higher man becomes—lord.

Have you understood this word, O my brothers? You are startled? Do your hearts become giddy? Does the abyss yawn before you? Does the hellhound howl at you? Well then, you higher men! Only now is the mountain of man's future in labor. God died: now *we* want the overman to live.

3

The most concerned ask today: "How is man to be preserved?" But Zarathustra is the first and only one to ask: "How is man to be overcome?"

I have the overman at heart, *that* is my first and only concern—and *not* man: not the neighbor, not the poorest, not the most ailing, not the best.

O my brothers, what I can love in man is that he is an overture and a going under. And in you too there is much that lets me love and hope. That you despise, you higher men, that lets me hope. For the great despisers are the great reverers. That you have despaired, in that there is much to revere. For you did not learn how to surrender, you did not learn petty prudences. For today the little people lord it: they all preach surrender and resignation and prudence and industry and consideration and the long etcetera of the small virtues.

What is womanish, what derives from the servile, and especially the mob hodgepodge: *that* would now become master of all human destiny. O nausea! Nausea! Nausea! *That* asks and asks and never grows weary: "How is man to be preserved best, longest, most agreeably?" With that—they are the masters of today.

Overcome these masters of today, O my brothers—these small people, *they* are the overman's greatest danger.

You higher men, overcome the small virtues, the small prudences, the grain-of-sand consideration, the ants' riff-raff, the wretched contentment, the "happiness of the greatest number"! And rather despair than surrender. And verily, I love you for not knowing how to live today, you higher men! For thus *you* live best.

• • •

FIRST BOOK: THE ANTICHRIST

Attempt at a Critique of Christianity

• • •

2

What is good? Everything that heightens the feeling of power in man, the will to power, power itself.

What is bad? Everything that is born of weakness.

What is happiness? The feeling that power is *growing*, that resistance is overcome.

Not contentedness but more power; not peace but war; not virtue but fitness (Renaissance virtue, *virtù* . . .).

The weak and the failures shall perish: first principle of *our* love of man. And they shall even be given every possible assistance.

What is more harmful than any vice? Active pity for all the failures and all the weak: Christianity.

3

The problem I thus pose is not what shall succeed mankind in the sequence of living beings (man is an *end*), but what type of man shall be *bred,* shall be *willed,* for being higher in value, worthier of life, more certain of a future.

Even in the past this higher type has appeared often—but as a fortunate accident, as an exception, never as something *willed.* In fact, this has been the type most dreaded—almost *the* dreadful—and from dread the opposite type was willed, bred, and *attained:* the domestic animal, the herd animal, the sick human animal—the Christian.

4

Mankind does *not* represent a development toward something better or stronger or higher in the sense accepted today. "Progress" is merely a modern idea, that is, a false idea. The European of today is vastly inferior in value to the European of the Renaissance: further development is altogether *not* according to any necessity in the direction of elevation, enhancement, or strength.

In another sense, success in individual cases is constantly encountered in the most widely different places and cultures: here we really do find a *higher type,* which is, in relation to mankind as a whole, a kind of overman. Such fortunate accidents of great success have always been possible and *will* perhaps always be possible. And even whole families, tribes, or peoples may occasionally represent such a *bull's-eye.*

5

Christianity should not be beautified and embellished: it has waged deadly war against this higher type of man; it has placed all the basic instincts of this type under the ban; and out of these instincts it has distilled evil and the Evil One: the strong man as the typically reprehensible man, the "reprobate." Christianity has sided with all that is weak and base, with all failures; it has made an ideal of whatever *contradicts* the instinct of the strong life to preserve itself; it has corrupted the reason even of those strongest in spirit by teaching men to consider the supreme values of the spirit as something sinful, as something that leads into error—as temptations. . . .

6

It is a painful, horrible spectacle that has dawned on me: I have drawn back the curtain from the *corruption* of man. . . . I understand corruption, as you will guess, in the sense of decadence: it is my contention that all the values in which mankind now sums up its supreme desiderata are *decadence-values.*

I call an animal, a species, or an individual corrupt when it loses its instincts, when it chooses, when it prefers, what is disadvantageous for it. A history of "lofty sentiments," of the "ideals of mankind"—and it is possible that I shall have to write it—would almost explain too *why* man is so corrupt. Life itself is to my mind the instinct for growth, for durability, for an accumulation of forces, for *power:* where the will to power is lacking there is decline. It is my contention that all the supreme values of mankind *lack* this will—that the values which are symptomatic of decline, *nihilistic* values, are lording it under the holiest names.

7

Christianity is called the religion of *pity.* Pity stands opposed to the tonic emotions which heighten our vitality: it has a depressing effect. We are deprived of strength when we feel pity. . . .

Suppose we measure pity by the value of the reactions it usually produces; then its perilous nature appears in an even brighter light. Quite in general, pity crosses the law of development, which is the law of *selection.* It preserves what is ripe for destruction; it defends those who have been disinherited and condemned by life; and by the abundance of the failures of all kinds which it keeps alive, it gives life itself a gloomy and questionable aspect.

Some have dared to call pity a virtue (in every *noble* ethic it is considered a weakness) ; and as if this were not enough, it has been made *the* virtue, the basis and source of all virtues. . . .

Pity is the *practice* of nihilism. To repeat: this depressive and contagious instinct crosses those instincts which aim at the preservation of life and at the enhancement of its value. It multiplies misery and conserves all that is miserable, and is thus a prime instrument of the advancement of decadence: pity persuades men to *nothingness!* Of course, one does not say "nothingness" but "beyond" or "God," or "*true* life," or Nirvana, salvation, blessedness.

. . .

In our whole unhealthy modernity there is nothing more unhealthy than Christian pity. To be physicians *here,* to be inexorable *here,* to wield the scalpel *here*—that is *our* part, that is *our* love of man, that is how *we* are philosophers, we *Hyperboreans.*

. . .

43

. . .

That everyone as an "immortal soul" has equal rank with everyone else, that in the totality of living beings the "salvation" of *every* single individual may claim eternal significance, that little pigs and three-quarter-madmen may have the conceit that the laws of nature are constantly broken for their sakes—such an intensification of every kind of selfishness into the infinite, into the *impertinent,* cannot be branded with too much contempt. And yet Christianity owes its triumph to this miserable flattery of personal vanity: it was precisely all the failures, all the rebellious-minded, all the less favored, the whole scum and refuse of humanity who were thus won over to it. The "salvation of the soul"—in plain language: "the world revolves around *me*."

The poison of the doctrine of "equal rights for all"—it was Christianity that spread it most fundamentally. Out of the most secret nooks of bad instincts, Christianity has waged war unto death against all sense of respect and feeling of distance between man and man, that is to say, against the *presupposition* of every elevation, of every growth of culture; out of the *ressentiment* of the masses it forged its chief weapon against *us*, against all that is noble, gay, high-minded on earth, against our happiness on earth. "Immortality" conceded to every Peter and Paul has so far been the greatest, the most malignant, attempt to assassinate *noble* humanity.

And let us not underestimate the calamity which crept out of Christianity into politics. Today nobody has the courage any longer for privileges, for masters' rights, for a sense of respect for oneself and one's peers—for a *pathos of distance*. Our politics is sick from this lack of courage.

The aristocratic outlook was undermined from the deepest underworld through the lie of the equality of souls; and if faith in the "prerogative of the majority" makes and *will make* revolutions—it is Christianity, beyond a doubt, it is *Christian* value judgments, that every revolution simply translates into blood and crime. Christianity is a rebellion of everything that crawls on the ground against that which has *height:* the evangel of the "lowly" *makes* low.

· · ·

57

· · ·

The *order of castes,* the supreme, the dominant law, is merely the sanction of a *natural order,* a natural lawfulness of the first rank, over which no arbitrariness, no "modern idea" has any power. In every healthy society there are three types which condition each other and gravitate differently physiologically; each has its own hygiene, its own field of work, its own sense of perfection and mastery. Nature . . . distinguishes the pre-eminently spiritual ones, those who are pre-eminently strong in muscle and temperament, and those, the third type, who excel neither in one respect nor in the other, the mediocre ones—the last as the great majority, the first as the elite.

The highest caste—I call them *the fewest*—being perfect, also has the privileges of the fewest: among them, to represent happiness, beauty, and graciousness on earth. Only to the most spiritual human beings is beauty permitted: among them alone is graciousness not weakness. . . .

. . . The most spiritual men, as the *strongest*, had their happiness where others would find their destruction: in the labyrinth, in hardness against themselves and others, in experiments; their joy is self-conquest; asceticism becomes in them nature, need, and instinct. Difficult tasks are a privilege to them; to play with burdens which crush others, a recreation. Knowledge—a form of asceticism. They are the most venerable kind of man; that does not preclude their being the most cheerful and the kindliest. They rule not because they want to but because they *are*; they are not free to be second.

The *second*: they are the guardians of the law, those who see to order and security, the noble warriors, and above all the king as the highest formula of warrior, judge, and upholder of the law. The second are the executive arm of the most spiritual, that which is closest to them and belongs to them, that which does everything gross in the work of ruling for them—their retinue, their right hand, their best pupils.

In all this, to repeat, there is nothing arbitrary, nothing contrived; whatever is *different* is contrived—contrived for the ruin of nature. The order of castes, the *order of rank*, merely formulates the highest law of life; the separation of the three types is necessary for the preservation of society, to make possible the higher and the highest types. The *inequality* of rights is the first condition for the existence of any rights at all.

A right is a privilege. A man's state of being is his privilege. Let us not underestimate the privileges of the *mediocre*. As one climbs *higher*, life becomes ever harder; the coldness increases, responsibility increases.

A high culture is a pyramid: it can stand only on a broad base; its first presupposition is a strong and soundly consolidated mediocrity. Handicraft, trade, agriculture, *science*, the greatest part of art, the whole quintessence of *professional* activity, to sum it up, is compatible only with a mediocre amount of ability and ambition; that sort of thing would be out of place among exceptions; the instinct here required would contradict both aristocratism and anarchism. To be a public utility, a wheel, a function, for that one must be destined by nature: it is *not* society, it is the only kind of *happiness* of which the great majority are capable that makes intelligent machines of them. For the mediocre, to be mediocre is their happiness; mastery of one thing, specialization—a natural instinct.

It would be completely unworthy of a more profound spirit to consider mediocrity as such an objection. In fact, it is the very *first* necessity if there are to be exceptions: a high culture depends on it. When the exceptional human being treats the mediocre more tenderly than himself and his peers, this is not mere politeness of the heart—it is simply his *duty*.

Whom do I hate most among the rabble of today? The socialist rabble . . . who undermine the instinct, the pleasure, the worker's sense of satisfaction with his small existence—who make him envious, who teach him revenge. The source of wrong is never unequal rights but the claim of "equal" rights.

What is *bad*? But I have said this already: all that is born of weakness, of envy, of *revenge*. The anarchist and the Christian have the same origin.

58

Indeed, it makes a difference to what end one lies: whether one preserves or *destroys*. One may posit a perfect equation between *Christian* and *anarchist*:

their aim, their instinct, are directed only toward destruction. The proof of this proposition can easily be read in history: it is written there in awful clarity. If we have just become acquainted with a religious legislation whose aim it was to "eternalize" the highest condition of life's *prospering,* a great organization of society—Christianity found its mission in putting an end to precisely such an organization *because life prospered in it.* There the gains of reason, after a long period of experiments and uncertainty, were to be invested for the greatest long-term advantage and the harvest to be brought home as great, as ample, as complete as possible; here, conversely, the harvest was *poisoned* overnight. That which stood there *aere perennius,* the *imperium Romanum,* the most magnificent form of organization under difficult circumstances which has yet been achieved, in comparison with which all before and all afterward are mere botch, patchwork, and dilettantism—these holy anarchists made it a matter of "piety" for themselves to destroy "the world," *that is,* the *imperium Romanum,* until not one stone remained on the other, until even Teutons and other louts could become masters over it.

The Christian and the anarchist: both decadents, both incapable of having any effect other than disintegrating, poisoning, withering, bloodsucking; both the instinct of mortal hatred against everything that stands, that stands in greatness, that has duration, that promises life a future. Christianity was the vampire of the *imperium Romanum:* overnight it undid the tremendous deed of the Romans—who had won the ground for a great culture *that would have time.*

It is not understood yet? The *imperium Romanum* which we know, which the history of the Roman provinces teaches us to know better and better, this most admirable work of art in the grand style was a beginning; its construction was designed to prove itself through thousands of years: until today nobody has built again like this, nobody has even dreamed of building in such proportions *sub specie aeterni.* This organization was firm enough to withstand bad emperors: the accident of persons may not have anything to do with such matters—*first* principle of all grand architecture. But it was not firm enough against the *most corrupt* kind of corruption, against the *Christians.*

.   .   .

THE MIND AND SOCIETY

Vilfredo Pareto

1848–1923

❧

Vilfredo Pareto was born into a prominent and prosperous Italian family. Although he started his career as an engineer, he soon became interested in the problems of political economy and in 1894 succeeded the distinguished Swiss economist Leon Walras to the chair of political economy at Lausanne.

Pareto's chief work, the *Trattato di Sociologia generale*, was published in 1916. He attracted relatively little attention in the English-speaking world until the appearance in 1935 of Arthur Livingston's highly regarded four-volume translation called *The Mind and Society*. Thereupon occurred what Ernest Sutherland Bates called the "Pareto craze" and such Pareto coinages as "residue" and "derivation" became part of the vocabulary of every social science seminar and avant garde drawing room. Even Aldous Huxley, whose writings hardly place him in the Pareto tradition, found perhaps with characteristic extravagance that Pareto's was "the best and most comprehensive hypothesis devised by any sociologist." There were, to be sure, strong dissenting judgments. William McDougall wrote with some acerbity that "Anyone who would defend Pareto's classification of residues * would defend anything." Another critic urged that Pareto's concepts were "like patients in a free clinic, each suffering from some disease." Although Pareto died in the year of Mussolini's march on Rome, his emphasis on the role of the non-logical in social conduct, and his insistence that an elite must be ready and willing to use force, made him especially welcome among apologists seeking an intellectual defense of fascism—especially Italian fascism—by an author with respectable academic credentials.

Vilfredo Pareto, from *The Mind and Society*, trans. Arthur Livingston (New York, 1935), I, 6, 23–24, 27, 75, 78, 171; III, 1419, 1422–27, 1429–32; IV, 1526–27, 1532–33, 1569, 1573–77, 1585–92, 1608–09, 1737–39. Reprinted with permission of The Pareto Fund. Certain footnotes which appeared in the original have been deleted.

* "Residues" as used by Pareto are so-called constants (instincts, drives?) in human nature. [Ed.]

CHAPTER I
THE SCIENTIFIC APPROACH

. . . "Humanitarian" sociologies we have to satiety—they are about the only ones that are being published nowadays. Of metaphysical sociologies (with which are to be classed all positive and humanitarian sociologies) we suffer no dearth. Christian, Catholic, and similar sociologies we have to some small extent. Without disparagement of any of those estimable sociologies, we here venture to expound a sociology that is purely experimental, after the fashion of chemistry, physics, and other such sciences. In all that follows, therefore, we intend to take only experience and observation as our guides. . . .

. . . [W]hen we are reasoning objectively, according to the logico-experimental method, we are not called upon to declare our sentiments either explicitly or by implication.

As regards proofs, a person stating a logico-experimental proposition or theory . . . asks them of observation, experience, and logical inferences from observation and experience. But the person asserting a proposition or theory that is not logico-experimental can rely only on the spontaneous assent of other minds and on the more or less logical inferences he can draw from what is assented to. At bottom he is exhorting rather than proving. However, that is not commonly admitted by people using non-logico-experimental theories. They pretend to be offering proofs of the same nature as the proofs offered for logico-experimental theories; and in such pseudo-experimental arguments they take full advantage of the indefiniteness of common everyday language.

. . . We are in no sense intending, in company with a certain materialistic metaphysics, to exalt logic and experience to a greater power and majesty than dogmas accepted by sentiment. Our aim is to distinguish, not to compare, and much less to pass judgment on the relative merits and virtues of those two sorts of thinking . . .

Again, we have not the remotest intention of bringing back through the window a conviction we have just driven out by the door. We in no wise assert that the logico-experimental proof is superior to the other and is to be preferred. We are saying simply—and it is something quite different—that such proof alone is to be used by a person concerned not to abandon the logico-experimental field.

In logico-experimental theories . . . principles are nothing but abstract propositions summarizing the traits common to many different facts. The principles depend on the facts, not the facts on the principles. They are governed by the facts, not the facts by them. They are accepted hypothetically only so long and so far as they are in agreement with the facts; and they are rejected as soon as there is disagreement. . . .

But scattered through non-logico-experimental theories one finds principles that are accepted *a priori*, independently of experience, dictating to experience. They do not depend upon the facts; the facts depend upon them. They govern the facts; they are not governed by them. They are accepted without regard to the facts, which must of necessity accord with the inferences deducible from the principles; and if they seem to disagree, one argument after another is tried until one is found that successfully re-establishes the accord, which can never under any circumstances fail.

.   .   .

CHAPTER II
NON-LOGICAL CONDUCT

So far we have stated our attitude in writing these volumes and the field in which we intend to remain. Now we are to study human conduct, the states of mind to which it corresponds and the ways in which they express themselves, in order to arrive eventually at our goal, which is to discover the forms of society. We are following the inductive method. We have no preconceptions, no *a priori* notions. We find certain facts before us. We describe them, classify them, determine their character, ever on the watch for some uniformity (law) in the relationships between them. . . .

.   .   .

. . . [A]t the very first glance induction leads to the discovery that non-logical actions play an important part in society. . . .

.   .   .

CHAPTER III
RATIONALIZATION OF NON-LOGICAL CONDUCT
.   .   .

. . . That runs counter to many sociological theories that either scorn or ignore non-logical actions, or else, in an effort to reduce all conduct to logic, attach little importance to them. The course we follow in studying the behaviour of human beings as bearing on the social equilibrium differs according as we lay the greater stress on logical or non-logical conduct. . . .

Non-logical actions are generally considered from the logical standpoint both by those who perform them and by those who discuss them and generalize

about them. Hence our need to do a thing of supreme importance . . . to tear
off the masks non-logical conduct is made to wear and lay bare the things they
hide from view. That too runs counter to many theories which halt at logical ex-
teriors, representing them not as masks but as the substantial element in conduct
itself. We have to scrutinize those theories closely: for if we were to find them
true—in accord with experience, that is—we would have to follow an altogether
different course from the one we would follow were we to discover that the substantial element in the conduct lies in the things that underlie the logical ex-
teriors. . . .

•   •   •

CHAPTER XI

PROPERTIES OF RESIDUES AND DERIVATIONS

•   •   •

Social Elites [1] and Their Circulation

Whether certain theorists like it or not, the fact is that human society is not
a homogeneous thing, that individuals are physically, morally, and intellectually
different. Here we are interested in things as they actually are. Of that fact, therefore, we have to take account. And we must also take account of another fact:
that the social classes are not entirely distinct, even in countries where a caste
system prevails; and that in modern civilized countries circulation among the
various classes is exceedingly rapid. . . .

. . . Suppose we begin by giving a theoretical definition of the thing we are
dealing with, making it as exact as possible, and then go on to see what practical
considerations we can replace it with to get a first approximation. Let us for the
moment completely disregard considerations as to the good or bad, useful or
harmful, praiseworthy or reprehensible character of the various traits in individuals, and confine ourselves to degrees—to whether, in other words, the trait in
a given case be slight, average, intense, or more exactly, to the index that may be
assigned to each individual with reference to the degree, or intensity, in him of
the trait in question.

Let us assume that in every branch of human activity each individual is
given an index which stands as a sign of his capacity, very much the way grades
are given in the various subjects in examinations in school. The highest type of
lawyer, for instance, will be given 10. The man who does not get a client will be
given 1—reserving zero for the man who is an out-and-out idiot. To the man who

---

[1] Kolabinska, *La circulation des élites en France*, p. 5: "The outstanding idea in the
term '*élite*' is 'superiority.' That is the only one I keep. I disregard secondary connotations of
appreciation or as to the utility of such superiority. I am not interested here in what is
desirable. I am making a simple study of what is. In a broad sense I mean by the *élite* in
a society people who possess in marked degree qualities of intelligence, character, skill, capacity, of whatever kind. . . . On the other hand I entirely avoid any sort of judgment on
the merits and utility of such classes." . . .

has made his millions—honestly or dishonestly as the case may be—we will give 10. To the man who has earned his thousands we will give 6; to such as just manage to keep out of the poor-house, 1, keeping zero for those who get in. To the woman "in politics," such as the Aspasia of Pericles, the Maintenon of Louis XIV, the Pompadour of Louis XV, who has managed to infatuate a man of power and play a part in the man's career, we shall give some higher number, such as 8 or 9; to the strumpet who merely satisfies the senses of such a man and exerts no influence on public affairs, we shall give zero. To a clever rascal who knows how to fool people and still keep clear of the penitentiary, we shall give 8, 9, or 10, according to the number of geese he has plucked and the amount of money he has been able to get out of them. To the sneak-thief who snatches a piece of silver from a restaurant table and runs away into the arms of a police-man, we shall give 1. To a poet like Carducci we shall give 8 or 9 according to our tastes; to a scribbler who puts people to rout with his sonnets we shall give zero. For chess-players we can get very precise indices, noting what matches, and how many, they have won. And so on for all the branches of human activity.

We are speaking, remember, of an actual, not a potential, state. If at an English examination a pupil says: "I could know English very well if I chose to; I do not know any because I have never seen fit to learn," the examiner replies: "I am not interested in your alibi. The grade for what you know is zero." If, similarly, someone says: "So-and-so does not steal, not because he couldn't, but because he is a gentleman," we reply: "Very well, we admire him for his self-control, but his grade as a thief is zero."

There are people who worship Napoleon Bonaparte as a god. There are people who hate him as the lowest of criminals. Which are right? We do not choose to solve that question in connexion with a quite different matter. Whether Napoleon was a good man or a bad man, he was certainly not an idiot, nor a man of little account, as millions of others are. He had exceptional qualities, and that is enough for us to give him a high ranking, though without prejudice of any sort to questions that might be raised as to the ethics of his qualities or their social utility.

In short, we are here as usual resorting to scientific analysis, which distinguishes one problem from another and studies each one separately. As usual, again, we are replacing imperceptible variations in absolutely exact numbers with the sharp variations corresponding to groupings by class, just as in examinations those who are passed are sharply and arbitrarily distinguished from those who are "failed," and just as in the matter of physical age we distinguish children from young people, the young from the aged.

So let us make a class of the people who have the highest indices in their branch of activity, and to that class give the name of *élite*.

For the particular investigation with which we are engaged, a study of the social equilibrium, it will help if we further divide that class into two classes: a *governing élite*, comprising individuals who directly or indirectly play some considerable part in government, and a *non-governing élite*, comprising the rest.

A chess champion is certainly a member of the *élite*, but it is no less certain that his merits as a chess-player do not open the doors to political influence for him; and hence unless he has other qualities to win him that distinction, he is not a member of the governing *élite*. Mistresses of absolute monarchs have often-times been members of the *élite*, either because of their beauty or because of their intellectual endowments; but only a few of them, who have had, in addition, the particular talents required by politics, have played any part in government.

So we get two strata in a population: (1) A lower stratum, the *non-élite*, with whose possible influence on government we are not just here concerned; then (2) a higher stratum, *the élite*, which is divided into two: (*a*) a governing *élite*; (*b*) a non-governing *élite*.

In the concrete, there are no examinations whereby each person is assigned to his proper place in these various classes. That deficiency is made up for by other means, by various sorts of labels that serve the purpose after a fashion. Such labels are the rule even where there are examinations. The label "lawyer" is affixed to a man who is supposed to know something about the law and often does, though sometimes again he is an ignoramus. So, the governing *élite* con-tains individuals who wear labels appropriate to political offices of a certain altitude—ministers, Senators, Deputies, chief justices, generals, colonels, and so on—making the apposite exceptions for those who have found their way into that exalted company without possessing qualities corresponding to the labels they wear.

Such exceptions are much more numerous than the exceptions among lawyers, physicians, engineers, millionaires (who have made their own money), artists of distinction, and so on; for the reason, among others, that in these latter departments of human activity the labels are won directly by each individual, whereas in the *élite* some of the labels—the label of wealth, for instance—are hereditary. In former times there were hereditary labels in the governing *élite* also—in our day hardly more than the label of king remains in that status; but if direct inheritance has disappeared, inheritance is still powerful indirectly; and an individual who has inherited a sizable patrimony can easily be named Senator in certain countries, or can get himself elected to the parliament by buying votes or, on occasion, by wheedling voters with assurances that he is a democrat of democrats, a Socialist, an Anarchist. Wealth, family, or social connexions also help in many other cases to win the label of the *élite* in general, or of the govern-ing *élite* in particular, for persons who otherwise hold no claim upon it.

. . .

If all these deviations from type were of little importance, they might be dis-regarded, as they are virtually disregarded in cases where a diploma is required for the practice of a profession. Everyone knows that there are persons who do not deserve their diplomas, but experience shows that on the whole such excep-tions may be overlooked.

One might, further, from certain points of view at least, disregard devia-tions if they remained more or less constant quantitatively—if there were only a negligible variation in proportions between the total of a class and the people who wear its label without possessing the qualities corresponding.

As a matter of fact, the real cases that we have to consider in our societies differ from those two. The deviations are not so few that they can be disregarded. Then again, their number is variable, and the variations give rise to situations having an important bearing on the social equilibrium. We are therefore required to make a special study of them.

Furthermore, the manner in which the various groups in a population intermix has to be considered. In moving from one group to another an individual generally brings with him certain inclinations, sentiments, attitudes, that he has acquired in the group from which he comes, and that circumstance cannot be ignored.

To this mixing, in the particular case in which only two groups, the *élite* and the non-*élite*, are envisaged, the term "circulation of élites" has been applied—in French, *circulation des élites* [or in more general terms "class-circulation"].

In conclusion we must pay special attention (1), in the case of one single group, to the proportions between the total of the group and the number of individuals who are nominally members of it but do not possess the qualities requisite for effective membership; and then (2), in the case of various groups, to the ways in which transitions from one group to the other occur, and to the intensity of that movement—that is to say, to the velocity of the circulation.

Velocity in circulation has to be considered not only absolutely but also in relation to the supply of and the demand for certain social elements. A country that is always at peace does not require many soldiers in its governing class, and the production of generals may be overexuberant as compared with the demand. But when a country is in a state of continuous warfare many soldiers are necessary, and though production remains at the same level it may not meet the demand. That, we might note in passing, has been one of the causes for the collapse of many aristocracies.

Another example. In a country where there is little industry and little commerce, the supply of individuals possessing in high degree the qualities requisite for those types of activity exceeds the demand. Then industry and commerce develop and the supply, though remaining the same, no longer meets the demand.

We must not confuse the state of law with the state of fact. The latter alone, or almost alone, has a bearing on the social equilibrium. There are many examples of castes that are legally closed, but into which, in point of fact, newcomers make their way, and often in large numbers. On the other hand, what difference does it make if a caste is legally open, but conditions *de facto* prevent new accessions to it? If a person who acquires wealth thereby becomes a member of the governing class, but no one gets rich, it is as if the class were closed; and if only a few get rich, it is as if the law erected serious barriers against access to the caste. Something of that sort was observable towards the end of the Roman Empire. People who acquired wealth entered the order of the curials. But only a few individuals made any money. Theoretically we might examine any number of groups. Practically we have to confine ourselves to the more important. We shall proceed by successive approximations, starting with the simple and going on to the complex.

   . . . The least we can do is to divide society into two strata: a higher stratum, which usually contains the rulers, and a lower stratum, which usually contains the ruled. That fact is so obvious that it has always forced itself even upon the most casual observation, and so for the circulation of individuals between the two strata. Even Plato had an inkling of class-circulation and tried to regulate it artificially. . . . The "new man," the upstart, the *parvenu*, has always been a subject of interest, and literature has analyzed him unendingly. Here, then, we are merely giving a more exact form to things that have long been perceived more or less vaguely. . . .

•   •   •

The upper stratum of society, the *élite*, nominally contains certain groups of peoples, not always very sharply defined, that are called aristocracies. There are cases in which the majority of individuals belonging to such aristocracies actually possess the qualities requisite for remaining there; and then again there are cases where considerable numbers of the individuals making up the class do not possess those requisites. Such people may occupy more or less important places in the governing *élite* or they may be barred from it.

In the beginning, military, religious, and commercial aristocracies and plutocracies—with a few exceptions not worth considering—must have constituted parts of the governing *élite* and sometimes have made up the whole of it. The victorious warrior, the prosperous merchant, the opulent plutocrat, were men of such parts, each in his own field, as to be superior to the average individual. Under those circumstances the label corresponded to an actual capacity. But as time goes by, considerable, sometimes very considerable, differences arise between the capacity and the label; while on the other hand, certain aristocracies originally figuring prominently in the rising *élite* end by constituting an insignificant element in it. That has happened especially to military aristocracies.

Aristocracies do not last. Whatever the causes, it is an incontestable fact that after a certain length of time they pass away. History is a graveyard of aristocracies. The Athenian "People" was an aristocracy as compared with the remainder of a population of resident aliens and slaves. It vanished without leaving any descent. The various aristocracies of Rome vanished in their time. So did the aristocracies of the Barbarians. Where, in France, are the descendants of the Frankish conquerors? The genealogies of the English nobility have been very exactly kept; and they show that very few families still remain to claim descent from the comrades of William the Conqueror. The rest have vanished. In Germany the aristocracy of the present day is very largely made up of descendants of vassals of the lords of old. The populations of European countries have increased enormously during the past few centuries. It is as certain as certain can be that the aristocracies have not increased in proportion.

They decay not in numbers only. They decay also in quality, in the sense that they lose their vigour, that there is a decline in the proportions of the residues which enabled them to win their power and hold it. The governing class is restored not only in numbers, but—and that is the more important thing—in quality, by families rising from the lower classes and bringing with them the vigour and the proportions of residues necessary for keeping themselves in power. It is also restored by the loss of its more degenerate members.

If one of those movements comes to an end, or worse still, if they both come to an end, the governing class crashes to ruin and often sweeps the whole of a nation along with it. Potent cause of disturbance in the equilibrium is the accumulation of superior elements in the lower classes and, conversely, of inferior elements in the higher classes. If human aristocracies were like thorough-breds among animals, which reproduce themselves over long periods of time with approximately the same traits, the history of the human race would be something altogether different from the history we know.

In virtue of class-circulation, the governing *élite* is always in a state of slow and continuous transformation. It flows on like a river, never being today what it was yesterday. From time to time sudden and violent disturbances occur. There is a flood—the river overflows its banks. Afterwards, the new governing *élite* again resumes its slow transformation. The flood has subsided, the river is again flowing normally in its wonted bed.

Revolutions come about through accumulations in the higher strata of society—either because of a slowing-down in class-circulation, or from other causes—of decadent elements no longer possessing the residues suitable for keeping them in power, and shrinking from the use of force; while meantime in the lower strata of society elements of superior quality are coming to the fore, possessing residues suitable for exercising the functions of government and willing enough to use force.

. . . .

Violent movements take place by fits and starts, and effects therefore do not follow immediately on their causes. After a governing class, or a nation, has maintained itself for long periods of time on force and acquired great wealth, it may subsist for some time still without using force, buying off its adversaries and paying not only in gold, but also in terms of the dignity and respect that it had formerly enjoyed and which constitute, as it were, a capital. In the first stages of decline, power is maintained by bargainings and concessions, and people are so deceived into thinking that that policy can be carried on indefinitely. So the decadent Roman Empire bought peace of the Barbarians with money and honours. So Louis XVI, in France, squandering in a very short time an ancestral inheritance of love, respect, and almost religious reverence for the monarchy, managed, by making repeated concessions, to be the King of the Revolution. So the English aristocracy managed to prolong its term of power in the second half of the nineteenth century down to the dawn of its decadence, which was heralded by the "Parliament Bill" in the first years of the twentieth.

. . . .

CHAPTER XII
THE GENERAL FORM OF SOCIETY

. . . In the fact, whether universal suffrage prevails or not, it is always an oligarchy that governs, finding ways to give to the "will of the people" that expression which the few desire, from the "royal law" that bestowed the *imperium* on the Roman Emperors down to the votes of a legislative majority elected in one way or another, from the plebiscite that gave the empire to Napoleon III down to the universal suffrage that is shrewdly bought, steered, and manipulated by our "speculators." Who is this new god called Universal Suffrage? He is no more exactly definable, no less shrouded in mystery, no less beyond the pale of reality, than the hosts of other divinities; nor are there fewer and less patent contradictions in his theology than in theirs. Worshippers of Universal Suffrage are not led by their god. It is they who lead him—and by the nose, determining the forms in which he must manifest himself. Oftentimes, proclaiming the sanctity of "majority rule," they resist "majority rule" by obstructionist tactics, even though they form but small minorities, and burning incense to the goddess Reason, they in no wise disdain, in certain cases, alliances with Chicanery, Fraud, and Corruption.

. . . Social stability is so beneficial a thing that to maintain it it is well worth while to enlist the aid of fantastic ideals . . . and this or that theology— among the others, the theology of universal suffrage—and be resigned to putting up with certain actual disadvantages. Before it becomes advisable to disturb the public peace, such disadvantages must have grown very very serious; and since human beings are effectively guided not by the sceptical reasonings of science but by "living faiths" expressed in ideals, theories such as the divine right of kings, the legitimacy of oligarchies, of "the people," of "majorities," of legislative assemblies, and other such things, may be useful within certain limits, and have in fact proved to be, however absurd they may be from the scientific standpoint.

· · ·

Let us imagine a country where the governing class, *A*, is inclining more and more in the direction of humanitarianism, is fostering, in other words, only the more harmful group-persistences, rejecting the others as outworn prejudices, and, while awaiting the advent of the "reign of reason," is becoming less and less capable of using force and is so shirking the main duty of a ruling class. Such a country is on its way to utter ruin. But lo, the subject class, *B*, revolts against the class *A*. In fighting *A* it uses the humanitarian derivations * so dear to the *A*'s, but underlying them are quite different sentiments, and they soon find expression in deeds. The *B*'s apply force on a far-reaching scale, and not only overthrow the *A*'s but kill large numbers of them—and, in so doing, to tell the truth, they are

---

* For Pareto, "derivations" are the devices by means of which men rationalize their actions. [Ed.]

performing a useful public service, something like ridding the country of a bane-ful animal pest. They bring with them to the seats of power a great abundance of group-persistences; and little it matters, if it matters at all, that these group-persistences be different in outward forms from the old. The important thing is that now they are functioning in the governing class and that owing to them the social fabric is acquiring stability and strength. The country is saved from ruin and is reborn to a new life.

If one judges superficially, one may be tempted to dwell more especially on the slaughter and pillaging that attend a revolution, without thinking to ask whether such things may not be manifestations—as regrettable as one may wish—of sentiments, of social forces, that are very salutary. If one should say that, far from being reprehensible, the slaughter and robbery are signs that those who were called upon to commit them deserved power for the good of society, he would be stating a paradox, for there is no relationship of cause and effect, nor any close and indispensable correlation, between such outrages and social utility; but the paradox would still contain its modicum of truth, in that the slaughter and rapine are external symptoms indicating the advent of strong and courage-ous people to places formerly held by weaklings and cowards. In all that we have been describing in the abstract many revolutions that have actually occurred in the concrete, from the revolution which gave imperial rule to Augustus down to the French Revolution of '89. . . . If the class governing in France had had the faith that counsels use of force and the will to use force, it would never have been overthrown and, procuring its own advantage, would have procured the advan-tage of France. Since it failed in that function, it was salutary that its rule should give way to rule by others; and since, again, it was the resort to force that was wanting, it was in keeping with very general uniformities that there should be a swing to another extreme where force was used even more than was required. Had Louis XVI not been a man of little sense and less courage, letting himself be floored without fighting, and preferring to lose his head on the guillotine to dying weapon in hand like a man of sinew, he might have been the one to do the destroying. If the victims of the September massacres, their kinsmen and friends, had not for the most part been spineless humanitarians without a particle of courage or energy, they would have annihilated their enemies instead of waiting to be annihilated themselves. It was a good thing that power should pass into the hands of people who showed that they had the faith and the resolve requisite for the use of force.

.   .   .

We need not linger on the fiction of "popular representation"—poppycock grinds no flour. Let us go on and see what substance underlies the various forms of power in the governing classes. Ignoring exceptions, which are few in number and of short duration, one finds everywhere a governing class of relatively few individuals that keeps itself in power partly by force and partly by the consent of the subject class, which is much more populous. The differences lie principally, as regards substance, in the relative proportions of force and consent; and as regards forms, in the manners in which the force is used and the consent obtained.

.   .   .

A governing class is present everywhere, even where there is a despot, but the forms under which it appears are widely variable. In absolute governments a sovereign occupies the stage alone. In so-called democratic governments it is the parliament. But behind the scenes in both cases there are always people who play a very important rôle in actual government. To be sure they must now and again bend the knee to the whims of ignorant and domineering sovereigns or parliaments, but they are soon back at their tenacious, patient, never-ending work, which is of much the greater consequence. In the Roman *Digesta* one may read truly splendid constitutions bearing the names of very wretched Emperors, just as in our day we have very fair legal codes that have been enacted by fairly brainless parliaments. The cause in both cases is the same: The sovereign leaves everything to his legal advisers, in some cases not even divining what they are having him do—and parliaments today even less than many a shrewd leader or king. And least of all King Demos! And such blindness on his part has at times helped to effect betterments in conditions of living in the face of his prejudices, not to mention much-needed steps in behalf of national defense. King Demos, good soul, thinks he is following his own devices. In reality he is following the lead of his rulers. But that very very often turns out to the advantage of his rulers only, for they, from the days of Aristotle down to our own, have made lavish use of the arts of bamboozling King Demos. Our plutocrats, like those of the late Roman Republic, are at all times busy making money, either on their own account or to sate the hungry maws of their partisans and accomplices; and for anything else they care little or nothing. Among the derivations which they use to show that their rule is to the advantage of a country, interesting is the assertion that the public is better qualified to pass on general questions than on special ones. The fact, in reality, is the precise opposite. One has to talk only for a very brief time with an uneducated person to see that he grasps special questions, which are usually concrete, much more clearly than general questions, which as a rule are abstract. But abstract questions have the advantage for people in power that whatever the answers that are given them by the public, they will be able to draw any inference they choose from them. The people sends to parliament men who are pledged to abolish interest on capital and "surplus value" in industry, and check the "greed" of the "speculators" (general questions) ; and those representatives now directly, now indirectly by helping others, increase the public debt beyond all bounds and consequently the interest paid to capital, maintain and in fact increase the "surplus value" enjoyed by manufacturers (many of whom fatten on political demagoguery), and put the government of the nation into the hands of speculators . . . .

The governing class is not a homogeneous body. It too has a government—a smaller, choicer class (or else a leader, or a committee) that effectively and practically exercises control. Sometimes that fact is visible to the eye, as in the case of the Ephors of Sparta, the Council of Ten in Venice, the favourite ministers of absolute sovereigns, or the "bosses" in parliaments. At other times it is more or less hidden from view, as in the "caucus" in England, the political convention in the United States, the cliques of "speculator" chieftains who function in France and Italy, and so on. The tendency to personify abstractions or merely to think of them as objective realities inclines many people to picture the governing class as a person, or at least as a concrete unit, and imagine that it knows what it wants and executes by logical procedures designs which it had conceived in advance. In just such terms do anti-Semites think of the Jews, and many Socialists of the *"bourgeoisie"* (though others, coming closer to realities, think of the middle class as a "system" functioning to some extent quite aside from any design on the part of its members). Ruling classes, like other social groups, perform both logical and non-logical actions, and the chief element in what happens is in fact the order, or system, not the conscious will of individuals, who indeed may in certain cases be carried by the system to points where they would never have gone of deliberate choice. In speaking of "speculators," we must not think of them as actors in a melodrama who administer and rule the world, executing wicked designs by stratagem dark. Such a conception of them would be no more real than a fairy-story. Speculators are just people who keep their minds on their business, and being well supplied with Class I residues, take advantage of them to make money, following lines of least resistance, as after all everybody else does. They hold no meetings where they congregate to plot common designs, nor have they any other devices for reaching a common accord. That accord comes about automatically; for if in a given set of circumstances there is one line of procedure where the advantage is greatest and the resistance least, the majority of those who are looking for it will find it, and though each of them will be following it on his own account, it will seem, without being so, that they are all acting in common accord. But at other times they will be carried along by the sheer force of the system to which they belong, involuntarily, and indeed against their wills, following the course that is required of the system. Fifty years ago "speculators" had no conception whatever of the state of affairs that prevails today and to which their activities have brought them. The road they have followed has been the resultant of an infinitude of minor acts, each determined by the present advantage. As is the case with all social phenomena, it has been the resultant of certain forces operating in conjunction with certain ties and in the face of certain obstacles. When we say that at the present time our speculators are laying the foundations for a war by continually increasing public expenditures, we in no sense mean that they are doing that deliberately—quite to the contrary! They are continually increasing public expenditures and fanning economic conflicts not in order to bring on a war, but in order to make a direct profit in each little case. But that cause, though an important one, is not the main cause. There is another of greater importance—their appeal to sentiments of patriotism in the masses at large, as a device for governing. Furthermore, the speculators in the various countries are in competition with each other and are using armaments to exact concessions from rivals. Other similar causes are operating, and they all are leading to increases in armaments without that's being in any sense the consequence of preconceived design. . . .

. . . .

For purposes of maintaining its power the governing class uses individuals from the subject class, who may be grouped in two divisions corresponding to the two principal instruments for holding power secure. . . . The one group uses force, and is made up of soldiers, police of one sort or another, and the *bravi* of a day gone by; the other uses skill, and ranges in character and in time all the way from the clientage of the old Roman politicians to the clientèles of our contemporary politicians. Those two groups are always with us, but never in the same actual proportions, nor, much less, in the same visible proportions. One extreme is marked by the Rome of the praetorians, where the chief *de facto* instrument of governing, and even more so the visible instrument, was armed force. The other extreme is represented by the United States of America, where the chief actual instrument of governing, and to a somewhat lesser extent the apparent instrument, is the political "machine." These cliques work in various ways. The principal way is the least conspicuous. The administration in power "looks after" the interests of the speculators, and often without any explicit understanding with them. A protectionist government, for instance, gets the confidence and the support of the manufacturers it protects without having to come to explicit terms with all of them, though it may have some agreement with outstanding individuals. The situation is the same with public works, though agreement with the big contractors is becoming the rule. Other ways are better known—they are less important from the social standpoint, but are commonly regarded as more important from the ethical standpoint. Among them is the bribery of voters, elected officials, government ministers, newspaper-owners, and other such persons, which has its counterpart under systems of absolutism in the bribery of courtiers, favourites, male and female, officials, generals, and so on— an old form of corruption that has not altogether disappeared. Such means have been employed in all periods of history, from the days of ancient Athens and republican Rome down to our own; but they are really the consequences of government by a class that forces its way into power by cunning and rules by cunning. And that is why the numberless attempts which have been made to "purify" politics have been failures and still remain such. Witch-grass may be cut as often as one chooses, but it sprouts only the more rankly if the roots are left untouched. Our democracies in France, Italy, England, and the United States are tending more and more to become demagogic plutocracies and may be following that road on the way to one of those radical transformations that have been witnessed in the past.

Barring some few exceptions, chief among them the conferring of honours and decorations by governments . . . , money has to be spent to secure the support both of armed force and of political "machines." It is not enough, therefore, to be willing to use such instruments—one has to be able to. That capacity is correlated with the production of wealth, and the production of wealth, in its turn, is not independent of the manner in which armed force and the political following are utilized. The problem therefore is a complex one and has to be considered synthetically. Analytically, one may say that armed force in many cases costs less than the "machine," but in certain other cases the "machine" may prove to be more favourable to the production of wealth; and that has to be taken into account in striking the balance . . . .

Evolution towards "democracy" seems to stand in strict correlation with the increased use of that instrument of governing which involves resort to artifice and to the "machine," as against the instrument of force. In ancient times that was clearly observable towards the end of the Republic in Rome, where there was a conflict between precisely those two instrumentalities, force winning the final victory in the Empire. It is even more apparent in our own day, when the régimes in many "democratic" countries might be defined as a sort of feudalism that is primarily economic . . . and in which the principal instrument of governing is the manipulation of political followings, whereas the military feudalism of the Middle Ages used force primarily as embodied in vassalage. A political system in which "the people" expresses its "will"—given but not granted that it has one—without cliques, intrigues, "combines," "gangs," exists only as a pious wish of theorists. It is not to be observed in reality, either in the past or in the present, either in our Western countries or in any others.

Such phenomena, long the subject of remark, are usually described as aberrations, or "degenerations," of "democracy"; but when and where one may be introduced to the perfect, or even the merely decent, state from which said aberration or "degeneration" has occurred, no one ever manages to tell. The best that can be said is that when democracy was an opposition party it did not show as many blemishes as it does at present; but that is a trait common to almost all opposition parties, which lack not so much the will as the chance to go wrong.

It is further to be noted that the defects in various systems of government may differ from each other, but, taking things as a whole, it cannot be held that one type of régime is very different in that respect from any other. The criticisms that are levelled at modern democracy are not greatly different from those that were levelled at ancient democracies, the Athenian, for instance; and if there are cases of corruption in democracies old and new, it would not be difficult to find cases just as bad in absolute and constitutional monarchies, in oligarchical governments, and in any other sort of régime . . . .

. . .

If we look at all these facts from the outside, trying as far as possible to free our minds of the ties of sectarian passions, prejudices of country and party, utopian perfections, ideals, and so on, we see that, substantially, and whatever the form of government, men holding power have, as a rule, a certain inclination to use that power to keep themselves in the saddle, and to abuse it to secure personal gains and advantages, which they sometimes fail to distinguish clearly from party gains and advantages and almost always confuse with the gains and advantages of country. Wherefrom it follows that: 1. Individuals holding power behave in more or less the same way under the various systems of government. The differences come in the substance, in other words, in the sentiments that prevail in the given population: the more (or less) honest the population, the more (or less) honest the government. 2. Uses and abuses of power will be the greater, the more extensive the government's interference in private business. As raw material increases, the amount that can be earned from it increases. In the United States, where the government tries to enforce morality by law, one notes gross abuses that are not observable in countries where there are no such restrictions or where restriction is on a smaller scale. 3. The governing class sees to appropriating other people's property not only for its own use, but also to share with such members of the subject class as defend it and safe-guard its rule, whether by force or by fraud—the support the client lends to the patron. 4. In the majority of cases neither patron nor client is fully conscious of violating the moral norms that prevail in their society, and even when they are, they justify themselves either on the ground that after all others would like to be doing as they do or on the convenient pretext that the end justifies the means—and from their point of view what better end can there be than to keep in power? In fact, not a few of them in all sincerity identify that end with the best interests of their country. There may even be persons who believe that they are upholding honesty, morality, and the public welfare, whereas in point of fact their activities are but a cloak for the intrigues of men who are out to make money. 5. The government machine consumes, at any rate, an amount of wealth that is correlative not only with the total amount of wealth belonging to the private enterprises in which the government interferes, but also with the instruments that the governing class uses to keep in power. . . .

· · ·

In the practice of the social sciences one must especially be on one's guard against intrusions of personal sentiments; for a writer is inclined to look not for what is and nothing else, but for what *ought* to be in order to fit in with his religious, moral, patriotic, humanitarian, or other sentiments. The quest for uniformities is an end in itself. Once they have been found, they may be made to serve other purposes. But to mix the two researches is harmful to both, and is in any case a serious and oftentimes insuperable obstacle to the discovery of experimental uniformities. As long as the natural sciences had to deal with such obstacles, they made little or no progress, and only as the obstacles became fewer in number and finally disappeared did they make the marvellous progress they show today. If, accordingly, one would remould the social sciences on the model of the natural sciences, one must proceed in them as in the natural sciences, reducing highly complicated concrete phenomena to simpler theoretical phenomena, being exclusively guided all the while by the intent to discover experimental uniformities, and judging the efficacy of what one has done only by the experimental verifications that may be made of it.

· · ·

THE RULING CLASS

Gaetano Mosca

1858–1941

❧❧

Of the contemporary critics of democracy Gaetano Mosca was one of the most able and scholarly. His *Elementi di Scienza politica* (1896), edited and revised by Arthur Livingston, and translated into English by Hannah D. Kahn as *The Ruling Class* (1939), is a contemporary classic. Mosca's basic ideas were first developed in the *Teorica dei governi e governo parlamentare* which appeared in 1884.

Born in Sicily, he taught mainly at Turin, where he was professor of constitutional law, and in Rome, where he was professor of political theory. He served for many years in the Italian Chamber of Deputies as a member of the Liberal Conservative party and in 1918 became a senator for life by royal appointment.

Among the constant facts and tendencies that are to be found in all political organisms, one is so obvious that it is apparent to the most casual eye. In all societies—from societies that are very meagerly developed and have barely attained the dawnings of civilization, down to the most advanced and powerful societies—two classes of people appear—a class that rules and a class that is ruled. The first class, always the less numerous, performs all political functions, monopolizes power and enjoys the advantages that power brings, whereas the second, the more numerous class, is directed and controlled by the first, in a manner that is now more or less legal, now more or less arbitrary and violent, and supplies the first, in appearance at least, with material means of subsistence and with the instrumentalities that are essential to the vitality of the political organism.

In practical life we all recognize the existence of this ruling class. . . . We all know that, in our own country, whichever it may be, the management of public affairs is in the hands of a minority of influential persons, to which management, willingly or unwillingly, the majority defer. We know that the same thing goes on in neighboring countries, and in fact we should be put to it to conceive of a real world otherwise organized—a world in which all men would be directly subject to a single person without relationships of superiority or subordination, or in which all men would share equally in the direction of political affairs. If we reason otherwise in theory, that is due partly to inveterate habits that we follow in our thinking and partly to the exaggerated importance that we attach to two political facts that loom far larger in appearance than they are in reality.

The first of these facts—and one has only to open one's eyes to see it—is that in every political organism there is one individual who is chief among the leaders of the ruling class as a whole and stands, as we say, at the helm of the state. That person is not always the person who holds supreme power according to law. At times, alongside of the hereditary king or emperor there is a prime minister or a major-domo who wields an actual power that is greater than the sovereign's. At other times, in place of the elected president the influential politician who has procured the president's election will govern. Under special circumstances there may be, instead of a single person, two or three who discharge the functions of supreme control.

The second fact, too, is readily discernible. Whatever the type of political organization, pressures arising from the discontent of the masses who are governed, from the passions by which they are swayed, exert a certain amount of influence on the policies of the ruling, the political, class.

But the man who is at the head of the state would certainly not be able to govern without the support of a numerous class to enforce respect for his orders and to have them carried out; and granting that he can make one individual, or indeed many individuals, in the ruling class feel the weight of his power, he certainly cannot be at odds with the class as a whole or do away with it. Even if that were possible, he would at once be forced to create another class, without the support of which action on his part would be completely paralyzed. On the other hand, granting that the discontent of the masses might succeed in deposing a ruling class, inevitably, as we shall later show, there would have to be another organized minority within the masses themselves to discharge the functions of a ruling class. Otherwise all organization, and the whole social structure, would be destroyed.

From the point of view of scientific research the real superiority of the concept of the ruling, or political, class lies in the fact that the varying structure of ruling classes has a preponderant importance in determining the political type, and also the level of civilization, of the different peoples. According to a manner of classifying forms of government that is still in vogue, Turkey and Russia were both, up to a few years ago, absolute monarchies, England and Italy were constitutional, or limited, monarchies, and France and the United States were classed as republics. The classification was based on the fact that, in the first two countries mentioned, headship in the state was hereditary and the chief was nominally omnipotent; in the second two, his office is hereditary but his powers and prerogatives are limited; in the last two, he is elected.

That classification is obviously superficial. Absolutisms though they were, there was little in common between the manners in which Russia and Turkey were managed politically, the levels of civilization in the two countries and the organization of their ruling classes being vastly different. On the same basis, the regime in Italy, a monarchy, is much more similar to the regime in France, a Republic, than it is to the regime in England, also a monarchy; and there are important differences between the political organizations of the United States and France, though both countries are republics.

As we have already suggested, ingrained habits of thinking have long stood, as they still stand, in the way of scientific progress in this matter. The classification mentioned above, which divides governments into absolute monarchies, limited monarchies and republics, was devised by Montesquieu and was intended to replace the classical categories of Aristotle, who divided governments into monarchies, aristocracies and democracies. What Aristotle called a democracy was simply an aristocracy of fairly broad membership. Aristotle himself was in a position to observe that in every Greek state, whether aristocratic or democratic, there was always one person or more who had a preponderant influence. Between the day of Polybius and the day of Montesquieu, many writers perfected Aristotle's classification by introducing into it the concept of "mixed" governments. Later on the modern democratic theory, which had its source in Rousseau, took its stand upon the concept that the majority of the citizens in any state can participate, and in fact *ought* to participate, in its political life, and the doctrine of popular sovereignty still holds sway over many minds in spite of the fact that modern scholarship is making it increasingly clear that democratic, monarchical and aristocratic principles function side by side in every political organism. We shall not stop to refute this democratic theory here, since that is the task of this work as a whole. Besides, it would be hard to destroy in a few pages a whole system of ideas that has become firmly rooted in the human mind. . . .

We think it may be desirable, nevertheless, to reply at this point to an objection which might very readily be made to our point of view. If it is easy to understand that a single individual cannot command a group without finding within the group a minority to support him, it is rather difficult to grant, as a constant and natural fact, that minorities rule majorities, rather than majorities minorities. But that is one of the points—so numerous in all the other sciences —where the first impression one has of things is contrary to what they are in reality. In reality the dominion of an organized minority, obeying a single impulse, over the unorganized majority is inevitable. The power of any minority is irresistible as against each single individual in the majority, who stands alone before the totality of the organized minority. At the same time, the minority is organized for the very reason that it is a minority. A hundred men acting uniformly in concert, with a common understanding, will triumph over a thousand men who are not in accord and can therefore be dealt with one by one. Meanwhile it will be easier for the former to act in concert and have a mutual understanding simply because they are a hundred and not a thousand. It follows that the larger the political community, the smaller will the proportion of the governing minority to the governed majority be, and the more difficult will it be for the majority to organize for reaction against the minority.

However, in addition to the great advantage accruing to them from the fact of being organized, ruling minorities are usually so constituted that the individuals who make them up are distinguished from the mass of the governed by qualities that give them a certain material, intellectual or even moral superiority; or else they are the heirs of individuals who possessed such qualities. In other words, members of a ruling minority regularly have some attribute, real or apparent, which is highly esteemed and very influential in the society in which they live.

·　　·　　·

What we see is that as soon as there is a shift in the balance of political forces—when, that is, a need is felt that capacities different from the old should assert themselves in the management of the state, when the old capacities, therefore, lose some of their importance or changes in their distribution occur—then the manner in which the ruling class is constituted changes also. If a new source of wealth develops in a society, if the practical importance of knowledge grows, if an old religion declines or a new one is born, if a new current of ideas spreads, then, simultaneously, far-reaching dislocations occur in the ruling class. One might say, indeed, that the whole history of civilized mankind comes down to a conflict between the tendency of dominant elements to monopolize political power and transmit possession of it by inheritance, and the tendency toward a dislocation of old forces and an insurgence of new forces; and this conflict produces an unending ferment of endosmosis and exosmosis between the upper classes and certain portions of the lower. Ruling classes decline inevitably when they cease to find scope for the capacities through which they rose to power, when they can no longer render the social services which they once rendered, or when their talents and the services they render lose in importance in the social environment in which they live. So the Roman aristocracy declined when it was no longer the exclusive source of high officers for the army, of administrators for the commonwealth, of governors for the provinces. So the Venetian aristocracy declined when its nobles ceased to command the galleys and no longer passed the greater part of their lives in sailing the seas and in trading and fighting.

·　　·　　·

On the other hand it may happen in the history of a nation that commerce with foreign peoples, forced emigrations, discoveries, wars, create new poverty and new wealth, disseminate knowledge of things that were previously unknown to cause infiltrations of new moral, intellectual and religious currents. Or again —as a result of such infiltrations or through a slow process of inner growth, or from both causes—it may happen that a new learning arises, or that certain elements of an old, long forgotten learning return to favor so that new ideas and new beliefs come to the fore and upset the intellectual habits on which the obedience of the masses has been founded. The ruling class may also be vanquished and destroyed in whole or in part by foreign invasions, or, when the circumstances just mentioned arise, it may be driven from power by the advent of new social elements who are strong in fresh political forces. Then, naturally, there comes a period of renovation, or, if one prefer, of revolution, during which individual energies have free play and certain individuals, more passionate, more energetic, more intrepid or merely shrewder than others, force their way from the bottom of the social ladder to the topmost rungs.

Once such a movement has set in, it cannot be stopped immediately. The example of individuals who have started from nowhere and reached prominent positions fires new ambitions, new greeds, new energies, and this molecular rejuvenation of the ruling class continues vigorously until a long period of social stability slows it down again. We need hardly mention examples of nations in such periods of renovation. In our age that would be superfluous. Rapid restocking of ruling classes is a frequent and very striking phenomenon in countries that have been recently colonized. When social life begins in such environments, there is no ready-made ruling class, and while such a class is in process of formation, admittance to it is gained very easily. Monopolization of land and other agencies of production is, if not quite impossible, at any rate more difficult than elsewhere. That is why, at least during a certain period, the Greek colonies offered a wide outlet for all Greek energy and enterprise. That is why, in the United States, where the colonizing of new lands continued through the whole nineteenth century and new industries were continually springing up, examples of men who started with nothing and have attained fame and wealth are still frequent—all of which helps to foster in the people of that country the illusion that democracy is a fact.

Suppose now that a society gradually passes from its feverish state to calm. Since the human being's psychological tendencies are always the same, those who belong to the ruling class will begin to acquire a group spirit. They will become more and more exclusive and learn better and better the art of monopolizing to their advantage the qualities and capacities that are essential to acquiring power and holding it. Then, at last, the force that is essentially conservative appears— the force of habit. Many people become resigned to a lowly station, while the members of certain privileged families or classes grow convinced that they have almost an absolute right to high station and command.

A philanthropist would certainly be tempted to inquire whether mankind is happier—or less unhappy—during periods of social stability and crystallization, when everyone is almost fated to remain in the social station to which he was born, or during the directly opposite periods of renovation and revolution, which permit all to aspire to the most exalted positions and some to attain them. Such an inquiry would be difficult. The answer would have to take account of many qualifications and exceptions, and might perhaps always be influenced by the personal preferences of the observer. . . .

As we have just seen, in fairly populous societies that have attained a certain level of civilization, ruling classes do not justify their power exclusively by de facto possession of it, but try to find a moral and legal basis for it, representing it as the logical and necessary consequence of doctrines and beliefs that are generally recognized and accepted. So if a society is deeply imbued with the Christian spirit the political class will govern by the will of the sovereign, who, in turn, will reign because he is God's anointed. So too in Mohammedan societies political authority is exercised directly in the name of the caliph, or vicar, of the Prophet, or in the name of someone who has received investiture, tacit or explicit, from the caliph. The Chinese mandarins ruled the state because they were supposed to be interpreters of the will of the Son of Heaven, who had received from heaven the mandate to govern paternally, and in accordance with the rules of the Confucian ethic, "the people of the hundred families." The complicated hierarchy of civil and military functionaries in the Roman Empire rested upon the will of the emperor, who, at least down to Diocletian's time, was assumed by a legal fiction to have received from the people a mandate to rule the commonwealth. The powers of all lawmakers, magistrates and government officials in the United States emanate directly or indirectly from the vote of the voters, which is held to be the expression of the sovereign will of the whole American people.

This legal and moral basis, or principle, on which the power of the political class rests, is what we have elsewhere called, and shall continue here to call, the "political formula." . . . [T]he various political formulas may be based either upon supernatural beliefs or upon concepts which, if they do not correspond to positive realities, at least appear to be rational. We shall not say that they correspond in either case to scientific truths. A conscientious observer would be obliged to confess that, if no one has ever seen the authentic document by which the Lord empowered certain privileged persons or families to rule his people on his behalf, neither can it be maintained that a popular election, however liberal the suffrage may be, is ordinarily the expression of the will of a people, or even of the will of the majority of a people.

And yet that does not mean that political formulas are mere quackeries aptly invented to trick the masses into obedience. Anyone who viewed them in that light would fall into grave error. The truth is that they answer a real need in man's social nature; and this need, so universally felt, of governing and knowing that one is governed not on the basis of mere material or intellectual force, but on the basis of a moral principle, has beyond any doubt a practical and a real importance.

Spencer wrote that the divine right of kings was the great superstition of past ages, and that the divine right of elected assemblies is the great superstition of our present age. The idea cannot be called wholly mistaken, but certainly it does not consider or exhaust all aspects of the question. It is further necessary to see whether a society can hold together without one of these "great superstitions"—whether a universal illusion is not a social force that contributes powerfully to consolidating political organization and unifying peoples or even whole civilizations.

. . .

. . . We shall not . . . attempt a systematic refutation of the theories on which universal suffrage is based. We shall simply refer to some of the main considerations that most seriously undermine the foundations on which universal suffrage as an intellectual edifice rests. We deem it sufficient for our purposes here to demonstrate that the assumption that the elected official is the mouthpiece of the majority of his electors is as a rule not consistent with the facts; and we believe that this can be proved by facts of ordinary experience and by certain practical observations that anyone can make on the manner in which elections are conducted.

What happens in other forms of government—namely, that an organized minority imposes its will on the disorganized majority—happens also and to perfection, whatever the appearances to the contrary, under the representative system. When we say that the voters "choose" their representative, we are using a language that is very inexact. The truth is that the representative *has himself elected* by the voters, and, if that phrase should seem too inflexible and too harsh to fit some cases, we might qualify it by saying that *his friends have him elected*. In elections, as in all other manifestations of social life, those who have the will and, especially, the moral, intellectual and material *means* to force their will upon others take the lead over the others and command them.

The political mandate has been likened to the power of attorney that is familiar in private law. But in private relationships, delegations of powers and capacities always presuppose that the principal has the broadest freedom in choosing his representative. Now in practice, in popular elections, that freedom of choice, though complete theoretically, necessarily becomes null, not to say ludicrous. If each voter gave his vote to the candidate of his heart, we may be sure that in almost all cases the only result would be a wide scattering of votes. When very many wills are involved, choice is determined by the most various criteria, almost all of them subjective, and if such wills were not coordinated and organized it would be virtually impossible for them to coincide in the spontaneous choice of one individual. If his vote is to have any efficacy at all, therefore, each voter is forced to limit his choice to a very narrow field, in other words to a choice among the two or three persons who have some chance of succeeding; and the only ones who have any chance of succeeding are those whose candidacies are championed by groups, by committees, by *organized minorities*. In order to simplify the situation for purposes of proof, we have assumed a uninominal ballot, where one name only is to be voted for. But the great majority of voters will necessarily have a very limited freedom in the choice of their representative, and the influence of committees will necessarily be preponderant, whatever the system of balloting. When the list ballot is used and the voter votes for a list of candidates, it turns out that the number of candidates with some chance of succeeding is less than double the number of representatives to be elected.

How do these organized minorities form about individual candidates or groups of candidates? As a rule they are based on considerations of property and taxation, on common material interests, on ties of family, class, religion, sect or political party. Whether their component personnels be good or bad, there can be no doubt that such committees—and the representatives who are now their tools, now their leaders or "bosses"—represent the organization of a considerable number of social values and forces. In practice, therefore, the representative system results not at all in government by the majority; it results in the participation of a certain number of social values in the guidance of the state, in the fact that many political forces which in an absolute state, a state ruled by a bureaucracy alone, would remain inert and without influence upon government become organized and so exert an influence on government.

. . .

The great majority of voters are passive, it is true, in the sense that they have not so much freedom to choose their representatives as a limited right to exercise an option among a number of candidates. Nevertheless, limited as it may be, that capacity has the effect of obliging candidates to try to win a weight of votes that will serve to tip the scales in their direction, so that they make every effort to flatter, wheedle and obtain the good will of the voters. In this way certain sentiments and passions of the "common herd" come to have their influence on the mental attitudes of the representatives themselves, and echoes of a widely disseminated opinion, or of any serious discontent, easily come to be heard in the highest spheres of government.

It may be objected that this influence of the majority of voters is necessarily confined to the broad lines of political policy and makes itself felt only on a very few topics of a very general character, and that within limits as narrow as that even in absolute governments the ruling classes are obliged to take account of mass sentiments. In fact the most despotic of governments has to proceed very cautiously when it comes to shocking the sentiments, convictions or prejudices of the majority of the governed, or to requiring of that majority pecuniary sacrifices to which they are not accustomed. But wariness about giving offense will be much greater when every single representative, whose vote may be useful or necessary to the executive branch of government, knows that the discontent of the masses may at almost any moment bring about the triumph of a rival. We are aware that this is a two-edged argument. The masses are not always any wiser in discerning and protecting their interests than their representatives are; and we are acquainted with regions where public discontent has created greater obstacles to desirable reforms than the mistakes of parliamentary representatives and ministries.

The representative system, furthermore, has widely different effects according as the molecular composition of the electoral body varies. If all the voters who have some influence, because of education or social position, are members of one or another of the organized minorities, and if only a mass of poor and ignorant citizens are left outside of them, it is impossible for the latter to exercise their right of option and control in any real or effective manner. In these circumstances, of the various organized minorities that are disputing the field, that one infallibly wins which spends most money or lies most persuasively.

The same thing happens if persons of ability and economic independence represent only a slender minority within the electing group and so have no way of influencing the vote of majorities directly. Then, as ordinarily happens in large cities, the majorities do not feel the moral and material influence of the "better elements." But when the "better elements" do succeed in withdrawing the majority from the influence of committees and "ward heelers" and win its vote, their control over the conduct of the organized minorities becomes effective. It follows, therefore, that the comparison of the merits and platforms of the various candidates will be relatively serious and dispassionate only when electoral forces are not entirely under the control of men who make a regular profession or trade of electioneering.

The real juridical safeguard in representative governments lies in the public discussion that takes place within representative assemblies. Into those assemblies the most disparate political forces and elements make their way, and the existence of a small independent minority is often enough to control the conduct of a large majority and, especially, to prevent the bureaucratic organization from becoming omnipotent. But when, beyond being organs of discussion and publicizing, assemblies come to concentrate all the prestige and power of legitimate authority in their own hands, as regularly happens in parliamentary governments, then in spite of the curb of public discussion the whole administrative and judiciary machine falls prey to the irresponsible and anonymous tyranny of those who win in the elections and speak in the name of the people, and we get one of the worst types of political organization that the real majority in a modern society can possibly be called upon to tolerate.

In governments that are based very largely on the representative principle the referendum is in some respects a fairly effective instrument. By it the mass of likes and dislikes, enthusiasms and angers, which, when they are truly widespread and truly general, constitute what may quite plausibly be called public opinion, is enabled to react against the conduct and enterprise of the governing minority. In a referendum it is a question not of making a choice, or an election, but of pronouncing a "yes" or a "no" upon a specific question. No single vote, therefore, is lost, and each single vote has its practical importance independently of any coordination or organization along lines of sect, party or committee. However, the democratic ideal of majority government is not realized even by the referendum. Governing is not altogether a matter of allowing or prohibiting modifications in constitutions or laws. It is quite as much a matter of managing the whole military, financial, judiciary and administrative machine, or of influencing those who manage it. Then again, even if the referendum does serve to limit the arbitrariness of the governing class, it is no less true that often it seriously hampers improvements in the political organism. Such improvements will always be more readily appreciated by a governing class, however selfish and corrupt it may be, than by the ill-informed majority of the governed. In many countries, for instance, if increases in taxes were to be submitted to referendum, they would always be rejected, even though they were of the most unqualified urgency and would be the most obvious benefit to the public.

. . . . .

. . . Social democracy is more than anything else the intellectual malady of our age. To be sure, it found a propitious moral environment. It found a soil prepared by all the rancors, ambitions and greeds that necessarily resulted from a long revolutionary period and from the shiftings of fortunes that were bound up with such a period. Supremely beneficial to it has been the world's disappointment with parliamentary democracy, which set out to inaugurate a reign of justice and equality in the world, and has failed miserably to keep that promise. Nevertheless this new doctrine originates in a system of ideas which is nothing, after all, but the logical consequence of the system in which the pure democracy of the old days found its inspiration.

Belief in the possibility that government can emanate from the majority; faith in the incorruptibility of the majority; confidence that once they have been emancipated from every principle of authority that is not rooted in universal consensus, from every aristocratic, monarchical and religious superstition, men will be able to inaugurate the political system that will best serve the general interests and the interests of justice—such is the content of the body of ideas and sentiments that has combated, and is combating, Christian beliefs in the people, and is the chief obstacle to any compromise with the church. Ideas and sentiments of the same sort have produced parliamentary democracy and, as we have seen, are now preventing the application of radical remedies to parliamentarism. The same body of ideas and sentiments, finally, is sweeping us inexorably toward socialism, and ultimately toward anarchy.

There is no stopping along the road. Once experience has shown that mere political equality as embodied in universal suffrage fails to produce political equality in the fact and maintains the political preeminence of a given class and of certain social influences, it is natural and logical that a system should be contrived which will destroy disparities in private fortunes and place all who aspire to rule over society, and therefore need the votes of the people, on an equal footing. And after a somewhat riper experience has made it clear, or made it merely plausible, that not even in that way can one get a government that is a genuine emanation of the majority will, much less absolute justice, we will have, as the final implication of a metaphysical concept that has vainly sought to concretize itself, a doctrine that favors ending any sort of social organization whatever, and therefore, anarchy.

Now democratic doctrine has rendered undeniable services to civilization. Embodied in the representative system, for which England set the pattern, it has contributed to important improvements in juridical defense, which have been attained through a system of free discussion that has been established in many parts of Europe. But now that we have come to its last logical implication, and men are trying to realize the principles on which it was based down to their remotest consequences, the same doctrine is disorganizing the countries in which it prevails and forcing them into their decline.

.   .   .

Things could not be otherwise with democracy because, at bottom, under pseudoscientific appearances, the democratic doctrine is altogether aprioristic. Its premises are not in the slightest degree justified by the facts. Absolute equality has never existed in human societies. Political power never has been, and never will be, founded upon the explicit consent of majorities. It always has been, and it always will be, exercised by organized minorities, which have had, and will have, the means, varying as the times vary, to impose their supremacy on the multitudes. . . .

.   .   .

. . . [O]ne might reasonably wonder at the slight practical influence which this new doctrine has had and is still having upon the development of political institutions and upon practitioners of official and nonofficial science. Even those who do admit the existence of a ruling class (and not to admit it would sometimes be equivalent to denying the obvious) often fail to reason as though the fact were inevitable—they do not draw the necessary consequences from it and so do not utilize the theory as the guiding thread that must steer us as we go looking into the causes that mature and produce the effects which at times lift societies to prosperity and power and at other times engulf them in anarchy and ruin. It is of no avail to credit the ruling class for successes, or to blame it for failures, unless we scrutinize the intricate mechanism, in the operation of which the explanation for the strength or weakness of the class can be found. And in this we have already glimpsed one of the causes for the failure of the new doctrine to bear more fruit in practice.

These causes we must, therefore, go into somewhat carefully. In order to make it easier to keep them in mind, suppose we divide them into two groups: extrinsic causes, which are foreign to the essence and structure of the doctrine proper, and intrinsic causes, which are due to defects or shortcomings in the doctrine itself.

First and perhaps foremost among the extrinsic causes is the fact that, so far, all the institutions that have been functioning in Europe have been based on other doctrines, some of which are different from the doctrine we are here concerned with, and, so to say, irrelevant to it, while others are directly antithetical to it. Representative governments now prevail almost everywhere in countries of European civilization. Some of them are modeled along the lines laid down by Montesquieu, who saw the essence and guarantee of political liberty in a tripartite separation of sovereign powers. More numerous are governments that follow the principle of Rousseau, that those powers only are legitimate which represent the will of the numerical majority of citizens, while the right of suffrage is regarded as an innate right from which no individual can reasonably and properly be barred.

Now in itself the democratic system probably has greater powers of self-preservation than other sytems. That is because its natural adversaries have to make a show of accepting it if they wish to avoid its consequences to a greater or lesser extent. All those who, by wealth, education, intelligence or guile, have an aptitude for leading a community of men, and a chance of doing so—in other words, all the cliques in the ruling class—have to bow to universal suffrage once it is instituted, and also, if occasion requires, cajole and fool it. On no other condition can they participate in the control of the state and reach positions from which they can best defend the interests of their particular clique. The fact, then, that the natural adversaries of democracy are obliged to pay official homage to it prevents them from openly declaring themselves followers of theories that explicitly deny the possibility of democratic government as commonly understood. And the same fact also impedes the formation of the coalitions of sentiments and interests that are necessary if a doctrine is to become an active force capable of transforming institutions—if it is to penetrate people's minds and so take hold of them as to modify the trend of a society at all appreciably. Michels has very properly stressed the point that, in countries which have representative governments, conservative parties are obliged to pay homage to democratic doctrines.

Then again, a new conception in politics or religion cannot have a very great efficacy in practice until the conception that has preceded it in the public consciousness has exhausted all its powers of expansion, or, better still, has carried out, so to say, the historic mission which it was born to fulfill and which explains its more or less rapid success. The modern democratic conception is hardly more than a century and a half old. It spread like wildfire because, first in France and soon after throughout western Europe, the new ruling class at once made use of it in order to oust the nobility and clergy from their privileges and in large part to supplant them. But rapid as its progress had been, the doctrine surely had not completed its historic task at the end of the nineteenth century, and it did not begin to influence the countries in eastern Europe till very recently.

.   .   .

. . . So far, in all the countries that have adopted universal suffrage more or less recently, the educated and well-to-do classes have maintained their rule under its aegis, though their influence has been tempered more or less by the influence of the petty bourgeoisie and of representatives of the interests of certain groups in the proletariat. That type of democracy is not so very different from the sort of government that Saint-Simon approved of and which he wanted Louis XVIII to use his authority to inaugurate—government by businessmen, scientists, scholars and artists. Democratic institutions may be able to endure for some time yet if, in virtue of them, a certain equilibrium between the various elements in the ruling class can be maintained, if our *apparent* democracy is not fatally carried away by logic, its worst enemy, and by the appetites of the lower classes and their leaders, and if it does not attempt to become *real* democracy by combining political equality with economic and cultural equality.

On the main intrinsic cause for the slight success that has so far been enjoyed by the doctrine that a ruling class necessarily exists, we have already touched very briefly.

A doctrine is a thread by which those who are examining a given body of facts try to guide themselves in the maze which the facts seem to present at first glance; and a doctrine becomes the more useful in practice the more it facilitates and simplifies the understanding and analysis of facts. In this matter of political theory, as in so many other matters, appearances are often as satisfactory to people as the substance would be. The old classifications of the various forms of government—the classification of Aristotle, who divided governments into monarchies, aristocracies and democracies, and the classification of Montesquieu, who trisected them into despotic, monarchical and republican governments— answered that purpose well enough. Following the Stagirite and the author of the *Esprit des lois*, anyone could get his bearings in political theory by deciding in just what category the government of his own country, or the governments of neighboring or even distant countries, belonged. Once that point was settled, he could well believe himself authorized to go on and point out the values, defects and dangers of this or that form of government, and to answer any objections that might be made to it by simply applying the precepts of the master he followed, or the master's successors.

On the other hand, merely to assert that in all forms of government the real and actual power resides in a ruling minority is to dismiss the old guides without supplying new ones—it is to establish a generic truth which does not take us at once into the heart of political happenings, present or past, and which does not explain by itself why certain political organisms are strong and others weak, nor suggest ways and means of preventing their decadence or repairing their defects. To assign all credit for the prosperity of a society, or all responsibility for its political decrepitude, to its ruling class is of little help when we do not know the various ways in which ruling classes are formed and organized. It is precisely in that variety of type that the secret of their strength and weakness must be sought and found.

The comprehensive and generic demonstration that a ruling class necessarily exists has to be supplemented, therefore, with an analytical study. We must patiently seek out the constant traits that various ruling classes possess and the variable traits with which the remote causes of their integration and dissolution, which contemporaries almost always fail to notice, are bound up. It is a question, after all, of using the procedure that is so much used in the natural sciences, in which no end of information that has now become an indestructible patrimony of human knowledge is due to happy intuitions, some of which have been confirmed, others modified, but all elaborated and developed by successive experiments and experiences. If it should be objected that it is difficult, and we might add, virtually impossible, to make experiments in cases where social phenomena are involved, one might answer that history, statistics and economics have by now gathered such a great store of experimental data that enough are available to permit us to begin our search.

Historians so far—following an opinion prevailing in the public at large—have especially stressed the achievements of the supreme heads of states, of people who stand at the vertex of the political pyramid, and occasionally, too, the merits of the lower strata in the pyramid, of the masses, who with their toil and often with their blood have supplied the supreme heads with the material means required for accomplishing the things they accomplished. If this new perception of the importance of the ruling class is to gain a hold, we must, without denying the great importance of what has been done at the vertex and at the base of the pyramid, show that, except for the influence of the intermediate social strata, neither of the others could have accomplished very much of any significance and permanence, since the type to which a political organism belongs and the efficacy of its action depend primarily upon the manner in which the intermediate strata are formed and function. Once that proof is obtained, it becomes evident that the supreme heads of states have, in general, been able to leave enduring marks on history only when they have managed to take the initiative in timely reforms of ruling classes, and that the principal merit of the lower classes has always lain in their inborn capacity for producing from within themselves new elements that have been able to rule them wisely.

. . . [I]n systems where everybody, or almost everybody, can vote—the chief task of the various party organizations into which the ruling class is divided is to win the votes of the more numerous classes, which are necessarily the poorest and most ignorant. These classes ordinarily live in submission to a government which often they do not care for, and the aims and workings of which more often still they do not understand. Their first, their natural, their most spontaneous desire is to be governed as little as possible, or to make as few sacrifices as possible for the state. Their second desire, which develops more especially with the exercise of suffrage, is to profit by government in order to better their economic situation, and to vent the repressed resentments and envies which often—not always—the man who is below feels for the man who is above, especially for the man who is his immediate superior.

When success in the struggle between the different groups in the ruling class depends upon the support and sympathy of the masses, the group that has the less effective means of influence at its disposal will unfailingly avail itself of the two desires mentioned, especially of resentments and envies, in order to draw the lower strata of society along with it. Connected with the group, now as a matter of sentiment, now as a matter of interest, are individuals who were born in the less favored classes but have managed by special talent and energy, or by exceptional cunning, to climb out of them. Michels has examined with great acumen the contribution to the management and organization of the socialist parties in the various countries that has been made by elements deriving from the middle classes and by elements issuing from the working classes themselves, and the rivalries and competitions that often arise between those two categories in the socialist general staffs.

Whatever their origins, the methods that are used by the people who aim to monopolize and exploit the sympathy of the masses always have been the same. They come down to pointing out, with exaggerations of course, the selfishness, the stupidity, the material enjoyments of the rich and the powerful; to denouncing their vices and wrongdoings, real and imaginary; and to promising to satisfy a common and widespread sense of rough-hewn justice which would like to see abolished every social distinction based upon advantage of birth and at the same time would like to see an absolutely equal distribution of pleasures and pains.

Often enough the parties against which this demagogic propaganda is directed use exactly the same means to combat it. Whenever they think they can profit by doing so, they too make promises which they will never be able to keep. They too flatter the masses, play to their crudest instincts and exploit and foment all their prejudices and greeds. A despicable competition, in which those who deliberately deceive lower their intellectual level to a par with those they deceive, while morally they stoop even lower!

.   .   .

The democratic tendency—the tendency to replenish ruling classes from below—is constantly at work with greater or lesser intensity in all human societies. At times the rejuvenation comes about in rapid or violent ways. More often, in fact normally, it takes place through a slow and gradual infiltration of elements from the lower into the higher classes.

In the past, violent renovations not infrequently came about as a result of foreign invasions. A conquering people would settle on the territory of the conquered and, without destroying the old inhabitants or driving them out, force its rule upon them. That happened in western Europe after the fall of the Roman Empire, in the Persia of the Sassanids after the Arab invasion, in England after the victory of William the Conqueror, in India after the invasion of the Mohammedans, in China after the invasion of the Mongols and again, later on, after the invasion of the Manchu Tatars. In such cases, remnants of the old native aristocracies have almost always crept into the new aristocracies of foreign origin. In the examples mentioned, also, the conquest by foreigners was usually facilitated by an incipient domestic decline. The indigenous ruling class had either weakened or disintegrated, or else had become alienated spiritually from the rest of the population.

In times more recent, violent and far-reaching renovations of old political classes have sometimes come about through internal upheavals. These would be "revolutions" proper. They occur when a wide breach opens between a people's official political organization and its customs, ideas and sentiments, and when many elements which would be competent to participate in government are artificially held in a subordinate status. The classic example of that situation would be the French Revolution. Another example is developing before our eyes in Russia today.

But cases where violent crises radically alter the criteria of selection for ruling classes, and change or modify their composition profoundly in the course of a few years, may be regarded as exceptional. They are characteristic of a few particular periods in history. Such overturns sometimes give a vigorous impetus to intellectual, moral and material progress. At other times they have been the beginnings, or else the results, of periods of decay and disintegration in civilizations. Even in normal times, one can almost always observe that a slow and gradual renewal of the ruling class is going on through infiltrations into the higher strata of society of elements emerging from the lower. But this tendency, which we have decided to call democratic, sometimes is outstanding in a civilization and operates in a more effective and rapid manner. At other times it proceeds covertly and therefore more blandly, because of the thousand obstacles that laws, habits and customs put in its way.

As we have seen . . . the democratic tendency is more likely to prevail in unsettled times, when new manners of thinking and feeling are undermining the old concepts on which the structure of social rankings has been based, when scientific and technical progress have created new ways of making money or produced changes in military organization, or even when a shock from outside has forced a nation to rally all the energies and capacities which, in quiet times, would have remained in a potential state. Revolutions and long wars give many new men a chance to assert themselves and make use of their talents. Had there been no French Revolution, Napoleon Bonaparte would probably have lived to be a good colonel of artillery, and had it not been for the wars of the Revolution and the Empire, some of his marshals would certainly have remained lieutenants. In general, changes in religion, new movements in philosophy and political thinking, invention of new weapons or new instruments of warfare, application of new discoveries to economic production and corresponding increases in economic production, are all elements that favor rapid translations and interchanges of the molecules that make up the various social strata. Such changes and interchanges come about more readily in new countries, where natural resources have not been very much exploited and still abound, permitting energetic and enterprising men to attain wealth and reputation with ease, or at least with less difficulty. The examples of Australia and the different countries in the Americas are apt to this point.

If it is confined within moderate limits, the democratic tendency is in a sense indispensable to what is called "progress" in human societies. If all aristocracies had remained steadfastly closed and stationary, the world would never have changed, and mankind would have stopped developing at the stage that it had attained at the time of the Homeric monarchies, or the old Near Eastern empires. The struggle between those who are at the top and those who are born at the bottom but aspire to climb has been, is and will ever be the ferment that forces individuals and classes to widen their horizons and seek the new roads that have brought the world to the degree of civilization that it attained in the nineteenth century. That high level of civilization made it possible to create in the political field the great modern representative state, which, as we have seen,* is of all political organisms the one that has succeeded in coordinating the largest sum of individual energies and activities and applying them to purposes that are related to the collective interest.

When the democratic tendency does not exert too great an influence, to the exclusion of other tendencies, it represents a conservative force. It enables ruling classes to be continually replenished through the admission of new elements who have inborn talents for leadership and a will to lead, and so prevents that exhaustion of aristocracies of birth which usually paves the way for great social cataclysms. Nevertheless, beginning with the end of the eighteenth century and continuing through the nineteenth, the dogma of human equality, modernized to accord with modern ways of thinking, has been taking on new vigor, and it has been deemed possible to make a complete application of it on the earth. Many people have believed and still believe, and not a few have feigned to believe and still feign to believe, that every advantage due to birth can, in time and by appropriate changes in our social system, be eliminated, and that the future will see human associations in which there will be an exact correspondence between the service a person renders to society and the rung he occupies on the social ladder.

The notion that in an ideally organized state there would be absolute corre-

---

* In Mosca's original, the following appears as part of the earlier text: [Ed.]

The representative system, as we have seen, resulted from notions and concepts that had been inherited from classical antiquity but were adapted to the requirements of nineteenth-century society—a very different sort of society from the society that had evolved the city-state of Greece and Rome. It was cut to a pattern that had been worked out in England in the two preceding centuries, almost empirically, and as the consequence of very special circumstances in English history. Nevertheless, the new constitutions corresponded amazingly well to the ways of thinking and the social requirements of the age that had adopted them. Maintaining a fairly good public order, and supported by marvelous scientific discoveries that supplied the means for achieving an economic progress that had not even been dreamed of before, they went hand in hand with a material prosperity that cannot be matched in the history of other ages and other civilizations. Not only that: During the whole nineteenth century they managed to maintain undisputed throughout the world a supremacy of the peoples of European civilization that had begun to take shape a century earlier. The preponderance of states of European civilization over states of Asiatic civilization became conspicuous early in the eighteenth century, when Turkey began to give signs of weakness as compared with the rest of Europe. That country had maintained its full offensive vigor down to the siege of Vienna in 1683. The English conquered India in the second half of the eighteenth century. The French might have done the same had they realized the importance of the game that was being played in the Orient in time. European preponderance held on unshaken during the nineteenth century. In our day it received its first powerful shock in the victory of Japan over Russia. The Asiatics are now beginning rapidly to understand that they can adopt the administrative and military organization of Europe and America and profit by western scientific progress, without abandoning their own type of civilization.

Now, there has been, as there could not help being, a profound and irremediable discrepancy between the theoretical assumptions of the new political system and its functioning in practice. In spite of the gradual adoption of universal suffrage, actual power has remained partly in the hands of the wealthiest classes, and in larger part still, especially in so-called democratic countries, in the hands of the middle classes. Those classes have always had the upper hand in the controlling cliques of political parties and in electioneer-

spondence between the service rendered by an individual to society and the rank
he comes to occupy in it was clearly formulated for the first time by Saint-Simon.
He presses the doctrine in many of his works under one form or another. Later
on the same concept became one of the tenets of the Saint-Simonian school,
which in other respects ranged far afield from the master's teachings. This
aspiration has never, perhaps, been so widely held and so clearly formulated as it
is today, but it would be absurd to imagine that it was first conceived in Saint-
Simon's time, or even a little less than two centuries ago. It has been the moral
basis of every attack that has ever aimed at renewing or rejuvenating ruling
classes. Whenever an effort has been made to remove the barriers that have separated an aristocracy, hereditary by law or in fact, from the rest of society, the
appeal has always been to the claims of individual merit as against the privileges
of birth, now in the name of religion, now in the name of the natural equality of
all men or at least of all citizens. In this respect, the democracies of Greece and
Rome, the Ciompi (wool carders) of Florence, the Anabaptists of Münster—
without, to be sure, having the Bill of Rights at their fingers' tips—thought and
acted like the French reformers of the eighteenth century and like the communists of today. Wat Tyler was the leader of a famous rebellion of the English
peasants against the lords which broke out in 1381. Some years before, while the
insurrection was brewing, a priest named John Ball wrote the often quoted
couplet that exactly expresses this attitude:

> When Adam delved and Eve span
> Who was then the gentleman?

But every time the democratic movement has triumphed, in part or in full,
we have invariably seen the aristocratic tendency come to life again through

---

ing committees, and they have supplied in large part, the reporting and editorial staffs of
the daily press, the personnel of the bureaucracies and army officers.

All the same, for the very reason that a combination of bureaucratic and elective
elements is inherent in the nature of the representative system, it has been possible, under
that system, to utilize almost all human values in the political and administrative departments of government, and the door has been left open to all elements in the governed
classes to make their way into ruling classes.

Specialization in the various political functions and cooperation and reciprocal control
between bureaucratic and elective elements are two of the outstanding characteristics of the
modern representative state. These traits make it possible to regard that state as the most
complex and delicate type of political organization that has so far been seen in world
history. From that point of view, and from others as well, it may also be claimed that there
is an almost perfect harmony between the present political system and the level of civilization that has been attained in the century that saw it come into being and grow to maturity.
That civilization may perhaps have shown itself inferior to some of its predecessors as
regards the finer perfections of artistic and literary forms, as regards depth of philosophical
thought and religious sentiment, as regards appreciation of the importance of certain great
moral problems. But it has shown itself far superior to all others in its wise organization
of economic and scientific production and in its exact knowledge and shrewd exploitation
of the forces of nature. There can be no question that the political system now prevailing
has won over the spontaneous energies and wills of individual human beings the same
victory which the complex of institutions, instruments, knowledge and aptitudes that form
the culture and the strength of our generations has won over the forces of nature.

efforts of the very men who had fought it and sometimes had proclaimed its suppression. In Rome, after forcing the doors that barred their access to high office, the rich plebeians fused with the old patriciate and formed a new nobility to which access by outsiders was legally permitted though in practice it was left very difficult. In Florence an oligarchy of "fat proletarians" supplanted the noble families whose political influence they had seen fit to destroy by the famous "ordinances of justice." In France the bourgeoisie of the nineteenth century in part replaced the nobility of the old regime. Everywhere, the moment the old barrier has been cast down a new one has been raised in its place, perhaps lower at times and less bristling with brambles and thorns, but high enough and hard enough to cross to offer fairly serious obstacles to anyone disposed to leap over it. Everywhere, those who have reached the top rungs on the social ladder have set up defenses for themselves and their children against those who also wished to climb.

It will be said that all that is a necessary product of private property, which makes wealth hereditary and smooths the road for those who inherit it to attain power and stay there. In that objection there is certainly a large element of truth—we do not say the whole truth, because the cultural level and the family connections of a parent can be passed on in part to his children, even when the family has no patrimony proper. But few people realize today that in a collectivist state the drawback mentioned, for which private property is at present held responsible, will not disappear. It will simply present itself in a graver form. As we have already demonstrated . . . (and as is now happening in Russia), the governors of a state that is organized along collectivist lines will have far greater resources and means of action than have the rich and powerful of today. The rulers of a collectivist state pile economic power on political power and so, controlling the lots of all individuals and all families, have a thousand ways of distributing rewards and punishments. It would be strange indeed if they did not take advantage of such a strategic position to give their children a start in life.

In order to abolish privileges of birth entirely, it would be necessary to go one step farther, to abolish the family, recognize a vagrant Venus and drop humanity to the level of the lowest animalism. It is interesting that in the *Republic* Plato proposed abolishing the family as an almost necessary consequence of the abolition of private property. He seems to have been inclined, however, to confine the two abolitions to his ruling class—the class of philosophers and warriors. He was not in favor of what would now be called "free love." He envisaged temporary unions, in which choice of the temporary mate was to be made by his philosophers. He further arranged that the children born of such unions should not know their parents, or be known by them, since the state should form one single family. A similar system is expounded and defended in Campanella's *City of the Sun*. Campanella also wanted to abolish private property and the family.

But we do not think that even provisions as radical as these would suffice to establish in the world an absolute justice that will never be realized, but which will always be appealed to by those who are trying to upset the system of social rankings that prevails in a given country at a given time. The Catholic clergy have not been allowed to have legal children. But whenever they have come to wield great economic and political power, nepotism has arisen in the Church. And we may well imagine that if nephews as well as sons were to be suppressed the human being would still find among his fellow men some whom he would love and protect in preference to others.

It is not so certain, meantime, that it would be altogether beneficial to the collectivity to have every advantage of birth eliminated in the struggle for membership in the ruling class and for high position in the social hierarchy. If all individuals could participate in the scramble on an equal footing, struggle would be intensified to the point of frenzy. This would entail an enormous expenditure of energy for strictly personal ends, with no corresponding benefit to the social organism, at least in the majority of cases. On the other hand, it may very well be that certain intellectual and, especially, moral qualities, which are necessary to a ruling class if it is to maintain its prestige and function properly, are useful also to society, yet require, if they are to develop and exert their influence, that the same families should hold fairly high social positions for a number of generations.

.   .   .

EPILOGUE

❧

The United States—
Mass or Class?

THE HIGHER CIRCLES

C. Wright Mills

1916–1962

≫≪

C. Wright Mills was a volcanic eminence among the members of his profession and perhaps the most widely read and translated sociologist in
this country. At a time when most of his colleagues were shunning value
judgments and bold generalization and engaged in rendering their
science dull and otiose, Mills combined crusading zeal with scholarly insight.

Mills taught sociology at Columbia University. Among his best
known and most translated books are *The New Men of Power* (1948),
The Causes of World War III (1958), *Listen, Yankee* (1960), *The Sociological Imagination* (1959) and *The Marxists* (1962). *The Power Elite*
(1956), from which the following selection is taken, is perhaps his most
famous work.

The powers of ordinary men are circumscribed by the everyday worlds in
which they live, yet even in these rounds of job, family, and neighborhood they
often seem driven by forces they can neither understand nor govern. 'Great
changes' are beyond their control, but affect their conduct and outlook none the
less. The very framework of modern society confines them to projects not their
own, but from every side, such changes now press upon the men and women of
the mass society, who accordingly feel that they are without purpose in an epoch
in which they are without power.

But not all men are in this sense ordinary. As the means of information and
of power are centralized, some men come to occupy positions in American society from which they can look down upon, so to speak, and by their decisions
mightily affect, the everyday worlds of ordinary men and women. They are not
made by their jobs; they set up and break down jobs for thousands of others;
they are not confined by simple family responsibilities; they can escape. They

C. Wright Mills, from *The Power Elite* (New York, 1956), pp. 3–29. © 1956 by
Oxford University Press, Inc. Reprinted by permission. Certain footnotes which appeared
in the original have been deleted.

may live in many hotels and houses, but they are bound by no one community. They need not merely 'meet the demands of the day and hour'; in some part, they create these demands, and cause others to meet them. Whether or not they profess their power, their technical and political experience of it far transcends that of the underlying population. What Jacob Burckhardt said of 'great men,' most Americans might well say of their elite: 'They are all that we are not.' [1]

The power elite is composed of men whose positions enable them to transcend the ordinary environments of ordinary men and women; they are in positions to make decisions having major consequences. Whether they do or do not make such decisions is less important than the fact that they do occupy such pivotal positions: their failure to act, their failure to make decisions, is itself an act that is often of greater consequence than the decisions they do make. For they are in command of the major hierarchies and organizations of modern society. They rule the big corporations. They run the machinery of the state and claim its prerogatives. They direct the military establishment. They occupy the strategic command posts of the social structure, in which are now centered the effective means of the power and the wealth and the celebrity which they enjoy.

The power elite are not solitary rulers. Advisers and consultants, spokesmen and opinion-makers are often the captains of their higher thought and decision. Immediately below the elite are the professional politicians of the middle levels of power, in the Congress and in the pressure groups, as well as among the new and old upper classes of town and city and region. Mingling with them, in curious ways which we shall explore, are those professional celebrities who live by being continually displayed but are never, so long as they remain celebrities, displayed enough. If such celebrities are not at the head of any dominating hierarchy, they do often have the power to distract the attention of the public or afford sensations to the masses, or, more directly, to gain the ear of those who do occupy positions of direct power. More or less unattached, as critics of morality and technicians of power, as spokesmen of God and creators of mass sensibility, such celebrities and consultants are part of the immediate scene in which the drama of the elite is enacted. But that drama itself is centered in the command posts of the major institutional hierarchies.

The truth about the nature and the power of the elite is not some secret which men of affairs know but will not tell. Such men hold quite various theories about their own roles in the sequence of event and decision. Often they are uncertain about their roles, and even more often they allow their fears and their hopes to affect their assessment of their own power. No matter how great their actual power, they tend to be less acutely aware of it than of the resistances of others to its use. Moreover, most American men of affairs have learned well the rhetoric of public relations, in some cases even to the point of using it when they are alone, and thus coming to believe it. The personal awareness of the actors is only one of the several sources one must examine in order to understand the higher circles.

[1] Jacob Burckhardt, *Force and Freedom* (New York: Pantheon Books, 1943), pp. 303 ff.

Yet many who believe that there is no elite, or at any rate none of any consequence, rest their argument upon what men of affairs believe about themselves, or at least assert in public.

There is, however, another view: those who feel, even if vaguely, that a compact and powerful elite of great importance does now prevail in America often base that feeling upon the historical trend of our time. They have felt, for example, the domination of the military event, and from this they infer that generals and admirals, as well as other men of decision influenced by them, must be enormously powerful. They hear that the Congress has again abdicated to a handful of men decisions clearly related to the issue of war or peace. They know that the bomb was dropped over Japan in the name of the United States of America, although they were at no time consulted about the matter. They feel that they live in a time of big decisions; they know that they are not making any. Accordingly, as they consider the present as history, they infer that at its center, making decisions or failing to make them, there must be an elite of power.

On the one hand, those who share this feeling about big historical events assume that there is an elite and that its power is great. On the other hand, those who listen carefully to the reports of men apparently involved in the great decisions often do not believe that there is an elite whose powers are of decisive consequence.

Both views must be taken into account, but neither is adequate. The way to understand the power of the American elite lies neither solely in recognizing the historic scale of events nor in accepting the personal awareness reported by men of apparent decision. Behind such men and behind the events of history, linking the two, are the major institutions of modern society. These hierarchies of state and corporation and army constitute the means of power; as such they are now of a consequence not before equaled in human history—and at their summits, there are now those command posts of modern society which offer us the sociological key to an understanding of the role of the higher circles in America.

Within American society, major national power now resides in the economic, the political, and the military domains. Other institutions seem off to the side of modern history, and, on occasion, duly subordinated to these. No family is as directly powerful in national affairs as any major corporation; no church is as directly powerful in the external biographies of young men in America today as the military establishment; no college is as powerful in the shaping of momentous events as the National Security Council. Religious, educational, and family institutions are not autonomous centers of national power; on the contrary, these decentralized areas are increasingly shaped by the big three, in which developments of decisive and immediate consequence now occur.

Families and churches and schools adapt to modern life, governments and armies and corporations shape it; and, as they do so, they turn these lesser institutions into means for their ends. Religious institutions provide chaplains to the armed forces where they are used as a means of increasing the effectiveness of its morale to kill. Schools select and train men for their jobs in corporations and their specialized tasks in the armed forces. The extended family has, of course, long been broken up by the industrial revolution, and now the son and the father are removed from the family, by compulsion if need be, whenever the army of the state sends out the call. And the symbols of all these lesser institutions are used to legitimate the power and the decisions of the big three.

The life-fate of the modern individual depends not only upon the family into which he was born or which he enters by marriage, but increasingly upon the corporation in which he spends the most alert hours of his best years; not only upon the school where he is educated as a child and adolescent, but also upon the state which touches him throughout his life; not only upon the church in which on occasion he hears the word of God, but also upon the army in which he is disciplined.

If the centralized state could not rely upon the inculcation of nationalist loyalties in public and private schools, its leaders would promptly seek to modify the decentralized educational system. If the bankruptcy rate among the top five hundred corporations were as high as the general divorce rate among the thirty-seven million married couples, there would be economic catastrophe on an international scale. If members of armies gave to them no more of their lives than do believers to the churches to which they belong, there would be a military crisis.

Within each of the big three, the typical institutional unit has become enlarged, has become administrative, and, in the power of its decisions, has become centralized. Behind these developments there is a fabulous technology, for as institutions, they have incorporated this technology and guide it, even as it shapes and paces their developments.

The economy—once a great scatter of small productive units in autonomous balance—has become dominated by two or three hundred giant corporations, administratively and politically interrelated, which together hold the keys to economic decisions.

The political order, once a decentralized set of several dozen states with a weak spinal cord, has become a centralized, executive establishment which has taken up into itself many powers previously scattered, and now enters into each and every cranny of the social structure.

The military order, once a slim establishment in a context of distrust fed by state militia, has become the largest and most expensive feature of government, and, although well versed in smiling public relations, now has all the grim and clumsy efficiency of a sprawling bureaucratic domain.

In each of these institutional areas, the means of power at the disposal of decision makers have increased enormously; their central executive powers have been enhanced; within each of them modern administrative routines have been elaborated and tightened up.

As each of these domains becomes enlarged and centralized, the consequences of its activities become greater, and its traffic with the others increases. The decisions of a handful of corporations bear upon military and political as well as upon economic developments around the world. The decisions of the military establishment rest upon and grievously affect political life as well as the very level of economic activity. The decisions made within the political domain determine economic activities and military programs. There is no longer, on the one hand, an economy, and, on the other hand, a political order containing a military establishment unimportant to politics and to money-making. There is a political economy linked, in a thousand ways, with military institutions and decisions. On each side of the world split running through central Europe and around the Asiatic rimlands, there is an ever-increasing interlocking of economic, military, and political structures. If there is government intervention in the corporate economy, so is there corporate intervention in the governmental process. In the structural sense, this triangle of power is the source of the interlocking directorate that is most important for the historical structure of the present.

The fact of the interlocking is clearly revealed at each of the points of crisis of modern capitalist society—slump, war, and boom. In each, men of decision are led to an awareness of the interdependence of the major institutional orders. In the nineteenth century, when the scale of all institutions was smaller, their liberal integration was achieved in the automatic economy by an autonomous play of market forces, and in the automatic political domain, by the bargain and the vote. It was then assumed that out of the imbalance and friction that followed the limited decisions then possible a new equilibrium would in due course emerge. That can no longer be assumed, and it is not assumed by the men at the top of each of the three dominant hierarchies.

For given the scope of their consequences, decisions—and indecisions—in any one of these ramify into the others, and hence top decisions tend either to become co-ordinated or to lead to a commanding indecision. It has not always been like this. When numerous small entrepreneurs made up the economy, for example, many of them could fail and the consequences still remain local; political and military authorities did not intervene. But now, given political expectations and military commitments, can they afford to allow key units of the private corporate economy to break down in slump? Increasingly, they do intervene in economic affairs, and as they do so, the controlling decisions in each order are inspected by agents of the other two, and economic, military, and political structures are interlocked.

At the pinnacle of each of the three enlarged and centralized domains, there have arisen those higher circles which make up the economic, the political, and the military elites. At the top of the economy, among the corporate rich, there are the chief executives; at the top of the political order, the members of the political directorate; at the top of the military establishment, the elite of soldier-statesmen clustered in and around the Joint Chiefs of Staff and the upper echelon. As each of these domains has coincided with the others, as decisions tend to become total in their consequence, the leading men in each of the three domains of power—the warlords, the corporation chieftains, the political directorate—tend to come together, to form the power elite of America.

The higher circles in and around these command posts are often thought of in terms of what their members possess: they have a greater share than other people of the things and experiences that are most highly valued. From this point of view, the elite are simply those who have the most of what there is to have, which is generally held to include money, power, and prestige—as well as all the ways of life to which these lead. But the elite are not simply those who have the most, for they could not 'have the most' were it not for their positions in the great institutions. For such institutions are the necessary bases of power, of wealth, and of prestige, and at the same time, the chief means of exercising power, of acquiring and retaining wealth, and of cashing in the higher claims for prestige.

By the powerful we mean, of course, those who are able to realize their will, even if others resist it. No one, accordingly, can be truly powerful unless he has access to the command of major institutions, for it is over these institutional means of power that the truly powerful are, in the first instance, powerful. Higher politicians and key officials of government command such institutional power; so do admirals and generals, and so do the major owners and executives of the larger corporations. Not all power, it is true, is anchored in and exercised by means of such institutions, but only within and through them can power be more or less continuous and important.

Wealth also is acquired and held in and through institutions. The pyramid of wealth cannot be understood merely in terms of the very rich; for the great inheriting families, as we shall see, are now supplemented by the corporate institutions of modern society: every one of the very rich families has been and is closely connected—always legally and frequently managerially as well—with one of the multi-million dollar corporations.

The modern corporation is the prime source of wealth, but, in latter-day capitalism, the political apparatus also opens and closes many avenues to wealth. The amount as well as the source of income, the power over consumer's goods as well as over productive capital, are determined by position within the political economy. If our interest in the very rich goes beyond their lavish or their miserly consumption, we must examine their relations to modern forms of corporate property as well as to the state; for such relations now determine the chances of men to secure big property and to receive high income.

Great prestige increasingly follows the major institutional units of the social structure. It is obvious that prestige depends, often quite decisively, upon access to the publicity machines that are now a central and normal feature of all the big institutions of modern America. Moreover, one feature of these hierarchies of corporation, state, and military establishment is that their top positions are increasingly interchangeable. One result of this is the accumulative nature of prestige. Claims for prestige, for example, may be initially based on military roles, then expressed in and augmented by an educational institution run by corporate executives, and cashed in, finally, in the political order, where, for General Eisenhower and those he represents, power and prestige finally meet at the very peak. Like wealth and power, prestige tends to be cumulative: the more of it you have, the more you can get. These values also tend to be translatable into one another: the wealthy find it easier than the poor to gain power; those with status find it easier than those without it to control opportunities for wealth.

If we took the one hundred most powerful men in America, the one hundred wealthiest, and the one hundred most celebrated away from the institutional positions they now occupy, away from their resources of men and women and money, away from the media of mass communication that are now focused upon them—then they would be powerless and poor and uncelebrated. For power is not of a man. Wealth does not center in the person of the wealthy. Celebrity is not inherent in any personality. To be celebrated, to be wealthy, to have power requires access to major institutions, for the institutional positions men occupy determine in large part their chances to have and to hold these valued experiences.

The people of the higher circles may also be conceived as members of a top social stratum, as a set of groups whose members know one another, see one another socially and at business, and so, in making decisions, take one another into account. The elite, according to this conception, feel themselves to be, and are felt by others to be, the inner circle of 'the upper social classes.' They form a more or less compact social and psychological entity; they have become self-conscious members of a social class. People are either accepted into this class or they are not, and there is a qualitative split, rather than merely a numerical scale, separating them from those who are not elite. They are more or less aware of themselves as a social class and they behave toward one another differently from the way they do toward members of other classes. They accept one another, understand one another, marry one another, tend to work and to think if not together at least alike.

Now, we do not want by our definition to prejudge whether the elite of the command posts are conscious members of such a socially recognized class, or whether considerable proportions of the elite derive from such a clear and distinct class. These are matters to be investigated. Yet in order to be able to recognize what we intend to investigate, we must note something that all biographies and memoirs of the wealthy and the powerful and the eminent make clear: no matter what else they may be, the people of these higher circles are involved in a set of overlapping 'crowds' and intricately connected 'cliques.' There is a kind of mutual attraction among those who 'sit on the same terrace'—although this often becomes clear to them, as well as to others, only at the point at which they feel the need to draw the line; only when, in their common defense, they come to understand what they have in common, and so close their ranks against outsiders.

The idea of such ruling stratum implies that most of its members have similar social origins, that throughout their lives they maintain a network of informal connections, and that to some degree there is an interchangeability of position between the various hierarchies of money and power and celebrity. We must, of course, note at once that if such an elite stratum does exist, its social visibility and its form, for very solid historical reasons, are quite different from those of the noble cousinhoods that once ruled various European nations.

That American society has never passed through a feudal epoch is of decisive importance to the nature of the American elite, as well as to American society as a historic whole. For it means that no nobility or aristocracy, established before the capitalist era, has stood in tense opposition to the higher bourgeoisie. It means that this bourgeoisie has monopolized not only wealth but prestige and power as well. It means that no set of noble families has commanded the top positions and monopolized the values that are generally held in high esteem; and certainly that no set has done so explicitly by inherited right. It means that no high church dignitaries or court nobilities, no entrenched landlords with honorific accouterments, no monopolists of high army posts have opposed the enriched bourgeoisie and in the name of birth and prerogative successfully resisted its self-making.

But this does *not* mean that there are no upper strata in the United States. That they emerged from a 'middle class' that had no recognized aristocratic superiors does not mean they remained middle class when enormous increases in wealth made their own superiority possible. Their origins and their newness may have made the upper strata less visible in America than elsewhere. But in America today there are in fact tiers and ranges of wealth and power of which people in the middle and lower ranks know very little and may not even dream. There are families who, in their well-being, are quite insulated from the economic jolts and lurches felt by the merely prosperous and those farther down the scale. There are also men of power who in quite small groups make decisions of enormous consequence for the underlying population.

The American elite entered modern history as a virtually unopposed bourgeoisie. No national bourgeoisie, before or since, has had such opportunities and advantages. Having no military neighbors, they easily occupied an isolated continent stocked with natural resources and immensely inviting to a willing labor force. A framework of power and an ideology for its justification were already at hand. Against mercantilist restriction, they inherited the principle of *laissez-faire;* against Southern planters, they imposed the principle of industrialism. The Revolutionary War put an end to colonial pretensions to nobility, as loyalists fled the country and many estates were broken up. The Jacksonian upheaval with its status revolution put an end to pretensions to monopoly of descent by the old New England families. The Civil War broke the power, and so in due course the prestige, of the ante-bellum South's claimants for the higher esteem. The tempo of the whole capitalist development made it impossible for an inherited nobility to develop and endure in America.

No fixed ruling class, anchored in agrarian life and coming to flower in military glory, could contain in America the historic thrust of commerce and industry, or subordinate to itself the capitalist elite—as capitalists were subordinated, for example, in Germany and Japan. Nor could such a ruling class anywhere in the world contain that of the United States when industrialized violence came to decide history. Witness the fate of Germany and Japan in the two world wars of the twentieth century; and indeed the fate of Britain herself and her model ruling class, as New York became the inevitable economic, and Washington the inevitable political capital of the western capitalist world.

The elite who occupy the command posts may be seen as the possessors of power and wealth and celebrity; they may be seen as members of the upper stratum of a capitalistic society. They may also be defined in terms of psychological and moral criteria, as certain kinds of selected individuals. So defined, the elite, quite simply, are people of superior character and energy.

The humanist, for example, may conceive of the 'elite' not as a social level or category, but as a scatter of those individuals who attempt to transcend themselves, and accordingly, are more noble, more efficient, made out of better stuff. It does not matter whether they are poor or rich, whether they hold high position or low, whether they are acclaimed or despised; they are elite because of the kind of individuals they are. The rest of the population is mass, which, according to this conception, sluggishly relaxes into uncomfortable mediocrity.

This is the sort of socially unlocated conception which some American writers with conservative yearnings have recently sought to develop. But most moral and psychological conceptions of the elite are much less sophisticated, concerning themselves not with individuals but with the stratum as a whole. Such ideas, in fact, always arise in a society in which some people possess more than do others of what there is to possess. People with advantages are loath to believe that they just happen to be people with advantages. They come readily to define themselves as inherently worthy of what they possess; they come to believe themselves 'naturally' elite; and, in fact, to imagine their possessions and their privileges as natural extensions of their own elite selves. In this sense, the idea of the elite as composed of men and women having a finer moral character is an ideology of the elite as a privileged ruling stratum, and this is true whether the ideology is elite-made or made up for it by others.

In eras of equalitarian rhetoric, the more intelligent or the more articulate among the lower and middle classes, as well as guilty members of the upper, may come to entertain ideas of a counter-elite. In western society, as a matter of fact, there is a long tradition and varied images of the poor, the exploited, and the oppressed as the truly virtuous, the wise, and the blessed. Stemming from Christian tradition, this moral idea of a counter-elite, composed of essentially higher types condemned to a lowly station, may be and has been used by the underlying population to justify harsh criticism of ruling elites and to celebrate utopian images of a new elite to come.

The moral conception of the elite, however, is not always merely an ideology of the overprivileged or a counter-ideology of the underprivileged. It is often a fact: having controlled experiences and select privileges, many individuals of the upper stratum do come in due course to approximate the types of character they claim to embody. Even when we give up—as we must—the idea that the elite man or woman is born with an elite character, we need not dismiss the idea that their experiences and trainings develop in them characters of a specific type.

Nowadays we must qualify the idea of elite as composed of higher types of individuals, for the men who are selected for and shaped by the top positions have many spokesmen and advisers and ghosts and make-up men who modify their self-conceptions and create their public images, as well as shape many of their decisions. There is, of course, considerable variation among the elite in this respect, but as a general rule in America today, it would be naïve to interpret any major elite group merely in terms of its ostensible personnel. The American elite often seems less a collection of persons than of corporate entities, which are in great part created and spoken for as standard types of 'personality.' Even the most apparently free-lance celebrity is usually a sort of synthetic production turned out each week by a disciplined staff which systematically ponders the effect of the easy ad-libbed gags the celebrity 'spontaneously' echoes.

Yet, in so far as the elite flourishes as a social class or as a set of men at the command posts, it will select and form certain types of personality, and reject others. The kind of moral and psychological beings men become is in large part determined by the values they experience and the institutional roles they are allowed and expected to play. From the biographer's point of view, a man of the upper classes is formed by his relations with others like himself in a series of small intimate groupings through which he passes and to which throughout his lifetime he may return. So conceived, the elite is a set of higher circles whose members are selected, trained and certified and permitted intimate access to those who command the impersonal institutional hierarchies of modern society. If there is any one key to the *psychological* idea of the elite, it is that they combine in their persons an awareness of impersonal decision-making with intimate sensibilities shared with one another. To understand the elite as a social class we must examine a whole series of smaller face-to-face milieux, the most obvious of which, historically, has been the upper-class family, but the most important of which today are the proper secondary school and the metropolitan club.

. . .

Such an elite may be conceived as omnipotent, and its powers thought of as a great hidden design. Thus, in vulgar Marxism, events and trends are explained by reference to 'the will of the bourgeoisie'; in Nazism, by reference to 'the conspiracy of the Jews'; by the petty right in America today, by reference to 'the hidden force' of Communist spies. According to such notions of the omnipotent elite as historical cause, the elite is never an entirely visible agency. It is, in fact, a secular substitute for the will of God, being realized in a sort of providential design, except that usually non-elite men are thought capable of opposing it and eventually overcoming it.*

* Those who charge that Communist agents have been or are in the government, as well as those frightened by them, never raise the question: 'Well, suppose there are Communists in high places, how much power do they have?' They simply assume that men

The opposite view—of the elite as impotent—is now quite popular among liberal-minded observers. Far from being omnipotent, the elites are thought to be so scattered as to lack any coherence as a historical force. Their invisibility is not the invisibility of secrecy but the invisibility of the multitude. Those who occupy the formal places of authority are so check-mated—by other elites exerting pressure, or by the public as an electorate, or by constitutional codes—that, although there may be upper classes, there is no ruling class; although there may be men of power, there is no power elite; although there may be a system of stratification, it has no effective top. In the extreme, this view of the elite, as weakened by compromise and disunited to the point of nullity, is a substitute for impersonal collective fate; for, in this view, the decisions of the visible men of the higher circles do not count in history.*

Internationally, the image of the omnipotent elite tends to prevail. All good events and pleasing happenings are quickly imputed by the opinion-makers to the leaders of their own nation; all bad events and unpleasant experiences are imputed to the enemy abroad. In both cases, the omnipotence of evil rulers or of virtuous leaders is assumed. Within the nation, the use of such rhetoric is rather more complicated: when men speak of the power of their own party or circle, they and their leaders are, of course, impotent; only 'the people' are omnipotent. But, when they speak of the power of their opponent's party or circle, they impute to them omnipotence; 'the people' are now powerlessly taken in.

More generally, American men of power tend, by convention, to deny that they are powerful. No American runs for office in order to rule or even govern, but only to serve; he does not become a bureaucrat or even an official, but a public servant. And nowadays, as I have already pointed out, such postures have become standard features of the public-relations programs of all men of power. So firm a part of the style of power-wielding have they become that conservative writers readily misinterpret them as indicating a trend toward an 'amorphous power situation.'

.   .   .

To say that there are obvious gradations of power and of opportunities to decide within modern society is not to say that the powerful are united, that they fully know what they do, or that they are consciously joined in conspiracy. Such issues are best faced if we concern ourselves, in the first instance, more with the

---

in high places, or in this case even those in positions from which they might influence such men, do decide important events. Those who think Communist agents lost China to the Soviet bloc, or influenced loyal Americans to lose it, simply assume that there is a set of men who decide such matters, actively or by neglect or by stupidity. Many others, who do not believe that Communist agents were so influential, still assume that loyal American decision-makers lost it all by themselves.

* The idea of the impotent elite . . . is mightily supported by the notion of an automatic economy in which the problem of power is solved for the economic elite by denying its existence. No one has enough power to make a real difference; events are the results of an anonymous balance. For the political elite too, the model of balance solves the problem of power. Parallel to the market-economy, there is the leaderless democracy in which no one is responsible for anything and everyone is responsible for everything; the will of men acts only through the impersonal workings of the electoral process.

structural position of the high and mighty, and with the consequences of their decisions, than with the extent of their awareness or the purity of their motives.

. . . .

The unity of the power elite . . . does not rest solely on psychological similarity and social intermingling, nor entirely on the structural coincidences of commanding positions and interests. At times it is the unity of a more explicit co-ordination. To say that these three higher circles are increasingly co-ordinated, that this is *one* basis of their unity, and that at times—as during the wars—such co-ordination is quite decisive, is not to say that the co-ordination is total or continuous, or even that it is very sure-footed. Much less is it to say that willful co-ordination is the sole or the major basis of their unity, or that the power elite has emerged as the realization of a plan. But it is to say that as the institutional mechanics of our time have opened up avenues to men pursuing their several interests, many of them have come to see that these several interests could be realized more easily if they worked together, in informal as well as in more formal ways, and accordingly they have done so.

It is not my thesis that for all epochs of human history and in all nations, a creative minority, a ruling class, an omnipotent elite, shape all historical events. Such statements, upon careful examination, usually turn out to be mere tautologies, and even when they are not, they are so entirely general as to be useless in the attempt to understand the history of the present. The minimum definition of the power elite as those who decide whatever is decided of major consequence, does not imply that the members of this elite are always and necessarily the history-makers; neither does it imply that they never are. We must not confuse the conception of the elite, which we wish to define, with one theory about their role: that they are the history-makers of our time. To define elite, for example, as 'those who rule America' is less to define a conception than to state one hypothesis about the role and power of that elite. No matter how we might define the elite, the extent of its members' power is subject to historical variation. If, in a dogmatic way, we try to include that variation in our generic definition, we foolishly limit the use of a needed conception. If we insist that the elite be defined as a strictly coordinated class that continually and absolutely rules, we are closing off from our view much to which the term more modestly defined might open to our observation. In short, our definition of the power elite cannot properly contain dogma concerning the degree and kind of power that ruling groups everywhere have. Much less should it permit us to smuggle into our discussion a theory of history.

During most of human history, historical change has not been visible to the people who were involved in it, or even to those enacting it. Ancient Egypt and Mesopotamia, for example, endured for some four hundred generations with but slight changes in their basic structure. That is six and a half times as long as the entire Christian era, which has only prevailed some sixty generations; it is about eighty times as long as the five generations of the United States' existence. But now the tempo of change is so rapid, and the means of observation so accessible, that the interplay of event and decision seems often to be quite historically visible, if we will only look carefully and from an adequate vantage point.

When knowledgeable journalists tell us that 'events, not men, shape the big decisions,' they are echoing the theory of history as Fortune, Chance, Fate, or the work of The Unseen Hand. For 'events' is merely a modern word for these older ideas, all of which separate men from history-making, because all of them lead us to believe that history goes on behind men's backs. History is drift with no mastery; within it there is action but no deed; history is mere happening and the event intended by no one.

The course of events in our time depends more on a series of human decisions than on any inevitable fate. The sociological meaning of 'fate' is simply this: that, when the decisions are innumerable and each one is of small consequence, all of them add up in a way no man intended—to history as fate. But not all epochs are equally fateful. As the circle of those who decide is narrowed, as the means of decision are centralized and the consequences of decisions become enormous, then the course of great events often rests upon the decisions of determinable circles. This does not necessarily mean that the same circle of men follow through from one event to another in such a way that all of history is merely their plot. The power of the elite does not necessarily mean that history is not also shaped by a series of small decisions, none of which are thought out. It does not mean that a hundred small arrangements and compromises and adaptations may not be built into the going policy and the living event. The idea of the power elite implies nothing about the process of decision-making as such: it is an attempt to delimit the social areas within which that process, whatever its character, goes on. It is a conception of who is involved in the process.

The degree of foresight and control of those who are involved in decisions that count may also vary. The idea of the power elite does not mean that the estimations and calculated risks upon which decisions are made are not often wrong and that the consequences are sometimes, indeed often, not those intended. Often those who make decisions are trapped by their own inadequacies and blinded by their own errors.

Yet in our time the pivotal moment does arise, and at that moment, small circles do decide or fail to decide. In either case, they are an elite of power. The dropping of the A-bombs over Japan was such a moment; the decision on Korea was such a moment; the confusion about Quemoy and Matsu, as well as before Dienbienphu were such moments; the sequence of maneuvers which involved the United States in World War II was such a 'moment.' Is it not true that much of the history of our times is composed of such moments? And is not that what is meant when it is said that we live in a time of big decisions, of decisively centralized power?

Most of us do not try to make sense of our age by believing in a Greek-like, eternal recurrence, nor by a Christian belief in a salvation to come, nor by any steady march of human progress. Even though we do not reflect upon such matters, the chances are we believe with Burckhardt that we live in a mere succession of events; that sheer continuity is the only principle of history. History is merely one thing after another; history is meaningless in that it is not the realization of any determinate plot. It is true, of course, that our sense of continuity, our feeling for the history of our time, is affected by crisis. But we seldom look beyond the immediate crisis or the crisis felt to be just ahead. We believe neither in fate nor providence; and we assume, without talking about it, that 'we'—as a nation —can decisively shape the future but that 'we' as individuals somehow cannot do so.

Any meaning history has, 'we' shall have to give to it by our actions. Yet the fact is that although we are all of us within history we do not all possess equal powers to make history. To pretend that we do is sociological nonsense and political irresponsibility. It is nonsense because any group or any individual is limited, first of all, by the technical and institutional means of power at its command; we do not all have equal access to the means of power that now exist, nor equal influence over their use. To pretend that 'we' are all history-makers is politically irresponsible because it obfuscates any attempt to locate responsibility for the consequential decisions of men who do have access to the means of power.

From even the most superficial examination of the history of the western society we learn that the power of decision-makers is first of all limited by the level of technique, by the *means* of power and violence and organization that prevail in a given society. In this connection we also learn that there is a fairly straight line running upward through the history of the West; that the means of oppression and exploitation, of violence and destruction, as well as the means of production and reconstruction, have been progressively enlarged and increasingly centralized.

As the institutional means of power and the means of communications that tie them together have become steadily more efficient, those now in command of them have come into command of instruments of rule quite unsurpassed in the history of mankind. And we are not yet at the climax of their development. We can no longer lean upon or take soft comfort from the historical ups and downs of ruling groups of previous epochs. In that sense, Hegel is correct: we learn from history that we cannot learn from it.

For every epoch and for every social structure, we must work out an answer to the question of the power of the elite. The ends of men are often merely hopes, but means are facts within some men's control. That is why all means of power tend to become ends to an elite that is in command of them. And that is why we may define the power elite in terms of the means of power—as those who occupy the command posts. The major questions about the American elite today—its composition, its unity, its power—must now be faced with due attention to the awesome means of power available to them. Caesar could do less with Rome than Napoleon with France; Napoleon less with France than Lenin with Russia; and Lenin less with Russia than Hitler with Germany. But what was Caesar's power at its peak compared with the power of the changing inner circle of Soviet Russia or of America's temporary administrations? The men of either circle can cause great cities to be wiped out in a single night, and in a few weeks turn continents into thermonuclear wastelands. That the facilities of power are enormously enlarged and decisively centralized means that the decisions of small groups are now more consequential.

But to know that the top posts of modern social structures now permit more commanding decisions is not to know that the elite who occupy these posts are the history-makers. We might grant that the enlarged and integrated economic, military, and political structures are shaped to permit command decisions, yet still feel that, as it were, 'they run themselves,' that those who are on top, in short, are determined in their decisions by 'necessity,' which presumably means by the instituted roles that they play and the situation of these institutions in the total structure of society.

Do the elite determine the roles that they enact? Or do the roles that institutions make available to them determine the power of the elite? The general answer—and no general answer is sufficient—is that in different kinds of structures and epochs elites are quite differently related to the roles that they play: nothing in the nature of the elite or in the nature of history dictates an answer. It is also true that if most men and women take whatever roles are permitted to them and enact them as they are expected to by virtue of their position, this is precisely what the elite need *not* do, and often do not do. They may call into question the structure, their position within it, or the way in which they are to enact that position.

Nobody called for or permitted Napoleon to chase *Parlement* home on the 18 *Brumaire*, and later to transform his consulate into an emperorship.* Nobody called for or permitted Adolf Hitler to proclaim himself 'Leader and Chancellor' the day President Hindenburg died, to abolish and usurp roles by merging the presidency and the chancellorship. Nobody called for or permitted Franklin D. Roosevelt to make the series of decisions that led to the entrance of the United States into World War II. It was no 'historical necessity,' but a man named Truman who, with a few other men, decided to drop a bomb on Hiroshima. It was no historical necessity, but an argument within a small circle of men that defeated Admiral Radford's proposal to bomb troops before Dienbienphu. Far from being dependent upon the structure of institutions, modern elites may smash one structure and set up another in which they then enact quite different roles. In fact, such destruction and creation of institutional structures, with all their means of power, when events seem to turn out well, is just what is involved in 'great leadership,' or, when they seem to turn out badly, great tyranny.

Some elite men *are*, of course typically role-determined, but others are at times role-determining. They determine not only the role they play but today the roles of millions of other men. The creation of pivotal roles and their pivotal enactment occurs most readily when social structures are undergoing epochal

---

* Some of these items are taken from Gerth and Mills, *Character and Social Structure*, pp. 405 ff. On role-determined and role-determining men, see also Sidney Hook's discussion, *The Hero in History* (New York: John Day, 1943).

transitions. It is clear that the international development of the United States to one of the two 'great powers'—along with the new means of annihilation and administrative and psychic domination—have made of the United States in the middle years of the twentieth century precisely such an epochal pivot.

There is nothing about history that tells us that a power elite cannot make it. To be sure, the will of such men is always limited, but never before have the limits been so broad, for never before have the means of power been so enormous. It is this that makes our situation so precarious, and makes even more important an understanding of the powers and the limitations of the American elite. The problem of the nature and the power of this elite is now the only realistic and serious way to raise again the problem of responsible government.

. . .

. . . The American elite is neither omnipotent nor impotent. These are abstract absolutes used publicly by spokesmen, as excuses or as boasts, but in terms of which we may seek to clarify the political issues before us, which just now are above all the issues of responsible power.

There is nothing in 'the nature of history' *in our epoch* that rules out the pivotal function of small groups of decision-makers. On the contrary, the structure of the present is such as to make this not only a reasonable, but a rather compelling, view.

There is nothing in 'the psychology of man,' or in the social manner by which men are shaped and selected for and by the command posts of modern society, that makes unreasonable the view that they do confront choices and that the choices they make—or their failure to confront them—are history-making in their consequences.

Accordingly, political men now have every reason to hold the American power elite accountable for a decisive range of the historical events that make up the history of the present.

It is as fashionable, just now, to suppose that there is no power elite, as it was fashionable in the 'thirties to suppose a set of ruling-class villains to be the source of all social injustice and public malaise. I should be as far from supposing that some simple and unilateral ruling class could be firmly located as the prime mover of American society, as I should be from supposing that all historical change in America today is merely impersonal drift.

The view that all is blind drift is largely a fatalist projection of one's own feeling of impotence and perhaps, if one has ever been active politically in a principled way, a salve of one's guilt.

The view that all of history is due to the conspiracy of an easily located set of villains, or of heroes, is also a hurried projection from the difficult effort to understand how shifts in the structure of society open opportunities to various elites and how various elites take advantage or fail to take advantage of them. To accept either view—of all history as conspiracy or of all history as drift—is to relax the effort to understand the facts of power and the ways of the powerful.

. . .

What I am asserting is that in this particular epoch a conjunction of historical circumstances has led to the rise of an elite of power; that the men of the circles composing this elite, severally and collectively, now make such key decisions as are made; and that, given the enlargement and the centralization of the means of power now available, the decisions that they make and fail to make carry more consequences for more people than has ever been the case in the world history of mankind.

I am also asserting that there has developed on the middle levels of power, a semi-organized stalemate, and that on the bottom level there has come into being a mass-like society which has little resemblance to the image of a society in which voluntary associations and classic publics hold the keys to power. The top of the American system of power is much more unified and much more powerful, the bottom is much more fragmented, and in truth, impotent, than is generally supposed by those who are distracted by the middling units of power which neither express such will as exists at the bottom nor determine the decisions at the top.

THE POWER ELITE
RECONSIDERED

Daniel Bell

1919–

❧❧

Daniel Bell has been an editor for *Common Sense* and *The New Leader*, and from 1948–1958 served as labor editor of *Fortune* magazine. He is now editor of a magazine called *The Public Interest*.

Bell has taught at the University of Chicago and is now chairman of the department of sociology at Columbia University.

A frequent contributor to academic and trade journals, he is the author of several books including *A History of Marxian Socialism in the United States* (1952), *The New American Right* (1956), *The End of Ideology* (1960), and *The Radical Right* (1963).

The article which follows was written by Bell as a critical commentary on C. Wright Mills' *Power Elite.*

Power is a difficult subject. Its effects are more observable than its causes; even the power-wielders often do not know what factors shaped their decisions. Its consequences are more refractory to control—and prediction—than any other form of human behavior. C. Wright Mills' *The Power Elite*, because it seeks to locate the sources of power in an identifiable constellation of elites, is one of those rare books in contemporary sociology that deal with the "world of causality" rather than mere description or methodological discussion. It is, in addition, something else: a political book whose loose texture and power rhetoric have allowed different people to read their own emotions into it: for the young neo-Marxists in England (*vide* the group around the *Universities and Left Review*)

Daniel Bell, from *The End of Ideology* (New York, 1960), pp. 43–67. Reprinted by permission of the author. This essay is a revised version of a paper first presented before the Columbia University Faculty Colloquium in Sociology and was printed in the *American Journal of Sociology*, November, 1958. Certain footnotes which appeared in the original have been deleted.

and the old orthodox Marxists in Poland (*vide* the reception by Adam Schaff, the Party's official philosopher), it has become a primer for the understanding of American policy and motives. This is curious, since Mills is not a Marxist, and, if anything, his method and conclusions are anti-Marxist. But because it is tough-minded and "unmasks" the naive, populist illusions about power, it has won a ready response among radicals.

The Mood and the Intent

The mood that pervades Mills' book—and most of his work—provides some clue to the response. In writing about labor (*The New Men of Power*), the white-collar class, and now the power elite—the range of classes in society—Mills is modeling himself on Balzac and writing what Balzac called the *étude de moeurs*, the "comedy" of morals. Some of the Balzac method is there: Balzac sought to reconcile the discoveries of science with poetry and to build up visual effects by the massing of factual detail. Mills takes statistic after statistic and clothes them with angry metaphors.

.   .   .

But whatever its initial emotional impulse, Mills' book is molded by more direct intellectual progenitors. These are: Veblen, from whom the rhetoric and irony are copied; Weber, for the picture of social structure, not, however, of classes, but of vertical orders, or *Standen;* and, most crucially, Pareto, but not for the definition of elite, which is much different from Mills', but the method. While the debts to Veblen and Weber are conscious, that to Pareto is probably not so. Yet there is the same scorn for ideas, and the denial that ideology has any operative meaning in the exercise of power. And by seeing power as an underlying "combination of orders," Mills parallels, in method, what Pareto was doing in seeing social groups as "combinations of residues." This leads, I think, despite the dynamism in the rhetoric, to a static, a historical approach. For *The Power Elite* is not an empirical analysis of power in the United States, though many readers have mistaken its illustrations for such an analysis, but a *scheme* for the analysis of power; and a close reading of its argument will show, I think, how confusing and unsatisfactory this scheme is.

The Argument

One can examine Mills' book by an alternate scheme but as a prior necessity one must write a textual analysis: identify the key terms, see how consistently they are used, and relate evidence to propositions in order to test the coherence of the argument. This, then, is an exercise in hermeneutics.

The argument, as it unfolds in Mills' opening chapter (the others are largely uneven illustrations rather than development or demonstration of the thesis), shuttles perplexingly back and forth on the key problem of how power is wielded.

One can show this only by some detailed quotation, a difficult but necessary burden for exposition.*

Within American society, says Mills, major national power "now resides in the economic, political and military domains." . . .

Thus power, to be power, apparently means control over the *institutions* of power . . .

It is shared by only a few persons . . .

But although these people make the key decisions, they are not the "history makers" of the time. The "power elite" is not, Mills says (p. 20), a theory of history; history is a complex net of intended and unintended decisions.

> The idea of the power elite implies *nothing about the process of decision-making as such:* it is an attempt to delimit social areas within which that process, *whatever its character,* goes on. It is a conception of *who* is involved in the process [p. 21].

Does then the elite make history? Sometimes it is role-determined, sometimes role-determining (pp. 22–25). Mills is obviously wrestling with a contradictory position. For if the power elite are not the history makers, why worry much about them? If they are, it seems to lead to a simple-minded theory of history. Finally Mills resolves the problem:

> It was no "historical necessity," but a man named Truman who, with a few other men, decided to drop a bomb on Hiroshima. It was no historical necessity, but an argument within a small circle of men that defeated Admiral Radford's proposal to send troops to Indochina before Dienbienphu fell [p. 24].

If we extract a residue from all this backing and filing, it is that a smaller number of men than ever before, holding top positions in government, economic life, and the military, have a set of responsibilities and decision-making powers that are more consequential than ever before in United States history—which, in itself, does not tell us very much.

But it is less the argument than the rhetoric which found an echo, and crucial to Mills' book are a set of objective terms—*institutions* (with which are interchanged freely, *domains, higher circles, top cliques*), *power, command posts,* and *big decisions*—the political use of which gives the book its persuasiveness. These are the key modifiers of the term "elite." What do they mean?

The Terms

(a) *Elite.* Throughout the book, the term elite is used in a variety of ways. Sometimes the term denotes "membership in clique-like sets of people," or "the morality of certain personality types," or "statistics of selected values" such as

---

* All italics, unless otherwise indicated, are [Bell's]. They are intended to underline key statements. All citations are from: C. Wright Mills' *The Power Elite*, New York, Oxford University Press, 1956.

wealth, political position, etc. In only one place, in a long footnote on page 366, among the notes, Mills explicitly tries to straighten out the confusion created by the profuse interchange of terms. He says that he defines elites primarily on the basis of "institutional position." But what does this mean?

(b) *Institutions, Domains, etc.* Behind men and behind events, linking the two, says Mills, are the major institutions of society: The military, the political, and the economic. But, actually, the military, the economic, the political, as Mills uses these terms, are not institutions but sectors, or what Weber calls *orders,* or vertical hierarchies—each with their enclosed strata—in society. To say that this sector, or order, is more important than that—that in some societies, for example, the religious orders are more important than the political—is to give us large-scale boundaries of knowledge. But surely we want and need more than that.

Such usage as "the military," "the political directorate," etc., is extraordinarily loose. It would be hard to characterize these as institutions. Institutions derive from *particular, established* codes of conduct, which shape the behavior of *particular* groups of men who implicitly or otherwise have a loyalty to that code and are subject to certain controls (anxiety, guilt, shame, expulsion, etc.) if they violate the norms. If the important consideration of power is *where people draw their power from,* then we have to have more particularized ways of identifying the groupings than "institutionalized orders," "domains," "circles," etc.

(c) *Power.* Throughout the book, there is a curious lack of definition of the word power. Only twice, really, does one find a set of limits to the word:

By the powerful we mean, of course, those who are able to realize their will, even if others resist it [p. 9].

All politics is a struggle for power: the ultimate kind of power is violence [p. 171].

It is quite true that violence, as Weber has said, is the ultimate sanction of power, and in extreme situations (e.g., the Spanish Civil War, Iraq, etc.) control of the means of violence may be decisive in seizing or holding power. But power is not the inexorable, implacable, granitic force that Mills and others make it to be. . . . And is it true to say that *all* politics is a struggle for power? Are there not ideals as a goal? And if ideals are realizable through power—though not always—do they not temper the violence of politics?

Power in Mills' terms is domination. But we do not need an elaborate discussion to see that this view of power avoids more problems than it answers, and particularly once one moves away from the outer boundary of *power as violence* to *institutionalized power,* with which Mills is concerned. For in society, particularly constitutional regimes, and *within* associations, where violence is not the rule, we are in the realm of norms, values, traditions, legitimacy, consensus, leadership, and identification—all the modes and mechanisms of command and authority, their acceptance or denial, which shape action in the day-to-day world, *without violence.* And these aspects of power Mills has eschewed.

(d) *The Command Posts.* It is rather striking, too, given Mills' image of power, and politics, as violence, that the metaphor to describe the people of power is a military one. We can take this as a clue to Mills' implicit scheme. But, being little more than a metaphor, it tells us almost nothing about *who* has the power. The men who hold power, he says, are those who run the *organizations* or *domains* which have power. But how do we know they have power, or what power they have? Mills simply takes as postulates: (1) the organization or institution has power; (2) *position in it gives power*. How do we know? Actually, we can only know if power exists by what people *do* with their power.

What powers people have, what decisions they make, how they make them, what factors they have to take into account in making them—all these enter into the question of whether position *can* be transferred into power. But Mills has said: "The idea of the power elite implies nothing about the process of decision-making as such—it is an attempt to delimit the social areas within which that process, *whatever its character*, goes on. It is a conception of who is involved in the process" (p. 21). Thus, we find ourselves stymied. *Who* depends upon position? But position, as I have argued, is only meaningful if one can define the character of the decisions made with such power. And this problem Mills eschews.*

Mills says, further, that he wants to avoid the problem of the self-awareness of the power holders, or the role of such self-awareness in decisions. ("The way to understand the power of the elite lies neither in recognizing the historic scale of events or the personal awareness reported by men of apparent decision behind the men and the institutions" [p. 15].) But if the power elite is *not* the history-maker (p. 20), as Mills sometimes implies, *then what is the meaning of their position as members of the power elite?* Either they can make effective decisions or not. It is true that many men, like Chanticleer the Cock, crow and believe that they have caused the sun to rise, but if such power is only self-deception, that is an aspect, too, of the meaning of power.

(e) *The Big Decisions.* The power elite comes into its own on the "big decisions." In fact, this is an implicit definition of the power of the elite: only they can effect the "big decisions." Those who talk of a new social balance, or pluralism, or the rise of labor, are talking, if at all correctly, says Mills, about the "middle levels" of power. They fail to see the big decisions.

But, curiously, except in a few instances, Mills fails to specify what the big

---

* In his extraordinary story of policy conflicts between the Army, Air Force and Navy on strategic concepts—policy issues such as reliance on heavy military bombers and all-out retaliation, against tactical nuclear weapons and conventional ground forces for limited wars, issues which deeply affect the balance of power within the military establishment—General James Gavin provides a striking example of the helplessness of some of the top Army brass against the entrenched bureaucracy within the Defense Department. "With the establishment of the Department of Defense in 1947," he writes, "an additional layer of civilian management was placed above the services. Furthermore, by the law, military officers were forbidden to hold executive positions in the Department of Defense. As a result the Assistant Secretaries of Defense relied heavily on hundreds of civil service employees, who probably have more impact on decision-making in the Department of Defense than any other group of individuals, military or civilian." From *War and Peace in the Space Age* (Harper and Brothers), reprinted in *Life*, August 4, 1958, pp. 81–82.

decisions are. The few, never analyzed with regard to how the decisions were actually made or who made them, are five in number: the steps leading to intervention in World War II; the decision to drop the atom bomb over Hiroshima and Nagasaki; the declaration of war in Korea; the indecisions over Quemoy and Matsu in 1955; the hesitation regarding intervention in Indochina when Dien Bien Phu was on the verge of falling.

It is quite striking (and it is in line with Mills' conception of politics) that all the decisions he singles out as the "big decisions" are connected with *violence*. These are, it is true, the ultimate decisions a society can make: the commitment or refusal to go to war. And in this regard Mills is right. They *are* big decisions. But what is equally striking in his almost cursory discussion of these decisions is the failure to see that they are not made by the power elite. They are the decisions which, in our system, are vested constitutionally in the individual who must bear the responsibility for the choices—the president. And, rather than being a usurpation of the power of the people, so to speak, this is one of the few instances in the Constitution where such responsibility is specifically defined and where accountability is clear. Naturally, a president will consult with others. And in the instances Mills has cited, the president did. Richard Rovere has written a detailed analysis (in the *Progressive*, June, 1956) of the decisions that Mills has cited and, as Mills defines this elite, has broadly refuted the notion that a "power elite" was really involved. Few persons, other than the president, were involved in these decisions: on the atom bomb, Stimson, Churchill, and a few physicists; on Korea, a small group of men whose counsel was divided, like Acheson and Bradley; on Quemoy and Matsu, specifically by Eisenhower; and on Dien Bien Phu, a broader group, the military and the Cabinet: but in this instance, "the" power elite, narrowly defined, was for intervention, while Eisenhower alone was against the intervention and decided against sending in troops, principally, says Rovere, because of the weight of public opinion.

Now it may well be that crucial decisions of such importance should not be in the hands of a few men. But short of a system of national initiative and referendum, such as was proposed in 1938–39 in the Ludlow amendment, or short of reorganizing the political structure of the country to insist on party responsibility for decision, it is difficult to see what Mills' shouting is about. To say that the leaders of a country have a constitutional responsibility to make crucial decisions is a fairly commonplace statement. To say that the power elite makes such decisions is to invest the statement with a weight and emotional charge that is quite impressive, but of little meaning.

The Question of Interests

So far we have been accepting the terms "command posts" and "power elite" in Mills' own usage. But now a difficulty enters: the question not only of *who* constitutes the power elite but how *cohesive* they are. Although Mills contends that he does not believe in a conspiracy theory, his loose account of the centralization of power among the elite comes suspiciously close to it. . . .

Yet we can only evaluate the meaning of any centralization of power on the basis of what people do with their power. What *unites* them? What *divides* them? And this involves a definition of *interests*. To say, as Mills does: "*All* means of power tend to become *ends* to an elite that is in command of them. And that is why we may define the power elite in terms of power—as those who occupy the command posts" (p. 23)—is circular.

What does it mean to say that power is an end in itself for the power elite? If the elite is cohesive and is facing another power group, the maintenance of power may be an end in itself. But is the elite cohesive? We do not know without first coming back to the question of interests. And the nature of interests implies a selection of values by a group, or part of a group, over against others, and this leads to a definition of particular privileges, and so on.

Certainly, one cannot have a power elite, or a ruling class, without *community of interests*. Mills implies one: the interest of the elite is in the maintenance of the capitalist system as a *system*. But this is never really discussed or analyzed in terms of the meaning of capitalism, the impact of political controls on the society, or the changes in capitalism in the last twenty-five years.

But even if the interest be as broad as Mills implies, one still has the responsibility of identifying the conditions for the maintenance of the system, and the issues and interests involved. Further, one has to see whether there is or has been a *continuity of interests,* in order to chart the cohesiveness or the rise and fall of particular groups.

One of the main arguments about the importance of the *command posts* is the growing centralization of power, which would imply something about the nature of interests. Yet there is almost no sustained discussion of the forces leading to centralization. These are somewhat assumed, and hover over the book, but are never made explicit. Yet only a sustained discussion of these tendencies would, it seems to me, uncover the *locales* of power and their shifts. For example: the role of technology and increasing capital costs as major factors in the size of enterprise; forces in the federalization of power, such as the need for regulation and planning on a national scale because of increased communication, complexity of living, social and military services, and the managing of the economy; the role of foreign affairs. Curiously, Soviet Russia is not even mentioned in the book, although so much of our posture has been dictated by Russian behavior.

Since his focus is on *who* has power, Mills spends considerable effort in tracing the social origins of the men at the top. But, in a disclaimer toward the end of the book (pp. 280–87) he says that the conception of the power elite does not rest upon common social origins (a theme which underlies, say, Schumpeter's notion of the rise and fall of classes) or upon personal friendship, but (although the presumption is not made explicit) upon their "institutional position." But such a statement begs the most important question of all: *the mecha-*

nisms of co-ordination among the power holders. One can say obliquely, as Mills does, that they "meet each other," but this tells us little. If there are "built-in" situations whereby each position merges into another, what are they? One can say, as Mills does, that the new requirements of government require increased recruitment to policy positions from outside groups.* But then, what groups—and what do they do?

At one point Mills says that the Democrats recruited from Dutton, Read, and the Republicans from Kuhn, Loeb. But the point is never developed, and it is hard to know what he means. One could equally say that in the recruitment of science advisors the Democrats took from Chicago and Los Alamos, and the Republicans from Livermore; but if this means anything, and I think it does, one has to trace out the consequences of this different recruitment in the *actions* of the different people. Mills constantly brings the story to the point where analysis has to begin—and stops.

•   •   •

The European Image

How explain this image of power and policy in terms of the intents of self-conscious groups of men having fixed places in society? The peculiar fact is that while all the illustrations Mills uses are drawn from American life, the key concepts are drawn from European experiences; and this accounts, I believe, for the exotic attractiveness—and astigmatism—of the power elite idea.

For example: having defined politics and power in terms of the ultimate sanction of violence, Mills raises the provocative question: Why have the possessors of the means of violence—the military—not established themselves in power more than they have done in the West? Why is not military dictatorship the more normal form of government?

Mills' answer is to point to the role of status. "Prestige to the point of honor, and all that this implies, has, as it were, been the pay-off for the military renunciations of power . . ." (p. 174).

Now, to the extent that this is true, this fact applies primarily to the *European* scene. On the Continent, the military did create and seek to live by a code of honor. Many European works deal with this code, and many European plays, particularly those of Schnitzler, satirize it. But does the concept apply in the United States? Where in the United States has the military (the Navy apart) been kept in check by *honor?* The military has not had the power—or status—in

---

* One key theoretical point, for Marxists, which Mills, surprisingly, never comes to is the question of the ultimate source of power. Is the political directorate autonomous? Is the military independent? If so, why? What is the relation of economic power to the other two? Mills writes: "Insofar as the structural clue to the power elite today lies in the enlarged and military state, that clue becomes evident in the military ascendency. The warlords have gained decisive political relevance, and the military structure is now in considerable part a political structure" (p. 275). If so, what is one to say then about the other crucial proposition by Mills that the capitalist system in the U.S. is essentially unchanged? [See section below on "The Continuity of Power."]

American life for a variety of vastly different reasons: the original concept of the Army as a people's militia; the populist image of the Army man—often as a "hero"; the "democratic" recruitment to West Point; the reluctance to accept conscription; the low esteem of soldiering as against money-making; the tradition of civil life, etc.

All this Mills sees and knows. But if "honor" and "violence" are not meaningful in our past, why conceptualize the problem of the military in terms of violence and honor as a general category, when the problem does not derive from the American scene in those terms? Unless Mills assumes, as many intellectuals did in the thirties, that we shall yet follow the European experience.

A similar pitfall can be found in the treatment of prestige. Mills says: "All those who succeed in America—no matter what their circle of origin or their sphere of action—are likely to become involved in the world of the celebrity." And further, "With the incorporation of the economy, the ascendency of the military establishment, and the centralization of the enlarged state, there have arisen the national elite, who, in occupying the command posts, have taken the spotlight of publicity and become subjects of the intensive build-up. *Members of the power elite are celebrated because of the positions they occupy and the decisions they command"* (p.71).

Now by celebrities, Mills means *those names that need no further identification.* But are the relationships of celebrity, prestige, status, and power as direct as Mills makes them out to be? Certainly celebrities and glamor exist in American life, but these are the concomitants or the necessary components, *not* of an elite, but of a *mass consumption* society. A society engaged in selling requires such a system of lure and appeal. But why assume that positions of power involve one in this system of glamor? And could even a sophisticated reader quickly identify the president and board chairman of the top ten corporations on the *Fortune* magazine list of 500 largest corporations, e.g., Standard Oil of New Jersey, A.T.&T., General Motors, etc.; the top-ranking members of military staffs, e.g., the Chairman of the Joint Chiefs of Staff, the head of the Army, the Naval Chief of Operations, Air Chief of Staff, General of S.A.C., etc., and name the members of the cabinet?

Again the confusion arises from Mills' unthinking use of older, European conceptions of prestige. In such feudal-like hierarchies, prestige was identified with *honor* and with *deference.* Those who held power could claim honor and deference. This was true in Europe. But has it been so in the United States? When Harold Lasswell first attempted in the late thirties to use deference as a key symbol, it already had a false ring. Mills, in effect, substitutes glamor or celebrity for deference, but toward the same end. But does power today carry the immediate glorifications and celebration of name? It is doubtful if, in the mass consumption society, the notions of celebrity, glamor, prestige, and power have the kind of connotations, or are linked, as Mills suggests.

History and Ideas

Now, if one is concerned with the question about changes in the source and style of power, or in the synchronization and centralization of power, one would have to examine the problem historically. Yet except in one or two instances, Mills ignores the historical dimensions. In one place he speaks of a periodization of American history wherein political power has replaced economic power. But this is too loose to be meaningful. In another place—the only concrete discussion of social change in historical terms—he cites an interesting statistic:

> In the middle of the nineteenth century—between 1865 and 1881 —only 19 per cent of the men at the top of government began their political career at the national level: but from 1905 to 1953 about one-third of the political elite began there, and in the Eisenhower administration some 40 per cent started in politics at the national level—a high for the entire political history of the U.S. [p. 229].

Even in its own terms, it is hard to figure out the exact meaning of the argument, other than the fact that more problems are centered in Washington than in the states and, for this reason, more persons are drawn directly to the national capitol than before. Surely there is a simple explanation for much of this. During World War II, with a great need for both national unity and for specialists, more outsiders were co-opted for cabinet posts and the executive branch than before. And, in 1952, since the Republicans had been out of top office for twenty years and would have fewer persons who had a career in government, they would bring in a high proportion of outsiders.

What is interesting in the use of this kind of data is the methodological bias it reveals. In using such data—and variables like lower or national levels—there is a presumption that in the different kind of recruitment one can chart differences in the character of the men at top, and that therefore the *character of their politics* would be different too. (Mills seems to imply this but never develops the point other than to say that, today, the *political outsider* has come into the ascendant. But as a counter-methodology, it would seem to me that one would start not with recruitment or social origins but with the *character of the politics*. Has something changed, and if so, what and why? Is the change due to differences in recruitment (differential class and ethnic backgrounds) or to some other reason? But if one asks these questions, one has to begin with an examination of *ideas and issues*, not social origins.

But Mills, at least here, is almost completely uninterested in ideas and issues. The questions in politics that interest him are: In what way have strategic positions changed, and which positions have come to the fore? Changes in power then are for Mills largely a succession of different positions. As different structural or institutional positions (i.e., military, economic, political) combine, different degrees of power are possible. The circulation of the elite—by which

Pareto meant the change in the composition of groups with different "residues" —is transformed here into the succession of institutional positions.

But how does this apply to people? Are people—character, ideas, values— determined by their *positions?* And if so, in what way? More than that, to see political history as a shift in the power position of "institutions" rather than, say, of concrete interest groups, or classes, is to read politics in an extraordinarily abstract fashion. It is to ignore the changes in ideas and interests. This is one of the reasons why Mills can minimize, in the striking way he does, the entire twenty-year history of the New Deal and Fair Deal. For him these twenty years were notable *only* because they fostered the centralizing tendencies of the major "institutions" of society, notably the political.

In this neglect, or even dismissal of ideas and ideologies, one finds a striking parallel in Pareto's explanation of social changes in Italy. For Pareto, the rise of socialism in Italy was a mere change in the "derivations" (i.e., the masks or ideologies) while the basic combination of residues remained (No. 1704).

In effect, the shifts of temper from nationalism to liberalism to socialism reflected shifts in the distribution of class II residues (i.e., the residues of group persistence). Thus changes in the political class meant simply the circulation of socio-psychological types. All ideologies, all philosophical claims, were masks "for mere purposes of partisan convenience in debate. [They are] neither true nor false; [but] simply devoid of meaning" (No. 1708).

Similarly, for Mills, changes in power are changes in combinations of constitutional position; and this alone, presumably, is the only meaningful reality.

> Except for the unsuccessful Civil War, changes in the power system of the United States have not involved important challenges to basic legitimations. . . . Changes in the American structure of power have generally come about by institutional shifts in the relative positions of the political, the economic and the military orders [p. 269].

Thus the extraordinary changes in American life, changes in the concepts of property, managerial control, responsibility of government, the changes in moral temper created by the New Deal, will become "reduced" to institutional shifts. But have there been no challenges to basic legitimations in American life? How continuous has been the system of power in the United States?

The Continuity of Power

If in his analysis of politics Mills draws from Pareto, in his image of economic power he becomes a "vulgar" Marxist. Mills notes:

> The recent social history of American capitalism does not reveal any distinct break in the continuity of the higher capitalist class. . . . Over the last half-century in the economy as in the political order,

there has been a remarkable *continuity of interests,* vested in the *types* of higher economic men who guard and advance them . . . [p. 147].

Although the language is vague, one can only say that an answer to this proposition rests not on logical or methodological arguments but on empirical grounds . . . the singular fact is that in the last seventy-five years the established relations between the system of property and family, which, Malthus maintained, represented the "fundamental laws" of society, have broken down. And this has meant too the breakup of "family capitalism," which has been the social cement of the bourgeois class system.

In his summation of economic control, Mills paints an even more extraordinary picture:

The top corporations are not a set of splendidly isolated giants. They have been knitted together by explicit associations within their respective industries and regions and in supra-associations such as the NAM. These associations organize a unity among the managerial elite and other members of the corporate rich. They translate narrow economic powers into industry-wide and class-wide power; and they use these powers, first, on the economic front, for example, with reference to labor and its organizations; and second, on the political front, for example in their large role in the political sphere. And they infuse into the ranks of smaller businessmen the views of big business [p. 122].

This is a breath-taking statement more sweeping than anything in the old TNEC reports or of Robert Brady's theory of *Spitzenverbande* (or peak associations) in his *Business as a System of Power.* That there is some co-ordination is obvious; but unity of this scope—and smoothness—is almost fanciful. Mills cites no evidence for these assertions. The facts, actually, point to the other direction. Trade associations in the United States have declined; they were primarily important during wartime as a means of representing industry on government boards. The NAM has become increasingly feckless, and there has been a decline in member interest and contributions. And industry has divided on a wide variety of issues including labor policy (e.g., the large steel and auto companies have been attacked by General Electric and other firms for accepting s.u.b.— supplementary unemployment benefits).

Mills speaks of "their large role in the political sphere." But against whom are the members of the power elite united, and what kinds of issues unite them in the political sphere? I can think of only one issue on which the top corporations would be united: tax policy. In almost all others, they divide. They are divided somewhat on labor. There are major clashes in areas of self-interest, such as those between railroads, truckers, and the railroads and the airlines; or between coal and oil, and coal and natural gas interests. Except in a vague, ideological sense, there are relatively few political issues on which the managerial elite is united.

The problem of *who unites with whom on what* is an empirical one, and this consideration is missing from Mills' work. If such co-ordination as Mills depicts does exist, a further question is raised as to how it comes about. We know, for example, that as a consequence of bureaucratization, career lines within corporations become lengthened and, as a consequence, there is shorter tenure of office for those who reach the top. Within a ten-year period, A.T.&T. has had three executive officers, all of whom had spent thirty to forty years *within* the corporation. If men spend so much time *within* their corporate shells, how do members of the "elite" get acquainted?

In this preoccupation with elite manipulation, Mills becomes indifferent to the problems of what constitutes problems of power in the everyday life of the country. This is quite evident in the way he summarily dismisses all other questions, short of the "big decisions," as "middle level" and, presumably, without much *real* meaning. *Yet are these not the stuff of politics*, the issues which divide men and create the interest conflicts that involve people in a sense of ongoing reality: labor issues, race problems, tax policy, and the like? Is this not the meaning of power to people as it touches their lives?

The use of the term elite poses another question about the utility of its limits for discussing powers. Why use the word *elite* rather than *decision-makers*, or even *rulers?* To talk of *decision-making*, one would have to discuss policy formulation, pressures, etc. To talk of *rule*, one would have to discuss the nature of rule. But if one talks of an elite, one need only discuss institutional position, and one can do so only if, as Mills assumes, the fundamental nature of the system is unchanged, so that one's problem is to chart the circulation at the top. The argument that the fundamental nature of the system—i.e., that of basic legitimations, of continuity of the capitalist class—is unchanged is a curious one, for if power has become so centralized and synchronized, as Mills now assumes, is this not a fundamental change in the system?

Yet, even if one wants to talk in terms of elites, there have been key shifts in power in American society: the breakup of family capitalism (and this is linked to a series of shifts in power in Western society as a whole), but most importantly—and obviously—the decisive role of the political arena.

From Economics to Politics

In the decade before World War I, the growing power of the trusts, the direct influence of the bankers in the economy, the ideological rise of socialism all tended to focus attention on the class system as the hidden but actually decisive element in shaping society and social change. A group of "realistic" historians, notably J. Allen Smith and, most importantly, Charles A. Beard, began the task of reinterpreting the early colonial and constitutional struggles in economic terms. The Beard interpretation, schematically, was roughly this:

The earliest struggles in American history were direct class struggles between the merchant group, represented by the Federalists, and the agrarians, represented by the Democrats. Society was split fairly cleanly between the two
groups with antagonistic interests (tariff, cheap money, etc.). The unadorned way
in which class conflict was discussed by the "founding fathers" could be strikingly documented in the Federalist papers. As in the later struggle between the
English landed gentry and the manufacturing class over the protectionist corn
laws, a decisive victory for either would have decided the basic character of the
society. But that early American plutocracy, the Eastern merchants, proved to be
an unstable social group that was incapable of maintaining the political initiative. So the Federalists lost. Yet the Democrats—in the face of the economic facts
of life of a burgeoning capitalism—could not really win, and the "Jeffersonian
revolution" was something that Jefferson found easier to promise than to execute.

But later historiography has considerably modified this crude chiaroscuro
and has drawn in many subtle tones between the black and the white. . . .

. . . The mutual defeat of attempts to establish exclusive domination left
the social system undefined from the very start. It was not predominantly mer-
cantile, slave, free, agrarian, industrial, or proletarian. The wealthy families,
having lost direct political control, sought to work indirectly through the politician. But in a rapidly shifting society, whose very hugeness casts up a variety of
conflicting interests, a politician can succeed only if he is a broker and the party
system an agency of mediation.

This is not to deny the existence of classes or the nature of a class system.
*But one cannot, unless the society is highly stratified, use the class structure for
direct political analysis.* A class system defines the *mode* of gaining wealth and
privilege in a society. (This mode can be land [real property], corporate title
["fictitious" property], skill [technical or managerial], mercenaries [*condottieri*], or direct political allocation [party, bureaucracy, or army], and this class
system has to be legitimated, in legal forms, in order to assure its continuity.
Often this wealth and privilege carries with it power and prestige, but there is no
direct correlation.) But most important, whatever the mode, class analysis does
not tell us directly *who* exercises the power, nor does it tell us much about the
competition within that mode for power. Unless that mode and its legitimations
are directly challenged, one rarely sees a class acting as a class in unified fashion.
Once a specific mode is established, competition for privilege within the system is
high, and various and different interests develop. The growing complexity of society necessarily multiplies those interests, regional or functional, and in an open
society the political arena—unless there is a conflict to overthrow the system—is
a place where different interests fight it out for advantage. That is why, usually,
the prism of "class" is too crude to follow the swift play of diverse political
groups.

In European society, the *political* issues, especially after the French Revolution, tended to fall along class lines, but even then, any detailed analysis risked falsification of events simply by focusing the issues in gross class terms. Such a classic of Marxist political analysis as *The Eighteenth Brumaire of Louis Bonaparte* comes alive only because Marx depicts so skilfully the play of diverse group interests, as these are manipulated so imperiously by Louis Napoleon, beneath the larger façade of class interests. In the United States, so heterogeneous from the start, and striated even further by diverse ethnic, national, and religious differences, it is difficult to read the political order—which after all became an independent road to privilege for the leaders of minority groups—as a reflection of the economic order. But even where there was some rough correspondence, the play of diverse interests was immense. As late as 1892, Marx's co-worker, Friedrich Engels, wrote in a letter to his friend Sorge: "There is no place yet in America for a *third* party, I believe. The divergence of interests even in the *same* class group is so great in that tremendous area that wholly different groups and interests are represented in each of the two big parties, depending upon the locality, and almost each particular section of the possessing class has its representatives in each of the two parties to a very large degree, though *today* big industry forms the core of the Republicans on the whole, just as the big landowners of the South form that of the Democrats. The apparent haphazardness of this jumbling together is what provides the splendid soil for the corruption and the plundering of the government that flourishes there so beautifully."

At one point in later American history, the dominant business class—the plutocracy, rather than any landed squirerchy—came close to imprinting a clear mark on American politics. By the turn of the twentieth century the growing industrial class had scored a smashing economic victory. With that victory came some efforts to dissolve the structure of group interests by developing a pervasive political ideology which could also serve the emergent national feeling. One such attempt was the doctrine of imperialism in the "manifest destiny" of Beveridge and the "Americanism" of Franklin Giddings. This was alien to a heterogeneous people, or at least premature. The second and more successful effort was in the identification of capitalism with democracy. The early commercial class had feared democracy as a *political* instrument whereby the "swinish multitude" (Burke) would prepare the way for a radical despotism. The ideology of victorious industrial capitalism defined democracy almost completely in agreeable *economic* terms, as liberty of contract.

If the dominant business class was unable to exercise direct political control of the society, it could establish its ideological hegemony. While in the period from 1880 to 1912 the middle class (small farmers and businessmen, and many professionals) had supported the sporadic antitrust and antimonopoly outbursts, such opinions and movements were dissolved by the subsequent two decades of war, prosperity, and propaganda.

This unity burst with the bubble of prosperity because the ideologists of free enterprise, rugged or otherwise, did not understand the realities of the "socialized" economy that had come into being. They had failed to grasp the degree to which this market economy imposes a particular type of dependency upon every-one.

In a pure market society, as Marx once phrased it, each man thinks for him-self and no one plans for all. Today it is no longer individual men who are in the market but particular collectivities, each of which tries—by administered prices, farm supports, uniform wage patterns and the like—to exempt itself from the risks of the market; inevitably, the measures each group resorts to for protection provoke governmental concern that the entire economy not be overturned in the anarchic stampede to safety.

De Tocqueville once wrote that historians who live in aristocratic ages are inclined to read all events through the will and character of heroic individuals, whereas historians of democratic times deal perforce with general causes. The dazzling aristocratic glamor of Franklin D. Roosevelt has often confused the efforts to put the New Deal period in historical perspective, and even now we lack an adequate political characterization of the era. There have been many histori-cal analogies inspired by the flavor and verve of Roosevelt himself: e.g., Roose-velt was a temporizing Solon whose political reforms sought to stave off the revo-lution of propertyless masses; Roosevelt was a Tiberius Gracchus, a patrician who deserted his class to become the people's tribune; Roosevelt was a Louis Napoleon, an ambitious politician manipulating first one class and then another, while straddling them all, to maintain his personal rule. Certainly, they shed little light on the way government action gives rise to new combinations of interests and the operation of these shifting coalitions.

The public face of the New Deal was a set of sweeping social reforms, and, quite naively, some writers, and, indeed, Roosevelt himself, have called the New Deal an assertion of human rights over property rights. But such terms carry little meaning, either philosophically or pragmatically. Are "support prices" for farmers a property right or a human right? In effect, what the New Deal did was to *legitimate* the idea of *group* rights, and the claim of groups, as groups, rather than individuals, for government support. Thus unions won the right to bargain collectively and, through the union shop, to enforce a group decision over indi-viduals; the aged won pensions, the farmers gained subsidies; the veterans re-ceived benefits; the minority groups received legal protections, etc. None of these items, in themselves, were unique. Together, they added up to an extraordinary social change. Similarly, the government has always had some role in directing the economy. But the permanently enlarged role, dictated on the one hand by the necessity to maintain full employment, and, on the other, by the expanded mili-tary establishment, created a vastly different set of powers in Washington than ever before in our history.

What is amazing, in retrospect, is that while the commitment to a politically managed economy could have been foreseen, we were quite badly deficient in organizing our economic thinking for it. . . .

In the emergence of the political economy a new kind of decision-making has taken place. In the market society, peoples' wants are registered by their "dollar votes," as part of the automatic interaction of supply and demand. The sum total of individual dollars-and-cents decisions, operating independently of each other, added up, as Bentham thought, to a social decision, e.g., the general consensus. Thus, when decisions on the allocation of resources operated through the market, dollars, not ideology, determined what was to be produced. In this sense, economics was the key to social power, and politics its pale reflection.

But politics, operating through the government, has more and more become the means of registering a social and economic decision. Here, instead of acting independently as in a market, the individual is forced to work through particular collectivities to enforce his will. Since in a managed economy, "politics," not dollars, determines major production, the intervention of the government not only sharpens pressure-group identifications but forces each to adopt an ideology which can justify its claims and which can square with some concept of "national interest."

The Types of Decisions

Ultimately, if one wants to discuss power, it is more fruitful to discuss it in terms of *types of decisions* rather than elites. And curiously, Mills, I would argue, ultimately agrees, for the real heart of the book is a polemic against those who say that decisions are made democratically in the United States. Mills writes:

> More and more of the fundamental issues never came to any point of decision before Congress . . . much less before the electorate [p. 255].

> Insofar as the structural clue to the power elite today lies in the political order, that clue is the decline of politics as genuine and public debates of alternative decisions . . . America is now in considerable part more a formal political democracy [p. 224].

Now, to some extent this is true, but not, it seems to me, with the invidious aspect with which Mills invests the judgment.

In many instances, even the "interested public" feels itself "trapped," so to speak, by its inability to affect events. Much of this arises out of the *security* nature of problems, so that issues are often fought out in a bureaucratic labyrinth. The decision on the H-bomb was one such issue. Here we had groups of scientists versus a section of the military, particularly SAC. Unless one assumes that everyone ever involved in decision-making is a member of the power elite—which is circular—*we have to locate the source of such decisions, for these are the central problems of a sociology of power.*

But another, equally important reason for being unable to affect events is the onset of what one can only call, inaptly, "technical decision making": the fact that once a policy decision is made, or once a technological change comes to the fore, or once some long crescive change has become manifest, a number of other consequences, if one is being "functionally rational," almost inevitably follow. Thus, shifts of power become "technical" concomitants of such "decisions," and a sociology of power must identify the kinds of consequences which follow the different kinds of decisions.

Three short examples may illustrate the point:

(1) *The federal budget as an economic gyroscope.* From 1931 to 1935, in the depth of the depression years, total federal budget expenditures of all kinds averaged 5.2 billion dollars. In the next four years, 1936 to 1940, it reached a new high of 8 billion dollars. (Income during this period was about 60 per cent of expenditures.) Four years later, the federal government was spending, yearly, a staggering total of over 95 billion dollars and accumulating a national debt which more than quintupled the debt of the previous decade. The figures are in constant dollars.

More importantly, these expenditures have to be compared with gross national product (g.n.p.), the sum total of goods and services produced during a year. During the depression decade, despite the then relatively high government spending, the federal budget "consumed" and pumped back between 5 to 10 per cent of g.n.p. During the war, the figure mounted to over 40 per cent. But while this represented an "abnormally" high figure, in the decade and a half since the end of the war, the government has become the "consumer" of nearly one-fourth of the total g.n.p. Except for one year, 1948, the one "peacetime" year in postwar history, when the federal budget reached a "low" of 33 billion dollars (against a g.n.p. of 257 billion), the expenditures in the Korean campaign and the sums required to maintain the arms pace of the cold war has kept the federal budget at record highs. In the last half of the 1950 decade it averaged about 70 billion dollars, with g.n.p. about 325 billion dollars. In 1960, the federal budget will reach over 80 billion (estimated), and g.n.p. over 400 billion. In the 1950's, the yearly interest alone on the public debt, over 7.2 billion dollars, was greater than the *total* federal government expenditures each year during the depression.

The fact is that this enormous rise in the expenditures of the federal government was not "willed" by any one man or group of men, but arose, inevitably, as a necessary outcome of the war and its effects. And the permanent role of the federal government as the economic gyroscope of the country is due to that fact.

(2) *The "dual economy" of 1950–55.* When the Korean war broke out in 1950, the government was faced with the immediate choice of either converting existing machinery production to war goods or encouraging new plants. The decision rested on an estimate of the type of war. If it seemed as if the Korean war might spread into a general war, then the order to convert civilian facilities could be constructed to build large stockpiles of arms. The decision, based on political-military estimates, was to build a "dual economy." The chief consequence, economically speaking, was the decision to speed new capital expansion by allowing firms to write off the costs of new facilities in five years, as against the normal twenty-five years. (Thus firms could deduct 20 per cent of the new costs from

profits and thus gain a considerable tax benefit.) This five-year tax amortization scheme encouraged an extraordinarily high rate of capital investment, undoubtedly spurred the prosperity boom of the mid-fifties, and was responsible for the overexpansion of capacity which was a contributing element to the recession of 1958–59.

(3) *Weapons technology*. The rapid emergence of new weapons decisively affects the relative weight of power and influence within the military, and within each arm of the military, of the different branches. Thus the rise of missiles reduces the importance of the battleship, once the mainstay of the navy, and of the army itself. In the new technology, for example, the missile-carrying submarine becomes a key arm of striking power, while the extension of the range of the missile makes the manned airplane obsolete. These changes in the composition of the armed forces, the requirements of new skill groups, of technicians and of technologists, mean a change in the profile of military power. Research and Development become more important than Operations, and the power of the scientist, the engineer, and the technologist grows accordingly.

All of these consequences grow out of the "big decisions" that Mills has talked about. But the fundamental policy issues which Mills mentions are primarily, as I pointed out before, decisions to be involved in war or not—or, more broadly, the question of foreign policy. And how can one discuss this question, which Mills completely evades, without discussing the cold war, *and the extent to which our posture is shaped by the Russians!* United States foreign policy since 1946—or, more specifically, since Byrnes' Stuttgart speech, which reversed our position on weakening Germany—was not a reflex of any *internal* social divisions or class issues in the United States but was *based on an estimate of Russia's intentions.*

Nor was this estimate made, in the first instance, by "the power elite." It was an estimate made by American scholarly experts, most notably by George Kennan and the policy-planning staff of the State Department. It was a judgment that Stalinism as an ideological phenomenon, and Russia as a geopolitical power, were aggressively, militarily, and ideologically expansionist, and that a policy of containment, including a rapid military build-up was necessary in order to implement that containment. This underlay Truman's Greco-Turkish policy, and it underlay the Marshall Plan and the desire to aid the rebuilding of the European economy. These policies were not a reflex of power constellations within the U.S. They were estimates of national interest and of national survival.

From the first decision, many others followed: the creation of a long-distance striking arm in the air (SAC), the establishment of a West European Defense Community (EDC, and following its failure, NATO, etc.). This is not to say that every strategic step followed inexorably from the first decision (after France rejected EDC, one had to rely more on Germany for military support), *but that the broad imperatives were clear.*

Once these broad lines were laid down, interest groups were affected, and

Congress was used—often disastrously—to pass acts which gave pressure groups larger allocations of aid money (e.g., the Bland Act, pressured both by the unions and maritime industry, which provided that 50 per cent of all Marshall Plan aid had to be carried in American bottoms) or to hinder the flexibility of the State Department (e.g., the Battle Act, which forbade trade with the Soviet bloc and, in effect, crippled Ceylon, when it was our ally, by threatening to stop aid if Ceylon sold rubber to China).

To ignore the problems of this type of "imperative" decision-making is, it seems to me, to ignore the stuff of politics as well as the new nature of power in contemporary society. The theory of the "power elite" implies a unity of purpose and community of interest among the elite that is not proven or demonstrated. It is simply asserted.

Coda

Much of Mills' work is motivated by his enormous anger at the growing bureaucratization of life—this is his theory of history—and its abettors; and this gives the book its appeal and pathos. Many people do feel helpless and ignorant and react in anger. But the sources of helplessness ought to be made clear, lest one engage, as I think Mills does, in a form of "romantic protest" against modern life. . . .

Complexity and specialization are inevitable in the multiplication of knowledge, the organization of production, and the co-ordination of large areas of political society. That these should lead to "bureaucratization" of life is not necessarily inevitable, particularly in a society of growing education, rising incomes, and multiplicity of tastes. More importantly, such ambiguous use of terms like "bureaucratization" and "power elites" often reinforces a sense of helplessness and belies the resources of a free society: the variety of interest conflicts, the growth of public responsibility, the weight of traditional freedoms (*vide* the Supreme Court, an institution that Mills fails to discuss), the role of volunteer and community groups, etc., etc. Like the indiscriminate use by the Communists of the term "bourgeois democracy" in the thirties, or by Burnham of "managerial society" in the forties, or the term "totalitarianism" in the fifties, *particular and crucial* differences between societies are obscured. This amorphousness leads, as in the case of *The Power Elite* with its emphasis on "big" decisions, to a book which discusses power, but rarely politics. And this is curious, indeed.

POSTSCRIPT

In truth, the United States is in transition between two worlds and does not easily fit into either. For this reason both of the preceding essays are slightly off target.

There is enough verisimilitude in Mills' thesis to make it a compelling commentary on our social structure. But the note it sounds has an archaic ring. One reads *The Power Elite* with a feeling that it is more apt to the twenties (the military excepted) than to our own time. One may applaud a similar note in Veblen, whose sublimated irony it imitates, but may sit on his hands after reading Mills just because, in books like *The Theory of the Leisure Class* (1899), Veblen was accurately depicting his time, whereas Mills suggests John Steinbeck writing *The Grapes of Wrath* during the 1950's. To be sure, there is still misery in the fields and, similarly, much of what Veblen had to say bears repetition and amplification. But with a difference. Daniel Bell's most effective criticism is Mills' failure to reckon with the massive changes of the last thirty-five years.

Even so, Mills' thesis received impressive support from a strange quarter when President Dwight Eisenhower, in his last speech before leaving the White House, warned that "we must guard against the acquisition of unwarranted influence, whether sought or unsought, by the military-industrial complex. The potential for the disastrous rise of misplaced power exists and will persist." He went on:

> We must never let the weight of this combination endanger our liberties or democratic processes. We should take nothing for granted. Only an alert and knowledgeable citizenry can compel the proper meshing of the huge industrial and military machinery of defense with our peaceful methods and goals, so that security and liberty can prosper together.

Even without such unexpected warning, one might safely contend that Daniel Bell is too prone to overlook, or to dismiss with a qualifying phrase, the concentrations of power that exist in our society and the unity in outlook and action that does prevail among the higher income echelons. Thus in chiding

341

Mills for exaggerating the unity prevalent among them, Bell would have been more accurate had he noted that the overwhelming majority belong to one party and that, at the time he was writing, they had a record of having opposed every social reform of the preceding thirty years. Other evidences of agreement might be found for Bell; for example, the already noted unanimity with which the business community condemned attempts by two Presidents to prevent management from initiating price increases that would have profoundly affected the economy as a whole.

However, when all this has been said, it may fairly be claimed that the revolution that began in the thirties is still with us in what may be called its quiet phase. It proceeds quietly because a large number of those who first opposed and still have the power to challenge it, have accommodated themselves to it. They have learned that this is a revolution with which they can live. They see that the new distribution of power, while it cramps, limits and even frustrates them, still leaves them free to enjoy a privileged position in the power structure. Their early premonitions of annihilation reflected in exaggerated fears and reckless charges of Communism have abated. They perceive that the price of challenging the new revolution is alliance with the most erratic and irresponsible members of the community. The latter are innocuous enough if contained in their town and country clubs, but at a political or professional convention they can run amuck and their tantrums can make a shambles of one's party.

Finally, and most importantly, responsible citizens who occupy the higher echelons of the power structure perceive at last that our fantastic wealth makes possible, *without significant sacrifice on their part*, the gratification of mass expectations on a scale utterly unique in the history of man.

This does not mean that, as a group, they have helped or hastened the revolution. Far from it. With notable exceptions, they have grumbled, fretted, and resisted. But their resistance has been within the framework of our basic consensus and they appear to be bowing gracefully before that consensus. This C. Wright Mills did not anticipate.

The most recent outlines of our quiet revolution are reflected in the Supreme Court reapportionment decisions beginning in 1962 with *Baker* v. *Carr* (p. 154) and the Civil Rights Act of 1965. The combined impact of these two blows will seriously cripple forces that, despite the redistribution of power effected in the thirties, have successfully blocked substantive reform legislation except in time of dire emergency.[1] The strength of these forces has depended in part on the disfranchisement of the Southern Negro and the disparity between rural and urban representation in our state legislatures. The former has given ascendancy to Southern advocates of the old power structure and the latter has enabled that power structure, North and South, to bulwark itself with states' rights that can

[1] The Employment Act was passed after the war, in 1946, when there was no emergency, but fear of a recurrence of pre-war mass unemployment made its passage possible. The Civil Rights Act of 1965 could not have been passed had not leaders of the civil rights movement deliberately, and Southern bitter-enders inadvertently, created a condition of emergency.

hardly seem so attractive now that urban populations will be exercising them. A preview of the results can already be read in the record of reform legislation enacted in the first year of the Johnson Administration, a record that must be construed not as a mere mopping-up operation in the train of the reforms of the thirties, but as the reflection of a new vision of the good society.

The sharing of power has not been an act of enthusiastic self-divestment. Nevertheless, it provides massive refutation of the Marxist thesis (which Marx himself qualified in the case of Great Britain, the United States, and Holland) that the ruling class will use force to retain its power. Likewise it disproves the contention that a capitalist system is incapable of self-reform. It would be a serious error to exaggerate the extent to which the power elite has been weakened. It is not yet clear that the community is free to act in such crucial areas as the pricing of basic commodities even though, as in the case of critical metals, the determination may vitally affect its welfare; or informing consumers accurately about what they are buying; or banishing the blight that infects our cities and spreads over our countryside. It would be an equally serious error to ignore the new winds of freedom. The ancient polarity between mass and class may soon be relegated to the limbo of great over-simplifications with the discovery that an affluent society with strong democratic traditions makes possible a new and creative interaction between the many and the few in which old antagonisms, if not superseded, are safely subordinated to the common good. We may be on the eve of that "reciprocal courtesy between all classes"—to which with characteristic Gallic elegance Alexis de Tocqueville referred—where "the Empire of democracy is slowly and peaceably introduced into the institution and manners of the nation."

SUGGESTED READINGS

General Readings

Auerbach, M. Morton. *The Conservative Illusion.* New York: Columbia University Press, 1959.

Babbitt, Irving. *Democracy and Leadership.* Boston: Houghton Mifflin Co., 1953.

Becker, Carl. *Modern Democracy.* New Haven: Yale University Press, 1941.

Bendix, Reinhard and Seymour M. Lipset, eds. *Class, Status and Power: A Reader in Social Stratification.* Glencoe, Ill.: The Free Press, 1953.

Blau, Peter M. *The Dynamics of Bureaucracy: A Study of Interpersonal Relations in Two Government Agencies.* Rev. ed. Chicago: University of Chicago Press, 1963.

Bryce, James. *Modern Democracies.* New York: The Macmillan Co., 1921.

Catlin, George E. G. *Systematic Politics: Elementa Politica et Sociologica.* Toronto: University of Toronto Press, 1962.

D'Antonio, W. V. and H. J. Erlich, eds., *Power and Democracy in America.* Notre Dame, Ind.: University of Notre Dame Press, 1961.

Dahl, Robert A. *A Preface to Democratic Theory.* Chicago: University of Chicago Press, 1956.

Ebenstein, William. *Modern Political Thought in Perspective.* New York: McGraw-Hill Book Co., 1957.

Frankel, Charles. *The Democratic Prospect.* New York: Harper & Row, Publishers, 1962.

Friedrich, Carl J. *Constitutional Government and Democracy: Theory and Practice in Europe and America.* Boston: Little, Brown and Co., 1941.

Heimann, Eduard. *Reason and Faith in Modern Society.* Middletown, Conn.: Wesleyan University Press, 1961.

Kornhauser, Arthur W., ed. *Problems of Power in American Democracy.* Detroit: Wayne State University Press, 1957.

Lippincott, Benjamin E. *Victorian Critics of Democracy: Carlyle, Ruskin, Arnold, Stephen, Maine, Lecky.* London: Oxford University Press, 1938.

Lipson, Leslie. *The Democratic Civilization.* New York: Oxford University Press, 1964.

Mayer, Kurt B. *Class and Society.* New York: Random House, Inc., 1955.

Merton, Robert K., and others, eds. *Reader in Bureaucracy.* Glencoe, Ill.: The Free Press, 1952.

Niebuhr, Reinhold. *The Children of Light and the Children of Darkness: A Vindication of Democracy and a Critique of Its Traditional Defence.* New York: Charles Scribner's Sons, 1944.

Parkinson, C. Northcote. *The Evolution of Political Thought.* Boston: Houghton Mifflin Co., 1958.

Rossiter, Clinton L. *Conservatism in America: The Thankless Persuasion.* 2nd ed., rev. New York: Alfred A. Knopf, Inc., 1962.

Sabine, George H. *A History of Political Theory.* 3rd ed. New York: Holt, Rinehart & Winston, Inc., 1961.

Sartori, Giovanni. *Democratic Theory.* Detroit: Wayne State University Press, 1962.

Talmon, Jacob L. *The Origins of Totalitarian Democracy.* New York: Frederick A. Praeger, Inc., 1960.

Tocqueville, Alexis de. *Democracy in America,* trans. Henry Reeve. New York: Schocken Books, Inc., 1961.

Weber, Max. *From Max Weber: Essays in Sociology,* trans., ed. H. H. Gerth and C. Wright Mills. New York: Oxford University Press, 1946.

On Represented Authors

JOHN LOCKE

Cox, Richard H. *Locke on War and Peace.* Oxford: The Clarendon Press, 1960.

Gough, John W. *John Locke's Political Philosophy: Eight Studies.* Oxford: The Clarendon Press, 1950.

Kendall, Willmoore. *John Locke and the Doctrine of Majority Rule.* Urbana: University of Illinois Press, 1959.

Locke, John. *Two Treatises of Government,* ed. Peter Laslett. Cambridge: Cambridge University Press, 1960.

Macpherson, C. B. *The Political Theory of Possessive Individualism: Hobbes to Locke.* Oxford: The Clarendon Press, 1962.

Pollock, Sir Frederick. "Locke's Theory of the State," *Proceedings of the British Academy 1903–1904.* Oxford: Oxford University Press, 1904.

JEAN JACQUES ROUSSEAU

Babbitt, Irving. *Rousseau and Romanticism.* Boston: Houghton Mifflin Co., 1935.

Chapman, John W. *Rousseau—Totalitarian or Liberal?* New York: Columbia University Press, 1956.

Cobban, Alfred. *Rousseau and the Modern State.* 2nd ed. Hamden, Conn.: The Shoe String Press, Inc., 1964.

Maritain, Jacques. *Three Reformers: Luther—Descartes—Rousseau.* New York: Sheed & Ward, 1947.

Osborn, Annie M. *Rousseau and Burke: A Study of the Idea of Liberty in Eighteenth-Century Political Thought.* London: Oxford University Press, 1940.

THOMAS JEFFERSON

Adams, James Truslow. *The Living Jefferson.* New York: Charles Scribner's Sons, 1936.

Boorstin, Daniel J. *The Lost World of Thomas Jefferson.* Boston: Beacon Press, 1960.

Bowers, Claude G. *Jefferson and Hamilton; The Struggle For Democracy in America.* Boston: Houghton Mifflin Co., 1929.

———. *Jefferson in Power: The Death Struggle of the Federalists.* Boston: Houghton Mifflin Co., 1936.

Chinard, Gilbert. *Thomas Jefferson: The Apostle of Americanism.* 2nd ed., rev. Ann Arbor: University of Michigan Press, 1957.

Reynolds v. *Sims*

Baker, Gordon E. *Rural versus Urban Political Power: The Nature and Consequences of Unbalanced Representation.* New York: Random House, Inc., 1955.

———. *The Reapportionment Revolution: Representation, Political Power and the Supreme Court.* New York: Random House, Inc., 1965.

DeGrazia, Alfred. *Essay on Apportionment and Representative Government.* Washington: American Enterprise Institute For Policy Research, 1963.

Schubert, Glendon A., ed. *Reapportionment.* New York: Charles Scribner's Sons, 1965.

PLATO

Barker, Sir Ernest. *Greek Political Theory: Plato and His Predecessors.* 4th ed. London: Methuen and Co., Ltd., 1951.

———. *The Political Thought of Plato and Aristotle.* New York: Russell & Russell, Inc., 1959.

Crossman, R. H. S. *Plato Today.* 2nd rev. ed. New York: Oxford University Press, 1959.

Havelock, Eric A. *The Liberal Temper in Greek Politics.* New Haven: Yale University Press, 1957.

Jaeger, Werner W. *Paideia: The Ideals of Greek Culture.* 3 vols. Oxford: Blackwell and Mott, 1939–1945.

Popper, Karl R. *The Open Society and Its Enemies.* Vol. I: *The Spell of Plato.* 4th ed. rev. Princeton, N.J.: Princeton University Press, 1963.

Sabine, George H. *A History of Political Theory.* 3rd ed. New York: Holt, Rinehart & Winston, Inc., 1961.

Taylor, A. E. *Plato, The Man and His Work.* 6th ed. London: Methuen and Co., Ltd., 1949.

Thorson, Thomas L. *Plato: Totalitarian or Democrat?* Englewood Cliffs, N.J.: Prentice-Hall, Inc., 1963.

Winspear, Alban D. *The Genesis of Plato's Thought.* 2nd ed. rev. New York: Russell & Russell, Inc., 1956.

ARISTOTLE

Barker, Sir Ernest. *The Political Thought of Plato and Aristotle.* New York: Russell & Russell, Inc., 1959.

Havelock, Eric A. *The Liberal Temper in Greek Politics.* New Haven: Yale University Press, 1957.

Jaeger, Werner W. *Aristotle: Fundamentals of the History of His Development.* Trans., with the author's corrections and additions, Richard Robinson. 2nd ed. Oxford: The Clarendon Press, 1948.

Kelsen, Hans. "The Philosophy of Aristotle and the Hellenic-Macedonian Policy," *Ethics,* 48 (October 1937), 1–64.

Randall, John Herman. *Aristotle.* New York: Columbia University Press, 1960.

Sabine, George H. *A History of Political Theory.* 3rd ed. New York: Holt, Rinehart & Winston, Inc., 1961.

EDMUND BURKE

Cobban, Alfred. *Edmund Burke and the Revolt Against the Eighteenth Century: A Study of the Political and Social Thinking of Burke, Wordsworth, Coleridge, and Southey.* 2nd ed. New York: Barnes & Noble, Inc., 1961.

Graubard, Stephen R. *Burke, Disraeli, and Churchill: The Politics of Perseverance.* Cambridge, Mass.: Harvard University Press, 1961.

Laski, Harold J. *The Rise of Liberalism: The Philosophy of a Business Civilization.* New York: Harper & Brothers, 1936.

Osborn, Annie M. *Rousseau and Burke: A Study of the Idea of Liberty in Eighteenth-Century Political Thought.* London: Oxford University Press, 1940.

FRIEDRICH NIETZSCHE

Brinton, C. Crane. *Nietzsche.* Cambridge, Mass.: Harvard University Press, 1948.

Danto, Arthur C. *Nietzsche as a Philosopher.* New York: The Macmillan Co., 1965.

Jaspers, Karl. *Nietzsche: An Introduction to the Understanding of His Philosophical Activity,* trans. C. F. Wallraff and F. J. Schmitz. Tucson: University of Arizona Press, 1965.

Kaufmann, Walter A. *Nietzsche: Philosopher, Psychologist, Antichrist.* New York: The World Publishing Co., 1956.

Morgan, George A. *What Nietzsche Means.* New York: Harper & Row, Publishers, 1965.

VILFREDO PARETO

Aron, Raymond. "Social Structure and the Ruling Class." *British Journal of Sociology,* I (March and June 1950), 1–16, 126–143.

Burnham, James. *The Machiavellians: Defenders of Freedom.* New York: John Day Co., Inc., 1943.

Friedrich, Carl J. *The New Image of the Common Man.* 2nd ed. Boston: Little, Brown and Co., 1950.

Homans, George C. and Charles P. Curtis. *An Introduction to Pareto, His Sociology.* New York: Alfred A. Knopf, Inc., 1934.

Meisel, James H. *The Myth of the Ruling Class: Gaetano Mosca and the Elite.* With the first English translation of "The Theory of the Ruling Class." Ann Arbor: University of Michigan Press, 1958.

————, ed. *Pareto and Mosca.* Englewood Cliffs, N.J.: Prentice-Hall, Inc., 1965.

Parsons, Talcott. "Pareto," in *Encyclopedia of the Social Sciences,* XI. New York: The Macmillan Co., 1933.

————. *The Structure of Social Action: A Study in Social Theory With Special Reference to a Group of Recent European Writers.* 2nd ed. Glencoe, Ill.: The Free Press, 1958.

GAETANO MOSCA

Burnham, James. *The Machiavellians, Defenders of Freedom.* New York: John Day Co., Inc., 1943.

Marx, Fritz M. "The Bureaucratic State," *Review of Politics,* I (October 1939), 457–472.

Meisel, James H. *The Myth of the Ruling Class: Gaetano Mosca and the Elite.* Ann Arbor: University of Michigan Press, 1962.

————, ed. *Pareto and Mosca.* Englewood Cliffs, N.J.: Prentice-Hall, Inc., 1965.

C. WRIGHT MILLS

Meisel, James H. *The Myth of the Ruling Class: Gaetano Mosca and the Elite.* With the first English translation of "The Theory of the Ruling Class." Ann Arbor: University of Michigan Press, 1958.

Mills, C. Wright. *"The Power Elite:* Comment on Criticism," *Dissent,* IV (Winter 1957), 22–34.

Parsons, Talcott. "The Distribution of Power in American Society," *World Politics,* X (October 1957), 123–143.